POPE PIUS XII LIB., ST. JOSEPH COLLEGE
3 2528 01291 5072

WORKING WITH TROUBLED CHILDREN

Working with Troubled Children

Victor Savicki, Ph.D.
Oregon College of Education
Monmouth, Oregon

Rosemary Brown, M.S.
Private Consultant in Child and Family Treatment
Salem, Oregon

Illustrations by Mark Gostnell

HUMAN SCIENCES PRESS, INC.
72 FIFTH AVENUE
NEW YORK, N.Y. 10011

72 Fifth Avenue, New York, New York 10011

Printed in the United States of America
123456789 98765432

Library of Congress Cataloging in Publication Data

Savicki, Victor.
Working with troubled children
Includes index.
Bibliography p. 391
1. Problem children—United States. 2. Helping behavior. 3. Helping behavior—Study and teaching—United States. I. Brown, Rosemary, 1947-joint author. II. Title.
HQ773.S23 362.7'4 LC 80-15953
ISBN 0-87705-087-2 Cloth
ISBN 0-89885-243-9 Paper

CONTENTS

To my children, Steven and Kristin,
for keeping me honest.

To my original mentor, Bill Murray, for laying
the foundations with his knowledge, wisdom,
and unwavering faith.

ACKNOWLEDGEMENTS

Kathy Savicki for her long–term commitment in supporting the effort, and the sacrifices she has made.
Roy and Alice Brown for their never–ending support, acceptance, and confidence.
Cherie Andrews for her love and spiritual guidance.
Tom Cherry for encouraging the conception of the training program.
Pat Smith for patiently and supportively sharing in the project from its beginnings.
Chris White for his enthusiasm, permission, and ego–building.
Bill Wellard for helping to prime the pump with his energy and humor.
Mary Murphy for her thoughtfulness, rich resources, invaluable lessons about process, and editorial comments.
Ray Peterson for early lessons in what child treatment is all about.
Mike Ebner for expanding a neophyte's awareness by cleaning the windshield of her perceptions and encouraging her to trust her knowing.
Prudie Gilbert for her encouraging comments and for being such a competent typist.
Maxine Warnath for her moral and practical support
Eric Stewart for being there without my having to ask.
. . . . and all the Poyama staff for being such willing and enjoyable guinea pigs.

In addition, the authors gratefully acknowledge permission to reprint the following:

An adaptation of a figure from Leary, T. *Interpersonal Diagnosis of Personality* on page 34: copyright Ronald Press 1957, reprinted by permission of John Wiley and Sons, Inc.

A flow chart about extinction by Benoit, R. B. and Mayer, G. R. on page 380 copyright 1974 reprinted with permission of American Personnel and Guidance Association.

A list of counterproductive fighting styles from Adler, R. and Towne, N. on pages 446 to 449: copyright Rinehart Press 1975, reprinted with permission of Holt Rinehart and Winston.

INTRODUCTION

This book addresses people who work with troubled children. We believe that the information in the book applies to many types of troubled children, to many types of helpers, and to many contexts in which children and helpers interact. Our experience in training people to work with troubled children comes from work with mental health professionals, teachers, college students, and parents working with delinquent, mildly retarded, or emotionally disturbed children in residential, day treatment, and home settings. The major impetus of the training sequence described in this book evolved from involvement over a 5-year period in training staff and parents to treat emotionally disturbed children between the ages of 3 and 12. Although the language and examples used apply to children, the skills easily transfer to adults as well; after all, adults are children grown up. Thus we see a wide generalization of the content of this book.

As we prepare ourselves to present this book to our readers, a feeling of anxiety emerges. At the base of this fear is the potential hazard inherent in the book's "nuts and bolts" format. The training sequence is organized skill by skill. This presents an artificial, static picture of the treatment process—it's too pat. We feel that it would be possible to follow all the rules, get good grades on all the tests, yet flunk the course, because the world is not neatly segmented into the somewhat arbitrary categories that we attempt to impose on it. Also, as treatment workers, we do not stand outside the treatment process and act on the child. It is not the "doer-doee" dichotomy that this sequence may imply. In reality, we are an integral part of the ongoing process of therapy that continually changes from moment to moment. We act on and are acted upon simultaneously. This reciprocal relationship *is* treatment. Thus, it is essential for treatment workers to be aware of, monitor, and use their responses in relating with the child. From this point of view, it becomes clear that the worker's unfinished business and "buttons" will be continually activated in this process, and it will be necessary for her to acknowledge and work on these so as not to cloud the child's issues with her's.

Another danger of the book's format is the potential confusion between methods of treatment and the purpose of treatment. As we see it, effective treatment establishes conditions that will free a child's potential capacities and energies and encourage the child's greater acceptance of self and others. Therapeutic skills do not solve problems. Rather, they assist the individual in becoming aware of alternatives, in being able to make choices, and, we hope, in accepting a positive image of self so that they feel deserving of positive choices.

This skill sequence could be mistakenly seen as "the answer" for treatment workers' desire to create a positive impact on children. The skills, in fact, crystallize effective helping behaviors, but they do not guarantee effective helping. That eludes absolute, concrete definition.

Treatment clearly is a complex process and requires a great deal of awareness and creativity in order to make the continual necessary decisions. There are not absolute formulas to derive answers for treatment questions. This can be especially disconcerting when the inevitable, seemingly unresolvable conflicts inherent in treatment arise. (See Table 1-1.) For instance, how can we deal with the reality of a situation when all we have are our various perceptions of reality? How can we accept the child and simultaneously push for change (which implies lack of acceptance)? How can we go with what the kid needs at the moment while maintaining a structure that may not always allow for the expression of needs? How can we work towards developing a child's responsibility for himself and be a helper, which means intervening for the child? These and many other questions constantly emerge in the course of child treatment. Only the blend of experience, awareness, information, creativity, and caring can provide adequate answers.

Table 1–1. Unresolvable Treatment Dilemmas

Caring	vs.	Rescue
Objective reality	vs.	Personal perceptions
Acceptance of the child	vs.	Expectation of change
Flexibility to meet individual needs	vs.	Structure to attain goals
Facilitating autonomy	vs.	Supplying concrete control

Our Approach

Our approach to training can be called pluralistic, that is, we believe that there exists more than one "reality" to become aware of. Depending on whom you talk to, you will find that the necessary ingredients for helping people differ greatly. Some approaches stress specific behavioral skills. Sometimes the skills of one approach are defined as opposite to skills of a different approach. For example, an Adlerian would use "the skill of encouragement" and condemn a Behavior Modifier's use of "shaping" although telling the two skills apart in practice may be quite difficult. On a behavioral skill level we subscribe to what Lazarus (1972) calls "technical eclecticism." In other words, we may put together, on a behavioral level, skills that are defined as being opposed on a theoretical level. By practical necessity we have had to use what works regardless of whether or not it was "supposed" to work on a more abstract level.

Others in the field of training helpers assert that what is important is not what you do (behavioral skill level) but how you do it, or whether or not you do it with good intentions. Rather than decide whether it is behavior, style, or intent that is most important, we accept all of these realities as valid. For us it is not "which is most important, the chicken or the egg?"; it is "well, what do we do with all these eggs and chickens?"

We assume that humans function as unified, holistic beings within a given context. That is, they use "everything they've got" in helping. Therefore, tapping as many levels of functioning as possible seems valid. Ivey (1977) uses the term "cultural expertise" to explain the idea of the helper-child-relationship-within-a-context. According to Ivey, "the individual with cultural expertise has communication competence or the possession of an adequate repertoire of verbal and nonverbal language varieties so as to achieve maximum communication with self, other individuals, groups and cultures" (1977 p. 297). Although more limited in scope, this book takes these same abilities as goals.

Levels of Helper Functioning

We will consider four levels of helper functioning in this book. (See Figure 1-1)

1. *Behavior.* Specific behavioral skills can yield therapeutic outcomes. This training sequence focuses most intently on skill development. Behavioral functioning can be most easily observed, and therefore most accurately described. Behavioral skills include not only "what to do" and "how to do it," but also some ideas about "when this skill can be used effectively."

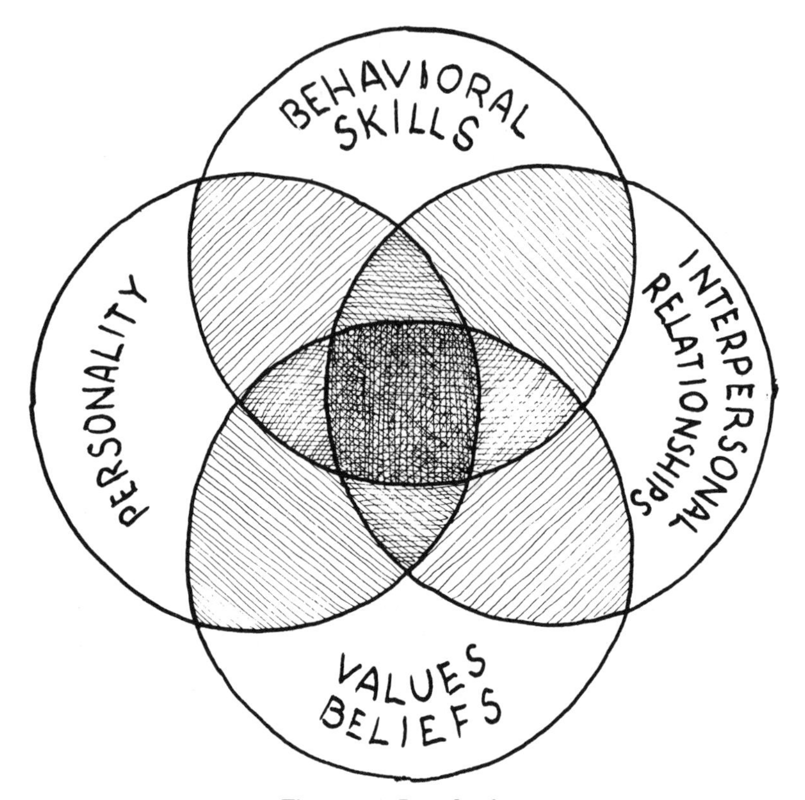

Figure 1-1. Introduction

2. *Interpersonal Relationship.* Because helping is interpersonal, the quality of interpersonal relationship becomes extremely important. Any behavioral skill occurs within the context of a relationship; therefore occasional conflict between skill performance and facilitative relationship must be resolved.
3. *Values and Beliefs.* Each of us carries with us beliefs about who we are and how the world works. We also have an emotional and behavioral commitment to specific values; we believe that our experiences "should" be consistent with our values. These values and beliefs filter our experience, and even promote actions to make our experiences consistent with our values. For better or worse, we carry such filtering and actions into helping situations.
4. *Personality.* Thank goodness we are not all stamped from the same mold. We each have unique personalities and emotional reactions. Since there is no one "helping personality," the helper's task becomes developing her awareness of personal attributes and finding a range of behavioral skills that complement those attributes.

The hoped-for general outcomes of this training sequence are:

1. Flexible use of an expanded range of therapeutically effective behavioral skills (i.e. accurate use in appropriate situations).
2. Awareness of self on the levels listed above (i.e., helper is able to observe self and report his performance accurately).
3. Movement towards research-identified "good helper" positions on relationship, values, and beliefs levels.
4. Development of a trained "intuitive" style in which the disconnected experience of training merges into a congruent, holistic pattern.

The last outcome, trained intuitive style, represents the ultimate outcome of training. Training often points towards "intuitive" responding by stressing alternative responses to a specific incident rather than stressing more generalized responses appropriate to a variety of incidents. The more traditional approach to training is somewhat akin to learning to read by memorizing single words. By contrast, the single skills approach to training as presented in this book is more like learning to read phonetically. Even though you may need to learn single sounds, those sounds recur in many words. A new reader saves time and effort by learning more generalizable skills. The same is true with the single skills approach to training helpers. Eventually, when confronted with a never-before-seen word, a phonetic reader can sound out the word. As a helper, especially a helper working with troubled children, you can predict with 100 percent accuracy that nothing will be 100 percent predictable in your work. Therefore, you also will need to "sound out" new situations. With experience you will develop a backlog of successful interventions, and you will expand your vocabulary of skills while increasing your comprehension of yourself, the people you work with, and your treatment setting.

As a final note, as you read this book and try new ways of functioning as a helper, be aware that you are attempting to change within a physical and social context. Be aware that it may be difficult to practice phonic skills in a situation in which everyone else does not know the sounds. The next chapter, "Effects of Training," will provide some information about how your home/work context may impact on your training (and vice versa).

Chapter 1

EFFECTS OF TRAINING

By definition, training in anything requires change. If a person does not change his or her perceptions, behaviors, or feelings as a result of training, then the content and process of the training has had no impact, and the person has, in fact, not been trained. Our experience in the Working with Troubled Children training sequence leads us to believe that change will occur. The purpose of this chapter is to examine the changes you might anticipate.

As you move through this training you are likely to experience certain predictable events. It is worth your while to consider these in the light of two questions:

1. "Given that these events may occur to me, is the gain I will achieve in increased competence, confidence, and effectiveness worth the risks and costs I must endure?" If after reading this chapter you choose to leave training, then so be it. It is better to save yourself time, energy, and discomfort. Your efforts might be better spent achieving more pressing personal goals. Not all people should be in the helping field.

2. "Having chosen to endure the possible risks and costs in order to achieve the goals set forth in this training sequence, what are the ways in which I can best maximize the benefits and minimize the costs?" We will address the second question in this chapter.

To accomplish the goals of this training sequence requires a commitment. Once you complete the sequence you will not be the same person you are now. This chapter is not meant to frighten you away; we are trying to give you information about training that most training sequences do not. We believe you ought to know what you are getting into.

Effects

Increased Competence and Challenge to Current Skill Performance. Your skill will skyrocket. You will find yourself able to handle situations that you previously found almost impossible, and you will find that your familiar and comfortable ways of doing things will be challenged and called into question. You may have to do as much unlearning as new learning, and you may feel some remorse at abandoning old ways of thinking, feeling, and behaving. An effective resolution of this problem comes through defining appropriate occasions for both old and new skills, or seeing old skills as signals that point out unfinished emotional issues. Acceptance of your current level of skills as a step in the process of growth also helps.

Increased Ability to Observe Oneself and Increased Tension or Discomfort with Nonfacilitative Facets of Self. You will look at yourself in ways you have never looked before. Your thoughts, feelings, and behaviors will become more clearly defined and differentiated. You will be better able to track your own functioning on a variety of different levels. And, you will be able to evaluate immediately if you "blew it." You will not be able to muddle along in ignorant bliss. Your own awareness will produce tension, so much tension at times that you may freeze because you have become self-conscious. Such hyper-self-awareness passes with practice and with centering. Actors learning a new role select a "point of concentration" to help them focus their energy. Once focused they can become "spontaneous within a role." As a treatment worker, your point of concentration will be on the child you are working with. If you can be self-aware *and* intensely focused on the child, your behavior will become spontaneous. All the information about "how to behave" stored in your brain will emerge in response to cues from the child. Trainees often make the mistake of "working too hard." To counter this, try to accept where you are, accept your mistakes (there will be lots of them) as opportunities, and trust yourself. New skills will grow more quickly given an accepting, even playful mood.

Increased Openness to Feedback and Temporary Increase in Fear of Negative Evaluation from Peers, Instructors, and Audio–video Tape. Feedback in this sequence is specific and centers on concretely focused issues rather than abstract, global personality traits that encompass the worker's whole being. Therefore, you will find yourself able to accept a tremendous amount of information without feeling threatened. Initially, trainees fear that others will think that they are lousy treatment workers, have crazy ideas, and are generally all-around inadequate people. With practice in both giving and receiving feedback, trainees not only develop a finely-tuned understanding of the skill involved, but also become more adept at asking for the kind of feedback they need and, therefore, satisfy their needs more fully by taking control of the feedback process.

Increased Carry-over of Facilitative Responses into Out-of-training Settings, and Temporary Negative Responses to Change from Others. As you practice the skills, you will find that they are effective in both work and non-work settings. The generalizability of the skills allows trainees to engage in facilitative behaviors with all manner of people. As with anything new, people will notice and oftentimes respond negatively, e.g., "Cut out all that 'therapy' stuff you're learning, I'm not a kid! Just be yourself." From a relationship point of view, your new behaviors move to redefine the relationship you have established with others. Initially, this change may be resisted by others unless you can arrange for them to support, or at least tolerate, your new skills. One suggestion: Avoid the zeal of the new convert. Persist in your new behaviors not as a gimmick and not as a means to manipulate others to change, but as a statement about your commitment to the new behavior. As others become familiar with your new style, they will accept and enjoy it.

Increased Awareness of Needs for Support and Contact, and Tension and Discomfort with Nonsupportive Environments. As you become more aware of yourself and your needs, as you become aware of how the skills you are learning provide supportive conditions, and as you practice providing and receiving contact and support from kids and peers during the training process, you will also become aware of how your needs for support and contact are met or not met in nontraining environments. If your needs are not met, you will feel discomfort and experience a tension to resolve the gap between what you want and what is there. Such motivation may lead you to redefine the relationships and physical environments in which you live. This means that you may have work to do with co-workers, parents, your own children, spouse, friends. Sometimes, if redefinition is impossible, you may choose to leave one environment in order to pursue your wants elsewhere.

Increased Ability to Facilitate Change in Children, and Frustration When Your Efforts Do Not Work as You Imagine They Should, as well as Fear of Doing Damage with Your Newfound Effectiveness. Being ineffective is like chicken soup: although it may not do any good, at least it cannot do any harm either. When you find that your behavior *can* make a difference, you must confront the limits of your power. Overestimating your impact can generate both frustration and fear. Frustration most often emerges when the treatment worker somehow blocks himself from doing an effective job. Some of these blocks will be reviewed in this chapter under the heading "Feelings and Issues for the Treatment Worker." Fear emerges from the realization that the life of the child you are working with will be changed to some extent in reaction to your behavior. The long-range implications of this can be overwhelming, especially if you are not sure whether your effect will be positive or negative. To some extent this fear safeguards you and your clients. Keep in touch with it and view it as a by-product and concrete demonstration of your effectiveness as a treatment worker.

Training as Treatment

This training sequence is not a place to work out problems that require professional help. At the same time, you will change in significant ways that will affect your life; this fact cannot be ignored. Our experience has been that new skills require integration into existing personality structures, and such integration may raise personal issues. Given a supportive context, these issues can be addressed. There is a balance between the two extremes of going through the training sequence in a closed and constricted manner, and disclosing problems and issues that would be better dealt with in professional counseling. As a compromise we suggest that you view training as an unprecedented opportunity to become aware of yourself. Tune into all of your awareness as potentially helpful to you for understanding and sorting out what may facilitate and what may hinder your performance as a treatment worker. As for feedback and validation from your trainer and peers, with all of that information in hand, you can decide which aspects of yourself you can work on in the training sequence, and which aspects you may want to seek aid for outside of training.

Emotional Education

We all learned to censor our perceptions and reactions as we grew up. We were taught to ignore, distort, or define as irrelevant certain cues and behaviors in ourselves and others. This training sequence will confront some of those early learnings. In other words, we will ask you to become aware of your environment, much as a child would, without preconceptions about what you are allowed or not allowed to perceive. You will learn to look in order to see, to listen in order to hear, to touch in order to feel, etc.

As a consequence of being asked to do things that (1) you now typically do not do, and (2) you may see as somehow not quite "right" on a gut level, some of the new learnings will seem "phony" and "put-on." Consider the sequence of emotional re-education as outlined by Maultsby (1975);

1. *Intellectual insight:* Learn the rudiments of the new task and develop a mental map. Some people visualize themselves doing the task, some talk their way through it, some rehearse the feelings of the task.

2. *Correct practice:* Practice it enough to be able to do it fairly smoothly.
3. *Cognitive dissonance:* You will come to the stage of doing the new task and doing it passably well, and even seeing that it has the desired impact, yet you will not feel "right" or completely congruent doing it. This is a crucial stage because although you have chosen rationally to prize the skill and you have worked diligently to "get the skill down," your more amorphous, slow-to-change emotional reactions are still conditioned to the "old" behaviors and beliefs. To pass through this stage, have confidence that your emotions will eventually readjust to the new pattern.
4. *Emotional insight:* Congruent performance on the job. Now it feels "right."
5. *Personality integration:* New behavior becomes part of your personality performed congruently in both work and nonwork settings.

Learning new treatment skills is like learning how to drive a car. First you read the driver's manual, play with the steering wheel, and kick the tires until you get an idea of what you need to do in order to drive. Secondly, you practice. You are cautious at first! You don't go too fast; you signal three blocks before you turn. But after a while, you get smooth. Thirdly, you know you can get where you want to go, but you are still very self-conscious. You worry about whether other drivers think you are too slow at a stop light. You feel funny moving out into an intersection to make a left turn. You wonder if you will ever feel as natural at the wheel as your friends do when they drive. You wonder if it would not be easier, after all, to take the bus or con someone into giving you a ride. Fourthly, you find yourself able to concentrate on the traffic and let yourself just do what needs to be done. You make all the right moves without having to work at it. You feel "right" behind the wheel, just as if you have always been doing it. Fifthly, you just assume that you are a "driver." There is no question in your mind that when you want to go somewhere, you will drive. Driving has become a "taken-for-granted" part of you.

Substitute, in this process, a treatment skill like reflecting or reinforcement and you will have the process through which you will proceed in that learning as well.

Professional Development

Depending on your experience in the helping professions, you may view this training sequence from various positions along a professional developmental continuum. The skills trained in the sequence have significance no matter where you are in your development. However, your development will alter your perception of the complexity and relevance of the skills.

Consider Peterson's (1975) professional developmental model; briefly the stages progress as follows:

1. *Novice:* "Help me make it through the night."
2. *Smug Sophomore:* "I made it, this isn't all that tough."
3. *Jittery Journeyman:* "Wow! Now I know how much I didn't know."
4. *Master:* "I'm ready for more."
5. *Teacher:* "I have something to share."

If you are a novice, you will see the skills in this sequence as lifesavers. If you are a master you will enjoy the refined points of the skills and find a good deal of self-confirmation. If you fall somewhere in between, your reactions will vary accordingly.

Feelings and Issues for the Treatment Worker

This section illustrates some very specific things that you may experience from yourself or from others.

"When will I be competent enough?" Two equally appropriate answers to this are "never" and "you already are." One of the problems of working in this field is that you cannot learn how to do treatment without doing treatment. So you must start at a less than proficient state. You may learn as much from your clients as they do from you, and that's okay. Another fact of learning to do treatment is that you are never done learning. You change, the people you work with change, the methods you use change. The task proceeds in an excitingly continuous way. For the moment assume that you can start now, and with training and supervision you will see yourself becoming more and more competent in more and more areas of a virtually limitless treatment landscape.

"It's nice to see you and I've got a little pain right here." You may hear such statements as people come to perceive you as a "helper." To some extent you may be flattered, yet taken to an extreme, the expectation that you are always "open for business" may wear thin. Protect yourself from working twenty-four hours a day by clearly stating your limits, and by asking for reciprocal support and nurturance from your friend-clients.

"Why are you going into that field? You know all these treatment people are a little bit crazy?" This question is often embarrassingly followed by the phrase "Present company excepted, of course." When people do not understand what you do or find treatment activities fearsome, they may deal with

that ignorance and fear by projecting negative attributes on the treatment people—and on you by association. Rather than accept this ricochetted discount, or fuming in silence, we suggest calmly insisting that neither you nor others you know of in the field are crazy. It is true that since you are more self–aware, you and your co-workers may be more in touch with the pain and vulnerability of the stresses of living and may communicate this more. Likewise, it is true that one of the popular motives for getting into the treatment area is to gain self-understanding. In any event, redefining the assumptions of the people you come in contact with shunts aside the possibility that you accept the myth embodied in the first sentence in this section.

"What's in it for me?" Treatment workers function effectively with a great variety of motives. Altruism exists alongside of other intentions that on the surface sound more crass and selfish. Whatever your motives (self-exploration, dominance, assuaging guilt, achievement, etc.) you can be sure that some effective treatment worker somewhere also has the same ones. The key is to translate these motives into effective action. To deny other than virtuous motives closes you off from their potential energy, and thus you lose a valuable resource. All of your motives are okay to start with. Use as your criterion for evaluating them their usefulness to you in doing treatment.

Behavioral Hints

You can make your life easier during training by following the suggestions below. All of them are easier said than done. But done, they make your experience in training potentially more useful.

Avoid thinking in terms of traits. Our language fosters the assumption that behavior has its origins within us. The catastrophic notion that there may be something terribly wrong with you because of what you do or do not do ignores the fact that behavior and internal states of being are not necessarily related on a one-to-one basis. You may act anxious in certain situations when you are not in fact an "anxious" person. You may be scared stiff on the inside, but carry off a calm exterior facade. This discontinuity between internal and external only illustrates the tremendous flexibility that humans possess. So we recommend suspending all labeling of behavior as representative of internal personality traits for the duration of training. Such labeling implies inalterability of behavior. Likewise, we recommend questioning all assumptions about personality traits you bring with you into training. Training is a time for possibilities.

Give yourself a break by assuming you have some positive intent even if your results are poor. This may come as a shock, but you are not perfect. Expecting yourself to attain over-idealized goals within the first five minutes of training will set you up to feel miserable. On the other hand you no doubt already do many things that make your treatment effective. Please take credit for those things. If you enter training expecting to discover all you do wrong, you will surely find those things and more. We suggest adopting the attitude that you have strengths to build on and a vast vista of new things to learn.

Relate your professional learning to your personal life. Although a personal/professional split is possible, we think that such a separation takes a great deal of effort to maintain. This book trains such basic communications and relating skills that you cannot help using them in any relationship. If you behave differently in your different relationships, the cost of monitoring yourself will tax relationships, or the skills you use will fall to a level midway between everyday behaviors and treatment skills. Experiment cautiously with the skills to find how they can be adapted to your nonprofessional life.

Go with the flow. Throughout the book you will encounter the "be spontaneous" paradox. Your task is to perform an unfamiliar behavior in a natural way. The key to mastering this task is developing a trust in your ability to process and react to events on a subconscious level. Allow the knowledge of the skills to recede into the background and allow your reactions to emerge without qualification. You will be surprised at yourself.

In summary, training will change you. Training has different effects on different people. How much you develop depends both on where you start from and on how much you allow and encourage yourself to experiment with the skills in the training sequence.

Part I

OBSERVATION AND LEVELS OF HELPER FUNCTIONING

In this part of the book our aim is to give you information and primary skills necessary to help you work towards the "therapeutic use of self." You are the instrument of treatment. As such, you can enhance the techniques you will be learning later, or you can block them. The key issue for this part of the book is to promote a sophisticated awareness of self that can be maintained through later skill chapters. Research on the good helper/poor helper and categories of personality functioning will aid you in developing the beginnings of an individual statement of who you are and what you want to be within the helping context. Observation, the most basic of all skills, provides the means to monitor yourself and others in a meaningful way. Clarity of perception forms the foundation for treatment skills and for adjustment of behavior. For each person, those adjustments and self-understandings will be unique and flexible. They will change with experience and with the addition of the skills to be learned later. Our personal experience is that our understanding and use of self continues to change as we expose ourselves to more treatment stituations. The sense of self that develops expresses itself through the medium of the techniques that we use. Therefore, in the long run, we urge you to work towards both differentiation of self and differentiation of skill. The more options you have both personally and in terms of treatment skills, the more able you will be to respond effectively to the demands of treatment. Many "right" ways exist to help people. Allow yourself the time to mature as a treatment worker. The beginnings of that maturation process proceed from an awareness of self.

Chapter 2

PERSONALITY

"Is the glass half full or is it half empty?" People's tendency to perceive themselves as "empty" or "full" depends to some extent on their early learning. We believe the full/empty, black/white, good/bad notion of personality taps only the extremes of functioning, thus, falsely implying that these categories lie in qualitatively different dimensions. We believe that any personality trait can be described positively or negatively. As the diagram below illustrates, the characteristic of dominance, for example, can be construed as positive, i.e., "teaching," or negative, i.e., "bossing." (Armas, 1957.) (See Figure 2-1.)

Thus, you can accept your personality "as is." It is the raw material with which you have to work. You need not exclude any parts of yourself. As a matter of fact, to do so, may deny yourself a rich resource for your development as a treatment worker. Oftentimes a person's greatest strength emerges as the obverse of his greatest weakness.

Personality is not generally a crucial factor in working with troubled children. That is, people of widely differing personalities can help troubled children. The crucial factor seems to be whether or not the skills and techniques the worker uses fit his personality. For example, both a somewhat disorganized, free-floating individual and a more organized compulsive one can be effective with kids if they choose skills that fit or mesh with their respective styles.

There are limits. Some people should not be in the helping professions given the present state of their personality. A person who is overwhelmed by others might better choose to become a lighthouse tender who has only

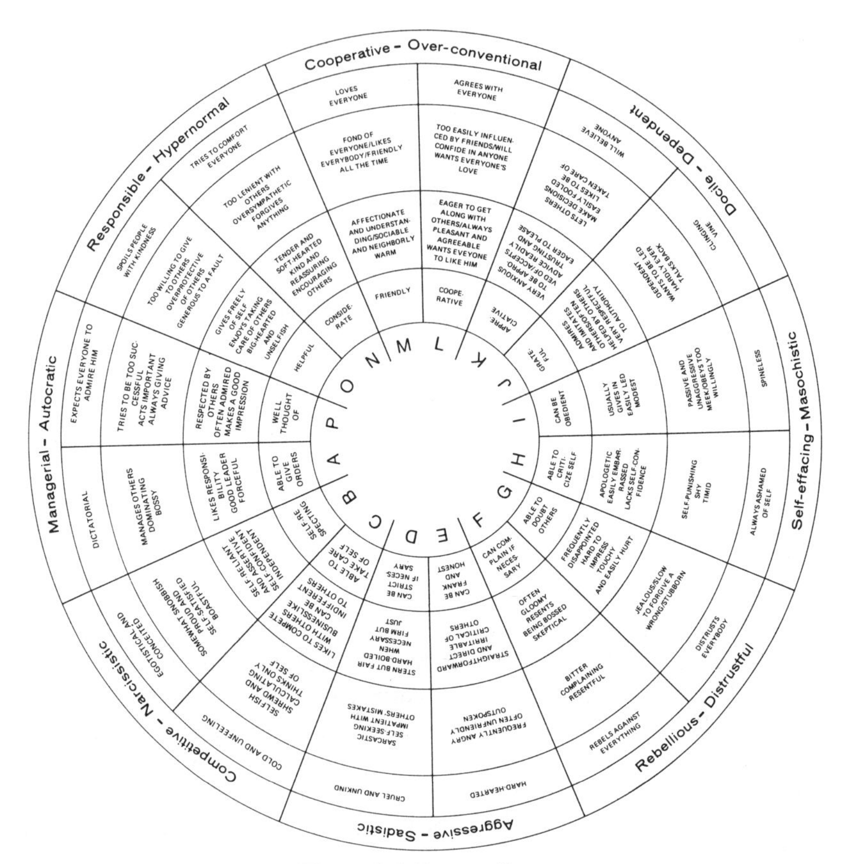

Figure 2-1. Personality

limited contact with others. Likewise, a person who relieves unresolved anger through indirect hostility toward the young would do better to work through his anger before intruding himself on troubled children.

The goals of this chapter are to explain some processes involved in personality, and to increase awareness of the interaction between personality and helping. Your training will help you to become aware of your own blind spots and vulnerabilities, and to anticipate and remedy difficulties with skills and types of children and co-workers. There is no such thing as a completely adaptable and flexible person who works equally well with all types of people and who performs all skills at a high level. We are not asking you to become a super-helper. There are, however, some things you can do to expand the range and sophistication of your abilities and personality.

Definition of Personality

Personality is an enduring (but not unchangeable) set of concrete habits of thought, feeling, and behavior which interacts with physical aspects of the person. In this chapter we avoid developing a typology of personality. Rather, we will explain some of the many processes that contribute to development and expression of personality.

One of the assumptions about personality that we want to avoid is the "trait" assumption. To see personality as a set of traits implies two things: 1) that personality is abstract and 2) that personality is unchanging. Often people take their own or others' evaluations of their own behavior to define the "self." For example, a child of average intelligence going to school in a class of geniuses may come to see himself as "dumb." In fact, he is less intelligent when compared to his peers in class, but to accept the label of "dumb" as valid for all time and in all places may lead the child to a faulty perception and definition of himself. Likewise, a person who has grown up without appropriate models for the expression of anger may vent his rage through hostile words and actions towards other people. That does not mean that he is forever and always a "hostile" person. It means that he lacks the skills necessary to deal with his anger in more constructive ways. If one assumes that personality is an abstract quality of the mind which cannot be touched, then people are stuck with labels like dumb or hostile. On the other hand, if we assume that personality is represented in concrete behavior, thoughts, and feelings, then we can move to deal with the concrete manifestations of personality. If we assume an unchangeable nature to personality, we can shrug our shoulders and forget about expending any energy on effecting change. In contrast, specific thoughts, feelings, and behaviors are changeable.

The decision to suspend trait thinking can be a difficult one to sustain. Our language and typical modes of thinking foster the trait approach. To help understand the eventual circularity of trait thinking, consider the following example.

We, as outside observers, notice several incidents in which George, a fictional treatment worker, behaves in a nurturant way towards kids. We see him comfort a child with a skinned knee. We see him offer his handerchief to a sniffling child. We see him rocking a child while reading that child a story. Our typical shorthand way of talking about these incidents is to label George rather than labeling his behavior. Thus George comes to be seen as a "nurturant" person rather than as a person who behaved nurturantly in three specific situations. This minor verbal shift implies a major difference in the ways we will expect George to act in the future. If George is a nurturant, person i.e. possesses nurturance (a trait), then we will expect him to react in a nurturant way at all times, in all situations, because, after all, that is the way he is. If he behaves differently, we will be surprised and may even comment to him, "George, that's not like you at all." We have assumed that behavior issues from the inside out, that the personality trait of "nurturance" must be present for nurturant behavior to occur. The truth is, as you will remember, that we have assumed that trait in George on

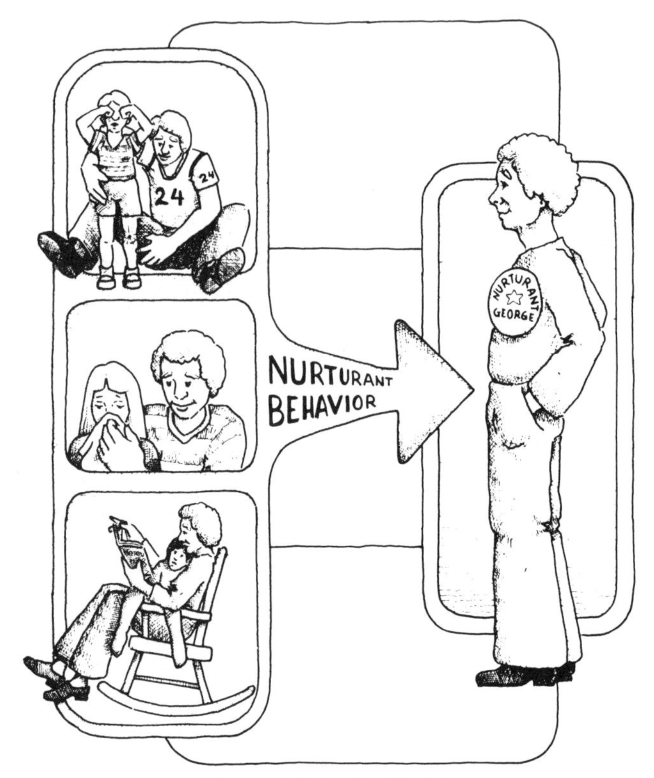

Figure 2-2. Trait Thinking

the basis of what we have observed him doing. Thus a trait attributed to a person on the basis of his behavior is expected to cause that behavior. It is like saying that night has the quality of darkness because of the absence of light; and there is an absence of light because it is dark. The terms do not explain each other, they merely label the same situation. (See Figure 2-2.)

In the following sections we will briefly survey some of the layers of self that contribute to personality. During this survey, pay attention to what "fits" for you. Try to get a feel for how the processes identified below can help you understand your personality more clearly.

Physical Aspects of Personality

Since we function as holistic beings, personality must take into account some of the physical as well as psychological aspects of human personality. We shall consider three general physical factors: temperament, cycles, and bodily characteristics.

Temperament

Temperament, as explained by Thomas & Chess (1977), is a "wired-in" behavioral style or physical responsiveness that refers to the *how* rather than *what* or *why* of behavior. It can be clearly defined in each individual as early as three months of age. This pattern of response to environmental stimuli seems fairly consistent over time. Its interaction with differing environmental situations yields differences among individuals. Below are listed the nine variables of temperament.

Activity Level: the motor component of a person's functioning as indicated by the daily proportion of active and inactive periods

Rhythmicity (Regularity): the predictability and/or unpredictability of any function, e.g., eating, sleeping

Approach or Withdrawal: the nature of the initial response to a new situation or stimulus

Adaptability: responses to new or altered situations. This variable measures not the nature of the initial responses but the ease with which such responses are modified in desired directions.

Threshold of Responsiveness: the intensity level of stimulation that is necessary to evoke a response, regardless of the way in which the response is expressed or the sensory modality affected

Intensity of Reaction: the energy level of a response, regardless of its quality or direction

Quality of Mood: the amount of pleasant, joyful, and friendly behavior, as contrasted with unpleasant, sad, and unfriendly behavior

Distractability: how much irrelevant environmental stimuli interfere with or alter the direction of ongoing behavior

Attention Span and Persistence: attention span concerns the length of time a person continues in a specific activity. Persistence refers to the person's continuation of an activity in the face of obstacles to continuation (Thomas & Chess, 1977). Although adults' temperamental patterns are affected by environmental learning, the basic patterns remain.

Cycles

Human behavior often follows cyclical patterns. Some of these cycles are easily observable while some are more obscure.

Yearly cycles: e.g., the post-Christmas depression that some people feel, response to seasons, spring fever

Monthly cycles: the menstrual cycle in women may be more obvious, yet males are also subject to such repeated patterns

Daily cycles: e.g., some people work more effectively in the early morning, while others cannot function effectively until late in the day

Biorhythms: this approach specifies three separate cycles: intellectual, physical, and emotional. The proponents of this approach say that people are vulnerable to environmental effects during "crossover" days, i.e., days when the cycles are moving from high or low to their opposite. Especially "critical" days occur when all three cycles crossover at the same time (Thommen, 1964).

Bodily Characteristics

We all are endowed with a body that has certain definable characteristics, for example, height, physical strength, endurance, color-blindness, hearing impairment, or other physical advantages or restrictions. Such differences among individuals will affect what we perceive and how we perceive it.

HABITS OF THOUGHT, FEELING, AND BEHAVIOR

Habits of Thought

Habits of thought can be viewed as both content and process and as both in and out of awareness. The historically developed content of our personal beliefs carry images and definitions of self that influence how we interpret reality and provide us with a private logic to justify our behavior and feelings. Script Analysis from Transactional Analysis theory (Steiner, 1971) provides one explanation of how such beliefs are formed and how they affect feelings and behavior.

We use specific processes of thoughts on a daily basis to think about events that impinge on us. Some of these processes lead us to erroneous conclusions based on the information presented to us. Examples include catastrophizing, (from Rational Emotive Therapy theory—Ellis & Harper, 1961), dichotomous thinking (from George Kelly's Personal Construct theory—Maher, 1969), stereotyping (from social psychological studies—Secord & Backman, 1969), and restricted perception and representation of information via selective sensory modalities (Grinder & Bandler 1976).

Habits of Feeling

Feelings associated with certain events and beliefs about acceptable channels of expression determine what we experience and express. Historically we have developed associations of internal feeling with external situations. Often the feelings we learned at the time served a practical purpose. For example, a child may learn to give his parents the answers that he thinks they want to hear rather than what he believes to be true because he fears a criticism or even physical harm. Some of these associations, however, may be carried on beyond their functional limits into situations in which the feared consequences are unlikely to occur. Thus, the child mentioned above may, as an adult, fear giving his true reactions to questions even when these reactions will be accepted and even approved of by others. This feeling response then is functionally autonomous (Wolpe, 1976).

Each of us develops his or her own favorite modes of expressing feeling. Although there may be many opportunities to experience and express a wide variety of feelings, most of us have a small set of favorite feelings (Rackets in Transactional Analysis terminology, James & Jongeward, 1973). These feelings often substitute for other feelings that might be more appropriately expressed, e.g., some people translate anger into guilt and depression, some people feel anger when they are afraid or hurt.

Habits of Behavior

Responses to everyday events grow out of our personal history as well as our efforts to maintain consistency among thought, feeling, and behavior. We learn our behavioral means of coping with the demands of life in several different ways. Sometimes we strive to meet ideal goals set by ourselves or others. For example, throwing a football fifty yards as a goal requires a specific sequence of actions before meeting that goal. Sometimes we try to behave in accordance with characteristics attributed to us by oneself or others. For example, if a child thinks she is "bright," she may persist in a difficult academic task until she finds a solution rather than giving up sooner. Some behavior is learned by trial and error while we are under duress. In such times our usual coping behaviors may not work effectively: therefore, we improvise in order to reduce the current stress. Other behavior is learned by design. Doing things in the ways that others do them (modeling) increases behavioral alternatives. Formal and informal teaching/learning situations such as classes or independent study may lead to new behavior.

Behavior tends to move toward consistency with thought and feeling. Some habits of behavior, consciously or unconsciously, complete a circle of interactions that repeatedly occurs in our lives. People often persist in trying to solve their problems or deal with their discomfort in ways that cause the problem or discomfort to continue (Watzlawick, Weakland & Fisch, 1974). For example, the child who vents his hurt or anger by destroying others' property or by acting aggressively toward others is likely to become more hurt and angry as a result of his actions. Therefore, he will vent more, etc.

Why Personality Affects Ability to Work with Troubled Children

The work environment is just another setting in which personality is expressed. Although some aspects of personality may appear only in specific situations, adults, more than children, use internal controls to carry consistent personality attributes across situations. Therefore, you can expect that most aspects of your personality will arise in the work setting.

Children somehow release very intense feelings in adults. Strong joy, attachments, frustration, and anger are shown by people working with children. Troubled children, almost by definition, require even more intense involvement because "normal" methods of dealing with them usually do not work well. This intensity will magnify adult personality characteristics, both the strengths and the vulnerabilities.

In addition, the stock in trade of the helper is interpersonal interaction on a daily basis. Personality and interaction cannot be downplayed or ignored. You will have to deal with children's personalities and children will have an effect on yours.

Effects of Personality on Working with Troubled Children

Because of the mesh of your personalities, you will find yourself attracted or repulsed with some children more than others. You will find yourself better able to work with some children than with others. You will also find yourself better able to work with some co-workers than others. You will feel more comfortable engaging in some skills than others. Each person's experience will be different. We have no sage advice that will make the process simple. We do, however, have some experience with people in the helping professions that may help you locate some specific personality vulnerabilities that could potentially cause you some difficulty. As an example, consider the issue of control in treatment. Each of the following persons may overcontrol, but the motivation for such overcontrol originates from the unique personality of each. Thus, the behavioral expression is similar although the origins in personality are different. Consider the following as examples, *not* personality types.

The Achiever. If you frame your definition of self on the basis of what you achieve, you may be vulnerable to intense frustration or depression by carrying that framework into the helping situation in which the evaluation of achievement is based on therapeutic outcome. Therapeutic outcome depends on you *and* your client. You alone cannot decide that the child will get better. Therefore, you are, in some respects, at the mercy of your clientele. To base your definition of self on the good will of other people opens you to the possibility that your failure to "make people better" will lead you to think poorly of yourself. The key here is to refocus your attention on the *process* of helping so that you can feel successful in the ways in which you have worked even if your client chooses not to change.

THE PEACEMAKER. Some people define their role as that of peacemaker—the one who makes things "all better." If you feel that your job is to help people feel better, you may fall prey to the urge to avoid pain. One of the hardest lessons for the peacemaker to learn is to allow other people their pain. Even harder is to see that pain can be an ally in the therapeutic process, because without it a good deal of the motivation for change may be defused. So rather than feeling guilty that someone feels pain, or anxious because they might undergo some pain-arousing experiences, you can cast pain as a team member working with you, not against you, for a more comprehensive resolution of the problematic situation.

THE RESCUER. Steiner (1971) thoroughly examines this pattern of thought, feeling, and behavior. For the moment we can compare a rescuer to the Boy Scout who helped the little old lady across the street even though she did not want to go. If you have a special place in your heart for the underdog, and find yourself helping people without invitation, you may be vulnerable to feelings of helplessness and powerlessness when the object of help indicates that she didn't want the help at all. Implied in the act of uninvited help is the assumption that the person you help is unable to work things out for himself. No matter how sweetly this assumption is couched, people are likely to rebel and lash out. One way to avoid the rescuer position is to make sure that you have an explicit agreement with your client as to how much of what kind of help is acceptable.

THE CATASTROPHIZER. Compare this pattern of response to the little Dutch boy with one finger already in the dike who suddenly sees ten more spurts of water gushing forth. He is all alone and he has only ten fingers; there are eleven holes and the safety of the whole country depends on him. If you find yourself working wildly to keep everything going smoothly and according to plan for fear that if you do not then something awful (real or imagined) will happen to your client and to you, then you fit in this pattern. Catastrophizers have a hard time allowing their clients to make their own mistakes. They feel overly responsible and so take control. The control comes not so much from a wish to manipulate others as an urgent need to prevent things from falling apart. The key with this pattern is to allow yourself to ask for and accept aid from other workers even if that aid is less effective or efficient than you would have done it yourself. Also, test your fear that the world will collapse by allowing little lapses of control in safe situations. Continued vigilance and overresponsibility stay the fear of catastrophy but lead to harried fatigue and resentment.

How Personality Relates to Skill Training

The skills in this book are presented "as if" each of us had the same personality—obviously that is not so. Students and trainers must take those differences into account because personality will affect skill training. *Genuine response* is a goal; that is, each of you works to develop a flexible set of skills that are compatible with your personality. *Flexibility of response* is a goal; that is, many genuine therapeutic responses are available for most personalities. At the same time skill training will affect personality. Competent performance of a broad range of skills may lead to a broadened personality. A restricted personality and restricted skills keep the effectiveness of the helper narrow. We suggest that you experiment with new skills that don't "feel right" so that you can adapt them to your style while maintaining the effectiveness of the skill, and you can thus provide yourself with behavioral alternatives that may lead to new habits of thought, feeling, and behavior. Also remember that trainees go through an uncomfortable, "cognitive dissonance" stage before their feelings converge with thoughts and behaviors (see "Effects of Training"). Prepare yourself to tolerate some discomfort in order to expand helping abilities.

When you discover apparent deficits or difficulties in your personality, we suggest that you reframe those originally negatively labeled qualities as resources for you. Although it sounds somewhat paradoxical, you can use all parts of your personality for positive goals. Therefore, when you find a seemingly negative facet, follow the steps below:

1. Determine the function of the personality facet. What does it do for you?
2. Ask yourself if you would be willing to allow yourself to use that negative facet of your personality as a valuable resource in your work towards becoming a good treatment worker.
3. If you can answer "Yes" to yourself, then think of two or three ways in which you can maintain that seemingly negative facet of personality while at the same behaving in ways that move towards your goal.

For example, you may dislike self–effacing, shy, and embarrassed parts of yourself. Yet by moving beyond the negative connotations of these characteristics, you can use them for positive ends by defining yourself as nondefensive, open to feedback, and self-examining. It is surprising the transformation that can occur in your perception of the specific personality facet when you can allow yourself to use that part of yourself as a help not a hindrance.

Finally, the relationship between skills and personality is never fixed once and for all. It is a continual process as your skills develop and as your personality changes. So, as a bit of sage advice, settle for a long journey with plenty of interesting sights and sounds along the way. There will be lots of bumps and jolts, but the view is great.

Chapter 3

VALUES AND BELIEFS

The ability to think is humankind's greatest blessing and curse. People are able to look at and understand events that impinge upon them from a variety of perspectives. This uniquely human talent can be very helpful. At the same time, thoughts and beliefs about the way the world "should" work act as filters that interpret reality. Thus, people may see and experience the world as they think it "ought to be" rather than the way it, in fact, is. And the difference between what "is" and what they believe "ought to be" may create tension, unhappiness, and anger. An awareness of the beliefs that helpers bring into their work will aid them in developing more consistency between what they believe and what they do.

BELIEFS

Before getting on to an explanation of values in the helping process, let us look at the concept of belief as the major component of values. Beliefs serve several functions. First, they filter our experience, thereby reinterpreting information to fit with previously used ways of conceptualizing events. Also, they make us more or less alert to events that agree or disagree with our preconceptions. Secondly, beliefs shape feeling and behavior. We feel and act in accordance with our interpretations of environmental events. The following illustration shows an abstract conception of how this shaping happens. For a more concrete example consider the following situation: Three people sitting on a park bench see a snake crawling toward them. One screams and runs away; the second yawns and returns to reading his newspaper; the third smiles and goes over to pick up the snake. On the basis of their behavior you can guess that the three people have different beliefs about the snake. Even though the snake is objectively the same to all three people, each responds on a feeling and behavioral level congruent with his or her belief about what snakes are and do. In treatment the process is the same. Three treatment workers can observe two children arguing over a toy. The first, believing that she must avoid conflict at all cost, might become fearful that a fight will ensue, so she would move in to resolve the potential violence. The second, believing that the children must work out their own disagreements even if they come to blows, would allow them to continue arguing and observe their behavior. The third, believing that one of the children does not have the skills to resolve the argument in a constructive way, would be excited by this opportunity to stand on the periphery and coach both towards resolving the conflict. Treatment workers respond to what they believe to be important. We believe that it is important for you to become aware of what is important to you. (See Figure 3-1.)

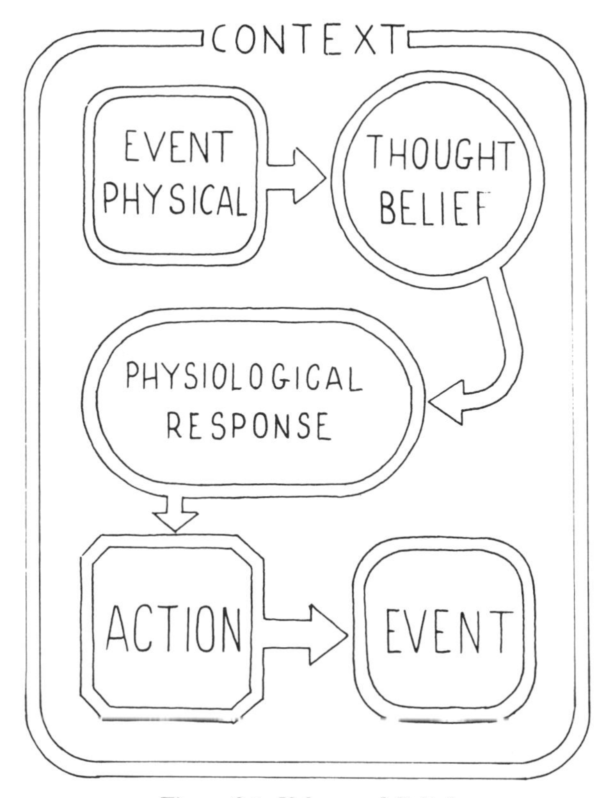

Figure 3-1. Values and Beliefs

Beliefs and Values

We will use the term "values" as a more inclusive concept that contains belief, feeling, and action. Thus, belief is a subpart of value.

Clear values, according to Raths, Harmin and Simon (1956) include three parts:

1. The value must be *freely* chosen from a set of alternatives.
2. The value must be *prized.* That is, a person must be willing to say publicly that he believes in this particular value and that he feels good about the value.
3. The value must be *acted upon* consistently.

A person with clear values shows the following characteristics: positiveness, purposefulness, enthusiasm, and pride.

The major consideration when examining values as they function in treatment is evaluating the congruence between belief, feeling, and action. People may do things that they do not believe in, or they may feel bad about the things they do, or they may not act on deeply cherished beliefs. Any of these situations illustrates unclear values.

Clear and Unclear Values

Given that there are three parts to a value, there can be many different examples of unclear values. We have found that the most common unclear-value situation persistently undermining good helping arises from those values that are freely chosen but not acted on, whether or not they are prized, and from those values that are not freely chosen and yet acted on, whether or not they are prized.

A value may be freely chosen, prized, but not acted upon. In this case, words and actions do not match. The person may believe that he is acting upon his chosen and prized values and yet may not be doing so. People in the helping professions often find themselves in this situation. A great deal of verbal support is given for spending time with children, yet paperwork and meetings consume large chunks of time and effort, limiting the person's ability to behave in accordance with her beliefs.

A value may be freely chosen, but not prized or acted upon. A person who believes in a child's right to express his feelings, and yet feels outraged by this and shuts off the child would be an example of this position.

A value may not be freely chosen, and yet prized and acted upon. In this case the person follows through on expectations in the roles in which he finds himself. For example, he may believe that a helper ought to be warm, accepting, and empathetic, and since he wants to be a helper, he may feel that he has no choice but to accept and prize this set of values, like it or not.

Values may be neither freely chosen nor prized, and yet may be acted upon. This is a situation in which a person may have grown up believing that she was basically introverted. She does not like this but finds herself acting on the expectation despite not liking it.

The values that you decide upon may not necessarily be those listed in this chapter. We do not demand that you act on and prize a set of beliefs that you do not freely choose, since that contradicts the goals of value clarification. However, by explaining some contrasts in beliefs, by exploring the various available alternatives, and by allowing discussion and debate of limits and the circumstances that may relate to each belief, you will hopefully clarify some of your values in relationship to working with troubled children.

It would be nice if we did not have to bother with all this effort at clarifying values, but the alternatives can be grim. No matter what we do or say, we express some values. And, sometimes we may act on values contrary to what we know to be therapeutic without being aware of the contradiction. By cloaking ourselves in the mantle of "proper beliefs" in the pursuit of becoming the "perfect helper," we cut off inevitable conflicts that arise between our actions and feelings. Thus we present a false portrait of ourselves to the children we work with. The major issue then becomes keeping in touch with the various ways in which we express values and monitoring the expression of those values in situations that may strain our abilities to remain clear. For example, someone may believe that children are able to solve their own problems given the proper support, and yet find himself faced with children of extremely limited abilities. How then can a worker's action be consistent with his belief in a situation that invites behavior contrary to it? The resolution of such paradoxical situations fuels the clarification process.

Throughout the skill chapters to follow in this book we will address some problematic beliefs that hinder appropriate use of the skills in the section entitled "Feelings and Issues for the Treatment Worker."

Functions of Belief Versus Behavior in Helping

We would like to avoid the possible misconception that all you have to do is "believe the right things" and you will be a wonderful treatment worker. Our emphasis on values as a comprehensive concept illustrates the necessity of responding totally. Thus, as we list below the values and perceptions of good versus poor helpers, remember that these alone will not lead to positive behavioral response in helping situations. Clear values, that is, the consistency of belief, feeling, and behavior, will allow a helper to respond to the ever-changing demands of the helping situation in a way that maintains therapeutic impact. There are many "right ways" to help people, and the good helper will have at his fingertips the specific behavioral responses that he must employ given the specific relations in which he finds himself at any particular moment.

Beliefs Characteristic of Good Versus Poor Helpers

The information in Table 3-1 from *The Helping Relationships* by Combs, Alvila, and Purkey (1971) comes from a series of studies of good versus poor helpers that covers several areas of beliefs: beliefs about others, beliefs about self, beliefs about the purposes of helping, beliefs about approaches to helping.

The variables in Table 3-1 are not meant to be dichotomous. The beliefs held by good versus poor helpers are not black or white; there are gradations between them. Thus, you may find yourself not agreeing 100 percent with all the beliefs that a good helper holds and at the same time, not quite disagreeing with the beliefs that a poor helper holds. You are likely to be somewhere in the middle. It is useful to look at the good versus poor helper beliefs as a continuum.

The list of comparisons is theoretical and represents ideal goals. When you compare yourself to these beliefs, you will most likely fall well below the level of perfection. Relax!! You are not alone. The idea of presenting these beliefs is to furnish a reference point. You may find yourself acting consistently with some of these beliefs already. If so, hurray. This list may help you become more articulate with your existing values. You may find that you act inconsistently with some of the beliefs. Your task then is to examine your beliefs using the values clarification format. In other words, Table 3-1 should be used as a source of information to perk your examination of your own values concerning treatment.

Research has indicated that there is no difference between good and poor helpers on their *verbal report* of what they believe about helping. But, observations of good versus poor helpers showed differences in behavior. So, it is not what a person says but rather how he follows through on those beliefs. Again look to the concept of values to gain consistency between thought, feeling and action.

When observing someone in order to determine his position on the continuum of beliefs, it is important to remember to observe in an "as if" fashion. Because you are unable to get inside another person's head and to observe his beliefs directly, all you can say is that they are behaving "as if" they're following a particular belief. Combs calls this *inferential observation* "reading behavior backwards" (see Chapter 5, "Observation"). Making the assumption that behavior and belief are consistent, you will read the behavior as an indicator of the person's belief. Even though the person verbalizes a contrary belief, his behavior speaks louder. Therefore, your focus is on what people do to act out their beliefs, as opposed to what they say to explain or justify their actions. You may be shocked at what other people read into your behavior, and others may be surprised at what you read into theirs. Attempt to receive the information as a gift, and keep rationalizing and self-justification to a minimum. When giving feedback, do so as objectively and caringly as you can.

One final note—the research that identified these good versus poor helper beliefs was not focused on people working with troubled children. The research included elementary school teachers, counselors, Episcopal priests, and college professors. The beliefs that differentiate good from poor workers with troubled children may vary from these. Therefore, look at this list of beliefs merely as good information as a jumping off place for you to clarify your own values. (See Table 3-1.)

Using the Beliefs Scales for Observation

Examining all of the variables in Table 3-1 will give you a chance to experience the breadth of values that affect good helping. If, however, you try to observe all these variables at once, you will find yourself overloaded with demands that split your attention too many different ways. We suggest that you choose three or four scales to observe at one time. Ideally, these scales should be selected according to the specific belief you wish to fit into the values clarification process. As an example, we include at the end of the chapter a rating scale that samples the beliefs used by Wasicsko (1975) in his research on teacher selection.

Behavioral Hints

As you engage in the values clarification process consider the following suggestions:

Attribute to Yourself Good Intentions. Some of the discrepancies between what you do and what you say will be disheartening. You may even have an urge to talk yourself down. Give yourself a break. The problem most often is not with your intentions, but with the way in which you carry them out. Look upon your awareness of the discrepancy as an opportunity to develop a clear and therapeutically relevant set of values.

When Considering Your Values, Ask Yourself the Following Values-Clarification Questions—

a. How did I come to hold this value? Was it freely chosen after careful consideration of many alternatives?
b. What are my feelings about this value? Am I willing to speak for it in public?
c. How is my value translated into action? Do I act on this value repeatedly over time?

Table 3–1. Beliefs that Differentiate "Good" versus "Poor" Helpers

	Good Helper	*Poor Helper*
Beliefs about others		
1. Able-Unable*	People have the capacity to deal with their problems. Given the appropriate conditions people can develop their own solutions.	People do not have the capacity to deal with their own problems. They need someone to do it for them.
2. Friendly-Unfriendly	People are friendly and do what they do through good intentions.	People are unfriendly and threatening. They do not have good intentions for their behavior.
3. Worthy-Unworthy	People have worth in their own right; therefore their dignity and respect must be maintained.	People are not worthy in their own right; therefore some people may be treated in ways that violate their dignity and respect.
4. Internally-Externally Motivated	People can actively direct their own lives in dynamic and creative ways.	People cannot direct their own lives and must passively wait for external events to direct them.
5. Dependable-Undependable*	People behave in understandable, lawful ways. Their behavior can dependably be related to meaningful principles of human behavior.	People behave in unpredictable capricious ways. Their behavior follows no dependable patterns. Who knows what they're going to do next and why?
6. Helpful-Hindering	People can help me grow and meet my needs. They are sources of satisfaction.	People will detract from me. They will block my needs and threaten my ability to gain personal satisfaction.
Beliefs about self		
1. Identified-Unidentified*	I belong. I am similar in many ways to everyone else. I can identify with the experiences of others.	I don't belong. I am different from other people. I feel alienated and removed from the experiences of others.
2. Adequate-Inadequate*	I have within me the resources to deal with my own problems.	I do not have within me the resources to deal with my own problems.
3. Trustworthy-Untrustworthy	I trust myself. I can depend on my own perceptions and abilities. I can cope with events competently.	I do not trust myself. I am unsure of my own perceptions and abilities. I am not sure about my abilities to cope with events competently.
4. Wanted-Unwanted	I am a likeable person. I can usually get other people to respond to me positively.	I am not a likeable person. I am usually ignored and rejected by other people.
5. Worthy-Unworthy	I am a worthwhile person. I have personal dignity and integrity. I am worthy of respect.	I do not count. My contributions are overlooked and discounted. I am not worthy of dignified, respectful responses from others.

Table 3–1. Continued

	Good Helper	Poor Helper
Beliefs about the purposes of helping		
1. Freeing-Controlling*	Helpers assist clients by facilitating the client's release of his/her own abilities to deal with a problem.	Helpers control the client by coercing or manipulating the client to behave differently.
2. Larger issues-Smaller issues*	Helpers view the clients' concerns in broad perspective. They are aware of the connotations and implications of events.	Helpers view the clients' concerns in narrow perspective. They focus on immediate and specific details of only the problem at hand.
3. Self-revealing-Self-concealing*	Helpers share themselves. They can treat their feelings and shortcomings as important and significant.	Helpers do not share themselves. They cover up feelings and shortcomings in the helping situation.
4. Involved-Alienated	Helpers commit themselves to the helping process. They become involved with their clients on a personal level.	Helpers remain aloof from the helping process. They do not allow themselves personal feelings about their clients.
5. Process oriented-Goal oriented	Helpers promote processes. They assist the client in the process of discovery of his solutions.	Helpers work towards preconceived solutions or helper-defined goal.
6. Altruistic-Narcissistic	Helpers use the helping situation to aid and assist others.	Helpers use the helping situation to satisfy personal goals.
Beliefs about approaches to helping		
1. People-Things	The helper's orientation focuses on people. Human responses and experiences are important.	The helper's orientation focuses on events, objects, rules, regulations, etc.
2. Perceptual-Objective*	The helper's orientation focuses on the clients' subjective experience or perception of events.	The helper's orientation focuses on objective reality of events.

SOURCE: Combs, A. W., Avila, D. L., and Purkey, W. W. *Helping Relationships: Basic Concepts for the Helping Professions*, Allyn and Bacon, Boston, 1971.
*Identified by research as significantly discriminating between good versus poor helpers.

USE YOUR ALREADY DEVELOPED SKILLS OF INFERENTIAL OBSERVATION. Most of us have already developed some skill in this area. The key in doing this with these variables is to keep focused on the list of beliefs in this chapter rather than introducing the concepts you might use in everyday inferential observation. By keeping focus you will be working from an agreed-upon set of definitions that you and others can refer to. After you become proficient at observing these variables, then you may want to branch out to others. Follow the steps below when making inferences—

a. Carefully examine the beliefs you have selected to observe. Read the definitions.
b. Observe some indicators of the beliefs: a segment of actual behavior, an audio- or videotape, a written account of a critical helping incident.
c. Reread the definitions of the beliefs and make your rating on the rating scales provided at the end of this chapter, or use other scales from Table 3-1. in this chapter.
d. Debrief with the person you observed. During the debriefing you may also want to include the person who was the target of the observed helping behavior. Children can provide a unique source of feedback to the helper.

ENGAGE IN COGNITIVE REHEARSAL OR ROLE–PLAYING TO EXAMINE THE EXTENT OF YOUR VALUES. Imagine seeing, hearing, and feeling how you might act out a value, or simulate a critical value situation and role-play your responses with a partner.

Attempt to resolve potential paradoxes between the good helper beliefs and actual situations you might encounter in your job.

HELPING BELIEFS RATING SCALE

BELIEFS ABOUT OTHERS

Able	*Unable*
People have the capacity to deal with their problems. Given the appropriate conditions people can develop their own solutions.	People do not have the capacity to deal with their own problems. They need someone to do it for them.

7 6 5 4 3 2 1

BELIEFS ABOUT SELF

Identified	*Unidentified*
I belong. I am similar in many ways to everyone else. I can identify with the experiences of others.	I do not belong. I am different than other people. I feel alienated and removed from the experiences of others.

7 6 5 4 3 2 1

BELIEFS ABOUT PURPOSES OF HELPING

Larger	*Smaller*
Helpers view the clients' concerns in broad perspective. They are aware of the connotations and implications of events.	Helpers view the clients' concerns in narrow perspective. They focus on immediate and specfic details of only the problem at hand.

7 6 5 4 3 2 1

BELIEFS ABOUT APPROACHES TO HELPING

People	*Things*
The helper's orientation focuses on people. Human responses and experience are important.	The helper's orientation focuses on events, objects, rules regulations, etc.

7 6 5 4 3 2 1

Chapter 4

RELATIONSHIP DIMENSIONS

A review of literature on positive outcome in counseling (Carkhuff, 1969) showed that the criterion that discriminates good from poor helpers was not their level of training, technique, or school of thought, but their ability to relate to their clients along certain dimensions. Although these dimensions grow out of client-centered or non-directive theory, their effects seem to exist within any theoretical approach. Ivey (1977) does caution, however, that behavioral indicators of these qualities may vary from culture to culture. The dimensions are defined below based on earlier work by Carkhuff (1969) and Gazda (1973).

Characteristics of a Facilitative Relationship

Warmth

A warm relationship is charcterized by compassion, kindness, and sensitivity to the feelings of the child. It is essential that the treatment worker communicate to the child, "I accept you. I see you as a worthwhile person even if I disagree with some important ideas you have." A person fostering warmth has the ability to care deeply without encouraging dependency relationships. Warmth from the treatment worker leads the child to an awareness that the counselor is kind and accepts him for what he is.

Respect

Respect is demonstrated through actions illustrating an intense belief that the child has the potential to deal constructively with her own problems —with appropriate help. Respect is communicated when the worker shows that she values the child enough to commit herself to a sharing rather than a controlling relationship. The treatment worker must be able to allow the child to work through her problem to her own solution in her own style. The worker's task is to affirm the child's abilities while helping to rally those abilities to cope with the problem at hand.

Empathy

To show empathetic understanding is to *know* how another feels and what he is experiencing without having to feel the same way yourself. To show empathy means to be able to infer accurately a child's feelings, attitudes, and beliefs (which are not observable) from what he is saying and doing (which is observable). The treatment worker must attempt to place himself in the position of the child. It is not sufficient for the worker to be aware only of feelings, beliefs, values, and future implications; he must also communicate these observations, inferences, and awareness. Worker empathy leads the child towards an awareness that the worker understands him.

Concreteness

This concept involves specific statements, that is, precise descriptions rather than generalities. Understandable vocabulary, examples, and eliciting of descriptive details lead to concrete understanding. The goal is fluent, direct, and complete expression of specific experiences and feelings by both worker and child. Concreteness on the part of the worker leads the child to an awareness that both she and the worker can communicate directly and completely about experiences and feelings that may have been previously avoided or unverbalized.

Genuineness

Genuineness is a congruence among actions, beliefs, values, and feelings. The concept has been used often by a variety of writers with a variety of meanings. Sometimes it seems to mean "honesty," at other times, "candid self disclosure." This dimension involves the ability to make what one does congruent with what one feels and to eliminate pretense from human interactions. Sensitivity to the needs of the client dictates that one does not always overtly *act* immediately upon his feelings; rather, congruence means that he is aware of his feelings and is free to choose his responses to them. Genuineness on the part of the worker leads the child to an awareness that the worker is not a "phony" pretending a facade, but that he is the person he represents himself to be to the child.

Self–disclosure

Through self-disclosure the worker provides models of behavior appropriate to a treatment context, and he or she demonstrates that he or she is just as human as the child. The key to facilitative self-disclosure is to use it to further the child's goals rather than to gratify the worker. Reacting in an honest, nondefensive manner to personal questions is also part of this characteristic. The key factors in making self-disclosure helpful are relevance to the child's goals, appropriate timing, and providing a model of an acceptable and constructive use of feelings, attitudes, and personal behavior.

Confrontation

A confrontation can be defined as a deliberate attempt to help another person examine the consequences of some aspect of his behavior. It expresses concern for the child and a wish to increase involvement. The purpose of a confrontation is to free the child to engage in more fruitful or less destructive behavior. In most cases this means confronting him in such a way that the child accepts the feedback. A worker's confronting the child leads the child towards an awareness that the worker cares deeply enough about him to insist that he look at behavior which may be growth inhibiting.

Immediacy

Immediacy focuses on the here-and-now interactions between worker and child. Using the worker/child relationship itself to work on problematic behavior and communication styles is the highest level of immediacy. Such a relationship allows the child to practice new ways of responding in a safe, personally supportive situation. Immediacy often involves drawing parallels between the worker/child relationship and other relationships, and insisting that the child relate her verbalization to herself as she is today rather than to people in general or to herself in the past.

Individual Versus Relationship

While we agree that it is important to foster the previously listed relationship qualities, we resist the often-made assumption that these qualities are characteristics of individuals. Our language labels traits or qualities of individuals more easily than it identifies traits or qualities of interaction. We agree with Gazda's statement (1973): "The nature of the interaction must be controlled by the helper. He is the expert on the conditions necessary for change to occur. Therefore, he must control his own behavior and create an atmosphere of security and trust that are prerequisites for the first step or goal in helping." His ability to exert such control does not mean that the quality of the relationship he maintains is located within him. The quality labels the relationship, not the person. (See Chapter Two on "Personality Factors.")

The task at hand is not to train a specific behavior labeled, for example, "empathetic." Rather it is to introduce a wide variety of alternative actions by means of which a helper may create and maintain "empathy" within a specific helping relationship. Therefore, in discussing and giving feedback to each other about these qualities we must avoid labeling traits of individuals, but rather must label effects of behavior.

The distinction here is difficult to express because our language does not represent relational issues very well. However, the major focus must be the responsibility of the treatment worker in developing and maintaining a facilitative relationship. Although the worker is accountable for the quality of the relationship, his performance in developing high or low facilitative qualities in any specific relationship may be seen as independent of personality traits. For example, a worker may be judged as "cool and aloof" by his peers but convey warmth and empathy in relationships with the children he works with. In this example a discrepancy clearly exists between how he behaves with his peers and how he behaves with child clients. Rather than insisting that the worker can "be" only one way or the other, we recognize that different relationships influence the worker to behave differently. Likewise a worker may convey warmth more easily to one child than to another. Rather than seeing the worker as somehow playing favorites, we can look at what the worker does and how she responds to what the child does. You may have known people who can create a warm and accepting atmostphere while they are "selling" something or feel they are "on stage," while "off stage," they sneer at and belittle others. Although this situation may lead to long-term problems for this person, it does not diminish the immediate positive effects of his behavior on those with whom he interacts. In giving feedback to yourself or others, you may want to use the following form: "I thought that you were promoting [*name the relationship dimension*] when you did [*describe the behavior*]."

Metaphorically you might consider the image of two people sitting on either side of a large cauldron, each contributing ingredients to the mutual stew that simmers between them. Some contributions make the brew fragrant and lucious, others create too much tartness or bitterness. Your task as a helper is to keep the simmering stew flavorful and nutritious by augmenting or by counteracting the contributions of your partner across the kettle. Therefore, when you observe yourself and others involved in relationships, you must track not only the flavor of the stew, but also the skill and artfulness of the helper's contributions. (See Figure 4-1.)

Emergent Qualities of the Relationship

Watzlawick (1978), in promoting an "interactional view" of therapy, explains that when two or more people interact, the result is more than the sum of the contributions of the individual members. This additional factor he labels an "emergent quality." An analogy in the physical sciences can be seen in the separate and joint characteristics of hydrogen and oxygen. As separate elements, hydrogen and oxygen at normal temperatures are gases that burn easily. When these elements are combined, however, in the form of H_2O, they form water, a liquid that puts out fires. Clearly, this

Figure 4-1. Relationship Dimensions

"emergent quality" does not reflect the characteristics of the separate elements.

In an example more relevant to working with troubled children, your separate meetings with a child and his or her parent may have been pleasant. Both may show a willingness to talk and cooperate in tasks you have requested of them in a calm, matter-of-fact way. When, however, you put them together, the child begins to whine and engage in passive resistance; the parent begins to sound critical and to control the child's behavior dictatorially. This whining/resisting-critical/controlling interaction often comes as a complete surprise to people who believe that they can predict the interaction of two people on the basis of their individual reactions. Thus, the "emergent qualities" of relationships cannot be assumed.

We propose that qualities such as "empathy," "warmth," "genuineness," etc. are "emergent qualities" that apply only in a relationship, not to an individual in isolation. These qualities come to light only in the individual in a relationship. "Emergent qualities" are the result of training behavior and perception, but they cannot be trained directly. Characteristics of the individual and of the relationship belong to different orders of being.

An Interactional View of the Demands of Relationship

In the interactional view the worker must develop the skills to elicit responses from the child which will fit the worker's thoughts and feelings about what is worthy of sincere warmth, respect, etc. Therefore, the worker must: (a) know her own tendencies for interpreting events in a helping framework, (b) elicit from the child responses that fit that framework, or (c) reframe the child's responses. Thus, the demands of the relationship influence the worker, and simultaneously the worker influences those relationship demands. Following this interactional view, you may find that you can develop a deep respect and admiration for some children you work with whom you might otherwise have avoided and even disliked.

Behavioral Hints

Some knowledge of the relationship scales, some suggestions on observing, and some hints on how to increase the quality of your relationships will help you in becoming more proficient in using the relationship dimensions in your work.

Expect Your First Attempts at Observing to be Difficult Because the Scales are "Mushy." We are asking you to pin down the characteristics of an abstract thing (a relationship) without reference to specific, unchanging behaviors, and that task occurs during an ever-changing series of events. It is like trying to shoot a polar bear in a blizzard while standing on a wildly rocking ice flow. Even if you could see what you are aiming at, you could not get anything to stand still long enough to take an accurate shot. We admit that your task is difficult. In the beginning it is not so important that you be 100 percent accurate, but that you begin to be able to see the interactional events and to use interactional language to describe them. With practice you will become more and more accurate. The later chapter on "Observation" will give you some more hints on evaluating the events.

EXPECT THAT THE EVALUATION THAT YOU MAKE WILL CHANGE BECAUSE THE SCALES ARE NOT ABSOLUTE. The rating scales in this chapter are meant to evaluate closeness or distance from the good or poor ends of the continuum. Although that continuum has been anchored by research, we are not asking you to use the scale as a rigid yardstick, but rather as a flexible tool for observing yourself and others. Your ratings of what a "5" is on any scale may change over time. That is okay. The point is that you use the dimensions to get and give feedback.

KEEP TRACK OF RELATIONSHIPS, BOTH PAST AND PRESENT, THAT YOU CAN NOW EVALUATE AS FACILITATIVE OR NONFACILITATIVE. Evaluate as objectively as you can your contribution to the relationship quality. This record will give you some clues about which of your actions contribute to or hinder the development of good relationship quality. You can also note which people and contexts aid or block this process.

PINPOINT WHAT MAKES IT EASIER FOR YOU TO MAINTAIN FACILITATIVE QUALITIES IN A RELATIONSHIP AND BE SURE TO ACTIVATE THOSE THINGS. You can take responsibility to act on the demands in a relationship as well as respond to them.

Observe and include in your repertoire *all* behavior: verbal as well as nonverbal. The quality of relationships can be markedly influenced by subtle facial expressions and tone of voice. Be prepared to observe minutely.

RELATIONSHIP DIMENSION SCALES

In order to observe the relationship dimensions in yourself or others, consider the following contextual factors prior to using the scales below.

1. Setting (e.g. classroom, counselor's office)
2. History of relationship (e.g. first meeting)

3. Immediate content focus (e.g. fight, stealing)
4. Role relationship (e.g. teacher-student)

(Not all interactions demand a response on all dimensions. If this is the case, note NA [not applicable] on the scale and explain your reasons for seeing the scale as not relevant.)

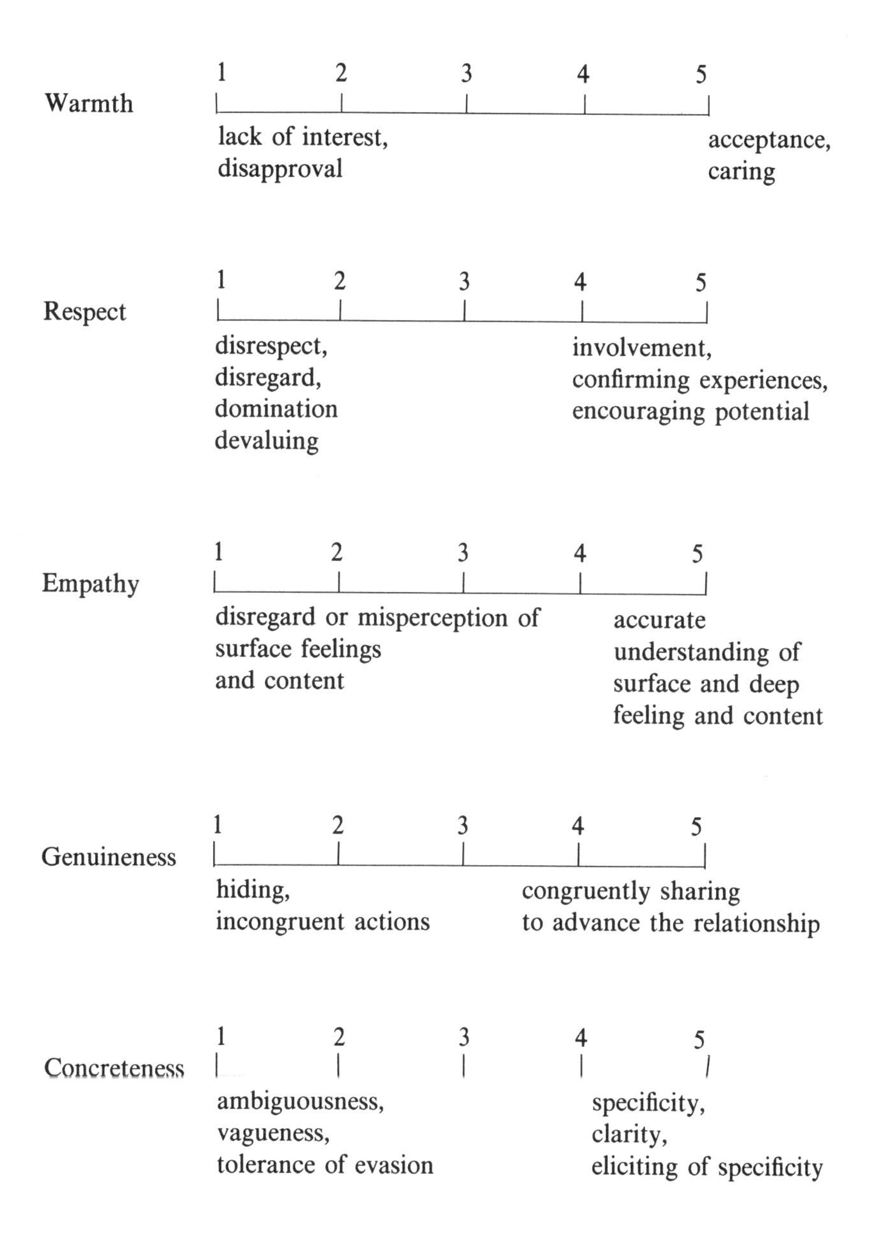

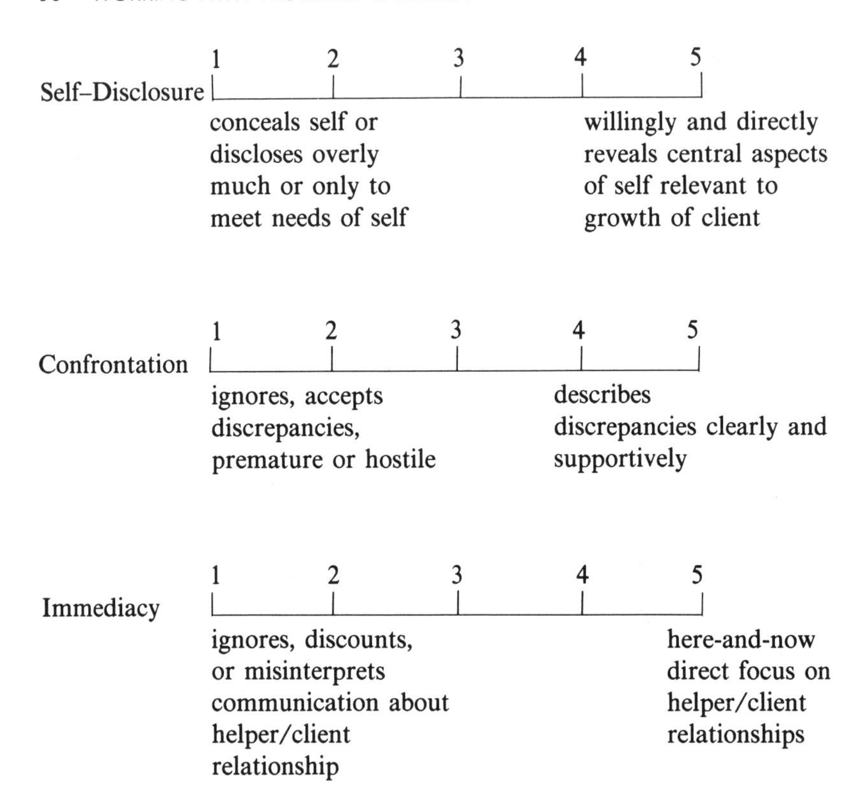
1
2
3
4
5
Self–Disclosure
conceals self or discloses overly much or only to meet needs of self
willingly and directly reveals central aspects of self relevant to growth of client
1
2
3
4
5
Confrontation
ignores, accepts discrepancies, premature or hostile
describes discrepancies clearly and supportively
1
2
3
4
5
Immediacy
ignores, discounts, or misinterprets communication about helper/client relationship
here-and-now direct focus on helper/client relationships

Chapter 5

OBSERVATION
Behavioral and Inferential

After mastering the information in this section you should be able to:—

1. describe specific, concrete observable behaviors;
2. describe a trait, motive, attitude, or feeling by identifying the key observable behaviors that indicate these internal states;
3. differentiate descriptions of internal states from descriptions of behaviors;
4. identify and define four methods of recording behavior;
5. use functional analysis to identify the antecedents and consequences of a behavior;
6. prepare an accurate running record of a sequence of behavior;
7. identify the necessary ingredients for accurate inferential observation;
8. identify several types of inferences that can be made;
9. identify three general categories of errors that can lead to inaccurate inferences.

For centuries the debate has raged over the question, "What is reality?" Some say there is a "real," "objective" set of things and events that each of us reacts to. Others say it is not the things and events that are important, but rather our internal perceptions and ideas about them. In this chapter we will define methods of observation for both external and internal realities.

In working with troubled children, observation skills provide the foundation for all of the other treatment skills. Before the worker can assess, treat, and evaluate a child's progress, she must be able to identify the significant events in the child's life. She must also be able to communicate those events to others who affect the child's life so that all concerned can attend to those events. In addition, observing herself will improve the worker's therapeutic skills. Behavioral and emotional blindspots can be damaging to both the children treated and to the worker. This chapter will focus not so much on what to look for or where to look for it, but on how to look. We do not believe that observation and keeping track of progress are inflexibly related to any theoretical position, be it behavioral, psychodynamic, or gestalt/existential. Observation as a method can be used in the service of any theory. It is atheoretical. It is, most of all, practical. Observation will help you become more effective.

Formal versus Informal Observation

Observation is an integral part of everday life both in and out of treatment. This chapter will elaborate several methods of formal observation. That is not to say that all your observation need be done in these ways. It is our intent to teach a few systematic ways of observing so that you can call upon those methods when necessary and so that your informal methods of observation become sharper.

Sensory Modes of Observing

Anything can be observed that can be seen, heard, felt, tasted, or smelled. Each of us, barring specific handicaps, can observe phenomena in each of those sensory modes. In growing up we have learned to experience and represent the world and ourselves by accenting or discounting some of the sensory modalities (Grinder & Bandler, 1976). This selection of modality usually comes about through the influence of our family. For example, the saying "Children are to be seen but not heard" represents a family rule legitimizing one modality and questioning another. Such rules can be carried into adulthood, limiting our abilities. As a general warning, be aware of your sensory orientation and do not allow yourself to exclude any mode.

Levels of Observation

The information that we take in and process when observing can be separated into three levels: 1) data level, 2) inference level, and 3) interpretaion level. In this chapter we will discuss only the data and inference levels. It is important at this time to be able to differentiate between the levels, to identify which level we are functioning in at any given time, and to know when and when not to use each level.

Data Level

At this level, there is no inference. Observation and reports of observation describe concretely and specifically the events that impinge upon our senses. Therefore, at the data level, the worker reports only what he or she can see, hear, feel, smell, or taste. The folowing is an example of data-level reporting.

> Georgie stomped into the room, muttering. Tears were streaming down his face. His face was hot and flushed, and he was panting.

Inference Level

Inferring is the process of drawing a conclusion from facts or evidence. Thus, when one infers, one goes beyond the data level to conclude how the observed data fit together. An inference based on the data in the example above might be that Georgie is angry. The large-muscle activity of stomping, the verbal activity of muttering, and the physiological cues of flushing and panting might fit together as an expression of Georgie's internal state of anger.

Inferring is natural and automatic. Since we as humans can think as well as observe, we naturally think about our observations. In fact, our experience tells us that most people *start* by inferring and making judgments about themselves and others.

Since inferential observation is less concrete, there is more room for error than with the data level. The solution to potential inaccuracy is not to stop all inference but to provide guidelines for a sophisticated use of inference. These guidelines will be explained later in the chapter under the heading of inferential observation.

Interpretation Level

When one interprets, one attributes meaning to data or inference. Interpretation usually follows a cause and effect model. If functioning on an interpretation level, one would say, "Georgie is angry because . . . "

Accurate interpretation takes into account a larger number and variety of factors than do the previous levels; therefore, it is a higher order process. Interpretation is one step more removed from the concrete level, and, like inference, can be inaccurate. This inaccuracy can occur for a number of reasons:

a. It may be based on incomplete or inaccurate data.
b. It may be based on inappropriate or erroneous assumptions.
c. It may not take into account the context in which the observed events occurred.

In summary, observation skills are basic and essential. The goal of training in these skills to identify the appropriate level of observation to be used, and to use these levels accurately and systematically. The remainder of this chapter will deal with the specifics of behavioral and inferential observation.

Behavioral Observation

Learning to observe behavior objectively and accurately forms the basis on which other skills are built. In dealing with human behavior and interaction, we are continually observing in order to gather the data necessary to make decisions about how and when to react. Often these observations are neither conscious nor systematic. The goal of this section is to develop the skills necessary to bring our observations systematically into conscious awareness and analyze them into discrete and describable pieces so that we can accurately assess our own and others' behavioral functioning.

Observed behavior forms the basis for communication about children and treatment. Although different people may use different vocabularies and theories, all planning and follow-through is based on observable events. People therefore need to be able to agree on those observable events.

The following sub-skills make up this section on observation: Description of Behavior, Recording Behavior, Functional Analysis.

Description of Behavior

When we talk about children, we need to understand each other clearly and avoid missing or distorting what actually happened in a specific situation. We need to be able to talk the same language; that is not always easy. Most of us have some trouble describing our own or a child's behavior clearly enough so that someone else really understands exactly what happened.

The language we usually use follows the *inside-out* idea. That is, instead of describing the outer behavior or actions of a person, we talk about what we think is inside the person. Some of the inside things we discuss are personality traits, motives, attitudes, feelings, and moods. Suppose a child throws his coat on the floor after coming in from playing. Is he lazy (personality trait)? Is he trying to make a mess so your supervisor will complain to you (motive)? Does he have an "I just don't care" attitude (attitude)? Is he angry (feeling)? Or, is he so depressed he hasn't enough energy to hang up his coat (mood)? Obviously the same outside behavior (throwing his coat on the floor) could mean many different things happening on the inside. The one thing we all can see and agree on is that he threw his coat on the floor. A description of the behavior is the place to start.

Describing Behavior. Describing behavior means letting others know what happened in a situation by presenting it specifically and clearly, that is, giving verbal instant replay as a movie camera or videotape machine would. This means telling only what can be seen, heard, touched, tasted, or smelled, without giving its meaning. Often people who give labels to behavior instead of describing it say more about themselves than about the person whom they observed. When describing behavior you focus on *what* a person did rather than *why*. If you find yourself saying, "She's crabby" (a trait), ask yourself the question, "What did she *do* to make me think she was crabby?" The "doing" description will usually lead you to verbalize behavior. Here is an example showing the differences between behavior description and labeling inside events. (See Figure 5-1.)

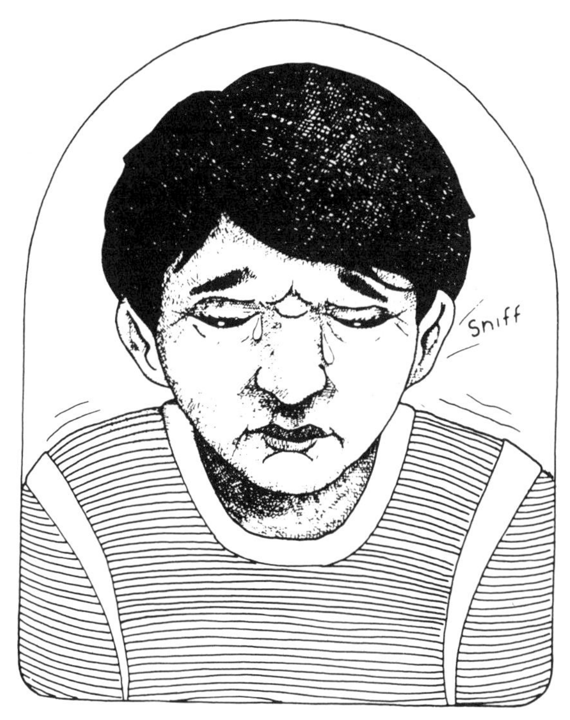

Figure 5-1. Observation

Behavior Description (crying)
head down, shoulders rounded
breathing in sobs
tears dripping down cheek
eyes red/partially closed
face flushed/pink/hot
making sniffling noises with nose
lips quivering
saying "Oh, my gosh"

A Few Possible Inside "Whys"

feelings:	He is sad, or happy, or angry
mood:	He has the blues
attitude:	He has a defeatist attitude
motives:	He is just trying to get my sympathy; he is trying to get my attention.
personality trait:	He is a weepy person; he has no guts.

Notice the variety of data that fit within the definition of behavior: physiological (breathing, flushed), large muscle (head down, shoulders rounded), small muscle (lips quivering), auditory (sobs, sniffling noises), verbal (saying "Oh, my gosh"), kinesthetic (face hot), visual (eyes red, face pink). All of these types of behavior are noteworthy.

One more type of behavior we will mention in passing is covert: thoughts, feelings, etc. These are observable only by the person within whom they are happening. You cannot observe this type of behavior directly in others. Therefore, we will not detail this type of behavior except to say that it is a valid target for self-observation.

HOW TO PUT NONBEHAVIORAL CONCEPTS INTO BEHAVIORAL TERMS. Once you have become clear about discriminating descriptions of behavior from nonbehavioral terms, you will come to the problem of wanting to observe something that is clearly nonbehavioral. Your task then is to find indicators at the data level for concepts at the inference or interpretive level. You will need to develop a "behavioral definition."

To do this you first list the actions that are associated with that nonbehavioral concept. For example, "a bad attitude toward school," a nonbehavioral term, may be indicated bybehavior such as "getting out of seat," "not finishing assignments," "handing in messy work," and "talking loudly to his neighbor during study time." Thus, the abstract attitude can be defined by means of listing the behavior which illustrates it.

When selecting behavioral indicators, you can refer to three criteria. First, the indicators should be *reliable.* That is, you and anybody you drag in from the street ought to be able to look at someone and agree that the action did or did not occur. Thus, "out of seat" must be defined clearly enough so that when the child punches someone in the next row while keeping one foot on his seat, you can agree whether or not he was indeed in or out of his seat. Secondly, the indicator should be *relevant.* You may be able to pick a completely reliable behavior that has nothing to do with the more abstract concept that you want to observe. Indicators must meaningfully represent the concept you are interested in. Thirdly, indicators should be *repeatable.* Such behavior has discrete beginnings and ends and happens more than once in a lifetime. Extremely low-rate behavior gives a tenuous indication of the more abstract concept you wish to infer.

You may want to observe several activities that "go together" as a natural grouping. For example, a child may refuse to follow instructions. Instead of making separate tallies of all of the ways in which he does not follow instructions, you may define a class of behavior called "noncompliance." Thus, instead of having one "ignoring request," one "looking out of window," and one "saying 'I won't'," you can count three non-compliances. This grouping of behaviors may save your time and effort and may more accurately represent the abstract area you are interested in.

Recording Behavior

After learning what a behavior is, the next step is to learn how to count and record the behavioral indicators you have chosen. Counting and recording are necessary in order to get an accurate picture of how often the behavior occurs and when. This information is important to know before starting to change a behavior, because by knowing where a behavior is today, it is possible to know where to expect it tomorrow. And you can monitor changes in relation to specific intervention or events. Formal methods of recording include frequency counts, measures of intensity, temporal recording, interval measures, and rate of behavior. We will briefly describe each below, along with some other considerations relevant to recording.

FREQUENCY RECORDING. With this method, *every* behavior is counted within a certain period of time. Here, we want to know exactly *how many times* a behavior occurs. A frequency count is most useful with a behavior that does not happen too often. You can imagine how frazzled you would be after counting someone's eye-blinks for five hours!

Example: Recording interruptions

	10:00									10:30
Interruptions	x	x	x	x	x	x	x	x	x	x

It can be seen that the subject is interrupted 10 times in 30 minutes.

INTENSITY/MAGNITUDE RECORDING. With some behavior, the intensity is of more concern than how often it happens. For example, when an observer is recording tantrums, he may rate them on a scale of 1 to 10. Intensity recording can accompany other types of recording. That is, you can count the frequency and estimate its intensity at the same time. The one big problem with estimating the intensity of a behavior is that the observer must make a judgment, and this allows room for error and inconsistency. A tantrum may seem more intense to a recorder if he has a headache. Therefore, attempt to remain objective and take into account personal variables.

TEMPORAL RECORDING. With some behavior, it is more important to know how *long it lasts.* In this case, it would be necessary to record the *duration* of time the person exhibits the behavior. For example, if you want to decrease a child's phone talking behavior, it would be more useful to time the calls than to count them. She may make only one phone call in a night, but it may last two hours.

Example: Phone calls between 5:00 and 9:00

October 1st	2nd	3rd	4th	5th
33 min.	1 hr. 1 min.	15 min.	45 min.	1 hr. 50 min.

Latency. Another type of temporal data, measures how long it takes for a child to respond to a specific event; i.e., how many seconds between a request to stop hitting and the actual stopping.

INTERVAL RECORDING. This type of recording is done by dividing a period of time into equal intervals and checking whether or not a certain behavior occurred in the specific interval. It does not matter how many times the behavior occurred; it could happen once or a hundred times. If the behavior occurs at all, check the interval. If not, leave it blank.

The intervals will vary in size according to the behavior. If it is a behavior that occurs often, such as talking, you may want to use small intervals such as 10 seconds. If it is a less frequent behavior, such as hitting, a 5–to 10–minute interval may be useful. Interval recording is a good method to use on high-rate behaviors whose frequency would be difficult to monitor or when recording for long periods of time.

Example: Intervals of 5 minutes

	1:00	1:05	1:10	1:15	1:20	1:25	1:30	1:35	1:40
Interruptions	x		x	x			x	x	x

It can be seen that interrupting occurred, regardless of how many times, in 6 out of 9 intervals.

RATE RECORDING. Rate recording simply merges frequency and temporal recording. Sometimes an observer records for different amounts of time from one day to the next or different amounts of time within a single day. When this happens, it is hard to compare the days in order to see whether the behavior is increasing or decreasing. At first glance, it may look like the behavior has doubled in occurrences, when it in fact has not. Twice as many actions may have been recorded, but twice as much time may have been used to record. Therefore the number per hour remain the same. This *number per hour* is called the *rate* of behavior.

The way to get a rate of behavior is to divide the number of times it occurred by the number of minutes, hours, or days you were recording. Imagine that you were keeping track of the number of times you said "hmmmm" for 10 minutes and found that you said it 10 times. Using the formula,

$\frac{\text{number}}{\text{time}}$, the rate would work out as $\frac{10}{10}\ \frac{\text{(number of “hmms”)}}{\text{(number of minutes)}}$,

or 1 "hmmm" per minute.

Using this formula, you will be able to compare behaviors from hour to hour or week to week.

TIME SAMPLING VERSUS CONTINUOUS RECORDING. Time sampling simply means that the observer limits the amount of observation time and "samples" rather than records all day. The amount of recording time used will depend on the behavior. In general, *more* frequent behaviors will need to be observed for a shorter period of time than *less* frequent behaviors. When using time-sample recording, it is important to choose a time when the behavior occurs the most. For example, if you are recording fights between children, it would be important to choose a time when they are in the same room. When using time sampling, you may record *intervals, frequency, duration,* or *intensity.*

It can be seen that the various methods will "color" the data somewhat by providing different pictures of the behavior. When choosing a method, consider closely the nature of the behavior, the information you want, and your own capability in terms of time, energy, and skill in observation.

Sometimes the mere act of observing will affect a behavior. For example, a spit-wad thrower may cease all spit-wad throwing when he realizes that you are counting that behavior. This result is called *reactivity.* That is, the behavior changed because of your observation even though you did not attempt to change it in any way. Sometimes you can use formal recording as an intervention technique (Armstrong & Savicki, 1971). However, if your concern rests primarily with accurate collection of data, then you may want to keep "private data" which are not accessible to the child. You may also want to use some behavior-monitoring technique that will not be perceived as "counting," such as unobtrusively shifting pennies from one pocket to another. Sometimes you will be unable to avoid reactivity because your mere presence will cause the child to act differently. If that is the case, interpret your information with caution.

FUNCTIONAL ANALYSIS

Once you have defined which behaviors to observe and how to count and record them, you will want to move towards understanding more fully the context within which that behavior occurs. In order to understand what elicits and maintains a behavior, it is important to look at the events occurring before and after it. These events can be observed and recorded in a *running record,* and then transferred to a chart that will facilitate the determination of the relationship between the behavioral events. This procedure is called a *functional analysis* because it helps to determine the function of the behavior, that is, what the person gets or avoids by the behavior.

A functional analysis is made up of three parts: 1) the antecedent, 2) the behavior, and 3) the consequence (the ABC format). The antecedent is the event occurring just before the behavior. The consequence is the event occurring just after the behavior. Many times, the consequence for one behavior is the antecedent for another. Functional analysis may include all the behaviors within a specified time period (generalized sequence) or it may focus on the antecedents and consequences surrounding a specific target (selected sequence). Which you choose will depend on the purpose you have for collecting information. For example, if you are clear on the behavior that you want to deal with therapeutically, the selected-sequence method will aid in specifying possible intervention techniques by highlighting the changeable environmental events surrounding that behavior. In instances in which the behavioral patterns are confused, the general-sequence method can serve to lend clarity.

The Running Record

Preparatory to recording, describe the setting, important objects and people, and their physical relationship to one another. Then, make a note of what was happening just before recording began. *General-sequence functional analysis* attempts to include as many sequential events as possible and to record the time at fairly regular intervals. In *selected-sequence functional analysis,* the occurrence of the target behavior will determine the frequency of recording. As soon as possible, write up notes in detail enlarging on some of the brief comments. Only behavior should be recorded; interpretations and inferences can be noted parenthetically. The running record is now ready to be transferred into a functional analysis following the ABC format.

Example: *Running record and general-sequence functional analysis*

Running Record

Date: July 15 Child: Tim
Time: 10:15 a.m.
Situation occurring before recording: Children arrived at 10:00 a.m. Free time until 10:10 a.m. During this time, Tim played in sandbox with Allen. They fought over a car. Resolved with help of staff. Entered meeting 1 minute late.
Setting: Morning meeting—in a circle on the floor

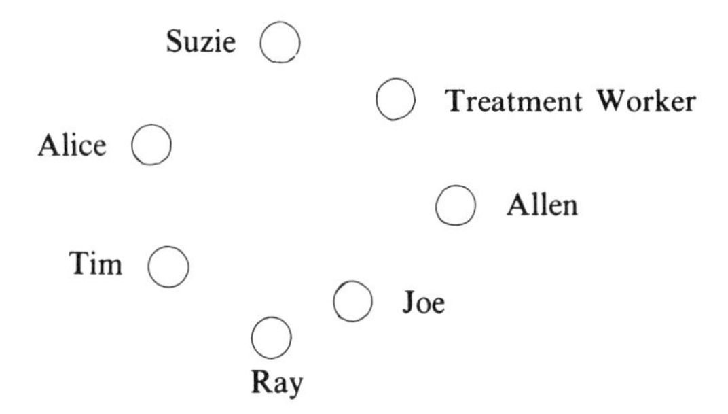

10:16 Tim (T.) sits on floor with a thud—face cast down—frown. Treatment worker (T. W.): "Thanks for joining the meeting, T." T. looks at T. W. with frown. T. W. smiles. T. continues eye contact with T.W.
Allen (A.) smiles—says, "Yeah, thanks" (mocking tone).
T. continues eye contact with T. W.
10:18 T.W.—"I like the way you ignored A., T." T. smiles. T. W. smiles.

Table 5–1. Functional Analysis General Sequence

Time	*Antecedent*	*Behavior*	*Consequence*
10:16		T. sits on floor with thud–face down–frown	TW: "Thanks for joining the meeting T."
	*S.C.	T. looks at TW–frown	TW smiles
	*S.C.	T. continues eye contact with TW	TW eye contact
	A. smiles–"Yeah thanks" (mocking tone)	T. continues eye contact with TW	TW: "I like the way you ignored A. T."
10:18	*S.C.	T. smiles	TW smiles

*S.C. denotes *Subsequent Consequence*. This notation is made when the consequence for one behavior serves as the antecedent for the next.

Notice that only behaviors are recorded. Inferences about internal states are omitted. Parentheses are used for words that describe a behavior when that description is interpretive.

The analysis suggests that the staff member's behavior elicits and maintains Tim's positive attending behaviors (i.e., sitting in group, eye contact, smiling, and ignoring) and that Allen's verbalizations and accompanying nonverbal behaviors are neutral for Tim. (See Table 5–1.)

Example: *Running record and selected-sequence functional analysis*

As an hypothesis you think that Jamie's disruptive behavior is preceded by a certain "look" on his face. You pinpoint that "look" as eyes looking down and smiling at the same time. The following running record forms the basis of a selected sequence of analysis around "the look" behavior.

Running Record Setting: Ms. Burt's classroom; class already started; Ms. B. giving general instructions to whole class.

Time: 9:30 a.m.

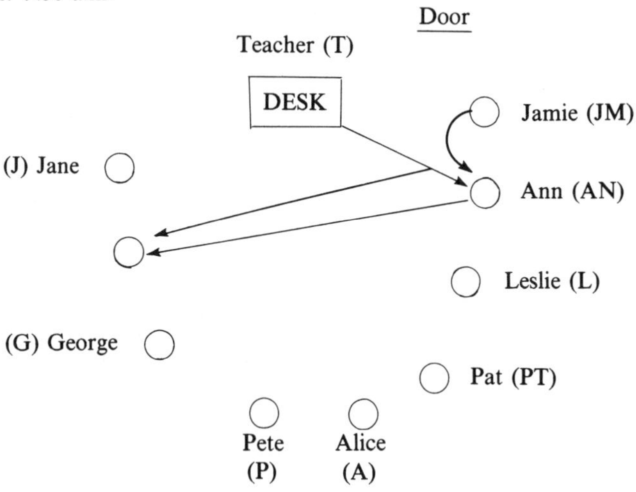

JM walks through the door slowly trailing hand over the door frame, head down. T sitting at desk smiles and says (in a harsh tone), "I'm glad you could make it, JM." JM not lifting head glances at T and with smile on face turns toward AN, looks down and steps on her foot. AN screams, "You big bully," and pulls feet under desk, puts head down, and cries while stroking foot. T gasps, stands up. T's eyes and mouth wide open—hands at her sides, fists clenched.

JM standing in front of L's desk smiles, looks up at AN and says, "I'm sorry." T moves left of desk, puts hands on hips, frown and yells, "Now you just get into your seat, you've caused enough disruption for one morning." JM with slight smile slowly walks toward his desk, head down, hands in pockets. T moves in front of AN's desk, leans over touching AN's head, looks at JM with mouth pursed and brow knitted. JM stands in front of desk with back to T, hands in pockets looking down. T takes rapid steps towards JM, grasps him by the shoulders, rapidly turns him. JM looks up, eyes wide open, hands out of pockets reaching backward toward desk. T still holding his shoulders pushes JM down into his seat. JM says "Umph," eyes down, tears up, smiles.

Table 5–2. Selected Sequence Functional Analysis

Antecedent	*Behavior*	*Consequence*
T sitting at desk smiles and says (in a harsh tone) "I'm glad you could make it JM."	JM *not lifting head* glances at T and with *smile on face* turns toward AN, looks down and steps on her foot.	AN screams "Ow! You big bully." And pulls both feet under desk, puts head down and cries softly while stroking foot.
T moves left of desk, puts hands on her hips, frowns and yells, "Now just get to your seat. You've caused enough disruption for one morning."	JM, with a *slight smile* walks slowly toward desk, *head down* & hands in his pockets.	T moves to front of AN's desk, leans over touching AN's head and looks at JM, mouth pursed & brow knitted.
T still holding his shoulders, pushes JM down into his seat.	JM says "Umph," *eyes look down* and *tears up*, *smiles.*	Unknown

This functional analysis shows that the teacher's negative response to Jamie (sarcasm, scolding, pushing) regularly preceded his disruptive behavior. Therefore, the data indicate that the first step in decreasing Jamie's disruptions may be to deal with the teacher's behavior toward him. (See Table 5–2)

Functional analysis is a useful tool in a child's assessment prior to and during treatment. This close scrutiny of behavioral data reveals patterns that often escape more casual notice. For example, a child may seem to the staff, through unsystematic observation, to be continually disruptive. Upon closer examination, through functional analysis, it becomes evident that he can attend for as much as thirty minutes without interrupting when he is seated next to a staff member who discusses issues in a calm tone and provides visual cues to keep him on track. The treatment worker can use this information to prescribe therapeutic interventions.

Although the procedures for functional analysis described in this chapter may seem finicky and protracted, we suggest them as an intermediate step to doing a functional analysis in your head. At that point the tool has become a part of you, and you can observe for greater lengths of time, and discern more subtle patterns as a matter of course.

Inferential Observation

As stated previously, the process of inferential observation involves drawing conclusions about nonobservable states based on behavioral data. Using this form of observation adds another dimension to the information that can be used for treatment or professional development. The reliability of inferential observation cannot equal that of behavioral observation because the events being reported are of differing complexities. However, since people naturally observe inferentially, making the inferences more reliable seems appropriate. Behavioral and inferential observation support and complement each other; ones does not discount or totally replace the other. One goal of training in these methods is to assist workers in being able to switch back and forth quickly between the methods, thus expanding the information available for assessment, treatment, and professional development.

Components Necessary for Accurate Inferential Observation

By its nature inference leaves room for error. To minimize the likelihood of error, attention needs to be given to the following components:

Accurate Behavioral Observation. All inferences are anchored in observable events. Mistakes on the data level lead to erroneous inferences. For example, if you see two children rolling on the ground in a yelling, arms-flailing embrace, you may infer either that they are fighting or that they are playing. The crucial cue necessary to discriminate between the two inferences may be the children's words and facial expressions. If you mistake gritted teeth for smiles, your inference will be in error. Thus, an ability to observe and describe data level information is indispensable.

Agreed-Upon Range and Type of Inferences That Contribute to the Fund of Information That May Be Used. If everyone is looking at different things, there may be disagreement about what is important. For example, if one member of a team interprets events from a behaviorist view, one from a psychoanalytic view and one from a gestalt view, they may agree on very few inferential concepts, and there will only be limited check for inaccurate inferences. They will both attend to different types of behavior and use different labels for the same behavior. If the person holding power takes idiosyncratic views, information used by a treatment team may be further confused; for example, if the team supervisor insists that astrological concepts take precedence over all others. The scales in the chapters on "Relationship Dimensions" and "Values and Beliefs" illustrate lists of inferential concepts.

AGREED-UPON DEFINITIONS OF INFERENTIAL TERMS. Inferential terms describe some abstract concept for which you must then find specific behavioral examples. To some extent, finding and agreeing on the behavioral examples will help define the more abstract term. However, careful discussion of the interferential term, its meaning and implications, will form a mental template or model against which you can compare specific events. Without an agreed-upon mental model, difficulties will arise both in identifying examples of inferences and in discriminating which inference is appropriate for a specific event. For example, you may agree on using the term "distraction" whenever a child attempts to guide a person's attention away from the ongoing event or subject, such as changing the topic in the middle of a discussion. However, always remember that "the map is not the territory" (Bandler & Grinder, 1975). Keep your mental template flexible enough to change with new data. Avoid modifying the data to fit the template.

After meeting the previous requirements for accuracy of inferential observation, a treatment team or whole agency will develop a set of assumptions and a language unique to itself. Thus, they will be able to communicate in a verbal shorthand that may sound like obscure jargon to someone outside. Words like "set up," "control-avoidant," "contracting," refer to specific concepts which may not correspond to usage outside of the treatment setting. It is important to remember that new workers, new ideas, and new settings require that the three previous accuracy requirements not be taken for granted, but be re-established and revised.

What Can Be Inferentially Observed

Inferences describe events metaphorically that cannot be measured objectively in everyday activity. Sadness or hostility cannot be read from a gauge; therefore, these emotional states have no objective representation. That does not mean such states are not concrete events. It only means that we do not have access to direct observation of the states in others. Therefore, we hope to explain the patterns we see through metaphorical, "as if," statements. Our language contains thousands of such shorthand statements; e.g., "You're looking down-in-the-mouth," "You're acting as if you think I tripped you on purpose." The catch comes when we forget that our statements are on the "as if" level and mistakenly believe our inferences represent objective facts, i.e., "You wanted to see me get hurt, that's why you tripped me." With this in mind, let us look at several types of inferences that can be made.

THOUGHTS. Obviously another person cannot observe your thoughts, nor you theirs. Yet, given the assumption that people's behavior is usually consistent with their thoughts and beliefs, you may infer thoughts or beliefs on the part of another. A useful question to ask yourself is "What would a person have to think or believe in order to do or say what he did?"

FEELINGS. Feelings are internal events which cannot be directly observed. We infer emotional states in other people from specific verbal and nonverbal cues and from the report of the other person. Often, others cover or disguise feelings; therefore, the usual reliable behavior cues are missing. Also, people may deny or become completely unaware of making their verbal report inaccurate. At those times, a useful question to ask yourself is "What would a person have to feel in order to do or say what he did?"

INTERACTIONAL QUALITIES. The interaction between individuals has a character and pattern beyond the contribution of the individuals, as explained in the "Relationship Dimension" chapter. Such interpersonal events can also be subject to inferences:

Thoughts—An example of relationship-system inference that may be understood as a thought is a "family rule" (Luthman & Kirschenbaum, 1975). This is a spoken or unspoken belief about what kind of behavior is permissible within the family: e.g., "Everything must be reasonable—no spontaneous expression of feeling is allowed."

Feelings—An example of a relationship-system in inference that may be understood as a feeling is "Family Atmosphere" (Dreikurs, 1958). The feelings that are and are not allowed expression by the family color the environment by their presence or absence. To help in infering these qualities, ask yourself the question "What would the interactors have to believe or feel in order to engage in these patterns of behavior?"

Problems and Errors

These errors in inferential observation can be grouped into the following categories:

ERRORS OF OBSERVATION. Many times we record events that have not actually occurred or miss events that did. Excluding observable information may occur because we use one primary sensory modality while ignoring others. Each of us has a preference for seeing, hearing, or feeling, as a mode of observing. A too-rigid reliance on one modality constricts the information that we allow ourselves to observe (Grinder & Bandler, 1976). Also the frame of reference through which we view the world colors our observation. Biases, stereotypes, and assumptions about what we are supposed to observe (selective vigilance) and what we are not supposed to observe (perceptual defense), induce us to include and exclude certain types of information. These processes often function below the level of conscious awareness.

ERRORS OF THINKING. Sometimes we make errors in inference because of how we think. Such errors often stem from the same types of presuppositions mentioned above. We fill in gaps in the information with what we assume ought to fit, rather than continuing to observe or leaving the gaps open. Also, insofar as we use language to articulate our observations, we can fall prey to the traps set by misuse of language. As examples consider the following problematic language forms:

Presuppositions—assume within one statement a previous unspoken statement. "He's more hyper than his father," assumes "His father is hyper."

Nominalizations—make static an active process, thereby implying that the process is unchangeable. "Your arguments cause me fear" immobilizes the more active processes of arguing and fearing. Less static would be "I am afraid when you argue with me."

Trait definitions—move transitory descriptive characteristics into fixed statements of unchanging traits. "He is excitable" fixes the excitation within the person; "He talks excitedly" labels the behavior (Grinder & Bandler, 1975).

ERRORS OF ASSOCIATION. Our past experiences with the events observed sometimes form a bias within us. Thus, we often feel that an inference is justified without being able to identify the logic behind that inference. For example, a child speaking in a loud, high-pitched voice may elicit irritation or guilt in a treatment worker because the worker has experienced irritation or guilt in the presence of such a vocal volume and pitch in the past. Even though the current situation is not at all related to the past events, the worker may have developed a complex equivalence in which the part (vocal volume and pitch) suggests the whole (the previous irritating or guilt-producing situation).

In summary, inferential observation can provide information about people that is invaluable to the treatment process in that it gives meaning to behavior. But inferences cannot be haphazard. Observation must be systematic, unprejudiced, and complete in order for inferences to be accurate. (See Table 5–3.)

Quality factors—Describe the worker's behavior in relation to the following:

1. A broad range of behaviors is described (physiological, small-muscle, large-muscle, sounds, words).
2. Reactivity is planned or avoided when a nonreactive measure is called for.
3. Definitions are reviewed by team to reaffirm consensus.

Table 5-3. Observation Checklist

For each observation, check the relevant items as they are demonstrated through written or verbal performance. Mark irrelevant items NA (for not applicable).

Positive performance	*Problematic performance*
Behavioral observation:	Behavioral observation:
____ Specific behaviors are identified	____ Non-behavioral terms used (e.g. attitude, trait, motive)
Behavioral definitions used are:	Behavioral definitions used are:
____ Reliable	____ Do not relate clearly to child's problem
____ Relevant	____ Are difficult to observe with accuracy
____ Repeatable	
Recording method selected:	Recording method selected:
____ Accurately reflects the quality and variation of the behavior	____ Obscures important qualities and variations of behavior
____ Promotes ease of recording	____ Is tiresome or overburdening to the observer
____ Is accurate	
Correct type of functional analysis for observer:	Incorrect type of functional analysis for observer:
____ Purpose	____ Events recorded out of sequence
____ Situational/contextual conditions noted	____ Inferences made without indication
____ Events recorded in correct sequence	
____ Behavioral events organized according to the ABC format	
Inferential observation:	Inferential observation:
____ Data level events anchor references	____ Inferences not related to data level events
____ Definitions have consensus of people using them	____ Inferences defined according to personal logic
____ Definitions are reviewed regularly	____ Data events not observed in drawing inferences
____ Inferential observation free of errors of observation, thinking, and association	____ Assumptions and biases distort inferences

Part II

COMMUNICATION FOR HELPING RELATIONSHIPS

The following ten chapters explain in detail some of the specific techniques that may be used to establish a helping relationship with the children in your care. The specific behaviors listed here provide the worker with a broad range of responses which must be flexibly applied in order to attain a positive outcome in treatment. As illustrated below (see Table 6-1.), these skills correlate approximately with the Relationship Dimensions explained in Chapter 4.

We introduce the communication skills here before behavior management or basic care techniques for a specific reason. Although the other techniques may be more useful in coping on a survival level with acting-out children, the communication skills form the backdrop against which the other methods gain credibility and depth. These techniques help to create a relationship in which the child experiences the worker as a person, not a mechanic. Also Phillips et al. (1975) indicate that the manner in which behavior management techniques are delivered can sometimes obviate the predicted effects. They now include social skill training for their group home staffs.

We would like to make several points about the communication skills. First, as we have already stressed, it is not the skills alone which effect change, but rather the coherent use of the skills consistent with the non-behavioral levels explained in Part 1. There is no one-to-one correlation between technique and problem solution. Secondly, the facilitative relationship, for all its power to effect change, may be inadequate. Especially with children whose contact and experience with reality may be somewhat limited or distorted, more active and directive methods will have to be used. Thus, as is true of treatment in general, you will eventually have to learn to do "everything all at once." For now, build your skills one at a time. Integration will come naturally as you move through the training sequence.

Table 6–1. General Relatedness of Relationship Dimensions and Communication Skills

Relationship Dimensions	*Behavioral Skills and Strategies*
Warmth	Open invitations to talk
Respect	Minimal encouragement to talk
Empathy	Paraphrasing and summary of content
	Reflection and summary of feeling
Genuineness	Cue congruence
Concreteness	Probing/use of language
Self-disclosure	Self-disclosure
Immediacy	
Confrontation	Confrontation

A final note: these techniques of communication draw heavily on the micro-counseling research of Ivey and his associates (1978). This method of training, using videotaped feedback, yields rapid results. We have found the following training format useful:

1) Reading and discussing the chapter
2) Video-or audiotaped skill practice in role play or for real
3) Immediately reviewing the tape using the behavior checklist at the end of each chapter,
4) Getting additional feedback from fellow trainees and/or from a supervisor, and
5) Recycling through steps 2 through 4.

Chapter 6

ATTENDING

After mastering the information in this chapter you should be able to—

1. define at least three verbal and three nonverbal cues that are subject to basic background rules of the culture;
2. list the effects of good attending for the worker/child relationship;
3. define the behaviors involved in attending and give examples of both good and poor performance.
4. relate attending behaviors to worker nonbehavioral levels of functioning as illustrated by "Feelings and Issues for the Treatment Worker."

The most basic of the relationship-facilitating communication skills is attending. It is so basic that oftentimes it is overlooked as being too trivial to consider. However, we believe attending to be the foundation upon which all other communication skills are built.

Attending includes the basic background communication rules of the culture, for example, rules about amount and type of eye contact, appropriate physical distance, body language and gestures, voice tone, pacing and tempo of speech, and follow-up of verbal content.

Each of us comes from a background in which we learned, usually unawares, some rules of interaction. When these rules are broken we may feel uncomfortable without being able to say why. And we may attribute characteristics to people to account for their rule-breaking behavior. The following example illustrates some of these culture-bound rules.

> A white middle-class teacher was talking to a girl of Puerto Rican background and was disturbed by the interaction. He felt that the youngster was being disrespectful and he was angry and irritated even though the child's words were very soft and compliant. Upon the teacher's invitation, a counselor observed the teacher/child interaction and found that although the teacher was working very hard to catch the child's eye, the child gave the teacher almost no eye contact. Later the counselor explained that in the child's Puerto Rican culture, respect was communicated by the nonverbal means of avoiding eye contact, while in the white middle-class background of the teacher, avoiding eye contact was an indicator of disrespect or even deceit. The teacher, not understanding the child's intent, attributed the motive of "disrespect" to her; the child, no doubt, thought the teacher strange for continually trying to make eye contact. The rules of interaction learned by each in their backgrounds were broken, and their relationship suffered as a result.

Sensitivity to nonverbal communication rules can help you become more adept at putting a child at ease and creating conditions for change. In this training sequence we will mention several attending behaviors. These have been used mostly with white middle- and lower-class children. If you work with children of other cultural origins, be aware that you may have to translate the form of some of the behaviors.

Effects of Attending

The effects of good attending help to create the conditions of a facilitative interpersonal relationship. The child will feel your respect through your close attention to what he has to say, which implies that he has something worthwhile to contribute. The accepting manner in which you give your undivided attention will be experienced as warmth. Your allowing the child the freedom to respond in his own way will permit him to express his thoughts more freely and more spontaneously.

Attending behaviors serve several functions for you as a worker. First, good attending helps you gather information. In order to understand the child and his situation, you must focus on the child. He is the person who holds the verbal and nonverbal information you need. He is his own best expert on what is going on in his life. Secondly, close attending will enable the treatment worker to pick up on signals that indicate what is important.

Both verbal and nonverbal behaviors contribute to good use of attending skills.

Nonverbal Behaviors

Relaxed Posture

Relax physically. Let your posture be comfortable and your movements natural so that you can focus on the child and not worry about yourself. If you usually move and gesture a good deal, feel free to continue. If your body is rigid, the message is that you are not receptive. At the opposite extreme, a slumped body suggests apathy. Frequent posture shifts may communicate nervousness. (see Figure 6-1. and Figure 6-2.)

Eye Contact

Look at the child while talking; vary your gaze rather than staring fixedly. With children, it is important to put yourself at their eye level. This will increase their comfort and thus ease their communication. Research

Figure 6-1. Rigid Posture

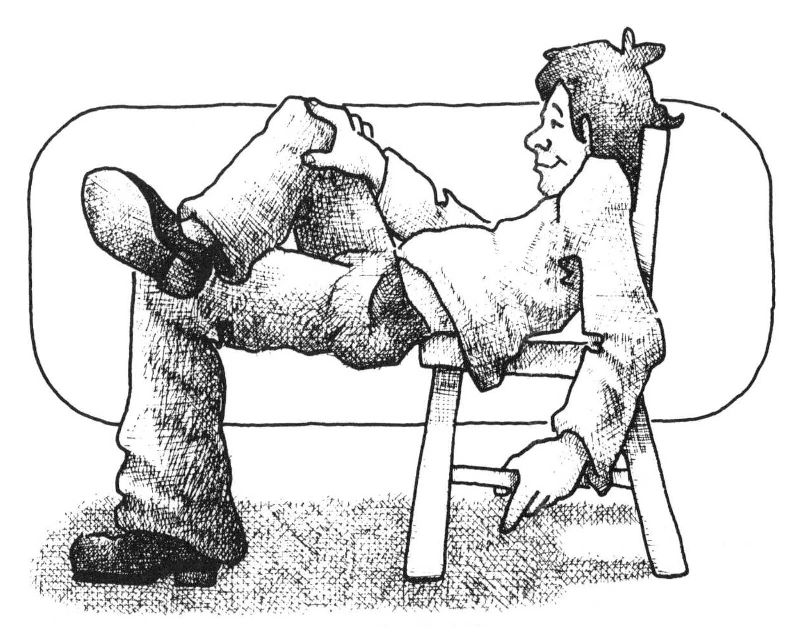

Figure 6-2. Slouched Posture

indicates that the face carries the largest percentage of meaning in spoken messages (Mehrabian, 1969):

Meaning = 55% facial expression + 38% tone of voice + 7% words. On the face, the eye area contains the most information. Therefore, eye contact yields a high level of information. (See Figures 6-3. and 6-4.)

Distance and Body Orientation

Close, but not too close, is the guideline here. Great distance conveys an attitude of avoidance. Too much closeness may invade the other's space. Different people have different personal spaces. The "too close" indicators will be their nonverbal behaviors; e.g., backing away, turning away, or looking down. Distance is especially crucial to gauge when you are on-the-move, as you often may be in talking with children e.g., walking, on the swings, in a play group.

Another way that people control distance and approachability is through body orientation. For the sake of simplicity let us look at the body as having three aprts: the head, the torso, and the hips and legs. Any one of these body parts may be oriented towards the child you are talking to or away from the child. Each of the body parts may be closed (e.g., arms crossed, legs crossed) or open. And the whole body may be angled more or less directly towards or away from the child. The most open (though not necessarily always the best) body orientation is one in which you are face

Figure 6-3. Non Eye-Contact

to face with the child, with all body parts oriented towards him and all body parts uncovered and uncrossed. The opposite extreme would be sitting back to back with all body parts covered and crossed.

Touching

With children especially, touching can facilitate communication. Your touch becomes a dominant focus in helping them ignore other distractions. This not only sends an "I am with you" message, but also is useful in maintaining their attention. (See Figure 6-5.)

The preceding discussion implies a static, sit down, face-to-face interview situation. In reality, child treatment is done "on-the-hoof" and the skills involved in attending can easily be translated into this kind of kinetic setting. Furthermore, many children become anxious and avoid or shut down in an isolated, verbal discussion. It is often far more useful to converse over some sort of mediating activity. Various activities will allow or inhibit the use of particular attending behaviors. In the end, it is the treatment

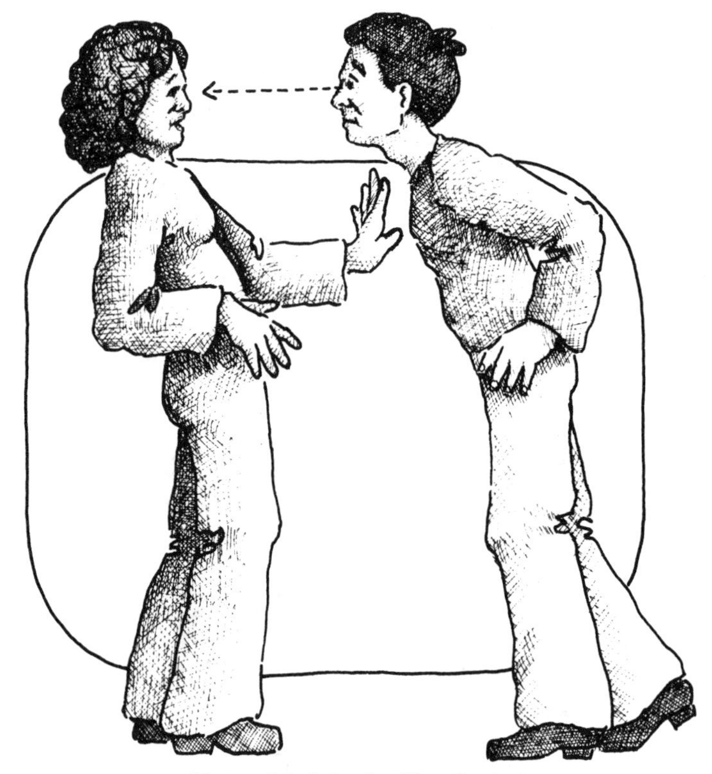

Figure 6-4. Intrusive Eye-Contact

worker's "trained intuition" that will determine the kind of attending best suited to give to a particular child.

Verbal Behavior

Verbal Following versus Topic Jumping

The basic goal of verbal following is to help the child explain and elaborate a topic that he has introduced. It is easier to react spontaneously when you are focusing on the child's reactions. You can always fit your own questions into the topics introduced by the child. Following the child reinforces and encourages his free expression so that he is then more likely to reveal crucial aspects of his situation or story.

If you do have to switch topics, use the skill of bridging by sharing your rationale for switching topics. Make a brief statement about how you see the two topics to be connected, or if they are not connected, why you

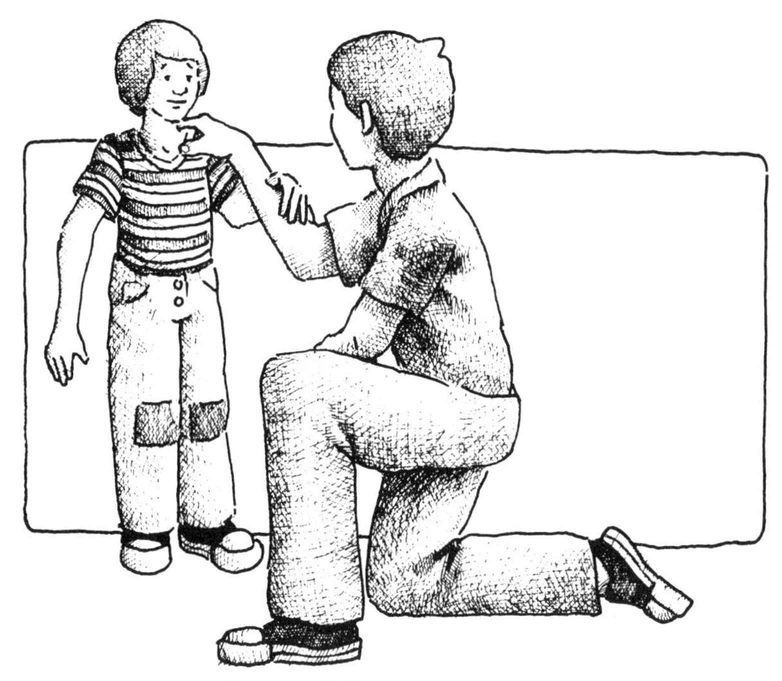

Figure 6-5. Touch for Attention

are going on to something else. To jump topics leaves the child floundering and suspicious of what you are after.

Poor Example:

CHILD: And I lost every game of cards last night, I'm really mad!
WORKER: Well, how's your math going today?

Good example:

CHILD: And I lost every game of cards last night, I'm really mad.
WORKER: You're mad about the cards last night and I saw you looking pretty mad doing your math today. How's your math going today?

Being Quiet versus Interrrupting

Sometimes it is very difficult for adults to keep their mouths shut when talking with children. Allowing time for the child to talk without interruptions shows that you are interested in what he has to say. Be especially attuned to "pregnant silences" when the child strains to find the words. Refrain from supplying words or talking over his response. This may require you to slow the pace of your talking considerably.

CHILD: My mom told me that I won't have to come here any more because she . . .
WORKER: Well, she didn't talk to me about that. [interruption—talking over]
CHILD: . . . . moving to a different state and taking me with her. And I feel . . . [thoughtful pause—pregnant silence]
WORKER: Well, you must feel frightened. [filling in]
CHILD: No, actually I feel relieved that mom finally decided to move away from my stepdad. He's been a . . .
WORKER: Wait! Stop! You mean you're really relieved? [interrupt]

Behavioral Hints

Relax Physically

If you are stationary, settle in; find a good posture and do all your fidgeting at once. Find your balance point, then start your conversation rather than starting with unresolved body tension. If you are on the move, minimize distractions (e.g., go to a more solitary place) and move at a pace that does not tax your abilities to focus on the child.

Create a Setting That Promotes Comfortable Posture

If you use a chair, find one that fits your own style: a chair with arms or without, a soft chair, a hard chair, a chair in which your feet can touch the floor. In an improvised setting you can use the floor, stairs, or even the merry-go-round. Create a setting in which you feel comfortable. You move the environment rather than allowing it to dictate to you.

Use Varied Eye Contact

Glance away and remake eye contact, as opposed to turning your head or body. Vary your eye contact. If the child does not make any direct eye contact with you, be aware that even though people fear it they do pick up some of your eye contact with peripheral vision. Stick with him, you have to pick up what eye contact he gives you. If he is fearful of too much eye contact, find an object or activity through which you can attend indirectly.

Focus on the Child and Follow What He is Saying

Take your cues from him. Don't topic jump. Try to keep your mouth shut during pregnant silences. Don't interrupt, or talk over the child. If you and the child start to say something at the same time, you stop. The child is about to say something that may be very important and you'll never know what he was going to say if you talk over him.

Build Bridges

If you have to switch from topic to topic, share with the child your reasons for switching.

Feelings and Issues for the Treatment Worker

Even though a worker may recognize the value of attending, he or she may block its appropriate use. The following include some blocks that we have seen:

"I Know What the Child is Going To Say So I'll Just Fill In."

By doing this, workers train the child to wait for someone to speak for him, and discourage the child's initiative to respond spontaneously. Even though you may have heard the child speak about a topic a hundred times, you can never be entirely sure that he is going to say the same thing. Be patient.

"I Know What Needs To Be Talked About So I'll Jump To The 'Right' Topic."

Children often have indirect means of communicating. They also have a feel for the right timing of expression. Allowing some indirectness in the service of spontaneity and building the relationship is useful.

"I'm Getting Frustrated and Anxious During Silences."

One of the things that workers may tell themselves during these silences is "I should hurry up and solve this kid's dilemma. Here he is silent and I'm falling behind." This thought is likely to make the worker feel anxious and helpless. Another thought may be "This kid is holding out on me, he's just trying to manipulate me." This is likely to lead the worker to feel frustrated and angry. Remember that the pacing of the conversation comes from the child, as does the final decision to choose to face his problems.

"It Is Impolite To Stare."

Some people learn this rule early in their development. Thus, they feel uncomfortable using eye contact to gather information. It's really okay, and even desirable to use balanced eye contact to find out more about the child you are working with.

"That's Not The Right Way To Communicate; There Must Be Something Wrong With That Kid."

Sometimes workers engage in in-group/out-group thinking. A worker may feel that the way he uses nonverbal cues is the "normal" or "right" way, and all other variations are therefore abnormal and wrong. Given this thought pattern, a child who deviates from his way of doing things is likely to be labeled "crazy" or "bad." The in-group/out-group mode of thought restricts people to a provincial and potentially destructive pattern of response. Acknowledging unfamiliar patterns of response as valid, even if not comfortable, will allow the worker to avoid labeling. (See Table 6-2.)

Table 6–2. Attending Behavior Checklist

Some of the following behaviors do not lend themselves to a simple frequency count. Therefore, use the following scale to indicate how often the listed behaviors occured: 0 = not at all; 1 = seldom; 2 = frequently; 3 = all the time.

Positive performance	*Problematic performance*
Posture:	Posture:
____ Relaxed, balanced	____ Extremely rigid and stiff
____ Natural gestures	____ Slumped, limp
	____ Overactive, posture shifts (legs and/or body)
Eye contact:	Eye contact:
____ Varied eye contact	____ Avoid eye contact
____ Initiate eye contact	____ Turn away (head or body) to break eye contact
____ Eye contact at child's eye level	____ Fixed stare
Distance and body orientation:	Distance and body orientation:
____ Maintains a comfortable speaking distance	____ Too far away
____ Approachable body orientation	____ Too close
	____ Body closed or turned away
Touching:	Touching:
____ Uses touch to help child focus attention	____ Touch is painful or distracting
Verbal following:	Verbal following:
____ Stays with main train of child's thought	____ Jumps topic
____ Bridges changes of topic	____ Talks over child's statement
____ Keeps mouth shut during pregnant silences	____ Interrupts child's statement

Quality factors—describe the worker's performance in relation to the following:

1. arrangement of the physical environment to facilitate communication (i.e., moving chairs closer, getting out from behind a table, moving away from distractions)
2. use of distance and body orientation to maintain comfortable communication atmosphere e.g., not leaning forward when already standing toe to toe
3. awareness of and verbalization about possible cultural differences in interactional rules between child and worker

Chapter 7

OPEN INVITATIONS TO TALK

After mastering the information in this chapter you should be able to—

1. describe the difference between the "Hide and Seek" pattern of communication and the open pattern of communication;
2. list the effects of Open Invitations To Talk for the worker/child relationship;
3. define the behaviors involved in Open Inivtation To Talk and give good and poor examples;
4. relate Open Invitations to Talk behaviors to non-behavioral levels of worker functioning as illustrated by "Feelings and Issues for the Treatment Worker."

After the basic background of attending has been taken care of, the next logical step in communicating is to provide yourself and the child a way of beginning and maintaining a fruitful pattern of communication. The potentially most fruitful pattern is one that helps the child focus his story yet allows spontaneous and voluntary disclosure. Open Invitations are open-ended questions and statements that allow the child tremendous flexibility of response while defining a *general* topic area. The spontaneous reactions of the child within the general topic area yield information and enthusiasm not as easily obtained when using closed methods.

Requesting more restricted responses from the child does have a place within the over-all area of facilitative communication. However, beginning workers are especially prone to use closed-ended techniques that result in unproductive patterns with children. The most common of these unproductive patterns can be seen as similar to the children's games of "Twenty Questions," "I've Got a Secret," or "Hide and Seek." The worker establishes and/or the child invites a situation in which the responsibility for the child's reporting his experience rests with the person who has least access to that information: the treatment worker. So you may witness a treatment worker asking questions such as: "Is it. . . . ?" "Could it be that. . . . ?" "Do you think it's. . . . ?" "Have you ever. . . . ?" (See Figure 7-1.)

The result of such a pattern is that the worker works much harder than he or she has to, becomes frustrated with the child for not volunteering information, and becomes frustrated with himself for not asking the "right" question. In this way you can be assured that the child will answer only those questions asked and may feel sufficiently pressured to be inhibited in his response. When the information later emerges, the treatment worker may wonder, "Why didn't you tell me?" The child's response, obviously, is "You didn't ask!" This response eloquently reflects the responsibility pattern that the worker has established. Open Invitations help to avoid the "Hide and Seek" pattern.

Effects of Open Invitations

There are a number of reasons for using Open Invitation To Talk. First, you get *more* information. It is a simple fact that if you make an open invitation the child will use *more words* than if you ask a closed question

Figure 7-1. Hide and Seek

which he can answer by a simple yes or no. Secondly, you get *richer* information because when the child can tell the story in his way he gives a broader range of information, some of which may not be relevant. Certainly you will find out some things that you would not ordinarily have found out had you asked limited questions. Thirdly, you get unbiased information because the child can express his own thoughts in his own words. The perspective is his rather than yours.

In contrast, the major function of closed techniques is to find out a specific piece of information. If you are in need of one definite fact, the best way to get it is to ask.

When you use Open Invitations To Talk, you must assume some verbal ability on the child's part. If the child has difficulty responding to the more abstract requests that Open Invitations employ, you may want to use other skills that tax his abilities less: e.g., reflection of feeling, or requests to act out an incident. If the child has the ability to respond but refuses, it may be necessary for you to use simple closed techniques just to get a minimal response from him. It is best at these times, after you have some verbalizing to work with, to switch from the closed techniques that started the talking, to more open ones that will yield more information.

As with attending, Open Invitations enhance your relationship with the child by showing *warmth* and *respect.* Your attention and interest are experienced as warmth. Your willingness to allow and encourage his free–form response is experienced as respect.

Behaviors

Open Invitations To Talk may take two forms:

1. *Open Statement*—a statement specifying a topic. For example, "You mentioned wanting to talk about your mother and father." "Your concerns about your school work are very noticeable." "Last time we talked about your feelings about leaving."
2. *Open Question*—a question about a general topic yet not requesting a specific response. For example, "How do you feel about your mother and father?" "What are your concerns about your homework?" "How have you been feeling since we talked about your feelings about leaving?"

The following are examples of closed questions that restrict the child's options:

1. *Yes/No or short answer.* This type of question specifies explicitly or implicitly a single type of acceptable answer. For example: "Do you want to talk about your mother and father? (Yes/No) "Were you aware that your concern for school work was noticeable to others?" (Yes/No)

"How many times have you talked about your feelings about leaving since we talked last?" (Short answer)

2. *True–false question.* This type of question is really two or more yes/no questions asked in a sequence. The questioner continues to ask until he gets an affirmative response. For example:
   WORKER: "Do you like your Mom?"
   CHILD: "No."
   WORKER: "Well, do you dislike her, then?"
   CHILD: "No."
   WORKER: "Well, do you feel kind of neutral?"
   CHILD: "I guess."
3. *Multiple choice question.* This type of question lists a number of alternatives for the child to pick from. For example:
   "Do you like your Mom or hate her or maybe are you just indifferent?" (or none of the above).

Behavioral Hints

Here are some behavioral hints about using open invitations:

Use the Child's Cues as a Topic Guide.

Practice attending and verbal following.

Start Questions With "What" and "How."

"What" and "how" ask for descriptive information in an open-ended way.

Use "How do You Feel About. . . . ?" to Focus on Feelings, and Use "What Does That Mean to You?" to Focus on Thoughts.

When you have nothing else to ask, these two Open Invitations can help because checking the person's thoughts and feelings about a situation is appropriate at any time.

Feelings and Issues for the Treatment Worker

Several things impede the effective use of Open Invitations. Some have to do with the beliefs workers have about themselves and the children they work with; others reside in the skill itself.

"How can I Get the Information I Want Without Letting the Child Know What I'm After?"

Often a worker feels reluctant to share with the child the intent of his line of questioning. He may feel that if he asks directly, the child will clam up, or he may underestimate the ability of a child to comprehend what it is the worker wants to know. He may also believe that he, as the worker, ought to know the "right" questions. Therefore, he avoids sharing with the child his confusion or lack of understanding. It is amazing how much children are willing and able to share once they understand what it is that you want to know. Even if you are not sure what to ask next, sharing that uncertainty with the child may give him the impetus to explore new information.

"Get to the Point, Will You!!"

Workers sometimes think that they ought to be able to fix up this kid immediately, if not sooner. Therefore, they are impatient with the seemingly irrelevant or tangential information that can accompany the child's full exploration of a topic. Sometimes the apparently "irrelevant" is in fact functional. Kids will sometimes use irrelevant information as a resting place between more intense parts of their story. Also, another person's logic or associations may be different enough from yours that what seems to you to be off the point, is in fact directly on for the child. In any event, before you cut off irrelevant topics, as sometimes you must, assess their function. If your assessment is that the child is avoiding the topic and would benefit from more directness at that point in her treatment, it may be that confrontation is indicated (see the chapter on "Confrontation").

"What do I Say When the Child Says. . . . ?"

Sometimes a worker may believe that she must respond to everything the child brings up. When the child introduces a broad range of information, the worker may feel overloaded by her self-imposed need to respond. With Open Invitations there is a balance between the freedom of response of the child, which is virtually unlimited, and the guidance of focus that the treatment worker gives by virtue of the fact that she responds to some aspects of the child's story but not to others. You must pick and choose what to respond to. Therefore, the answer to the question above can be "nothing."

"Oh, No! I've Just Asked Another Closed Question! Won't I ever Get It?"

While learning the skill of Open Invitations, most people feel very self-conscious about the frequency with which they ask closed questions. An informal survey of our trainees indicates that the everyday percentage of closed versus open questions is about ninety percent closed to ten percent open. Thus, you have a great deal of unlearning to do. Also, you must stifle the strong impulse to pay so much attention to whether or not you are complying with the Open Invitation expectation that you forget to focus on the child. The best course, though not the easiest to follow, is to relax and let the skills flow from your connection with the child. Also, it is perfectly permissible to stop in the middle of a closed question and say, "What I meant to say was. . . ." Children are usually very tolerant.

"Why Not Ask 'why' Questions?"

Although "why" questions are open-ended, they can give you faulty information and possibly lead to defensiveness in the child. There are three things to keep in mind when using "why" questions. First, "why" is often used in critical, angry, or accusatory rhetorical questions such as "Why can't you ever . . ." or "Why do you always . . ." Thus, the word "why" may have negative associations and arouse defensiveness. Secondly, "why" sometimes leads to a rationalization of defensiveness on the part of the child. A lot of times people really do not understand why they do the things they do, but since you ask them they will construct a logical reason. It may not be the real reason but they will think of a reason that seems satisfactory to you. Thirdly, "why" questions may get you in trouble because oftentimes children have an erroneous interpretation of their behavior. For example, a child might believe her father got sick because she was angry with him. So the best thing for you to do is to get descriptive information first. It is important to find out the child's interpretation of his own behavior or situation, but it is more useful if you have a good idea of why *you* think he behaves the way he does. (See Table 7-1.)

Quality factors—Describe the worker's performance in relation to the following:

1. Open Invitations used to—
   a) initiate a topic
   b) elaborate a topic
2. "Why" questions avoided or used in nonjudgmental manner

Table 7–1. Open Invitations Behavior Checklist

Record the frequency of the following behaviors:

Positive performance	*Problematic performance*
_____ Open questions	_____ Yes/No questions
_____ Open statements	_____ Guessing questions (true/false or multiple choice)

Chapter 8

MINIMAL ENCOURAGEMENTS TO TALK

After mastering the information in this chapter, you should be able to—

1. define the term Minimal Encouragement and explain the origin of the cues;
2. list the effects of the good use of Minimal Encouragements on the worker/child relationship;
3. define six types of Minimal Encouragements and give examples of good performance;
4. relate Minimal Encouragements To Talk behaviors to nonbehavioral levels of worker functioning as illustrated by "Feelings and Issues for the Treatment Worker."

Once the child has begun to tell his story, your task is to help him continue to talk, elaborate, and explain. You really need do very little since the less you say the more time there is for the child to tell his story. Minimal Encouragements are subtle cues and signals that we all use from time to time in everyday conversation. However, you will use these cues in a more focused and systematic way in order to facilitate the child's talking.

Although these cues are minimal, they are much more powerful than their intensity indicates. They are called minimal for two reasons. First of all they are very small interventions; they are usually very subtle and oftentimes very easy to overlook as they fade into the background of everyday conversations. Secondly, they are minimal in the sense that they impose a very small direction on the focus or direction of the interview. They merely indicate that your attention was directed towards one topic rather than another.

Effects of Minimal Encouragements

Minimal encouragements serve several functions for you as a treatment worker. First, they help you keep the child talking, so that you will get more information. Secondly, Minimal Encouragements focus the child's attention. The topic is still the child's but you help him explore with more depth. Finally, Minimal Encouragements facilitate voluntary sharing of information. Through use of subtle cues, you get out of the "Hide and Seek" pattern and the child is able to react more spontaneously.

Minimal Encouragements help to create a facilitative interpersonal relationship. By the interest and attention they communicate, Minimal Encouragements create a condition of *warmth* for the child. By allowing and inviting the child to continue his own story in his own words, you communicate *respect.*

Behaviors

Many behaviors may be used as Minimal Encouragements.

Head Nods—

The Minimal Encouragement head nod is sometimes almost imperceptible in social conversation. Different people nod their heads in different ways. Some people do short head nods from the top of their necks, some people nod from the base of their neck, some people even nod from their chest. The head nod you use is your style, but be aware that small head nods of a short arc are indications of attention; head nods of a wide arc tend to be more indicative of approval. (See Figure 8-1.)

Um Hum—

"Um Hum" is a simple, small, grunt-like sound. Interspersed in the other person's talking, it will encourage him to keep talking; it is an indication that you are listening. Tone of voice is very important. A harsh tone may indicate criticism. "Um hum" can also be said in a disbelieving, sarcastic, or nonaccepting tone of voice. Other words such as "yeah," "okay," "right," "yes," are also sometimes used. However, research shows the noise "um hum" is most effective. Other words such as "I see," or "I understand" can hurt more than they help as will be explained later in this chapter.

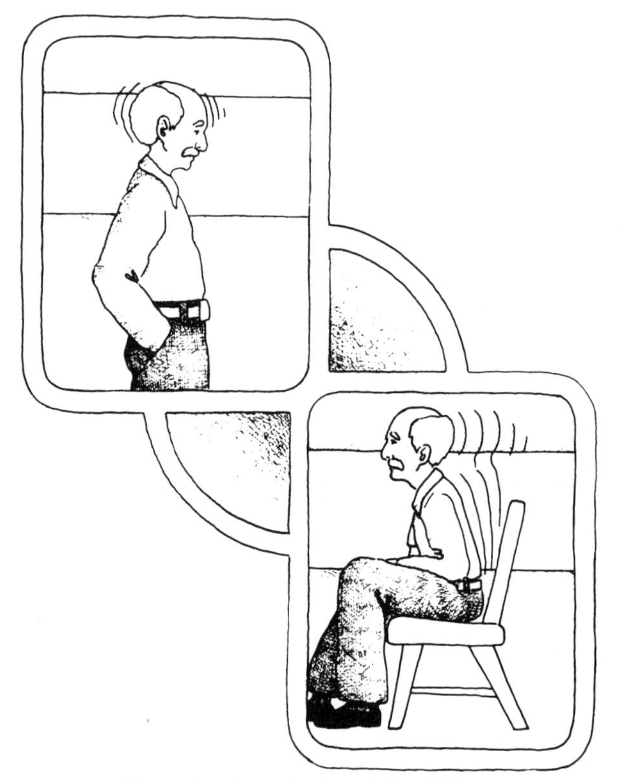

Figure 8-1. Two Styles of Head-Nods

Questioning Inflection—

Sometimes a child will start a discussion and all you have to say is "Oh?" "And?" to keep him talking. A simple little word with a questioning inflection will help him continue to elaborate and focus more depth on his topic.

Repeating Key Words—

Oftentimes a child will say words that represent key concepts in his story. All you need to do is repeat those key words and he will continue to explain those words in more detail. For instance, a child may say "Last week I sprained my thumb, my dog ran away, I'm feeling really bad because I don't have enough money for my Mom's birthday present." There are a number of key words to follow up on. You could say, "Not enough money?" or "Dog ran away?", and direct the focus of the interview. Sometimes repetition of key words with a questioning inflection will be responded to as a Yes/No question. If this is the case, avoid the questioning inflection and drop your voice pitch at the end of the key words. Thus, you will have a statement rather than a question.

Brief Questions, Statements, and Phrases—

"Tell me more," is a brief statement. "What do you mean by that?" and "What else?" are brief questions. "For example" is a brief phrase. Such words will help the client to elaborate more.

Body Language—

Each of us has in our repertoire some nonverbal Minimal Encouragements that we may be aware of. Some examples include a quizzical facial expression, a subtle head-cock as an indication of puzzlement, a raised eyebrow, leaning forward with hands spread, palms up. (See Figure 8-2.)

Behavioral Hints

There are several things you can do to make your use of Minimal Encouragements more effective.

Figure 8-2. Body Language Minimal Encouragement

Use A Variety Of Minimal Encouragements

If you stick with one and one only, it becomes stilted and stale and begins to appear gimmicky.

Attend To The Child For Cues On When To Use Minimal Encouragements.

When you do not understand what the child is saying or when the child says something that seems ambiguous, ask him to clarify it by using a simple "for instance," or "what do you mean?" Sometimes children will ask for Minimal Encouragements. They will look at you to see if you are listening, they will even say things like, "You know what I mean?" At this point a simple statement such as "Go on" is sufficient.

Time Your Minimal Encouragements.

Sometimes it is better to keep your mouth shut than to intrude. Usually there is a pause or a change in the child's voice when he has become most receptive to a Minimal Encouragement. An appropriate time may be at the end of a sentence, when a key word emerges, when the child looks thoughtful, or when he looks like he is trying to figure and pauses to consider how to express another, you might say, "And?" "But?" as a way to get him to tell the other side.

Attend To The Child For Cues On How To Use Minimal Encouragements.

The child will give you many key words. You can focus on those key words and ask him to explain some of them by saying "Give me an example," or "Tell me more." Most of the time the child will give more key words than you are able to use at the moment. File some of them in the back of your mind to use at a later date. Finally, when all else fails, use the simple phrases that invite the child to continue: "What else?" "Go on." "Tell me more." You can use these "carry on" cues with great regularity when you can think of nothing else to say.

Feelings and Issues for the Treatment Worker

There are several ways that workers can use Minimal Encouragements to shut off conversation, and also several ways that they can rationalize to themselves why they should not use this technique.

"It's a Gimmick."

This statement is usually made by people with a limited pre-training repertoire of Minimal Encouragements. They feel uneasy using so many different types of Minimal Encouragements. The problem here stems from viewing the systematic use of Minimal Encouragements as gimmicky and seeing the random use as natural. The question is not whether or not to use Minimal Encouragements (since we all use them) but how. Using these cues systematically may feel gimmicky at first, but with practice and adaptation to your style, they will become a valuable tool.

"I Feel So Dumb Doing That."

Related to the previous issue is the worker's feeling "foolish" at carrying on a conversation with such small contributions. It is hard for some people to believe that a conversation will actually take place if they use very many Minimal Encouragements. Sometimes workers will defeat the value of Minimal Encouragements by using an appropriate one and immediately following it with some longer explanation of what they "really meant," as if the child could not possibly grasp the meaning of such a small intervention. Even though you may feel uneasy at first, brave the discomfort and you will find that, with practice, Minimal Encouragements will often get you more information than more time-consuming techniques.

"Sure, Sure, I See, I Understand, Um Hum. . . ."

Misusing the minimal cues listed in this chapter can be minimal *discouragements.* Since the same cues can just as powerfully shut off conversation as prolong it. Below are some ways minimal cues can be used as discouragements.

a) The phrases *"I see," "I understand,"* and similar phrases may limit talk. First of all, workers usually do not "see" or "understand" until after a great deal of discussion and observation. However, they use these words all the time. Thus the child can feel that you are lying or that you do not really understand but are just trying to be reassuring. Secondly, such phrases are often used to get people to end what they are saying so that the listener can get his two cents worth in. If you find yourself rapidly saying, "I see" three or four times in a row within space of fives seconds, ascertain if you are not "seeing" at all but trying to get the other person to shut up.

b) *Tone of voice* can stop a conversation dead. Accusatory or indifferent, bored tones used with any of the minimal cues listed above will undo their positive effect. Remember that tone of voice and facial expression carry more meaning than do words.

c) *Overuse of one type of Minimal Encouragement* may be seen by the child as a means to manipulate him. If a worker nods her head and says "Um Hum" sixty times a minute, the child will soon see these cues not as encouragement but as deterrents. Appropriate use of Minimal Encouragements includes a variety of cues and proper timing.

"If I Nod My Head, Won't She Think I Approve Of Or Even Want Her To Do More Of The Things That Have Gotten Her Into Trouble?"

Sometimes people will interpret your Minimal Encouragements as approval, or they will even overtly ask for your approval. If this is the case you can do a number of things. First, examine your pattern and type of minimal responses. You may, in fact, be approving rather than encouraging talk. If so, alter your behavior to match your intent. For example, speed up and shorten up your head nods. Secondly, you can make the intent of your Minimal Encouragements more explicit by verbally labeling your activity. Pairing a head nod and "Um hum" with the phrase "I hear you," or "I'm listening," may help to clarify your intent. Finally, if all else fails, you can examine the worker/ child relationship which invites either of you to mistake attention for approval. (See the chapter on "Confrontation" for ways to do this). (See Table 8-1.)

Table 8–1. Minimal Encouragements Behavior Checklist

Record the frequency of the following behaviors:

Positive performance	*Problematic performance*
_____ Head nods (small arc)	_____ "I see"
_____ Um Hum's	_____ Rapid "um hum" of other minimal cues to stop child talking
_____ Word or phrase with questioning inflection	_____ "Ah," "er," and other vocal markers which discourage child from spontaneously continuing
_____ Repetition of key word	
_____ Brief question (e.g. "How do you feel about . . . ?")	
_____ Brief statement (e.g. "Tell me more.")	
_____ Body language cue	

Quality factors— Describe the worker's performance in relation to the following:

1. variety of Minimal Encouragements used
2. appropriate timing i.e., not overused, responsive to the child
3. tone of voice indicating attention when using the verbal or vocal cues

Chapter 9

PARAPHRASING AND SUMMARY OF CONTENT

After mastering the information in this chapter, you should be able to—

1. explain potential trouble spots in the communication process and give examples of how paraphrasing can help to remedy them;
2. explain the effects of good paraphrasing on the worker/child relationship;
3. define the behaviors involved in paraphrasing and give examples of both good and poor paraphrasing;
4. explain the concept of "working from the point of agreement";
5. list at least three types of cues for when to use paraphrases and give examples;
6. differentiate between paraphrases and summaries of content;
7. list at least four types of cues for when to use summaries of content;
8. relate paraphrasing and summary of content to non-behavioral levels of worker functioning as illustrated by "Feelings and Issues for the Treatment Worker."

When using the skill of paraphrasing, the treatment worker acts as a clarifying mirror by verbally reflecting the meaning of verbal and/or acted-out messages from the child using the worker's own words. The worker thus helps the child express her concerns fully and demonstrates to the child his understanding.

The general goal of paraphrasing is to understand the child's situation from her point of view, although you need not agree with that point of view. Indeed, your ability to verbalize to the child her meanings from her point of view while maintaining your own point of view gives you the opportunity to be both empathetic and understanding, yet confronting and objective when you need to be.

Paraphrasing and the Communication Process

Communication is a complicated process fraught with potential for errors and distortion. The illustration below simplifies this process and shows several trouble spots for clear communication. (See Figure 9-1.)

The diagram illustrates how human communication is a two-party process. Starting at Number 1 in the upper left corner, the sender sends his message out of his particular frame of reference and experiences. At Number 2, he encodes it; he puts it into words or action.

After the message has been encoded, it goes across to the receiver. At Number 3, noise and interference in the environment may distort the message. At Number 4, the receiver hèars it, then decodes it. At Number 5, he takes the message and puts it into his particular frame of reference.

In this process, the trouble spots are:

1. between 1 and 2—the sender may not express in words or actions exactly the idea he wishes to convey

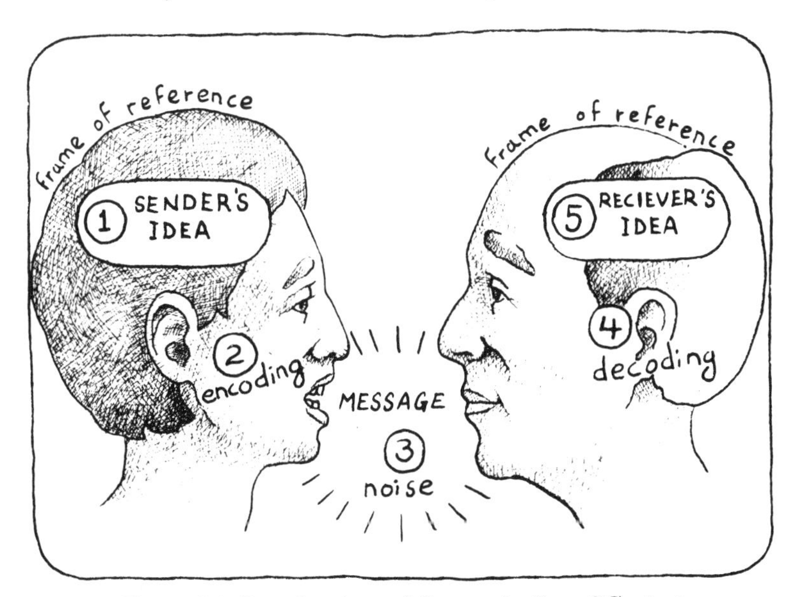

Figure 9-1. Paraphrasing and Summarization of Content

2. at 3—garbled speech, a noisy room, a plane passing overhead, all may obliterate or distort the message received
3. between 4 and 5—the receiver may change the message to fit into his frame of reference rather than seeing it as the sender intended
4. in addition, the sender's and receiver's frames of reference may be so different that they cannot find a common meaning.

Paraphrasing allows correction of all but the last of these communication problems.

The Effects of Paraphrasing

Paraphrasing Aids Understanding the Child's Point of View.

When paraphrasing, the worker attempts to say back to the child the important aspects of the child's message (i.e., those things that help the worker figure out what he really means).

Paraphrasing Helps to Make Complicated or Confusing Messages More Concise.

In order to gain an understanding of the total meaning of a client's message, you need to reflect back the essence of what the client has said. If what he said is confusing or rambling, the worker's job is to articulate the essential meaning. Doing so many times helps the child to understand what he or she is trying to say.

Paraphrasing Helps to Confirm or Disconfirm the Interviewer's Perception.

This is perception checking. The worker must check out whether or not her perception of the message contains the meaning that the child intended.

People very seldom take time to understand the real meaning of messages, and to work at trying to see the world from the other person's point of view. The major effect on the child of summaries of content and paraphrasing is *empathy;* that is, helping the child to feel that somebody really understands.

Behaviors

The essentials of paraphrasing can be illustrated in the following formula: "I perceive that you mean ____________." Each part of the formula contains important information.

I. When you claim direct ownership of the paraphrase, the child does not feel that this perception has been passed down from faceless or nameless beings. Instead, he can react to you as a person.

PERCEIVE. Labeling the paraphrase as a perception rather than a certain fact allows debate and/or disagreement. The child recognizes the tentative nature of the paraphrase.

YOU. Again, ownership is the issue. By indicating the child as the owner of the meaning, you make more immediate and personally relevant your interpretation of the child's meaning.

MEAN. This part of the formula focuses attention on the content of the message rather than on the feeling.

Obviously you cannot go around always saying "I perceive that you mean ________" when paraphrasing. You would sound like a stuck record. Luckily our language is full of similar phrases such as:

I hear you saying ________.
It seems to me you're saying ________.
Let me see if I've got this right. You're saying ________.
I get the impression that you mean ________.
I sense you're saying ________.
If I hear you correctly, you're saying ________.
In other words, you mean ________.
I guess I'd say the same thing this way ________.
Do you mean to say ________?
By what you're doing, I think you're telling me ________.

Try a variety of these, remembering to say or imply all the parts of the paraphrasing formula.

Another behavior relevant to paraphrasing is waiting for and/or *requesting confirmation or disconfirmation* of your paraphrase. Good treatment is more likely to occur when the worker and child are *working from the point of agreement.* This means that you and the child agree on the child's perception. This does not necessarily mean that you agree with how the child views his world, but that he confirms that you understand his perception. In order to determine whether or not the child agrees that your perception of his meaning is correct, you must get a response from the child. There are many ways to get this response:

a) *Keep your mouth shut after paraphrasing.* If you do this, the child may spontaneously confirm your perception directly by saying "yes" or "that's right." Or he may confirm it indirectly by continuing to explore in more depth on the topic you paraphrased.

b) *Request a reply.* You may have to ask for feedback as to whether or not your paraphrase was correct. Questions can include: "Is that right?" "How does that fit with you?" "What do you think of my last statement?"

c) *Request correction.* If the worker gets any indication that the paraphrase is wholly or even partially incorrect, ask for clarification so that you can move toward the point of agreement. Responses can include: "I guess I don't fully understand then." "Tell me again." "Say it differently for me." "Tell me what I missed."

When to Use Paraphrases

There are many situations in which paraphrases can be used. One is *when the child is confused or unsure,* that is, when the child is communicating that she is having trouble making sense of her experience. At this point, rephrasing the message will reflect it back to her and will enable the child to clarify whether or not the words she used accurately expressed her intent.

A second is *when the worker is confused or unsure.* Many times the child knows exactly what he means, but his point of view may be different from yours. Your confusion becomes a cue for you to reflect the message in order to check your understanding.

Finally, there are several situations in which *the language used may carry more than one meaning.* In these cases paraphrasing can clarify the child's intent. Examples of messages with more than one meaning include: abstract versus concrete meanings, words with double meanings, implied feeling cues, implied imperatives, figures of speech, cue discrepancy (see chapters on "Use of Language and Cue Congruence").

Summary of Content

The "when to use" suggestions for paraphrasing also apply to summary of content. Summary of content is really just a paraphrase covering a longer duration. Paraphrase deals with a child's last few sentences or a short paragraph. A summary combines a number of paragraphs, an entire interview session, or a number of sessions, in order to pull things together.

A summary is sometimes used at *the beginning of a session* to describe what has occurred to date, to consolidate various encounters, and to serve as a starting ground. At other times, a summary can be used to pull together confusing or rambling child statements. The child may talk on and on and on, and the worker can pull out the essence of the message, consolidate it, and then go on.

A further situation when summary is appropriate occurs when the worker wants to *consolidate the child's thoughts after the child has expressed them fully.*

Finally, summarizing content can be used to review important understandings and conclusions *at the end of an interview* or when a mutual child/worker agreement is needed in order to plan what to do next. Summaries make explicit the agreement in perceptions between worker and child. This is important if the worker is *moving into a new phase* of the interview, if he has finished exploring the problem and is ready to go on and try to figure out what to do about it, or if he is ready to move from one exploration phase into planning actions.

Behavioral Hints

Use "I" Statements.

Remember that paraphrasing is restating what you hear in your own words. Therefore, you need to take responsibility for your perceptions. The best way to do that is to say, "Hey, this is mine; this is the way I see it." Saying things like "It seems to me," "I get the feeling," "I hear you saying," acknowledges that it is *you* who are sharing your perceptions with the child.

Request a Reply.

You need to confirm or disconfirm your perception by saying such things as: "Well, is that right?" "Does that sound right to you?" "How does that fit?"

Translate the Child's Message.

You can translate by using more *specific terms,* more *general terms,* or by *inverting the meaning.* You make a child's general statement more specific. For instance, if he says, "I don't like George—he's too sloppy," a paraphrase might be "I think you mean that you don't like the way he dresses." If a child makes a very specific statement, you might want to make it more general. If the child says something like, "I hate the way George's shirt tail always hangs out," a paraphrase might take the form of "It seems to me that George's habits of dressing are getting to you." Or you can invert the meaning of a child's statement. If the child says something like, "George is so messy," you might say, "I hear you saying you might feel better if George were neater."

Attend to All the Child's Cues When You Listen.

Some of these cues are verbal and nonverbal messages. Others depend upon the sequence of messages. That is, the message may be distorted if taken out of context (see Cue Congruence).

Note the Context of the Interview.

Is the child coming in because he has just been arrested? Is he coming in to get off probation? Is he coming in to solve a problem with a friend?

Time Paraphrases Carefully.

Paraphrasing repetitively can be gimmicky. Too much paraphrasing can be intrusive. Your goal is to use it to help the child clarify his own perceptions, not merely to demonstrate your skill at paraphrasing.

Paraphrases can easily become *interpretations.* If you interpret, you give the child your point of view. The idea of paraphrasing is to help the child understand what he has said, and this is different from *contributing additional meanings.*

The behavioral hints for paraphrasing also apply to summarizing. Because summarizing covers a greater span of content, additional hints are useful to its practice.

Attend to Unifying Themes or Threads of the Interview.

There will usually be a theme or consistent pattern in what the child is saying. Summaries try to identify and crystallize those consistent patterns.

Use Summaries Infrequently.

Summarizing after every other statement is ineffective because at these points, there is not enough to summarize.

Feelings and Issues for the Treatment Worker

Worker perceptions, child responses, and some subtleties of the use of paraphrases lead to possible reluctance or misuse of this skill, as illustrated below.

"Oh, No. Why Do I Always Ask a Question When I Want to Paraphrase?"

People bring into training a style of relating to others that tends to be either question-or reflection-oriented. If your first inclination in response to a child is to ask a question, you will have to learn to delay your response long enough to allow yourself to recognize that a paraphrase might also be used in that situation. Even in demonstrating their understanding of a child's meaning, people with a questioning style prefer phrasing their reflections as questions, e.g., "Do I hear you saying that your perception is . . . ?" Both styles are equally good. Either questions or reflections used exclusively lead to a stilted style that is likely to be unresponsive to the unique needs of some children. Flexible use of both skills is preferred.

"It's So Obvious."

Often workers will complain that paraphrases only restate the obvious and therefore have limited worth. Sometimes an angry or hostile child will reinforce this view by responding to your paraphrase by saying, "Your grasp of the obvious is amazing!" Even though paraphrases can be an obvious restatement of what the child had just said, such repetition rises beyond the realm of the obvious when your restatement allows the child to understand himself or his situation in a slightly different way. As an analogy, you know what to expect every time you look in the mirror, and yet there are always subtle variations between your idea of what you will see and the image that is reflected (e.g., a pimple you did not know you had or a wayward strand of hair). Through your interchange with the mirror you can adjust yourself to more closely approximate your idea of what you want to look like. The same effects take place through your verbal mirroring. Sometimes people will not like what they see in themselves through your reflecting, and they may blame the mirror. At these times you might expect some attempts to get you to distort their image in the direction of their ideal. In any event, even when paraphrases are obvious, they have potential value.

"Now, Isn't It Really Best to Go Ahead and Say What You Know the Child is Really Thinking, Even If He Hasn't Gotten Around to Saying it Yet?"

There is a fine line between paraphrases and leading questions. A paraphrase *reflects* back to the child what he has already expressed through some mode of communication. A leading question *projects* onto the child an assumption or prejudice of the worker before the worker sees evidence to support his idea. "Aren't you really saying that you're going to quit your job?" is a leading question. "It seems to me you're saying you're not quite sure if this job is right for you" is a paraphrase.

Often you may have a hunch or guess about what the child "really means," even though he has not clearly stated his meaning. In that case, you might own your guess or hunch, or express what your reactions might be in a similar situation. "In a situation like that I might say, 'The hell with it,' and walk off. Did you experience anything like that?" This strategy can be leading in itself, even though you clearly separate your projection from the experience of the child. Use it with care.

"But When I Paraphrase, Nothing Happens!"

When you ask a question, you get some immediate feedback from its answer. You can tell right away whether or not you had the desired effect through the child's answer. With paraphrasing, the feedback can be just as concrete, but you may not be alert to cues that confirm or disconfirm your response. Sometimes a child will say "Yeah!" in a tone of wonder, and lean back to ponder the new insight you have given him. More often he will just say "Yes" to your paraphrase. Sometimes he will not even acknowledge your contribution, but will continue with his story in a more intense and enthusiastic way. And, another more confusing cue is total denial of the paraphrase. Avid protests often signal that the paraphrase has hit a tender spot ("The lady dost protest too much"). Although you may be right, this is not the time to push for confirmation by the child.

All of these are signs that your paraphrase has been accurate. Also, because reflections leave the problem-solving more on the shoulders of the child, this skill takes longer in helping a child resolve his difficulties. Thus, this skill requires treatment workers to tolerate ambiguity longer rather than when using more directive skills.

"Sometimes When I Paraphrase, the Child Stops Talking Altogether."

Sometimes you will give a wonderful paraphrase or summary and the child will stop her story cold in response. For example,

WORKER: I get the sense that even though you would like for you and your mother to get along, you have pretty much given up on that ever happening. Does that fit with your point of view?

CHILD: Yeah . . . [*silence—stops dead*]

Several things may be happening when you get the stop-dead effect. First, you may have reflected or summarized so well that the child feels he has finished and doesn't know what to say next. This may be a time for a transition to the next phase of problem-solving. Secondly, at these times the child may be virtually struck dumb by the significance of what you have just said. At these times, it is important to allow the child some time to ponder the new information, and then follow up on her reactions to it.

Thirdly, and most simple to correct, you may be using paraphrases that sound like Yes/No questions: e.g., "Are you saying that you would like to leave home?" If you get the stop-dead effect in these cases, work to avoid the Yes/No phrasing. If you still get silence, be sure to ask an open-ended follow-up question or continue to reflect, e.g., "Looks to me like you're having a hard time responding to my last statement." (See Table 9-1.)

Quality factors—Describe the worker's performance in relation to the following:

1. paraphrases appropriately timed
2. paraphrases used as perception checks
3. paraphrases used to crystalize confusing client content

Table 9–1. Paraphrasing and Summary of Content Behavior Checklist

Record the frequency of the following behaviors:

Positive performance	*Problematic performance*
Paraphrase:	Paraphrase:
____ "I" statement paraphrase	____ Does not own perception
____ Paraphrase with invitation for child feedback	____ Inaccurate response to content
	____ Ignores important content
Summary of content:	Summary of content:
____ Used to pull together several of client's comments	____ Used to end exploration before the client has finished
____ Used to review past sessions	____ Used as basis for planning action without checking
____ Used to begin further exploration of an area	

Chapter 10

REFLECTION AND SUMMARY OF FEELING

After mastering the information in this chapter, you should be able to—

1. explain difficulties involved in communicating on the feeling level;
2. explain and give examples of three different methods of putting feelings into words;
3. identify five different types of observable feeling cues;
4. explain the effects of good reflection of feeling on the worker/child relationship;
5. define the behaviors involved in reflection of feeling and give examples of both good and poor performance;
6. relate reflections and summary of feeling to non-behavioral levels of worker functioning as illustrated by "Feelings and Issues for the Treatment Worker."

Reflection and summary of feeling are the feeling-level counterpart to paraphrasing and summarization of content. The difference between these skills lies more in the focus of communication rather than in the form of the skill.

Virtually all communication can be responded to as either content or feeling. Your task in reflection and summary of feelings is to verbalize the feeling-level message. If you can accurately sense the world that the child is feeling and perceiving, you can help the child move towards self-understanding and self-awareness. Being alert to and responding to the feeling being expressed, rather than solely to the content of what the child says, requires selective attention to feelings. *What* the child is saying is the *content* portion of the message. *How* the child is saying what she is saying may indicate the *feeling* part of the message. For example, using identical words, one child may sit up on the edge of her chair and speak quickly and rapidly, communicating enthusiasm; another child may slouch over and speak more slowly, communicating discouragement.

Most of us have had little or no training in identifying, labeling, and dealing with feelings. We use the skills we learned growing up in a family and a culture that had certain rules about what, if anything, could be communicated about feelings. As a result of these limitations, feelings can be viewed as confusing, nebulous, and often scary. Some of these reactions to feelings arise because feelings are tied to more primitive and diffusely reacting parts of our body. Therefore, the ways of understanding and the labels used by the more evolved and specifically reacting parts of ourselves do not always match internal events we also perceive. Reflections of feeling can help children become aware of their emotional reactions and find more accurate and useful ways of labeling and expressing them. With a more sophisticated description of those previously mysterious internal events, the confusion and fear around feelings decreases.

Effects of Reflections of Feeling

There are several functions of reflection of feeling. The first is to *gain an understanding of the child's emotional experiences.* Your goal is to perceive the world as the child feels it in order to understand him more clearly. If the worker does not acknowledge or does not explore the child's feelings, he has cut out a whole part of the child's experience that could aid in understanding her.

The second reason to use reflection is to *clarify unclear or confused expressions of feelings* on the child's part. Words are only one way of expressing and communicating feelings, and most of us have a limited feeling vocabulary. Our usual way of expressing feelings in words is analogous to a color-blind person talking about colors: the person may perceive only black, white, and shades of gray. On the other hand, an artist perceives not only red, blue, green, and orange, but also heliotrope, chartreuse, magenta, and other shadings. So, when you want to help a child clarify a feeling, it helps to give him a vocabulary—words that he may not be aware of or familiar with.

Also, reflection and summary of feeling are used to *confirm or disconfirm your perception of the child's feelings.* Remember, you are trying to get an idea of how the child feels. This is many times difficult to determine because different people express their emotions differently. Also, the same person may express different emotions similarly or may express the same emotions in different ways at different times. For example, people cry because they are sad, because they are happy, and because they are angry. If you have a crying child with you, what does that mean? A reflection of feeling can confirm or disconfirm your perception.

There are several effects of the good use of reflections and summary of feelings on the child. First, *empathy* is enhanced: the child will feel that you really care and understand because you are taking the time and effort to understand how it feels to be in his shoes.

Secondly, the child will feel *permission to express feelings.* By your acknowledging the child's feelings, he will feel that it's okay to talk about feelings with you. Many settings and many people do not allow feelings to be expressed. They do not see feelings as a valid part of the human experience. In those settings, people are likely to say things like "Well, you shouldn't feel that way," or "It won't do any good to talk about the way you feel. Why don't you forget about it." Sometimes people imply that feelings only get in the way by saying "Well, when you're ready to talk sense, I'll listen, but I don't want to listen to all that feeling crap." Reflecting feelings says that feelings are a valid part of a person's experience. A slogan for children who do not quite believe that you are really giving permission is "Feelings aren't good or bad—they just are."

Finally, reflections of feeling help the child gain *new understanding* of his situation. The child may be denying part of his experience by not acknowledging a feeling. Recognizing this feeling may mean recognizing the experiences associated with the feelings. Or, her way of expressing the feeling may be so restricted that she is unable to differentiate between the types or the intensity of feelings she is having. In this case, reflection may help her to explore the feeling and give her some new understandings. Learning to *label his feelings and differentiate between different kinds of feelings* is a major insight for the child. Through your use of reflections, the child can also learn that feelings and behaviors are connected, i.e., that he behaves in certain ways because he feels certain ways, and that these behaviors result in more feelings.

BEHAVIOR

A reflection of feeling is similar in form to that of a paraphrase, with one obvious difference.

"I perceive that you feel . . ."

1. Again, ownership of the reflection must be claimed by the treatment worker, especially in the realm of feelings. Because feeling states can be ambiguous, people project labels and value judgments onto feeling expressions. Therefore, you must make an extra effort to pin your reflection to you as a person rather than to some more abstract or general value.

PERCEIVE. The tentativeness of your interpretation of the child's feeling must be conveyed. Labeling feelings is an act of inferential observation; therefore, no certainty can be attained. Also labeling your reflection as a perception allows the child to correct your perception rather than only accept or reject it.

YOU. By identifying the child as the owner of the feeling you have reflected, you make immediate and personally relevant your interpretation of the child's emotional experience.

FEEL. In reflections of feeling, this is the part of the formula that causes the most difficulty. Finding and maintaining the focus on feelings defines this technique. Yet, staying with the feelings can be the most difficult part.

All the sentence stems for paraphrasing also apply to reflection of feeling. You need not use "I perceive you feel . . ." exclusively. As an aid to expanding the variety of feeling words you may use, consider Table 10-1. on "Feeling Types and Intensities."

In addition to using specific feeling words, you can use figures of speech to capture feelings in words. For example: "You look as if your heart is soaring." "Sounds like you could cry your eyes out." "You're saying you felt like a bump on a log."

And, you can use descriptions of action urges to capture feeling: i.e., statements of what the child would like to *do* while experiencing the feeling. For example: "I sense you feel like running away right now." "It seems like you feel like telling everyone you see about your new friend." With children, de-scriptive phrases are especially effective when they use images, analogies, and activities from the child's world.

The major problem with staying with the feeling level of the child's expression comes from our imprecise usage of the word "feel." The word *feel,* as used commonly, can mean "feel" ("I feel sad") or "think" ("I feel that we shouldn't have done that") or "say" ("He felt I was right"). A sure giveaway that an attempted reflection of feeling expression is leaving the feeling level is the phrase "feel that" as in "I feel that you are wrong." As soon as you hear "feel that" you can be certain that thoughts not feelings are revealed. Also, be sure that *feeling terms* are used rather than *trait or personality terms.* For example, say "Sounds to me that you feel excited" rather than "Sounds to me that you feel excitable." The difference of only a few letters in the spelling of the word implies a much larger difference in terms of how the labeled feeling is thought of. "Excited" identifies a transient stage of being; "excitable" implies a set and somewhat unchanging characteristic of the person's personality. Some feeling descriptions do not

Table 10–1. Feeling Types and Intensities

Unpleasant types	*Low*			*High*
1. Blaming	suspecting	accusing	blaming	persecuting
2. Hate	dislike	contempt	disgust hate	loathing despising
3. Anger	irritated annoyed	resentful bitter	angry	fury rage
4. Sadness	unhappy gloomy	sad forlorn	dismal morose	despair/grief depressed
5. Guilt	ashamed	regretful	guilty	
6. Fear	worried nervous edgy	anxious apprehensive	fearful scared	terrified horrified
7. Loneliness	withdrawn	lonely alienated	isolated forlorn	abandoned rejected
8. Helplessness	fed-up frustrated	futile ineffectual	helpless inadequate	impotent hopeless
9. Fatigue	tired	weary	fatigued	exhausted
10. Boredom	tuned-out	indifferent	bored	apathetic
11. Hurt	distressed discomfort	pain hurt	anguished suffering	misery agony
12. Embarrassment	self-conscious bashful	inhibited shy	embarrassed	humiliated
13. Confusion	mixed-up puzzled	baffled	confused	bewildered
14. Disappointment	discontent	disappointed	dissatisfied	cynical
Pleasant types	*Low*			*High*
1. Accepting others' respect	respect	acceptance concern	approval caring	esteem
2. Loving	liking	warmth	affection tenderness	loving adoration
3. Content/Peaceful	untroubled	content	satisfied	peaceful
4. Happy	pleasure	happiness jolliness	delight elation	ecstasy
5. Confidence	importance	confident self-reliant	usefulness worth	pride
6. Calm/Relaxed	at ease comfortable	relaxed	calm patient	serene
7. Closeness	approachable	friendly	close	intimate
8. Competence	capable	strong	potent	powerful
9. Secure	snug	sure	safe protected	secure
10. Enthusiasm/Excitement	alertness	eagerness	enthusiasm	excitement
11. Well Being/Wholeness	well being	alive energetic	vibrant together	actualization wholeness
12. Spontaneity/Joy	uninhibited	spontaneity	freedom	passion joy
13. Understanding/Clarity	awareness	sensitivity	intelligent understanding	inspired intuition
14. Hopeful	trusting	hopeful	optimistic	assured

differ from their trait counterparts at all, so that the sentence in which they are used conveys the meaning. For example: "You're saying that you are inadequate" (trait) versus "You're saying that you feel inadequate" (feeling). Obviously the implied potential for change in the child's perception of his ability to make progress can make a large difference.

As in paraphrasing, work from the point of agreement, request a reply, and request correction.

Cues for Using Reflections of Feeling

Being alert to and responding to the feeling being expressed is always appropriate, regardless of the *nature* of the feeling, (e.g., positive, negative, or ambivalent) and regardless of the *direction* of the expression (e.g., toward himself, towards other people, towards you, and towards the treatment situation).

Some of the more specific cues that may indicate feeling states are illustrated below.

The first of the emotional cues are *physiological.* These would include such things as flushing, perspiration on the brow, sweaty palms, activity level, twitching, tics, trembling, goose bumps, and watery eyes. (See Figure 10-1.)

Another one is *body language:* posture, facial cues, voice tone and pitch and volume distance from others. Each of these may indicate a particular feeling. (See Figure 10-2.)

Emotion–motivated behavior will also tip you off. If a behavior looks emotionally based, a reflection would be appropriate. For instance, if the child regularly avoids certain topics you might look at this evasion as a feeling cue. Other emotion-motivated behavior might be flunking a test, quitting in the middle of a baseball game, or laughing at a story about a dog dying.

Another cue to look for is *direct or indirect emotionally laden words.* For instance, words like "angry," "sad," "ecstatic," or "loving," label feeling directly. As previously mentioned, these words may be limited. As an indirect expression the child may instead use words that are reports of action urges. Some examples of action word phrases are: "I could have strangled him." "I could have hugged him." "I could have cracked his head open." Children may also use metaphors and other such figures of speech as "I was down in the dumps," "I blew up," "I popped my lid," or "It was a real trip". At that point a reflection of feeling would be used to crystallize the feeling and confirm your perception.

Certain situations tend to induce certain feelings. In a situation involving a child's wants being blocked, a child will very likely feel frustrated. If

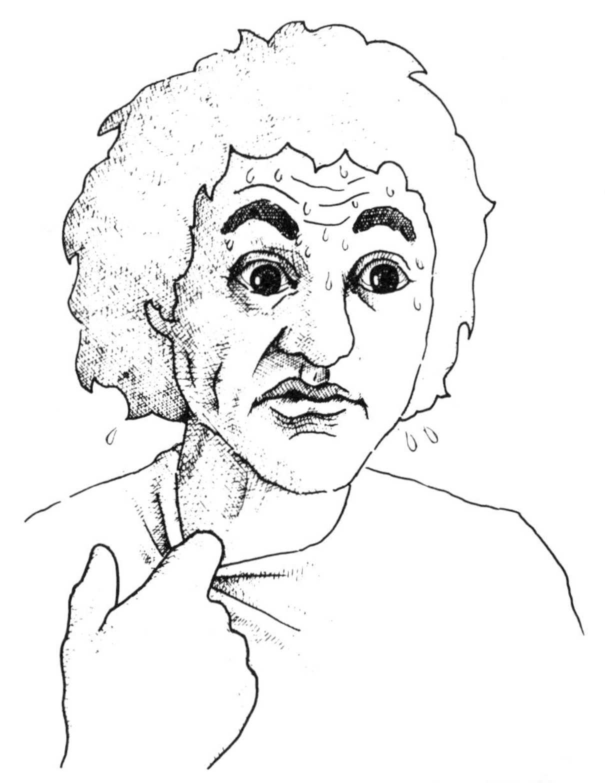

Figure 10-1. Reflection and Summarization of Feeling

there is a situation in which he is threatened, he may feel hurt, angry, or depressed. It is important here to check out how the child reacts on a feeling level to particular kinds of situations. You may respond to these *situational cues* by understanding the underlying psychological mechanism by imagining yourself in the child's situation. Remember that different people may react to the same situation in different ways. Also remember that if the reaction is very discrepant from the general population, e.g., smiling after being punched in the stomach, the child may very well be disguising one feeling with another. In these cases, which are common with emotionally disturbed children, it is important for the treatment worker to assess the feeling dynamics of the child and read these back, thus clarifying the child's confusing process.

Cues for Using Summary of Feeling

All of the guidelines for reflections apply to summary. In addition, summarizing can be used to verbalize emotional undertones expressed

Figure 10-2. Reflection and Summarization of Feeling

throughout the interview. That means making connections and focusing on ambivalent feelings. Many times, children will express one kind of feeling in one part of an interview and another kind in another part. Reflections can be used to explore those feelings when they happen, but to pull them together requires summarizing.

Behavioral Hints

Reflection of feeling is the feeling-level counterpart of paraphrasing, so some of the hints will be similar.

Use "I" Statements.

A reflection is your perception and the child needs to know that it is your perception. It is important that the child see that you are not trying to tell her she is feeling something that she is not.

Request a Reply.

This will tell you whether or not your reflection is accurate. If it is not, you need to readjust your understanding to take into account what the child is really trying to express.

Translate the Child's Expression of Feeling into Descriptions, Action Urges, or Figures of Speech.

Many times children are unable to use descriptive words. Sometimes they are unable to use words at all. Your task is to verbalize for the child by describing the feeling.

Use all Child Cues to Identify Feeling.

All of the cues previously mentioned are tremendously informative. Feelings are expressed through any or all of those cues at once. You need to be alert to all of them in order to pick up on the actual feeling present.

Be Aware of Timing.

You need to time your reflections to fit with the important feelings that the child is expressing. It is not necessary to label everything that is going on with the child.

The hints that apply to reflections are also applicable to summaries. In addition, *attend to threads and themes* of feeling to see if you can pull together the general feelings that are going on throughout the interview.

Secondly, summarizing involves *pulling together expressions of differing emotions on the same topic.* This would be a way of verbalizing ambivalence, or bringing into the child's awareness feelings of ambivalence that he had not yet considered.

Finally, *summarize at the end of the interview* after the important feeling topic has been fully explored. This will provide closure before going on to the next subject.

Feelings and Issues for the Treatment Worker

Several facts about feelings can help workers to keep themselves clear about their emotional contribution to reflecting feelings and thus help them to use this skill more often and more effectively.

"I'm Afraid I'll get Overwhelmed by the Intensity of the Child's Feelings."

Each of us has some feelings that will be more easily aroused while working with troubled children. Workers need to understand their vulnerable and "blind" spots in order to cope with these feelings. One way workers can become emotionally over-involved with a child is by taking responsibility for the child's feelings. If you believe that you must "make it all better" for the child, then you will frustrate yourself since the child himself is the only one who can control his feelings.

You may also place yourself in the target position for the child's emotions when you do not belong there. If a child expresses anger during your conversation with him, that does not necessarily mean that he is angry with you. If you believe that any emotion expressed in your vicinity is directed towards you, you will be less willing to encourage people to express unpleasant emotions.

Some children will be working on emotional issues that you have not satisfactorily resolved for yourself. When this is so, you may find yourself overreacting to this situation because you are bringing along your own feeling backlog, and you may need to pass the child on to someone else who can deal with the issue more dispassionately. Or you can make an extra effort at maintaining the separation between your own and the child's responses. If your emotional vulnerabilities are inflamed frequently during your work with children, we suggest that you take steps to work through those areas. All of us have our tender spots. We are not saying you have to be 100 percent well-adjusted to be working with troubled children—if that were the case, very few people would be available to work with them. Rather, become aware of your vulnerabilities and learn to use them, to work through them, or to refer those children with whom you cannot work effectively because of them.

"How Do I Get Onto The Feeling Level?"

Because our everyday conversation about feelings is usually superficial and/or nonexistent, we have had little practice at getting feeling information. The first of several hints in this regard is to use feeling words. Although our feeling vocabulary is woefully inadequate to describe the nuances of emotional experience, using a word brings those ambiguous, amorphous experiences into the realm of content, and as content, feeling words gain connectedness to feeling experience. Second, recognize that people may have negative associations to specific feeling words, e.g., some people will not admit to being angry. You could argue with them all day and they would not agree with that label for their expressions. However, they might accept a synonym, e.g., irritated. Words are merely referents for internal states, so do not get caught in semantics unless it is crucial. Use the labels that the child brings as a starting point. Third, the easiest ways to get to the feeling level are to ask ("How do you feel about that?") or reflect ("I perceive that you feel . . ."). Be sure that when you request a feeling response from a child that he or she gives you a feeling, not an idea or another nonfeeling response such as traits or opinions.

"What Do I Do Once I Get On The Feeling Level?"

Some workers are befuddled once they find that they can get to feelings so easily. They do not know what to say next after the child says "I'm sad." Once a feeling word is used, that word becomes part of the content of the interview. As such, it can be treated as any other content-level idea or concept. That is, you can ask questions about the feeling, reflect feelings about the feeling, probe the circumstances surrounding the occurrence of the feeling, use Minimal Encouragements to keep the child talking about the feeling, etc.

"Feelings Must Be Understandable."

Sometimes workers discount the child's feelings because they do not believe, or have difficulty understanding, the feelings that the child expresses. Remember that feelings are confusing and difficult to sort out even for adults who have more experience and greater verbal facility. If you believe that a child is misrepresenting his feelings, accept his statement as a first approximation which has face validity for the child. As you and the child explore the feelings in more detail, he may come to understand his experience differently, or you may come to understand that your initial perception was inaccurate. Do not tell children that they feel something; rather, *share your perception* of what they are expressing. Own your perception as yours and share the cues you observe that make you think that a specific feeling is occurring. Such reflecting of physical cues to feeling expression may help the child to pair the words you are using with the internal reactions that he experiences. At the same time, it is all right for you and the child to continue to disagree in your perceptions of the feelings represented by a specific expression. The child may discount his own feelings. You do not have to change your perception to fit his discount. You may end up "agreeing to disagree."

"Feelings Must Be Justified And Reasonable."

People feel exactly as they "should" feel given their belief system, past conditioning, and millions of other factors. We often feel compelled to explain our feelings rationally when no "logical" justification is necessary. We all attempt to explain confusing and ambiguous events with concepts that we understand. So, if a child expresses a feeling without apparent justification or for the "wrong" reasons, all that means is that she is not using concepts that you would use. If we admit that we often feel what we feel for "who knows what reasons," then we can accept feelings at face value rather than trying to over explain or justify them. (See Table 10-2.)

"When Is It Okay To Get Off The Feeling Level?"

Although feelings are important, they are not the only aspect of the child that you consider. Here are some reasons to get off of addressing feelings:

The child becomes blocked by feelings for which he has few or inadequate controls. You may want to teach the child how to defend against being overwhelmed so that he can move beyond the block.

The child uses feeling expression as a ploy to accomplish some other end. You can reflect the anger a child experiences at being given a command, but that does not mean he can avoid the command or the consequences of his behavior.

Table 10–2. Reflection and Summarization of Feeling Behavior Checklist

Record the frequency of the following behaviors:

Positive behavior	*Problematic behavior*
Reflection of feeling:	Reflection of feeling:
_____ "I" statement reflections	_____ Completely inaccurate reflection of here-and-now feelings (verbal or nonverbal)
_____ Reflection with invitation for the child to feed back	_____ Partially accurate reflection of here-and-now feelings (verbal or nonverbal)
_____ Accurately reflects here-and-now nonverbal cues	_____ Ignores obvious here-and-now feelings (verbal or nonverbal)
_____ Accurately reflects probable there-and-then feelings aroused by client experience	
Summary of feeling:	Summary of feeling:
_____ Summary used to integrate several feeling cues or reactions of client	_____ Summary used to end exploration of feeling before client is done
_____ Summary used to review past feeling expressions	_____ Summary used without allowing client time to confirm or disconfirm
_____ Summary used to bring together possible conflicting expressions	

Quality Factors— Describe the worker's performance in relation to the following:

1. reflection and summaries include more than one feeling when appropriate
2. flexible use of feeling vocabulary
3. allow disagreement of perception of feeling without discounting self or child

Chapter 11

CUE CONGRUENCE

After mastering the information in this chapter, you should be able to—

1. explain three basic truths about communication and how they affect the worker/child relationship;
2. identify the relationship dimension directly related to cue congruence;
3. explain the assumptions regarding the origins of cue congruence;
4. identify and explain ten different types of cues that function in human communication;
5. explain the paradoxical nature of practicing congruence;
6. relate cue congruence to nonbehavioral levels of worker functioning as illustrated by "Feelings and Issues for the Treatment Worker."

Any time you interact with anyone you are communicating through *many different channels* at the same time. You may be communicating *many different messages* at the same time. Human beings communicate as total organisms. Our faces, tones of voice, clothes, postures, gestures, the things we talk about, where we talk about them, all indicate meaning. The child will monitor not only the overt messages that you are sending through your words, but he will also monitor the rest of the messages which indicate something about the relationship between you and the child you are working with. Cue congruence, the focus of this chapter, means that the content-level and the relationship-level messages match and augment each other.

When this match occurs, people learn that you mean what you say, that you are trustworthy, that you are genuine rather than phony. The congruence of the cues is observable both in you and in the children you work with.

This chapter is different from previous chapters in that cue congruence is not an active skill: rather it is a characteristic of persons engaged in communication at all times in any setting. Congruence will emerge if we allow it to. The assumption is that all of us are cue congruent to begin with, but we unlearn it as we grow up. This chapter will focus on what to be aware of to allow yourself to be cue congruent.

Communication and the Worker-Child Relationship

To understand the impact of cue congruence we will first focus on some basic truths about communication. The first truth is that *you cannot avoid communicating.* You and the children you work with are always sending messages. Even silence is a message. For example, if you ask a child to hand you a toy, think of the meaning of the following responses: a) the child quietly hands you the toy; b) he throws the toy at you; c) he says "I won't"; d) he looks at you blankly and then turns away without complying.

The second truth is that *you cannot avoid qualifing a message.* Just by the fact that you are sending a message, you are sending it through some medium of expression. The way in which medium of expression is used has the potential of intensifying or diluting the original message. You may be sending a message on one channel that really is different than the message you are sending on the other channels. This difference is the basis of cue discrepancy. For example, you can say the words "good job" in a positive tone of voice and convey approval, or you can say them in a harsh tone of voice and communicate sarcasm and disapproval. So, the tone of voice is the qualifying cue. Think of how many ways you can say the word "no": "*No*!" "noooo", or "no?" Thus, a person may send a double message negating in one channel what she is asserting in another. (See Figure 11-1.)

The third fact about communication is that *you cannot avoid defining a relationship* in terms of what is permissible in the relationship. For example, an adult might catch a child with his hand in the cookie jar. The adult might send several congruent messages: (Frown and harsh voice) "You know you're not to be in that cookie jar," or (Smile and mellow voice) "It's all right, why don't you take two?" But, what is the child to do if the adult says, (Frown and harsh voice) "Go on, take as many as you like." In the first two examples the message is clearly to stop or to continue getting cookies. In the last example, it is not clear whether taking cookies is permissible or not. The mixed message leads to confusion about how the child is to understand the adult. Potential punishment or reward are both possible

Figure 11-1. Cue Discrepancy

as the basis of this communication. Thus the child is left in a quandry that leads to mistrust and a nonfacilitative atmosphere. When you are cue congruent you avoid this kind of subverting of the relationships with the children you work with. When you are congruent you communicate that "This relationship is one in which I will be sincere and I expect you to be sincere." The consequence of your being congruent is that the relationship is more genuine.

Allowing Cue Congruence

In monitoring your own and others' cue discrepancy and congruence, it helps to pretend to be a Martian; that is, to be like an objective visitor from another planet with no preconceptions of what should and should not be communicated. In growing up, we have all learned not to see, not to hear, not to feel, and not to comment on cue discrepancies. Through practice most of us have learned to override the powers of observation we were born with. As Martians we would have learned no such restrictions. As treatment workers, it is just these restrictions that we must overcome in order to monitor our own and others' cue congruence and discrepancy. So get ready to violate some of those early prohibitions such as, "don't stare," "don't act like you know so much," "if you can't say anything nice, don't say anything at all," "don't act so smart," "we don't talk about such things." You must sharpen your senses of seeing, hearing, and feeling. The restrictions on these functions are lifted; you have permission to be observant, to be smart, to know a lot about cue congruence and what it means, and to discuss cue congruence and discrepancy with others, even the children you work with.

Types of Cues

Below are different kinds of cues with a brief explanation of the dimensions along which the cues vary.

Verbal Cues

Along with the specific meanings of words as described in a dictionary, words have other characteristics that may be communicated by their selection or implication.

Denotative Cues: These are words that describe what is going on. They can vary from concrete to abstract. Concrete descriptive words are pinned to particular specific incidents. Abstract descriptive words are general and deal with qualities separated from specific objects or events.

Concrete	Abstract
"My nose is running and my head aches."	"I'm sick."

Connotative or Feeling Cues: Feeling words vary from objective to evaluative. For example, in the saying, "I am independent, you are stubborn, he is pig-headed," each adjective describes the same characteristic but evaluates it with different emotional implications.

Objective	Evaluative
"You didn't do what I asked."	"You're a real turkey."

Implied Imperatives: These are statements that can be heard as a demand for action on the part of the receiver. For example, if a close friend says, "My back itches and I can't reach it," does that mean that you should just acknowledge that fact saying, "Oh, that's too bad," or should you scratch the itch? The imperative cue varies in directness.

Indirect	Direct
"I can't tie my shoe."	"Please tie my shoe."

Accessibility of Information: This cue indicates how easy it is for the person to be aware of information and dredge it up out of his experiences. Is it easy to disclose or is the information repressed and very difficult to share?

Accessible	Inaccessible
"I'm sad about my mom leaving."	"I feel bad and I don't know why."

TOPIC TRACKING: A person's preference for certain topics and his ability to stay with some topics indicates feelings associated with those topics. Does the person talk freely about particular topics? Does he avoid particular topics?

WORKER: How was your math class today?

Tracking	Distracting
CHILD: "Rough! The teacher started to explain fractions."	"My math class had no class. It was sleazy."

ASSOCIATIONS: These can vary from logical to irrational. A logical association occurs when the child says something and then moves to something related. The irrational associations are more like Freudian slips and double meanings. For example, if you are talking to a potential suicide and he is talking about killing time, that certainly could have a double meaning.

WORKER: "What's it like to be going back to school?"

Logical	Irrational
CHILD: "It's like when I moved to my new house last year. . . . really strange."	"It's as much fun as a barrel full of turkeys—ah—I mean monkeys."

Para–Verbal Cues

These cues are not words, but they go along with words. They add meaning to the meanings expressed.

VERBAL FILLERS: These are miscues and fillers such as "er," "well," "ah," "you know," and stammers. A speech pattern containing few fillers tends to indicate relaxation; many indicates tension.

Many	Few
"Ah. . . . well. . . . er. . . could I. . . . well. . . you know. . . could I have a. . . little. . . a little. . . ah. . . you know. . . a little smooch."	"May I kiss you?"

SILENCE: Timing of silence and ability to tolerate silence conveys meaning. Is there a lot or just a little bit of silence? When does the silence occur?

Silence Intolerant	Silence Tolerant
"Well, what do you think about that fight between Jeff and George? [pause half a second] Now you know that disrupted the whole class, dont you? [pause half a second], Well, what's the matter, don't you have a tongue?"	"Well, what do you think about that fight between Jeff and George?" [pause five seconds].

IMMEDIACY: Is the content of what the person is talking about in the here and now, or is it generalized and abstract? Here-and-now topics tend to be more immediate and useful. Generalized topics are used by people who want to get away from what is going on in the here and now to intellectualized discussion.

Immediate	Generalized-Abstract
"I like you."	"Sometimes people are attracted to each other without any observable rationale."

SIGHS AND BREATHING SOUNDS: Sighs, snorts, sudden intakes of air, gasps, all are signs of a change in breathing patterns. These cues vary from few to many.

Vocal Cues

Vocal cues are hard to describe in writing. Everyday language has a limited vocabulary to differentiate vocal qualities. In addition, print cannot transmit vocal qualities. A person's tone of voice can vary along three dimensions.

QUALITY OR TIMBRE: A voice tone may be harsh, breathy, mellow, shrill, or other ways that convey the feeling of the speaker.

VOLUME: Variations in loudness or softness of speech can indicate the intensity of feeling about the given issue.

PITCH: Variations in how high or low the pitch of a person's voice is may indicate differing feelings attached to the words.

Body Language Cues

The body conveys messages.

Figure 11-2. Body Orientation

POSTURE: A person may slump, with shoulders rounded over, or sit rigidly, with a straight back.

BODY ORIENTATION: The torso may be oriented with the feet and legs directly towards the other person. Or the body may be split, with the feet and legs oriented towards the other while the chest turns away.

Add into this configuration whether or not the head is oriented directly or away and you can see the body orientation can be a complex cue. (See Figure 11-2.)

BODY OPENNESS: The crossing or uncrossing of legs and arms closes or opens either the upper or lower parts of the body. Upper and lower openness do not necessarily go together. (See Figure 11-3.)

BODY LEAN: Leaning toward indicates interest or attention. Leaning back is more relaxed; in the extreme it may indicate relaxation to the point of lack of interest or even contempt.

GESTURES: Gestures can vary from expressive to symbolic. Winks or a finger in front of the lips tend to be symbolic. Cleaning out your ears when somebody is telling you something you do not want to hear or throwing your hands up into the air are expressive.

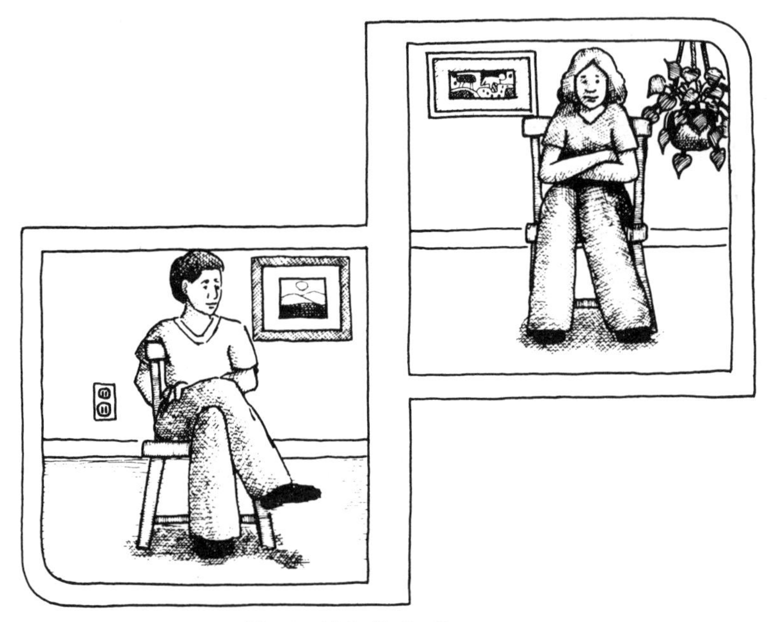

Figure 11-3. Body Openness

Facial Cues

The face is the most informative area of the body. Facial cues can be divided into two general categories: subtle or gross. Gross facial cues are movements like a big smile, sneer, or a wink or a frown. Subtle cues are things like slight tremors under the eyes, slight tremors of the lip, and relaxation or tension on jaw muscles. Each of these may indicate various kinds of feelings and emotions.

Eye Contact

The way in which people initiate, maintain, and break eye contact conveys messages. This cue varies from fixed staring at one extreme to absence of eye contact on the other. Balanced and varied eye contact seems to elicit more comfort and trust from others.

Physiological Cues

Some activity of the autonomic nervous system can be directly observed. Some of the observable cues include: blushing, perspiring, breathing rate, and tempo of body movement. Each of these cues may vary from mild to intense.

Intense	Mild
Blushing, face bright red, large red splotches on neck	Blushing, tips of ears pink, cheeks pink

Time and Space Cues

The ways in which people move through space and time convey messages.

DISTANCE: How far does the person sit from you? A small distance tends to indicate interest and attraction while a greater distance may indicate avoiding the other person.

USE OF SPACE: Personal space can be arranged to invite or discourage contact with others. The way a person arranges his furniture or his life space usually indicates something about the person. Is the furniture arranged so that people can look at and talk to each other, or is it centrifugal so that people look away from each other?

USE OF TIME: The way a person uses time can convey messages. How time is allotted indicates personal priorities. Another aspect of use of time includes a person's punctuality.

> Example: Harold gets dressed and is out in the gym for basketball practice early. He dawdles in the locker room and comes late to his regular physical education class.

Context Cues

Although these cues are often overlooked, they are potent, that is, an activity or statement may be consistent or discrepant with its context.

SIMULTANEOUS CONTEXT: Simultaneous context is discrepant when two different messages are being given at the same time. Is something happening right now that is different from the message? For example, saying "Come to me" while holding your hand up to stop the person is discrepant. Another example is the little kid who wants to be loved but has a face and hands smeared with chocolate. He comes up to his mother and says, "Mommy, I love you, how about a hug?" That certainly is not a situation that promotes good receptivity on the mother's part.

CONTEXT: Quiet reading time in class

Discrepant	Consistent
[*George jumping up and* down, yelling] "Oh boy, oh boy! I really like this quiet time. Let's be quiet and read some more."	[*George raises his hand and whispers to teacher*] "Oh boy, oh boy! I really like this quiet reading time. Let's read some more.

SUCCESSIVE CONTEXT CUES: These cues indicate the consistency of messages within a context over time. Inviting a child to play with an expensive vase when you have previously punished him for playing with it is not consistent and invites confusion.

CONTEXT: Lunch time, eating chicken

Discrepant	Consistent
"Don't you know how to eat properly? You don't have to use a knife and fork for chicken."	"I know I've insisted that you use your knife and fork for meals before, but in this case, eating chicken, you can use your fingers."

LOGICAL CONTEXT: Verbal parts of messages may agree logically, or they may convey a paradoxical message. Paradoxical cues at first glance do not make sense together. For example, the statement "If I didn't love you so much, I couldn't hate you as much as I do" seems illogical because love and hate are opposites. A command to "Be independent" is paradoxical because if you tell someone to be independent, he cannot be independent because independence means doing it without being told.

Empathy Cues

Empathy cues focus on your internal reactions to the child you are working with rather than the external cues of the child. Often workers will detect "something wrong" and react internally before they are able to pinpoint the discrepant cues of the child. This type of cue has sometimes been called intuition. The worker's task is to recognize his own internal reactions, and then to find the objective discrepancy of the child that has activated his subjective reaction. You may become aware of confusion, frustration, anxiety, anger, or sadness, all of which once you tune into them, can have significance.

Example: Internal reaction: The worker becomes aware of his boredom, daydreaming, and wandering attention as Sally talks about her trip to Disneyland.

External discrepancy: Sally uses works like "exciting," "fun," "super," "wonderful," but speaks in a monotone voice and her face is unexpressive.

It is important to monitor and become aware of feelings that accompany ingenuine behavior. First of all, these feelings can be a signal to you to take steps to avoid behavior patterns that are ingenuine, such as false reassurance. You can also use empathic responses to make you aware of ingenuine behavior in the child. For example, experienced treatment workers use their feelings as cues that something isn't quite right. When they start feeling uncomfortable with a child, they use that information first of all to scan themselves and to question if that reaction comes from a stereotype, from unfinished business, or from some internal personal process. They ask, "Is the feeling I'm feeling really my problem, or is it something that's going on out there?" If they are convinced that their reaction is due to some subtle combination of cues that they were not consciously aware of out there, then they take a look. By reacting to empathic cues, you may be aware of and respond to child cues before being able to observe them specifically.

Additional Notes on Cue Congruence

By definition, no *one* cue can demonstrate cue discrepancy. It is the combination of cues that is either discrepant or congruent. Human beings function as unified organisms and one's whole being is in any message given. Therefore, the message is conveyed not from the mouth alone but from the whole body. Sometimes we feel like we have really gotten ourselves "together." At those times, our whole body usually sends the cues together, all with the same message. When we feel pulled in two directions at once, split on an issue, and we are aware of how ambivalent or unintegrated we feel, our cues are probably fragmented and contradictory.

The assignment to be congruent is a paradoxical bind; that is, the logical context is discrepant. Congruence is a spontaneous reaction. By *trying* to be congruent you are not being spontaneous; therefore, you cannot be congruent. You *can* work on becoming more congruent by removing those behaviors, thoughts, and feelings that hinder your spontaneous and natural expression. So, you can remove blocks to genuineness but you cannot be unspontaneously congruent.

Congruence is not a license to be vindictive. Some people think they have to be brutally honest, that a truly genuine person will say what is on his mind no matter what. This is *not* the case. The worker can time and phrase his remarks in such a way that the child will understand and use the worker's reactions to become more self-directing. Directness goes along with caring.

Finally, there is no point in trying to hide strong reactions in a treatment situation. The message will leak out in some channels no matter how hard you try to disguise it. Because of this leakage, the problem is not whether or not to communicate your reactions, but how you will communicate them.

When to Look for Cue Discrepancy

Monitoring cue discrepancy may be appropriate at different times.

Be Aware Of Your Own Reacting On More Than One Level At A Time.

Examples include: a) ambivalence, feeling more than one way about an issue, and b) stifling your reactions by overcompliance to worker-role expectations.

You Or The Child May Overreact To A Topic Or Situation.

Such overreaction may indicate previously unexpressed feelings.

You Or The Child May Discount Perceptions Or Feelings.

Such discounting may indicate that the person is unwilling to accept a part of his experience.

You Or The Child May Use Sarcasm.

By definition, sarcasm expresses both positive and negative messages at the same time; that is positive words are accompanied by negative nonverbal cues.

You Or The Child Are Working On Something The Two Of You Have Not Agreed To Deal With.

Hidden agendas do not allow people to be direct about their desires.

You And The Child May Hold Conflicting Values.

Either of you supressing your position will lead to discrepant communications.

You Or The Child May Have Behavioral Blind Spots.

You may be especially vulnerable to specific issues and emotions. For example, your learning history may be such that you associate someone's expressing helplessness to you with attempts at manipulation and blame. If you have not dealt with that association well enough, you may impulsively react with sarcasm, guilt, or some other emotion when the child's expression of helplessness requires a different reaction.

You Or The Child May, For The Best Of Reasons, Lie.

Deceit involves incongruence and it usually shows in cue discrepancy. Often this discrepancy can be monitored only at a physiological level, as with a polygraph lie detector.

Familiar Facade Transactions Often Mask Contradictory Feelings.

For example, the answer "okay" to the polite inquiry "How are you feeling?" may slide over feelings that are not "okay."

Trite Clichés Also May Cover Contradictory Feelings.

For example, "It's okay . . . I guess," or "All people do that," or "That's just the way it's got to be," are sayings people use to slough off their unpleasant feelings.

BEHAVIORAL HINTS

Finally, let us look at some behavioral hints for cue congruence. Remember, you cannot be unspontaneously congruent. You can tune into yourself and the children in your care and work on some of the things that block you from being congruent:

Observe all of the child's cues.

Observe all your own cues.

Remember to communicate with your whole body.

Tune into your internal cues: Monitor your emphathic responses to things that are going on in the child and be aware of what is going on inside of you.

Avoid personal behavior patterns that set up cue discrepancy: Doing things for clients that they can do for themselves and shutting off feeling expression are two common kinds of behavior patterns that lead to incongruence.

Feelings and Issues for the Treatment Worker

Workers may block congruent expression by adhering to rules about how they "should" respond, rather than tuning in to how they "are" responding. Also, certain fears are associated with direct communication.

Along with the role of treatment worker go some real and some fantasized expectations about what is appropriate behavior. These expectations may come from our own stereotypes, from the subtle responses of others, from the demands of the work situation, or from an idealized theoretical assumption of what a worker "ought to be." Sometimes workers *force* themselves and their clients to meet those expectations when such a meeting is not possible. It is like forcing a round peg into a square hole. You can get it to fit by shaving and twisting, but that process is destructive for both the peg and the hole. Some of the role expectations that worker may hold include:

"I'm Here To Help, Even If It Kills Me—Or You."

Some workers want so much to be helpful that they take away the child's opportunities to learn to help himself. At the same time, these workers become frustrated and angry at children who do not change in the ways that the workers believe they should. Sometimes children may choose not to change. Acknowledging that choice as a valid, if not preferable, option allows workers to disengage themselves from literally "killing" themselves trying to change someone who does not want to be helped.

"I'm Not Supposed To Show My Feelings To The Children I Work With."

Some workers assume that all relations with clients ought to be cognitive, problem-solving, rational relationships. And, therefore, feelings only get in the way of a solution. After all, it's okay for kids to have temper tantrums, cry, or be frightened, but certainly treatment workers shouldn't (note the sarcasm). This belief put treatment workers in the position of having to work so hard at covering their own feelings that they have little energy left to respond to the child. In addition, denying the value of worker feelings in the problem solving-process makes unavailable a potent input into the worker/child relationship. It is okay to laugh, cry, rage, and frolick with the children you work with. Solving problems is not all there is to do with a child. And the input of workers feelings into the problem-solving process makes that process more effective (see the chapter on problem solving).

"I'm The Counselor, I Ought To Know The Answers."

When a child asks you what to do, you may feel compelled to come up with an answer even if you have no idea of what to do. When put in the spot of thinking he ought to know but realizing he does not know, the worker may experience guilt, anger, frustration, etc. Sometimes workers will "fake it" by making up something, or changing the topic and avoiding the question until later. It's okay not to know the answer. After all, it is impossible to know everything. In addition, it's a good idea for kids to develop a realistic notion of adults, even smart adults, as fallible. Certainly your not knowing the answer opens up the possibility of you and the child engaging in a problem-solving process that would never have occurred if you had just given him the answer.

"If I Can't Fix This Kid Within A Given Time Period [One Week, One Month, One Year], I've Failed."

A number of assumptions are embedded in this expectation. The first is that treatment can meet a specific time-line. Such projections in time are unrealistic because treatment is an incredibly complex process that may be influenced by many factors not under your control. The second assumption is that a "fixed" or "cured" kid is an objectively definable entity. There may be specific improvements that can be identified, and the combination of those specific changes may convey an overall impression of "fixedness"; however, there is no agreement on what is the end-point. A child may look "fixed" to one person and "messed up" to another. One way out of the problems associated with this assumption is to define specific concrete goals that can be realistically attained within a given time period, and which do not depend on influences outside of your control.

It is possible to "fail" with troubled children in the sense that you may persist in doing things that have no effect. If that is the case, consultation about your treatment with the child is in order. New workers particularly have unrealistic expectations of how people change. Realistic information about those processes also helps to defuse the time pressure.

"They're Only Tears" Versus "Ahha! She Scratched The Left Side Of Her Nose With Her Right Index Finger And That Means She's Hostile."

A worker's observing and commenting on the cues listed in this chapter may be distorted by adherence to either of two opposing tendencies: discounting cue significance and overanalyzing cues. Often there are non-message-related explanations for the occurrence of cues. For example, someone's crying might be explained by "something in my eye," or someone trembling as being "cold," someone's closed body position and averted body orientation as "Oh, I always sit this way." Of course, such cues may be accounted for by non-message-intending factors. However, habitual discounting of the significance of cues removes a large chunk of message-sending behavior from scrutiny.

On the other hand, some workers become so intrigued with the meaning of cues that they read vital significance into single behaviors. They jump to erroneous conclusions on the basis of overanalyzing cues out of context. Some balance of these extreme views acknowledge that message cues come from a variety of channels; yet each cue must be taken along with all other cues occurring at that moment. Repetition of cue patterns leads to a more solid inference of meaning (See "Inferential Observation").

"I Must Be Honest No Matter What."

Congruent expression may be used inappropriately when the worker values "honest communication" above common sense. Sometimes workers, in an attempt to be totally congruent, share with children half-formed ideas, negatively toned evaluations, and impulsive reactions. These workers reactions may overwhelm the child if he does not recognize the tentative nature of the reactions. A very angry or vindictive person may find cue congruence an excuse to vent those feelings at children. To vent anger about non-child-related matters on the child may tax the child's ability to place the worker's reactions in perspective.

Therapeutic outcome is the final test of any treatment skill. The benefit of congruent responding is diminished if the person receiving the message cannot understand it, or is not emotionally able to deal with it. In a later chapter on "Confrontation," we will discuss guidelines for constructive congruent expression of negative reactions.

Chapter 12

USE OF LANGUAGE

After mastering the information in this chapter, you should be able to—

1. explain the effects of good use of language on the worker/child relationship,
2. explain and give examples of metacommunication, symbols and referents, and qualities of language,
3. identify and give examples of factors influencing specificity of language,
4. relate use of language to nonbehavioral levels of worker functioning as illustrated by "Feelings and Issues for the Treatment Worker."

The most often used tool of our trade is words. In its infancy, psychotherapy was called the "talking cure." We do not intend to foray into the land of formal semantics and psycholinguistics. Rather, we will deal with aspects of language which we have found affect working with troubled children. Specifically, we will focus on the words treatment workers use to express themselves.

All of the aspects of use of language that will be considered in this chapter enhance *concreteness* in the worker/child relationship. By conveying his meaning clearly, directly, and specifically, the worker demonstrates to the child that he values accurate communication. The child then trusts that the worker will talk to him in ways that the child can understand.

Language and the ways people use language have been analyzed more ways than we can possibly deal with in this chapter. We will, however, review the following concepts: metacommunicating, referents, and qualities of language.

METACOMMUNICATION

In a sense, we are now engaged in metacommunication. Metacommunication means communicating about communicating. In the realm of child treatment, you and I may argue, for example, about whether or not kids should be "responsible" for the mess they make at the lunch table. Each of us may have a different definition of how "responsibility" is to be manifested. For you it might mean they have to clean up; for me it might mean they lose their play privilege for a week. We could continue to argue about the *content* of what the kids have to do to show "responsibility." If we continued, the likely outcome would be anger and disagreement. On the other hand, if we talked about the *process* of how we were talking to each other, we would soon find that we needed to come to some agreement on the definition of "responsibility" before we could agree on a plan to help kids develop it. The shift from arguing about content to discussing the process does not come about easily. It takes an awareness of "something wrong" in the communication pattern, and a willingness to shift levels. (See Figure 12-1.)

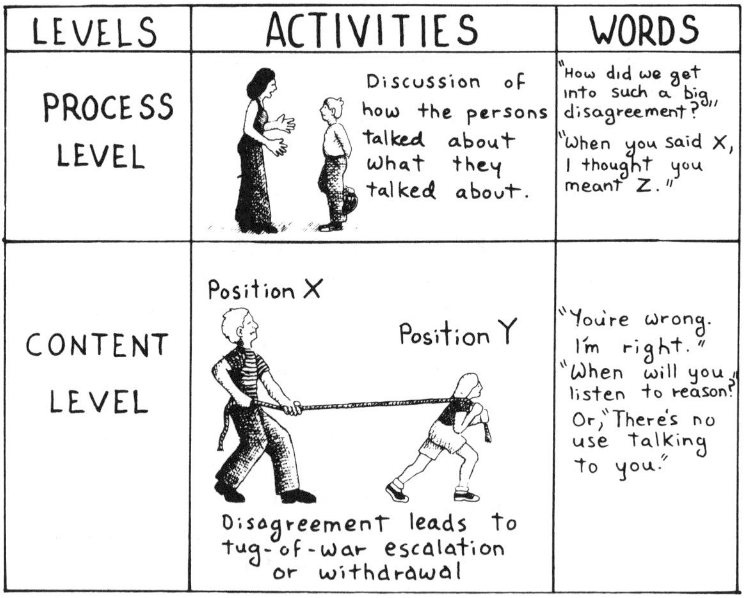

LEVELS	ACTIVITIES	WORDS
PROCESS LEVEL	Discussion of how the persons talked about what they talked about.	"How did we get into such a big disagreement?" "When you said X, I thought you meant Z."
CONTENT LEVEL	Position X Position Y Disagreement leads to tug-of-war escalation or withdrawal	"You're wrong. I'm right." "When will you listen to reason?" Or, "There's no use talking to you."

Figure 12-1. Use of Language

"Verbalize the process" is a shorthand phrase that means shift to metacommunication. Shifting requires the ability to see beyond yourself and your position to how you *and* the person you are communicating with fit into a dyadic pattern. That is, instead of saying to yourself, "I'm trying to convince *him* of the proper position," you might say, "*We're* fighting." Using metacommunication will not guarantee that everyone will agree with you, but at least you will have a clearer idea of what you disagree about.

All of the information to follow about language gives more specific descriptions of how content-level language can go awry. The shift to metacommunication can help you extricate yourself from a content-level morass.

Symbols and Referents

Words mean nothing in and of themselves. They are merely a conglomeration of sounds that people utter at each other. They gain their meaning as symbols for a specific referent. If you were learning Chinese and your teacher put his finger on a ball and said "win-chow," you might assume that the sounds "win-chow" were the symbols for ball. He may, in fact, have been pointing to a star on the ball, or a point on the star. Words acquire meaning by their regular association with the things they symbolize: their referents. Often people err by assuming that there is only one referent for each symbol, and that the referent he knows is obviously *the* one. There are over 14,000 definitions for the 500 most commonly used everyday words. Thus, it is more probable that people misunderstand each other than they will understand.

There are great advantages in the human ability to manipulate symbols in place of actual referents. For example, a child can symbolically annihilate his parents using words, perhaps saving both him and his parents from his doing it in reality. Thus, the symbol-referent system yields both advantages and disadvantages. The safest course for a therapist seems to be to recognize that miscommunication occurs frequently and request clarification. In addition, awareness of the complexities of language allows a therapist to use language therapeutically even though it may not be clear, e.g. by use of metaphors.

Qualities of Language

Levels of Literalism

Any communication may be interpreted on a literal or an idiomatic level. That is, we may respond to the specific words spoken, or to the more abstract intent of those words as defined by the social and cultural context.

Imagine a sign on the principal's door saying "Please Knock." On an abstract level we understand that the principal wants people to knock on his door before entering his office. However, taken on a literal level the sign would urge us to knock on his door whether or not we wished to enter. Children traveling back and forth past his door during the day could drive him crazy by dutifully responding to the concrete level of the sign's message.

A child looking for loopholes in a behavior contract may become a "Philadelphia Lawyer" pinpointing each phrase that we meant in an idiomatic sense by gleefully saying, for example, "But you didn't *say* not to hit Georgie with the baseball bat, you *said* keep your *hands* to yourself." Some of the shifts in levels of abstraction can be funny: e.g., "Won't you join me in a cup of coffee?", "Please make me a sandwich and step on it, I'm in a hurry!" "The drinks are on the house."

Denotative, Connotative, and Imperative

Words carry more than one meaning in that they can refer to different things. In addition, words have emotional associations based on our experiences with them and words request or demand certain actions. If you and I were looking at a 1955 Chevrolet (the referent), we might agree on the denotative word "car," disagree on connotative words: e.g., "It's a classic!" or "What a clunker." The connotations reflect our different views.

Words spoken within the context of a relationship also convey requests for behavior: this is the imperative level. Picture the following interchange.

CHILD: My shoe lace is untied.
WORKER: Oh? Yeah, I see. It sure is untied.
CHILD: [pause—sniffle/whine] You don't care about me, do you?
WORKER: What do you mean, of course I do.
CHILD: Then how come you'd let me trip over my shoelaces and hurt myself?

The worker ignored the child's indirect invitation to tie the shoelace. The child then responded as if she had made a request clearly rather than implying it.

Figurative Language

Figures of speech convey a variety of meaning. In an effort to develop concrete language, you should take care not to squelch your own or the child's richness of expression. Figures of speech are a simple yet dramatic avenue leading to the discovery of a child's pattern of thought and to the influence of that pattern. If a child finds himself ambivalent about going back to public school from the treatment setting, his shorthand expression of those feelings might be "I'm on the fence." One course of action in response to his metaphor would be to "play" with the image. Have him describe the fence: How high is it? What is it made of? What is on either side of it? Is there a gate in it? Using the image of him sitting on a fence may provide a concrete set of words which you and he can later interpret more abstractly. You also can be more sure that he understands the vocabulary the two of you are using because, to some extent, you are mutually defining it as you talk.

Specificity

Being specific means being concrete, definite, and particular. Specificity leads to clarity. Understandable vocabulary, examples, and elaboration of descriptive details lead to concrete understanding of specific experiences and feelings by both the treatment worker and the child. It is important to use words that convey exact meaning. Below are illustrations of factors influencing specificity of language.

NON-EQUIVOCAL VERSUS EQUIVOCAL. Equivocal words and phrases are those that can be interpreted in more than one way. For example, when one refers to a "good citizen," does one mean that he accepts their community or country the way it is, or that he is critical and works for change?

DEFINITE VERSUS RELATIVE. Relative words are those that gain their meaning only by comparison. For example, "big" and "small" only have relative meaning. Certainly, a big whale is not the same as a big sardine. A more definite description would include an estimate of actual measurement.

EXACT VERSUS BROAD. Broad words cover a greater than intended area. For example, if you ask a child to clean everything" off of the drain board, he may interpret this to mean the canisters as well as the dirty dishes. Exact language would describe only those items intended by the speaker.

DESCRIPTION VERSUS EUPHEMISM AND HYPERBOLE. A euphemism understates or "softens" the message, while a hyperbole overstates it. One may euphemistically say that another's behavior "concerned" him when in fact it angered him. Or, another may use hyperbole to describe her hard work as "beating my brains out."

NON-JUDGMENTAL VERSUS JUDGMENTAL. Judgmental words ascribe "good" or "bad" value. In treatment, as in all human communications, judgments add to defensiveness and they impede the receiver's listening. One may describe the same child in a good light by describing his "great tolerance for ambiguity" or in a bad light by describing him as "wishy-washy."

CONCISE VERSUS RAMBLING. Rambling and tangential verbalizations tend to lose the receiver. Omit unnecessary words.

VOCABULARY. Consider the vocabulary and your audience and use language within its bounds. Avoid talking either down to a person or over his head. Anchor your language in shared experiences: e.g., "When I say 'set up,' I mean what you did with Gary at recess."

BEHAVIORAL HINTS

Attend To Both Content And Process And Verbalize The Process.

By noting both content and process you will become aware of where the miscommunication lies—in your words or in your relationship with the child.

Develop A Mutually Understandable Language.

In your efforts to communicate clearly with words you may have to abandon some of your familiar sets of symbols in favor of (a) synonyms the child can identify, (b) figures of speech that convey the image of the idea you want, (c) examples, or even (d) brief gestures that become a shorthand symbolic sign for a mutually understood concept.

Listen To Yourself.

Your goal is to be specific and clear. If you find yourself using general terms, mixing concrete and abstract levels, or adding unintended connotations and imperatives, stop and rephrase your message. Most children will wait patiently as you clarify your use of language.

FEELINGS AND ISSUES FOR THE TREATMENT WORKER

Several assumptions about children and about the communication process lead workers to avoid or misuse concrete language.

"Well, If I'm Not Specific, At Least I'll Be Less Likely To Be Wrong."

Some workers do not use concrete language because they fear making a mistake. To protect themselves, they hedge, qualify, and intellectualize. In some cases there may be some merit in getting the child to be specific before the worker gives his specific reation. However, there is no sense in trying to avoid errors. You will be wrong at times. Other people will become angry, hurt, and guilty because of what you say. You can take responsibility for being wrong by correcting your mistakes. You need not take responsibility for the feelings of others; their reactions belong to them. At least with a specific response you know exactly what is wrong. With ambiguous statements you don't know anything for sure.

"Everybody Knows What I Mean, And Those Who Don't Are Just Trying To Be Difficult."

Some workers have the egocentric point of view that everyone does, or at least "ought to," think the way they do. With such a belief it is easy to attribute negative motives or attributes to people who do not understand what is said. A somewhat pathetic example of this belief in action is the American tourist who cannot communicate with a foreign native. The typical response is to talk slowly, as if the native were an idiot, then to yell angrily as if the person were deliberately not understanding. After such an encounter, the American may be heard to utter disparaging remarks about the person's ancestry and national character. Only rarely does the tourist consider his insufficient language skills the problem. This same pattern may be seen in treatment. A good deal of what is called client "resistance" may in fact be worker frustration at his own inabilities at communicating.

"In Order For Communication To Be Meaningful, It Has To Be Abstract."

Some workers believe that specific incidents do not have meaning unless they can be attached to some broader, conceptual explanation. Therefore, they hurry over the details to get to the "real stuff." In doing this, they are likely to use abstract concepts and labels that may indeed apply, but are unintelligible to the child. Sometimes the child will resent and resist the broader labels; for example, "What do you mean I'm defensive, and what's a 'rationalization' anyway? All I said is I threw the cat down the well because I wanted to teach it how to swim." A good strategy is to keep the abstract concept in your head and find specific examples of how that concept is expressed in action. Even more basic is the notion that all behavior may not be related to larger concepts in any direct way. Much behavior can change with focus on the specific incidents without reference to broader concepts at all. Abstractions may indeed be irrelevant.

"The Kid Wouldn't Understand Anyway, So Why Should I Waste My Time Getting Into Specific Details."

It is true that children have differing levels of cognitive ability, and their verbal comprehension may be less than that of an adult. However, children understand a great deal if the information is couched in language

that they can comprehend. Sometimes you may be more specific than the child wants you to be, as is sometimes the case with information about sex and reproduction. But most often adults err on the side of assuming the child cannot cope with information that in fact the child reacts to matter-of-factly. One other negative side-effect of the "kids wouldn't understand" assumption is that workers then do not take time to teach kids how to listen and comprehend. This becomes self-fulfilling prophecy. (See Table 12-1.)
Quality factors—Describe the worker's performance in relation to the following:

1. Treatment worker can use the child's vocabulary as a starting point rather than insisting that the child use the worker's.
2. Worker uses language playfully, seeing general, abstract, implied, and figurative communications as opportunities to extend the limits of language meanings in order to demonstrate to the child an unconstrained flexibility of perception.

Table 12–1. Use of Language Behavior Checklist

Record the frequency of the following behaviors:

Positive behavior	*Problematic behavior*
_____ Uses metacommunication	_____ Ignores obvious problems in the communication process
_____ Responds to the level of abstraction communicated by the child	_____ Misses or ignores the connotative level of communication
_____ Responds to or comments on the connotative level of communication	_____ Misses or ignores the imperative level of communication
_____ Responds to or comments on the imperative level of communication	
_____ Uses metaphors and figures of speech as a means of discussing concrete reactions with the child	
Specific language:	Non-specific language:
_____ Non-equivocal	_____ Equivocal
_____ Definitive	_____ Relative
_____ Exact	_____ Broad
_____ Descriptive	_____ Euphemism or hyperbole

Chapter 13

PROBING

After mastering the information in this chapter you should be able to—

1. identify the goals of probing;
2. list the effects of good probing on the worker/child relationship;
3. identify and give examples of the funnel and inverted funnel strategy;
4. identify the criteria for good topic tracking;
5. identify and give examples of content levels and relationship levels of topic choice;
6. explain how to evaluate the relevance of the child's information;
7. identify three processes that constrict people's representation of their experience;
8. give examples of four pairs of good versus poor probing responses that clarify a child's discussion of a topic;
9. relate probing to nonbehavioral levels of worker functioning as illustrated by "Feelings and Issues for the Treatment Worker."

Probing is a skill which elicits information. Probing has two general goals. The first is to obtain information meaningful for the topics that you choose as important. The second is to obtain honest, unbiased, and complete information about those topics. Probing presupposes that the interviewer will take more control over the interview than when using some of the other skills.

There are several reasons for probing. The first is to get *complete* information. Having the child respond to you in a complete way and not accepting evasiveness makes it easier to understand the child. The second reason is to get *clear, concrete* information. Because you are asking the child to be specific, and to give examples, the information will be clear and concrete rather than a series of general statements. Another reason to probe is to get *unbiased* information. Probing presupposes that you ask for information in an unbiased way, that you do not give hints to the child as to the answer you want. In this way, the child will be able to respond from her own view. Finally, probing elicits *relevant* information. Probing allows you to direct the topics in order to fill in gaps in your knowledge about the child and to confirm your hunches about why the child behaves the way she does.

Effects of Probing

There are several effects of probing on the child, all of which promote *concreteness.* Since you are asking the child to explain to you in much greater detail and depth than usual, he has a chance to *clarify* his own thoughts. You are also asking him to *perceive* the experience differently because you are encouraging him to report details and examples. Another effect on the child is that he will be able to *explore topics in depth.* Rather than allowing the child to flit from topic to topic, or rather than giving the answers to the child, you guide the child into a concentrated exploration of the subject which can lead to greater understanding. *Warning:* poor probing generates defensiveness. If you push the child too hard and if you ask the child questions in biased or judgmental terms, he will find it difficult to give you information because of the defensiveness generated under these conditions.

In this chapter we will consider three general skills that contribute to good probing: strategy of information gathering, topic tracking, and clarification of expression.

Strategy of Information Gathering

Complete and unbiased information on the categories that you choose may be best elicited by means of following a specific information gathering strategy. The "funnel" strategy starts with general topics and narrows them to specifics. An example of the probing funnel starts with a statement like "Describe your school experiences" (very general), narrows down to "How are you doing academically?" (more specific), and finally asks "What grades did you receive?", which is the most specific of all. (See Figure 13-1.A)

Sometimes children have difficulty answering general questions and you may have to resort to what is called the "inverted funnel" by asking specific questions first to lead up to more general questions. Keep this in mind especially with reticent children. An example of the inverted funnel starts with a question such as "Do you like Nancy?" (specific, closed question), moves on to "What happens to your feelings when you go from

Nancy's room to Alan's?" (a more general question), and finally ends with the most general question, "How do you react to men as compared to women?" As the child begins to respond, switch to the funnel approach. Staying with the inverted funnel runs the risk of getting into the "twenty questions" pattern. (See Figure 13-1.B)

Topic Tracking

Topic tracking follows and elaborates on the themes presented by a child. Experienced treatment workers make mental notes of most, if not all, possible choices of topics. Their immediate response is a compromise between reacting to the topic at hand and probing for information to confirm their hunches. Several skills are involved. The first is recognizing the choices available. Recognizing choices means being aware of the variety of topics presented, verbally or nonverbally, glimpsing the implications of following each choice. The second skill is pure memory, that is, remembering the bits so that they may be pieced together as more information appears. The third is evaluating what information will be most useful to help you frame your probes. Finally, an emerging idea of "what it all means" provides cues to the relevance of specific topics.

Recognizing Topic Choices

Three factors affect choices about what topics to track: 1) different topics, 2) different content levels, and 3) different relationship levels.

TOPIC: The most obvious choice of topics to follow occurs when blatantly different content areas appear in a single message: for example, "I can't do my English because my mother doesn't love me." "English" and "mother" are topics that may be pursued.

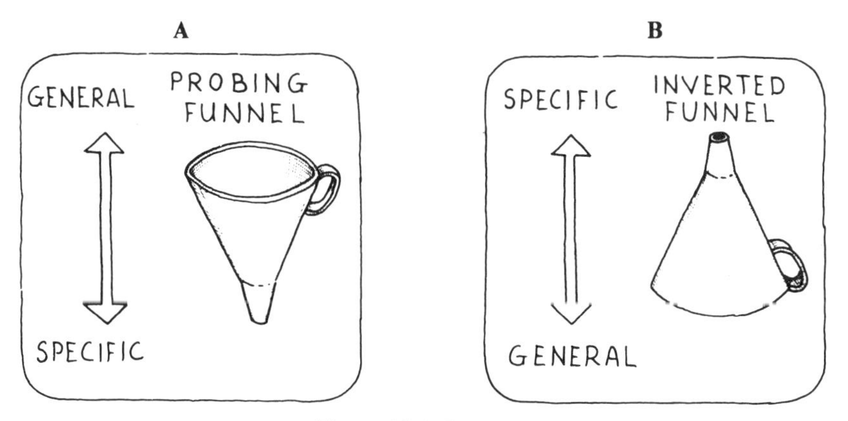

Figure 13-1. Probing

CONTENT: The choices become more difficult to recognize when only one topic is mentioned that shows more than one level of content. For example, "After he called me 'stupid,' I felt like punching him out. But I thought to myself, 'He's not worth it'; so I just turned and walked away." The general topic is the child's reaction to being called "stupid." However, he reacted on three different levels: 1) feelings (anger—"I felt like punching him out"), 2) thoughts (rationalization—"He's not worth it"), and 3) behavior (withdrawal—"I just turned and walked away").

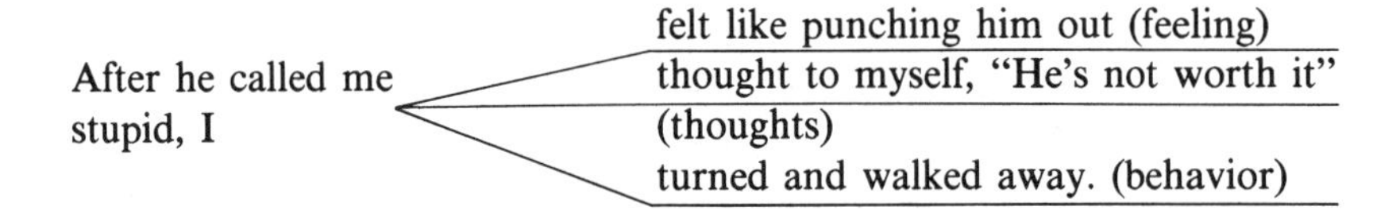

Thus, levels of content also yield topic choices. A simple probe on any level of content might be "tell me more about ______." To add complexity, a worker might follow up one topic choice by using probes of the other levels of content:

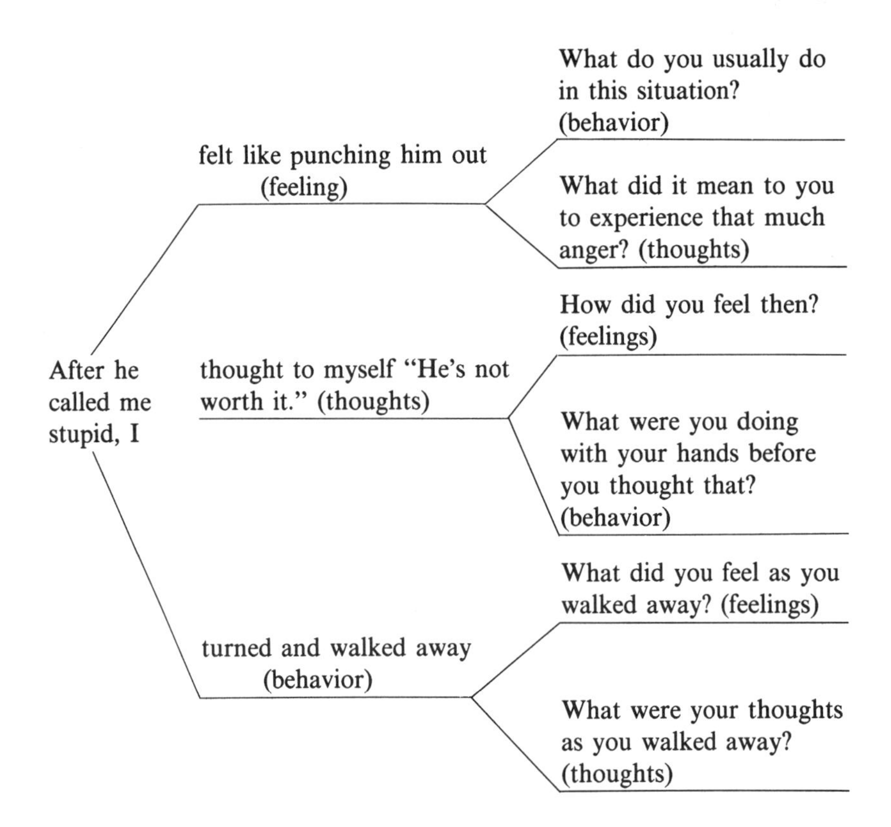

RELATIONSHIP: Another source of choices within a general topic area is the level of relationship that the child describes or implies. Relationship levels can be differentiated by person, setting, and time frame. For example, a child says:

> I really burn when people tell me what to do—like my mother always did. People who are trying to be helpful act phoney because they just try to prove they're better than me.

The general topic area is the child's reaction to people who give her advice. (See Table 13-1.)

As the diagram shows, different parts of the child's message can be represented directly or by implication at different levels of relationship. Given that the child is in the treatment setting to receive help with some problem in her life, her reference to "people who are trying to be helpful" strongly implies that the treatment worker fits as one of the "people." Thus, a worker might probe section one by asking "do you mean you're burnt about the suggestions that I've given you in the past?" A section-two follow-up might be "Are you saying that I am coming across as phoney to you?" A section-three probe might be "How do you want me to give you suggestions so that I don't seem like I'm trying to be better than you?" Since you have switched relationship levels, even though you are in the same general topic area, the child may be shocked that you "took it personally."

Often children may be only partially aware of the implications of their statements. Even if the child denies that he meant to include you in his statement ("Present company excepted of course") the topic is still fruitful to explore in your relationship. Likewise, if you are running a group or interviewing more than one person at once (e.g., the family) the here-and-now relationship level extends to include the other persons as well. Outside the interview session the setting and person variables of relationship dimension become very broad.

Table 13-1. Time Frame

Setting	*Past*	*Present*	*Future*
Interview Session	1) try to prove they're better	2) act phoney	3) try to prove they're better
Person	*Interviewer*	*Interviewer*	*Interviewer*
Outside Person	4) mother always did	5) "People tell me what to do."	6) try to prove they're better
Person	Mother	Helpful people	Helpful people

A probe for section four might include "In what situations did your mother do that?" (setting) or "Who else did that to you?" (person). Probes for sections five and six certainly require a clarification of who the helpful people are, were, or may be: "Give me some examples of people who are telling you what to do or giving you advice now or in the past." (person) "Who do you suppose might be doing these things to you in the future: at home? at school? at work?" (setting and person).

To review, topics to pursue at any given moment in an interview can be differentiated by: 1) actual topic differences, 2) levels of content within the same topic area, and 3) levels of relationship within the same topic area. You will not always be aware of all the choices all the time. Although theoretically all child statements may be probed on *all* of the content and relationship levels, some probes will seem more appropriate than others and will be dictated by the current treatment issues and the child's present readiness to deal with the issues. A good memory for what went on in the interview will allow you to recall and follow up a statement made earlier in the session or in previous sessions. Beginning treatment workers often experience the "I missed it and it was as plain as the nose on your face" frustration when recalling some child statements. Practice at recognizing possible choices is the first step towards effective topic tracking.

EVALUATING INFORMATIONAL QUALITY

In evaluating the quality of the information given to you by a child, consider the guidelines explained in the chapters on "Observation," "Cue Congruence," "Use of Language," and those that are yet to come in "Self-Disclosure." In brief, probe for information that is—

1. immediate rather than generalized;
2. descriptive rather than evaluative or interpretive;
3. concrete rather than abstract.

These criteria may be used to evaluate both topics offered by the child and probes used by the interviewer. Many a dead-end topic could be headed off by interviewers who probe for high-quality information rather than choosing low-quality topics and follow-ups.

EVALUATING CLIENT-RELEVANT INFORMATION

A skilled treatment worker realizes that the topic under discussion at a given time is only one of many topics to be tracked. Because individuals are multi-faceted and their behavior is multi-determined, tracking only one topic through to its conclusion would require tunnel vision. The problem, however, is to judge which of the topics are relevant and which are not according to three guides:

1. his theory about the way people behave,
2. the problems and themes in the child's life that he pieces together from the child's information and from background records,
3. an on-the-spot determination of what further information will be most useful to his understanding of the child.

Suffice it to say that the task of determining central rather than peripheral topic choices requires an awareness of many different topics at once plus a constant reference back to theories and themes. A series of questions for the treatment worker to ask himself in order to evaluate whether his probe of the child's information is central rather than peripheral is: 1) What inforamtion do I have already? 2) How does it fit together? 3) What does it mean? 4) If the meaning is unclear, what else do I need to know to make it clearer? and finally, 5) What is the best way to get that needed information? Data that are peripheral to one topic may be central to another. So, even though you may not follow up on a child's statement because it is peripheral to one topic, file it away because it may be central to a parallel topic that you will deal with later.

Clarification of Expression

Bandler and Grinder (1975) have elaborated three processes by which people construct and constrict their representation of themselves and the world around them: generalization, deletion, and distortion:

"Generalization is the process by which elements or pieces of a person's model become detached from their original experience and come to represent the entire category of which the experience is an example."

"Deletion is a process by which we selectively pay attention to certain dimensions of our experience and exclude others."

"Distortion is the process which allows us to make shifts in our experience of sensory data." The result of such distortion is that we literally do not see, hear, feel certain experiences as they occur.

When a treatment worker understands these processes, he or she can learn to listen for what is being left unsaid and learn to help children clarify generalizations or distortions of actual events. Below are examples of good and poor probing that illustrate these processes.

Good Example	*Poor Example*
The worker helps child specify in adequate detail	The worker accepts inadequate answer a) partial answer with parts deleted b) overall statement without detail (generalized) c) intensity of response as indicator of details (distorted)

Inadequate answers may take several forms. For example, if you ask a child a question like, "Tell me something about your family," a *partial* answer would be something like "Well, I have two brothers and sisters," which tells you little about the whole family. Another response might be "Well, we're a happy family," which would be an *overall statement,* without any detail about what that happiness means. A third response might be, "Wow, our family is really fantastic." You might interpret this *intense response* as meaning that the family is very nice, when in fact, fantastic could mean fantastically bad. A probe would be to help the client specify in detail by saying something like "Give an example" or "Tell me more about what you mean by that."

Good Example	*Poor Example*
The worker urges client to give meaningful response when	The worker accepts evasiveness
a) indecisive	a) "I don't know" or "I guess" unprobed (deleted)
b) confused	b) Unrelated answer unprobed (deleted/distorted)

If you want to learn about a child's family, you might say, "Well, tell me about your family. How do you get along with your family?" The child might say, "Well, they enjoy baseball. I play on Saturdays. I play a regular league every week, etc. etc." This is an evasive answer because it does not pick up and follow the main point, but rather goes off on a tangent. In order to probe indecisive or confused "I don't knows," you might say something like, "Well, think about it a little more," or "It must be difficult to figure out," or you may ask her for detail. Here you must be prepared to accept moments of silence.

Good Example	*Poor Example*
The worker uses non-evaluative manner when asking questions	The worker uses biased responses with a) leading questions b) cross examination questions c) begging questions d) assumptive statement e) sarcasm

When probing, it is important not to invite distortion by your manner of asking. All of the examples explained below contain within them a presupposition about what the answers ought to be. Such treatment worker behaviors will bias the child's response, thus leading to generalized or distorted information and run the risk of setting up defensiveness. The following are examples of biased behaviors used in questioning a child about his/her mother:

LEADING QUESTIONS: These imply that you already know the answer when in fact you do not: e.g., "You like your mother, don't you?"

CROSS EXAMINATION QUESTIONS: These imply that you do not believe what the person is saying: e.g., "Are you sure you don't like your mother?"

BEGGING QUESTIONS: Here, one assumes the answer to an unspoken question while asking the next: e.g., "When did you stop liking your mother?"

ASSUMPTIVE STATEMENTS: These infer something not yet stated by the person: e.g., "Well, most boys your age like their mothers."

SARCASM: This usually conveys disbelief by tone of voice: e.g., "Sure, sure I believe you. Right, you don't like your mother."

Good Example	*Poor Example*
The worker rephrases question if client a) does not respond appropriately b) is unclear about what is wanted	The worker hints at possible answers

For example, if you ask the child something like, "Tell me about any trouble you may be having at home," and the child says, "Well, what do you mean by troubles?", a poor probe would be "Well, for instance, do you and your father fight?" or "How do you and your brothers and sisters get along?" These questions hint at specific areas of family relationship and fill in missing or unclear data from the treatment worker's frame of reference rather than from the child's. They run the risk of the child's focusing on subjects initiated by the treatment worker rather than on subjects which are of concern to him. A good probe would rephrase without hinting by asking questions such as "Well, what kind of things are bothering you at home?"

Behavioral Hints

First Be Aware of Branching Points in the Client's Statement.

Often, there are more areas to probe about than you have time for. At these points remember that you want to pick out things that are *central* rather than *peripheral* and things that are *immediate* rather than *abstract.* If you are talking to a child about being busted for marijuana, the central concerns are her experience in the arrest, or her experience while obtaining the marijuana. Peripheral issues would be, for example, discussions of the drug laws, or the way she lost her dope, etc. Immediate issues focus on the here-and-now experience of the child and not, for example, the abstract concern over whether drug laws are just.

Arrange You Probes in a Sequence from General to Specific:

The funnel effect. A general question may elicit much information that is relevant. Ordering from general to specific gives you more information, richer information, and allows you to select topics for further probing, and thus, to structure the interview.

Thirdly, Probe with Non–directive Skills, such as Reflections of Feeling, Paraphrases, Minimal Encouragements, and Open Invitations.

They are useful in checking your understanding with the child, and in getting the child to elaborate more about specific topics.

Fourthly, Use Evasive Replies as a Cue for You to Probe.

If the child is evasive it may be an opportune moment to say to yourself, "Well, maybe I need to know more about that, or maybe he needs to know more about that." Likewise, use your own puzzlements as a cue to probe. If you are confused, if you do not understand, it is very likely that the child has not conveyed his understanding very well or that he is not clear about what he is saying.

FEELINGS AND ISSUES FOR THE TREATMENT WORKER

Workers may misuse or avoid probing because of assumptions about their role in the interview process and because of their confusion about how an interview progresses.

"But I'm Not Supposed to be So Directive."

There are times and places for both directive and non–directive responses. During a counseling relationship with a child it will be necessary to gather information that the child does not volunteer. That is the time to use probing.

"But I Know What She's Going to Say; Why Not Just Skip Over the Crap in the Middle and Get Right to the End?"

Workers sometimes find waiting for the children to unfold a story extremely frustrating. They like to jump in the middle and hurry the process. In some cases speeding the process may be okay. In more cases specific topics have a schedule: certain things follow in sequence. Therefore, skipping over some important steps may lead to confusion that you will have to clear up later. In addition, it is not only where you are going but how you get there that is the issue. A child encouraged to tell her story in a logical way may develop new insights during the process. Telling her the insights will have less impact than if she finds them on her own. And the worker may find herself ending in a different place than she thought when she began probing.

"I Could Probe Forever; Everything is Important," or "Well, We Got to the End of That Topic; Now What?"

If a worker takes the broad view, she can indeed probe everything. New topic leads crop up like weeds in the spring. The issue here is how to select the most important ones to follow. Selection depends on what you think is important. If you have no idea how to determine what is important, consult your theory about how people work, consult the treatment plan, and consult other workers who have some experience. On the other end, workers may get caught in a one-track probe. Every probe can be carried to its extreme. However, each topic is only a sub-part of the total understanding of the child and his situation. Workers may have a difficult time moving to another relevant topic after they have been overly committed to the topic they have probed completely. At those times, you might again consult the sources mentioned before. And you might consult the child; for example, "We've about finished talking about your school problem; what else would you like to deal with?"

"I Thought We Were Discussing His Reactions to His Foster Family, And All of a Sudden I Found Myself Asking Him About His Little League Team."

Sometimes workers wander off of the initial topic. This happens because in most child statements more than one possible topic can be followed. Selecting central rather than tangential or peripheral topics keeps the probing on course. Many times the topic choice points whizz by faster than workers can cope with. Many times also workers do not recognize possible topic choices when they do occur. As you become more adept at the treatment process, you will be better able to slow down the process so that you can see the choice points. And you will speed up your own observations. In the meantime, feel free to backtrack and bridge topics back to the original concern.

"When I Try to Probe, I Get So Concerned About Figuring Out What the Child is Saying that I Lose Some of My Other Skills."

Treatment is a multilevel activity. Workers must track: a) what the child is communicating, b) how they are reacting to the child, c) what they are going to do next, and d) how what the child says fits together into some meaningful explanation. New workers in particular find that as they add one new level of tracking, the older levels deteriorate temporarily. It seems impossible to do everything at once. However, the human organism has marvelous potential. We can function well beyond the capabilities we use in everyday life. You will learn to function on all those levels with practice. Treatment takes energy and commitment. The multilevel functioning is one example of how the energy is expended.

"The Child I'm Working With is Doing Something That Makes It Almost Impossible for Me to Probe."

There are four types of communication patterns that children use which can make probing very difficult: distracting, tangential, overspecific, overgeneral.

1. The distractor brings up obviously irrelevant topics in response to cues known only to him; for example, "Look at that wonderful wallpaper."
2. The tangential child brings up topics almost, but not quite, related. This pattern can be very subtle because the new topic does bear some relation to the original. However, the tangentor goes further and further afield with each new tangent.

3. The overspecific child comes in saying she has something very important to tell you, and then reviews each detail of the week preceding the event in excruciating completeness. There is often muttered debate over who was there, what time of day it was, and what everyone was wearing—all of which are irrelevant to the main point.
4. The overgeneral child relates his story in nonspecific terms which he believes to be specific. He usually can be more specific only with great pain and suffering.

In each of these cases the problem is likely to be compounded by the fact that the worker cannot get a word in edgewise because the client talks so much. In these cases the worker will have to interrupt, refocus the topic, and frequently verbalize the pattern that the child uses to get the topic off track. This might be a good time to introduce hand signals. It is best to frame your difficulty in probing as your problem and elicit the child's cooperation in helping you. (See Table 13-2.)

Table 13–2. Probing Behavior Checklist

Count frequency of the behavior listed. Use the scale shown above those items.

Positive performance	*Problematic performance*
____ Probes ambiguity with minimal encouragement	____ Accepts evasive client comment without probe
____ Probes ambiguity with open question	____ Uses leading questions
____ Probes ambiguity with closed question	____ Uses cross examination questions
____ Probes ambiguity with reflection of feeling or paraphrase	____ Uses begging questions
	____ Uses assumptive statement
	____ Uses sarcasm
	____ Hints

For the following behaviors use the scale: 0 = not at all; 1 = seldom; 2 = frequently; 3 = all the time

Positive performance	*Problematic performance*
____ Probes central topics	____ Inconsistent jumping between broad and narrow focus
____ Probes peripheral topics	____ Allows extensive off-topic rambling
____ Maintains general to specific exploration (funneling)	
____ Uses specific to general exploration (inverted funneling)	

Quality factors—Describe the worker's performance as it relates to the following:

1. chooses which topics to maintain or return to central issues
2. flexibly probes content and relationship levels within a topic
3. evaluates quality and relevance of child information and moves to increase both

Chapter 14

SELF-DISCLOSURE

After mastering the information in this chapter, you should be able to—

1. explain two factors contributing to the intensity of self-disclosure;
2. identify the social penetration process;
3. explain what factors contribute to perceived risk in self-disclosure;
4. list the advantages of self-disclosure by treatment workers in the treatment setting;
5. identify and explain the uses and misuses of self-disclosure and there-and-then events;
6. explain how owning language relates to the relationship dimension of immediacy;
7. list and explain categories of owning and disowning language;
8. relate self-disclosure to non-behavioral levels of worker functioning as illustrated by "Feelings and Issues for the Treatment Worker."

The ways in which a treatment worker uses his or her *self* in dealing with troubled children has great impact on the progress of treatment. Sharing *yourself* through self-disclosure provides one way of using yourself in a very direct way. In this chapter we will examine the self-disclosure process and how it relates specifically to treatment.

In everyday living, people show themselves to each other in a variety of ways. The Johari Window (Luft, 1969) indicates some of the areas that may be disclosed.

Known to Others	Known to Self	Not Known to Self
	Area of free activity Public self	Blind area
Not Known to Others	Avoided or hidden area Private self	Area of unknown activity

Only those areas known to you can be self-disclosed. The blind area —things about yourself that you do not know but others do—is public information. Examples of blind areas are an open fly, bad breath, and frequently saying, "You know?" The area of unknown activity is unknown to everyone; therefore, it is not usually an issue. The areas known to self that may be shared include the "public self" that is, the obvious everyday information that is available for all to see: color of hair, height, gregariousness, etc. When the public self does not match the private self, there may be problems of cue discrepancy. In addition, people may try to present themselves consistent with some image they have of themselves, rather than being who they are. This "on stage" performance creates feelings of dissonance.

The crucial area of consideration in the process of self-disclosure is the avoided or hidden area. People define their psychological space much as they do their physical space—in territories ranging from safe to vulnerable. A person will allow only trusted people into a vulnerable or intimate physical area; the same is true of allowing people to share in psychological space.

The circles below illustrate how people divide their knowledge about themselves into a continuum of public to private information. With advancing intimacy each type of information is shared with people whom the discloser increasingly trusts. (See Figure 14-1.)

Sometimes the individual labels self-knowledge in grosser gradations. In the figures person "A" perceives all self-knowledge beyond public self as nondisclosable. This person erects a barrier against sharing everyday self-information, because innocuous personal information is undifferentiated from embarrassing private information. When he does disclose, this person is likely to embarrass others because he will share very intimate information at inappropriate times. Person "B" has no barriers or gradations at all. She will share even the most private personal information with a total stranger. Such a person makes others feel uncomfortable because she violates the usual patterns of self-disclosure by "intruding" on others. The

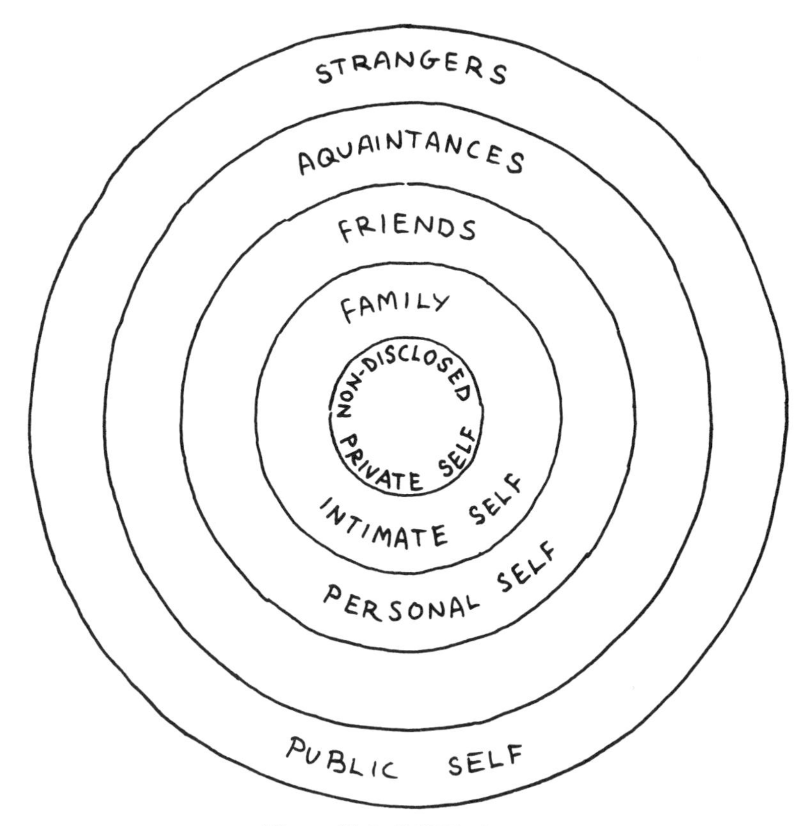

Figure 14-1. Self-Disclosure

others may then feel that they must respond with similar information, yet they don't trust person "B". (See Figure 14-2.)

People who self-disclose frequently have well-differentiated levels of self-information; they can see fine distinctions between what they want to share and what they do not. They also feel in control of how much they share. In addition, such self-disclosers tend to feel comfortable with themselves; therefore, shared information is less likely to be embarrassing or hurtful even if the receiver responds in a critical way.

The Interpersonal Effects of Self–Disclosure

On a day-to-day basis, people engage in both verbal and nonverbal self-disclosure as a means of solidifying interpersonal relationships, of meeting their needs for social contact, and of learning more about themselves. To clarify the latter goal, Culbert (1967) entitled his paper on self-disclosure "The interpersonal process of self-disclosure: It takes two to see

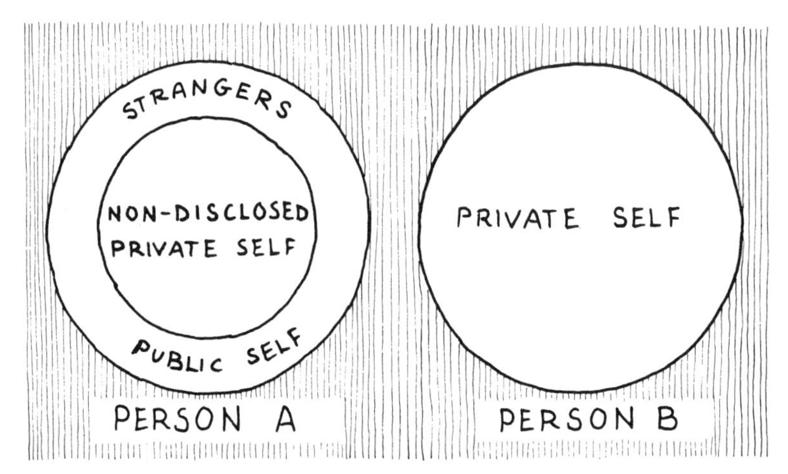

Figure 14-2. Self-Disclosure

one." Both in everyday interaction and in treatment, sharing one's self allows another person to voice feedback and reaction. That feedback and reaction helps the discloser see himself and his behavior in perspective. We learn about who we are from the reactions of others to us. Certainly such a process is important for troubled children, and for the people who work with them.

Culbert (1967) created a schematic formula to explain the interrelationship of several factors affecting a person's willingness to expose the hidden or avoided areas of self (risk).

$$\text{Risk} = f\left[\frac{\text{Intensity}}{\text{Pr (Intention) X Pr (Expected Reactions)}}\right]$$

That is, the risk in self–disclosure is a function of the intensity or importance the communicator places on the disclosure, divided by the product of the probabilities that the receiver will hear the disclosure as the communicator intended and that the receiver will react as the communicator expected. The greater the risk, the more the communicator is thought to be vulnerable with respect to the disclosure.

Intensity

Self-disclosure varies in intensity along two dimensions: depth and breadth.

DEPTH OF SELF-DISCLOSURE is related to the perceived intimacy of the statement. Altman and Taylor (1973), in their research on the social penetration process, identify gradations in intimacy of topics. Some of the more shallow topics include biographical information: school and work, interests, hobbies and habits. Some of the deeper topics include: love, dating, sex, one's own marriage and family, parental family, religion, money, emotions, and feelings. Also, speaking of topics in immediate, here-and-now terms, shows depth of disclosure because of the unavoidable identification of the topic with the speaker. As the depth of intimacy increased, the risk involved to the discloser is perceived as increasing.

BREADTH OF SELF-DISCLOSURE is related to the time or extent any particular topic is discussed. The longer one discusses a topic the more information is likely to be revealed. Therefore, a person may feel comfortable disclosing deeply intimate topics for only short periods but talk for hours on a shallow topic, for example, at a cocktail party.

Intention

If a listener does not understand the self-discloser's information in the way he intended, miscommunication will occur. Even a benign miscommunication can be frustrating. With increased intensity of self–disclosure the need for someone else to "understand" becomes even more important, and misunderstanding becomes more frustrating. Some people even interpret another's misreading of a message as a hostile act. Certainly they would be less likely to share with the other person at a later time.

Expected Reactions

The discloser's prediction of listener reaction helps the self-discloser determine whether or not to trust the receiver with his information. A predictable negative reaction by the receiver indicates low-level sharing at most. Predictable positive reaction indicates high-level sharing. Unpredictable listener reactions are likely to invite a person to share and then introduce negative responses later. A person who responds unpredictably is not trustworthy; therefore, he is a very risky person with whom to share personal information.

In the usual "getting to know you" process that people engage in when they are developing a relationship, the disclosures follow a shallow to deep, narrow to broad progression. In addition, people usually exchange disclosures on the same level of intimacy before they go on to the next level. It is almost as if each has to confirm that the other responds positively and predictably before they are willing to share the next level of intimacy. In treatment, this same process occurs. However, the rules of the interaction are somewhat different in that some of the preliminary shallow topics are rushed through and more time is spent on deep topics, e.g., family, feelings and emotions. Children carry with them some of the expectations of mutual disclosure into the treatment relationship. Therefore, they will invite, if not directly ask for, disclosures on the worker's part.

Effects of Worker Self–Disclosure in Treatment

Research has indicated that in a treatment setting worker self-disclosure increases self-disclosure on the child's part (Powell, 1968), apparently by accomplishing several ends. First, *workers demonstrate their understanding of the social penetration process* by not expecting only to receive self-disclosure. Outside of treatment, a person who discloses without getting disclosure in return risks the other person's using that revealed information in some harmful way. It is almost as if the mutual self-disclosure pattern safeguards the participants because each has an arsonal of weapons with which to respond, should the other violate his trust. So in treatment, the child takes incredible risks in disclosing information that he would share with very few individuals. And he does his sharing without a directly reciprocal response from the treatment worker. Thus, his trust in the worker has to be very great. One way to increase that trust is to use self-disclosure. That does not mean that you have to swap stories. All it means is that you recognize that disclosure on your part will give at least some recognition to the social penetration process.

Secondly, self-disclosure on the worker's part *provides a model for appropriate sharing of intimate information.* Definitions of appropriate behavior in the treatment setting are different, but new clients may not understand the permission to disclose on intense levels. Some early congruent self-disclosure on the worker's part provides concrete illustrations of how self-disclosure on intense levels can be shared without overbearing anxiety. Risk on the worker's part makes comparable risk on the child's part more likely. Some research indicates that even in social situations outside of treatment, intense self-disclosure by one person will be matched by another (Savicki, 1972). This intimacy-disclosure matching occurs even with people who typically disclose only at very low levels (Jourard & Resnick, 1973).

Finally, worker self-disclosure can *provide children glimpses of alternative ways of responding.* One of the feelings that clients often carry with them is the feeling of isolation: "I'm the only one who ever felt this way —I must be really weird." Children are sometimes surprised and taken aback that the workers whom they trust and admire also felt, and may yet feel, the way the child does. Worker self-disclosure can provide the child with more realistic, nonjudgmental labels to attach to their reactions. For example: "You know, John, I've felt left out and lonely too. I think most people feel that way at times. As a matter of fact, I felt that just yesterday when my husband decided to go bowling with the boys rather than stay home with me. You know what I did with those lonely feelings? I called a friend and we talked for an hour on the phone. After that I felt much better."

Issues with Worker's Self-disclosure

Several issues must be considered when workers use self-disclosure in the treatment setting. First, workers must keep in perspective how they are using self-disclosure. The ultimate criterion to evaluate any treatment approach is the outcome as measured by the growth of the child. Worker self-disclosure must be offered in ways that further that outcome. One inappropriate way of using self-disclosure is to provide more intimate information than the child can usefully process. This misuse is especially important to monitor with children, since their experiences and perspectives are limited and they may be easily overwhelmed.

Poor Example

"I've felt sad too. I never felt like my mom and dad loved me; they just ripped me apart whenever I made a mistake. I think I'll never get over that . . ."

Good Example

"I've felt sad too. My parents were critical of me, and I felt hurt."

Another misuse of self-disclosure in a treatment setting is using the child as a listener for disclosures that satisfy only the needs of the worker. The treatment setting is not a place for a worker to hash out his own problems. If a worker has some unresolved personal issues to deal with, personal counseling independent of his work with children is a better setting in which to meet those needs.

Poor Example

"I'm really furious with your mother for not letting me know that she has a new boyfriend. I'm just really hurt . . . and you can tell her that for me!"

Good Example

(To the child)
"Is your mom at home today? I want to call her . . .
(To self)
"I'm really more angry than the situation calls for. I'll work that out with my counselor."

Finally, another misuse of self-disclosure is "impression management." Each of us would like to make a certain impression on other people. Each of us also may go to different lengths to make sure that our desired impression is produced. One way of creating an impression is to use self-disclosure. Some of the impressions that can be transmitted: "Look, I've got it all together now. I've had some problems but they're all in the past. See how open and free I am? Ask me anything. I'm not shy." Of course only selected disclosures are shared in creating the above impression.

A good use of self-disclosure in a treatment setting is to *share your here-and-now reactions,* be they confusion, frustration, or inadequacies, as they relate to the treatment relationship. For example, an appropriate response to a request for 'The Answer' is "I don't know, let's figure it out together." If you are confused about what a child is saying, "I'm confused" is a good self-disclosure. If you and the child have been working on a problem for some time but you are making no headway, "I'm frustrated" is a good self-disclosure. Keeping the child in touch with your reactions to her as they are happening provides many opportunities for self-disclosure.

With some regularity, children will ask workers *personal questions,* or questions requesting an opinion. There are several schools of thought on how a worker should respond. We have found that what works well is a brief and direct answer to the question followed by a probe as to how the information will be used. Immediately attempting to find out "why" the child is asking the question implies a reluctance to share information about yourself, and it may induce defensiveness in the child. Following through as if the child were engaged in the social penetration process avoids reacting in a way that will make the child less likely to self-disclose in the future.

GUIDELINES

The behaviors included in self-disclosure can be divided roughly into two categories: there-and-then and here-and-now. There-and-then disclosures apply to out-of-the-treatment-setting incidents; these have been discussed in the previous paragraphs. Self-disclosures should be—

appropriate to maintain positive outcome. Self-disclosures should not be too aloof, nor should they overwhelm the child.

relevant to the treatment process. Self-disclosures should have a direct bearing on the child and the issues he is dealing with in treatment. Therefore, avoid self-disclosures aimed at satisfying only your needs, and avoid impression management self-disclosures.

Responsive to the social penetration process. Self-disclosures in response to direct questions, and self-disclosures at higher levels of intensity will advance the comfort of the child in sharing herself.

Owning Language for Here-and-Now Self-Disclosure

Owning language focuses on words used to express personal here-and-now experience and awareness. When people talk about events, even events that have happened in the past or that may happen in the future, they experience feelings and thoughts about those events in the present. Often people block their awareness of their present reactions by denying, distorting, or projecting their thoughts and feelings elsewhere. The words with which they choose to talk about their experience can either own or disown their present experience.

Contact between worker and child can be more intimate when the communication reflects the immediate reactions and concerns of the dyad. Owning language encourages *immediacy* of contact. A direct self–disclosing message follows the general form "I am saying something to you in this situation".

I (the sender)
am saying something (the message)
to you (the receiver)
in this situation (the context)

If one or more of these parts of a communication is disqualified in some way, the message is not clear and direct. In an immediate, here-and-now counseling context, all facets of the communication are evident.

I (sender)
am irritated (message)
at you (receiver)
when you switch topics each time we have talked about your
father today (context)

At other times disowning language is harder to spot. The contrasting words listed below illustrate some owning/disowning language.

"I" versus "It"

People use "it" to depersonalize their experience of situations; for example: "It's a real drag working with Betty." Owning language identifies the experience as belonging to the speaker; for example: "I'm bored when I work with Betty."

"I" versus "You"

"You-talk" includes two general types of disowning. The first is the "editorial you." For example: "Well, you never know when you might need to leave." Here, the person talks in general terms that distance his experience. An owning expression of the same experience would acknowledge the person's own reactions; for example: "I'm not sure how long I'm going to stay." The second type of "you-talk" hurls blame and accusation rather than owning anger or hurt; for example: "You never take me anywhere any more" versus "I'm feeling hurt that we don't spend as much time together as we used to."

"I" versus "We," "Everybody," "No one," "One," "Some People"

Sometimes pronouns such as "we," et al. fit because the speaker is expressing discussed and agreed upon consensus of a group of people. For the most part "we" et al. represents diluting responsibility for personal feelings by attributing those reactions to others as well as to self; for example: "We think that everybody will agree that no one ought to have bad breath when working with kids, because one never knows when some people might take offense." A riskier but straighter way to say the same thing is "I don't like working with you when you have bad breath."

"Won't" versus "Can't"

Sometimes people have a difficult time telling the difference between what they can and cannot accomplish. More often than not they put restrictions on themselves that are more limiting than the limits provided by the situation. In contrast, some people continue to fling themselves at a realistically unattainable goal by following the dictum "There's no such word as can't." Children and workers both need help in discovering the discrimination between real and self-imposed limits. Realistic "can't": "I can't reach the apples on the top branch without a ladder." Self-restricting "can't": "I can't possibly reach the apples on the top branch."

Also, "can't" is used as a more polite, less responsibility-assuming word than "won't". If we have no choice in being unable to do something, how can we be blamed? If, on the other hand, we actively *choose* not to do something, we must bear the displeasure and pressure of others. The common excuse "I can't make it" is many times less than accurate. Often, it is a way to be less specific about our choice not to go.

"Choose to" versus "Have to" or "Must"

For most people there is more choice available than is exercised. One way people limit their perception of choice and/or deny some of the responsibility for their choice is to phrase their actions in forced-compliance rather than free-choice terms. A responsibility-diluting statement is "I had to take Georgie's lunch. He hit me and I didn't know what else to do." A more direct statement might be "I chose to get back at Georgie by taking his lunch away."

"Want" versus "Need"

"Need" implies a more basic nonnegotiable deficit than does "want." Children and adults may define their needs as those that will send them into panic if unmet; for example: "But I need to come along with you to the store." Also, "need" implies an unchosen quality. Sometimes children learn that if they are impertinent enough to ask for what they "want," they will be denied. But if they make requests on the basis of "need," they will more likely get what they want. A "want" carries more risk and more choice; for example: "I want very much to go to the store with you."

"And" versus "But"

"But" is often used to take away, discount, or disqualify a previous statement. The word "but" means "except" or "on the contrary". When appropriately used, it highlights a contrast; for example: "I could have gone to the movies, but I wanted to study." "And" expresses connection between two ideas—"I want to lose weight, and I will stop snacking." The problem comes when a person phrases as opposites ideas or feelings that go together; for example: "I like your help cleaning the table, and/but I'd like you to stack the dishes too." In the previous statement, "but" dilutes or erases the positive statement in the first half of the sentence. The speaker gives, then takes away, the positive comment. "And" used instead allows the positive to remain while adding a further instruction. Following the same reasoning, using "but" also implies that only one part of a multipart statement is valid; for example: "I'm angry at my teacher, but I'm scared to tell her."

"I Feel" versus "You Make Me Feel"

Each of us feels exactly as we should feel given our interpretations of events. Since each of us has slightly different perceptions and belief systems, each of us reacts individually and consistent with our interpretations. Therefore, to lay the responsibility for our feelings on someone else, using "make-feel" language, denys the origin of our feelings. A disowning statement is "You make me so angry because you laugh at me that way." More accurate is "I get very angry when you laugh at me that way." In the second example, the speaker avoids the language of causality.

"I Will" versus "I'll Try"

"I'll try my best" is a phrase sometimes used to fend off someone who is attempting to obtain a commitment. Roughly translated it means "I'll give it a try, but I don't expect to succeed." "I will" does not qualify or quibble about doing what is agreed to. For example, a noncommitted statement is "I'll try to remember to hang up my coat after I come in, but you know how poor my memory is." "I will hang up my coat when I come in" is more direct. Our culture values "giving one's best" and "the old college try." The problem arises when "trying" means going through the motions without the desired outcome. Workers often mistake an agreement to "try" for an agreement to attain results. They then become angry when results are not forthcoming.

"Imagine," "Fantasize," or "Guess" versus "Know"

Each of us reacts to incomplete information by imagining what the completed information will be. We do this on the basis of past experience and our assumptions about how the world works. Some of us are quite accurate at making inferences, but no matter how accurate a person is, he cannot "know" until an event occurs how it will turn out. Therefore, even the best "guesser" is only that, a guesser not a "knower." However some guessers get ossified in their fantasy. The real issue with prematurely rigid fantasies is that they can become self-fulfilling prophecies. We can selectively perceive and selectively react to make events turn out as we imagine they could; for example: "I just know I'll flunk my English exam, I always do poorly on essay tests." More accurate would be "My fantasy is that I'll do poorly on my English exam."

Active Verbs versus Passive Verbs

In the passive voice, actions are phrased as someone's being "done to" rather than "doing." This phrasing implies that the person has little control or responsibility for her life. Habitual use of passive voice may lead a person to give away her personal power and impact; for example: "I was placed among the top ten kids in my class. I was seen as the best speller." A more owning construction is "I earned one of the top ten spots in my class. I spell better than the others."

Statements versus Questions

Sometimes rather than risking a direct statement of an opinion, feeling, or want, people ask a question that includes an implied statement. Rhetorical questions are one type of implied statement. A rhetorical question is a question that the speaker already knows the answer to. The question "Now don't you really think that kids get away with murder these days?" might be more directly expressed as an opinion, "I think these kids get away with murder these days." Another type of question with an implied statement is a question with a request for action imbedded in it; for example: "Did you notice how drafty it is in here?" Better would be "Please close the door."

Unqualified Statements versus Qualified Statements

"May," "maybe," "possibly," "I guess," and other qualifiers dilute a message. In addition they imply both positive and negative responses; for example: "I may tell Eve how much I like her . . . and then again I may not." "I guess I can agree to stop bugging Nancy" is much less direct than if "guess" were excluded from the statement

All of the previous categories of owning language can be used to promote more immediate sharing and intimate disclosing. Sometimes a worker will use non-owning language when introducing an interpretation that taps intimate levels of the child's self. Thus, rather than saying "I can see that you feel terrified at changing" when the child clearly is struggling to keep his terror from overwhelming him, a worker might use a less personal introduction to this concept, "Sometimes kids get real nervous about the idea of changing. I wonder if that's true for you?" By keeping the topic a little distant at first, the worker can allow the child to discharge a bit of the fear before going on to his own specific situation. As always, flexibility is important.

Feelings and Issues for the Treatment Worker

Workers may block themselves from using self–disclosure because of adherence to personal beliefs and assumptions.

"I'll Be Able To Hide My Reactions; They Will Never Know."

Workers assume that they hide more than they do, for here-and-now reactions with the child are especially difficult to cover completely. Also cloaking one's self in a role of dispassionate helper cannot completely hide the fact that some reactions are taking place. The question then is not how to hide these reactions, but how to use them effectively. Direct, owning self–disclosures offer a constructive way to share oneself in a treatment and non–treatment setting.

"If I Say I Like Him, He'll Know About The Sexual Fantasies I've Had About Him."

Some workers do not perceive differences between low-intensity disclosures and high-intensity disclosures. Therefore, they are reluctant to share even the most trivial self-information for fear that they will then be vulnerable to baring their innermost feelings. One way to develop more differentiation is to practice. With a trusted partner, test your ability to share only what you want to share. You will find that you have much more flexibility than you thought. Also, you can use disowning language to defuse some of the more intense disclosures to people and in contexts that you perceive as high risk, and save owning language for selected persons.

"It's Inappropriate To Share With Clients."

One of the old sayings sometimes repeated to beginning counselors is "Don't make friends of your clients or make clients of your friends." This statment reflects a reluctance to muddy the differing role expectations of friendship and therapy. Implicit in this saying is the assumption that it is not good to become too close to your clients. While keeping one's objectivity may be more difficult with a friend than with a client, the potential positive outcome of a close relationship with a client makes untangling those functions well worth the effort. Another possible limiting belief that blocks developing a sharing relationship with clients is the "let's keep it in the family" rule that some people learn. Parents may convey that no sharing outside of the family is permitted. If a person follows such a rule, then she limits her support and intense personal contact to people inside the family. Family members are not likely to meet all the needs of an individual at all times, especially when that individual violates family dictums. Therefore, breaking that family rule may be necessary in order to insure a person's well-being and growth.

"If I Share Myself, I Might Impose On My Children, And I Don't Have A Right To Do That."

Appropriate self-disclosure is not imposing. Often workers feel they are imposing because of a belief that they should not be important. Tied to this belief about self may also be a belief that good counselors do not influence their children. First, in a child's eyes there is no way that his worker can be unimportant. Your investment and caring make you important to the child in a personal sense. Therefore, self-disclosing to the child or to adult clients is not imposing, it is another demonstration of caring through sharing. Secondly, it is impossible not to influence someone with whom you are in relationship. Remember all the basic truths about communication that we discussed in the chapter on "Cue Congruence." You will influence whether you want to or not. Therefore, to make your influence more caring and personal, use self-disclosure to show your reasons and feelings about the actions that you take. You will provide a model not only for the actions but also for self-disclosing. (See Table 14-1.)

Table 14–1. Self-Disclosure Behavior Checklist

Record the frequency of the following behaviors:

Positive performance	*Problematic performance*
There-and-then self-disclosures:	There-and-then self-disclosures:
____ Self-disclosure given to match or slightly increase the child's level of disclosure	____ No self-disclosures
____ Self-disclosure relevant to child's treatment	____ Self-disclosures shallow and aloof
____ Self-disclosure in response to child's verbal or nonverbal request	____ Self-disclosures too intense for child
	____ Self-disclosure irrelevant to child's treatment
	____ Defensiveness/protectiveness in response to child's verbal or nonverbal request for disclosure
Here-and-now self-disclosures:	Here-and-now self-disclosures:
____ "I" language	____ "It," "you," "we" in place of "I"
____ "Won't," "choose to," "want," active voice used to indicate active choice	____ "Can't," "have to," "need," passive voice used to imply lack of responsibility for choice
____ "And" used to connect ideas that go together	____ "But" used to contradict ideas that go together
____ "I feel" used to take responsibility for feelings	____ "You make me feel" used to deny responsibility for feelings
____ "I will" and unqualified statements used to affirm commitment to a course of action	____ "I'll try" and qualified statements used to avoid commitment to a course of action
____ "Imagine," "fantasize," or "guess," used to describe guessing about unknown information	____ "Know" implying certain knowledge about unknowable information
____ Statements used to proclaim personal opinion or position	____ Questions used as disguised statements

Quality factors—Describe the worker's performance in relation to the following:

1. Nonverbal as well as verbal means used to self-disclose.
2. Timing of self-disclosures augment child's process, do not distract or hinder.

Chapter 15

CONFRONTATION

After mastering the information in this chapter, you should be able to—

1. define confrontation and identify its two sub-parts;
2. give examples of the types of discrepancies that a treatment worker may use as cues for confrontation;
3. explain the positive function of negative feedback;
4. explain how confrontation functions within the worker; child relationship;
5. identify six effects of confrontation on the child;
6. identify ten qualities of effective and acceptable confrontation;
7. identify and give examples of seven types of confrontation;
8. relate confrontation to non-behavioral levels of worker functioning as illustrated by "Feelings and Issues for the Treatment Worker."

A confrontation may be defined as a deliberate attempt to help a child examine the consequences of some aspect of his behavior. It is a subtle or direct invitation to self-examination. A confrontation originates from a desire on the part of the confronter to involve herself more deeply with the child, not to punish him. The treatment worker calls upon the child to notice and potentially take steps to resolve some discrepancy between his behavior and some other aspect of his situation.

Thus confrontation contains two parts: awareness of discrepancies and ways of calling attention to those discrepancies. Some of the discrepancies have been articulated in the chapter on "Cue Congruence." Other discrepancies that may exist include the child's plans versus probable outcomes, the child's intent versus his actions, the child's commitment to a course of action versus his follow–through, the child's awareness of expectations versus his compliance.

In calling attention to discrepancies, the treatment worker uses the *principle of divergent feedback.* Divergent feedback indicates that the child is not proceeding towards a certain goal, or that she is in fact proceeding away from the goal. Such feedback focuses on the differences rather than the similarities between intent and action, thus helping the child to reassess her position. It can help her evaluate her behavior in comparison with where she wants to be and then self-correct. As a brief aside, even positive information such as praise and affection may be discrepant with the child's evaluation of herself and thus may be seen as divergent feedback.

Treatment worker information provides the vehicle through which treatment confrontation is given (See Figure 15-1.). Such information may be discrepant with the child's views and the discrepancy must be evaluated on its utility for the child rather than on its agreement with some notion of "true reality." You can allow the child his reality while at the same time challenging its usefulness for him. For example:

CHILD: I wasn't trying to hurt myself when I jumped off the merry–go–round. I was just having fun.
MOTHER: I hear that it was your way of having fun. I also see that you bruised your arm.

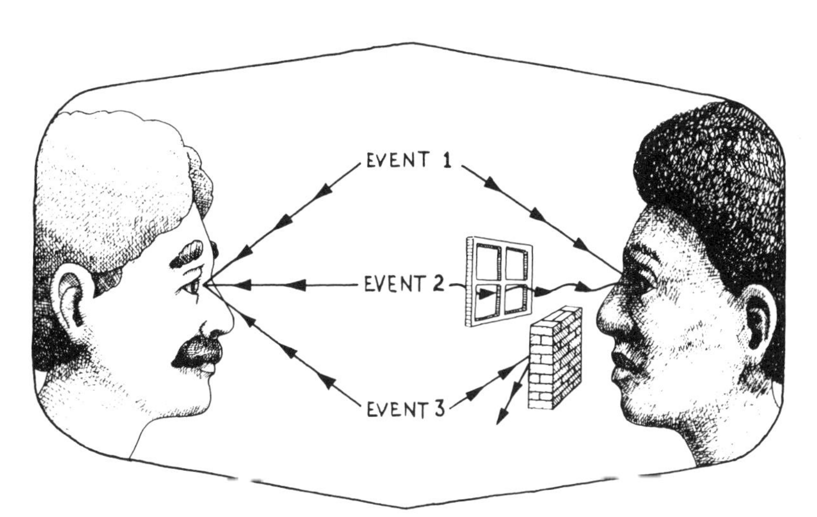

Figure 15-1. Confrontation

Constructive confrontation may take the form of assertion. That is, the treatment worker neither passively accepts clearly discrepant information from the child, nor aggresively demands that his own perceptions define the only reality. The worker can allow disagreement to persist, maintaining his own perceptions as valid and allowing the child the same right. He does not discount the child or himself by demanding agreement to unacceptable views.

Confrontation is the other half of empathy. Empathy means that the treatment worker understands the world as the child sees it yet keeps his own objectivity. Confrontation means that the treatment worker differs with the child's perception of his situation and understands the child's view as well. Confrontation asks the child to compare his perceptions with those of the treatment worker. Although both perceptions may have some basis in reality, the comparison of the different points of view teach the child two things: (a) there is more than one way to view his experience and (b) a different view may result in more desirable feelings and behaviors. Thus the treatment worker breaks the self-imposed limits of the client's way of seeing his situation.

Effects of Confrontation on the Child

Confrontation promotes honest and direct recognition and expression of perceptions. A confronted child may experience challenge, exposure, and threat on the one hand; and respect and excitement on the other. Like any powerful technique, confrontation has potentially both good and bad effects.

Effective confrontation gives the child an *honest* and *immediate* experience of himself. He feels the impact he can have on another and begins to realize his impact on himself.

Confrontation also signals to the child a measure of *respect* for his increasing capacity for self-determination. The treatment worker is not coddling him for fear of overwhelming, hurting, or shaping him. By directly communicating his own position to the child, the treatment worker allows or prompts the child to make his own stand clear and to evaluate it against the treatment worker's viewpoint.

Within the process of confrontation, the child has a model for accepting and expressing his own thoughts and feelings. It also provides experience with *alternative ways of viewing* his situation.

Through confrontation the child learns that two people can disagree without harboring hostile feelings for each other. Disagreement does not mean dislike, nor does it imply only conditional acceptance. It is possible to like the child without liking his behavior. However, the most instinctive response to confrontation is to perceive it negatively as a threat, a condemnation, a judgment, or a punishment.

If a confrontation is responsible—that is, if it is really an invitation to self-examination—the hoped for response (but not the easiest) is self-examination and not the more instinctive responses of defense and counter-attack. It is often far easier for the child to respond to the implied negative messages than to the substance of the confrontation itself.

Urge the child to listen to what you are saying and not just to the feelings that are evoked. You may have to confront the child about his reaction to the confrontation. In most cases this means that you want to confront in such a way that the child being confronted takes the feedback seriously but does not become so defensive that he refuses to accept or use the feedback.

General Qualities of Confrontation that Make it More Effective and Acceptable

Remember that the information the treatment worker exposes is not the only confrontational aspect; the behavior of the treatment worker while pointing out that information is also confrontational. If confrontation goes wrong, it is usually *how* it is expressed rather than *what* is said. Some of the previous communication skills need to be integrated into confrontation, e.g., reflection of feeling, cue congruence, self-disclosure and use of language. These facilitate a worker/child relationship that is empathic, genuine, immediate, and concrete. In addition, consider the following:

Timing

The confrontation must be timed so that the person is open to receiving the information without becoming overly defensive.

Changeability

This refers to the ability of the person to act upon the confrontation. The more he is able to use the confrontation to change his behavior, the more likely he is to accept it. For example, a confrontation of a child about his avoiding reading aloud during reading group will not be well received if the child cannot read the material. Your request for his participation calls on a skill he does not possess.

Relevance

Confrontation that bears some resemblance to what the child sees as relevant to her experience will receive more positive results than confrontation about an issue to which the child does not feel connected.

Tentativeness

Confrontation may be an inference about the other person's behavior. Thus you should not present your perception or interpretation of the other person's behavior as self-evident fact, but rather as an opinion which may or may not be correct. The important point to remember is that in a relationship, facts should be presented as facts, feelings as feelings, and inferences as inferences. Avoid confusing feelings and opinions as facts.

Relationship Intensity

The stronger the relationship, the more powerful the confrontation may be.

Emotional Readiness

Children function most effectively when their feelings are at an optimal level, i.e. neither overwhelming nor weak. Many of the people you will deal with will need "uncovering" efforts, that is, therapeutic techniques to help them bring their emotional responses into greater awareness. Confrontation is a powerful tool for this purpose. However, many children need to stay where they are or even "cover over" some feelings in order to maintain optimal emotional intensity for therapeutic change. To follow are some cautions about using confrontation when emotions may be too intense. Be cautious of pressing for more free expression of feeling if—

1. the child's emotional coping mechanisms are (a) presently severely underdeveloped or distorted, e.g., delusions, extreme anger, hysterical tendencies, (b) strained by current crisis or emotionally demanding pressures, or (c) reduced in ability to deal with emotional topics as a result of past unresolved emotional crisis,
2. the treatment worker's emotional life is in turmoil,
3. enough time is not available for working through the feelings to a comfortable (for the treatment worker) stopping level.

FUNCTIONAL TYPES OF CONFRONTATION

There are at least seven functional types of confrontation involving many different behavioral skills. Although some of the same behaviors may be used in all of the types, the function of each type differs so that the behaviors are used differently. Each type of confrontation focuses on a different kind of information. The type of confronting information defines the function, not the separate skills that may combine to form a particular confrontation.

Self-Confrontation

The goal is to help the child verbalize an existing awareness he has about himself or his situation.

WORKER: I notice that as we talk about how angry you are at Frank for ripping up your painting, you're getting tears in your eyes.
CHILD: Yeah. I'm mad but I'm sad too.

Guided Self-Confrontation

The goal is to help a child connect related pieces of information that he is aware of in new ways so that he discovers a new understanding of himself or his situation.

WORKER: Before Frank grabbed your painting, what was happening?
CHILD: I was painting . . . and kind of teasing him about how funny his picture looked. I was a little irritated at the way he was using my yellow paint without asking.
WORKER: What does it mean to you that Frank ripped up your paper just after you teased him?

Shared Perceptions

The goal is to share perceptions from your point of view in order to offer an alternative way of understanding mutual information about thoughts, feelings, and behaviors that you have about the child and his situation.

WORKER: Seems to me that you weren't being direct with Frank about his using the yellow paint, but teased him instead. He played the same game by ripping your paper instead of telling you about his anger and hurt. What do you think?

Clarification of Consequences

The goal is to make understandable to the child the positive and/or negative consequences of his present reactions or alternate reactions (reactions include behaviors, feelings, thoughts).

WORKER: "What happened when you teased Frank about his painting as a way of getting back at him for using your yellow paint? (pause) What else could you have done to express your irritation?"

Clarification of Relationship

The goal is to comment on, discuss, and negotiate what is acceptable and not acceptable in the relationship you have with the child.

CHILD: Don't you think Frank ought to be punished for ripping up my painting? It's not fair!

WORKER: Let's be real clear that I'm not going to fight your battles for you. What I will do is help you figure out what *you* could do about it.

Shared Feelings

The goal is to use your feelings as an undeniable, personal, immediate consequence in the treatment setting to some child behavior.

CHILD: You're just stupid. You don't care if Frank gets away with murder, but you jump all over me for nothing.

WORKER: I'm getting angry at you right now. I've told you clearly what I'm willing to do with you and I hear you insulting me and trying to push me into a different decision.

Direct Suggestion

The goal is to provide the child with constructive alternatives to his present behavior.

WORKER: "If you're angry or hurt with me right now, I want you to say that directly and we'll figure out how to work it through."

BEHAVIORAL HINTS

The following suggestions may help you confront more effectively:

Modeling

The principal goal of the treatment worker in using confronting is to challenge the child to include honest feeling in his statements and acknowledge all the aspects of his situation rather than denying or shutting out perceptions or feelings. One of the keys to this condition is to model these expectations yourself.

Direct Questions

A confrontational way to get children to express feelings is to ask them to do so. Some examples are: "What are you feeling right now?" "You've described some facts about your situation; how do you feel about it?" "You have been saying how you feel about school but I haven't sensed very intense feelings about it yet. How strongly do you feel about it?" Also, in non–feeling areas a direct question pinpoints specific information and commitment: "Will you change your behavior?" "Do you mean to say that you're going to run away from home?"

Non–Punishing Expression

If you confront merely to punish another you might find some satisfaction (for instance, relief from anger), but you are doing little to enhance interpersonal contact between you and the other. Undeniably, confrontation will always have some punitive side effects (none of us likes to be challenged for behavior discrepant with our self-definition), but punishment cannot be the rationale of confrontation. Merely punitive confrontation inevitably elicits either defensiveness or counterattack, and both of these are detrimental to growth. This brings up the observation that confronting information can be positive. Many people will not accept positive remarks about themselves. Ethical use of confrontation requires that the user examine his own motive in confronting. Sometimes you may opt to work out your own problems in counseling before using particular types of confrontation on particular types of topics.

Confront Behavior

Be slow to confront motivation. Use behavior description. Do not attribute motives or attitudes. Do not label a person's personality traits or states of motivation.

Confront Clearly

Indicate what is fact, what is feeling, and what is hypothesis. Do not present interpretation as facts.

Keep It Short.

Use Your Nonverbal Behavior As Confrontation

You need not rely on words to confront. Nonverbal responses often carry more power; e.g., not responding to manipulative gambits by a client, not laughing at painful, tense laughs of a client, employing hand signals to request attention.

Confront On Small Issues Continuously Rather Than Large Ones Once In Awhile

If you store up negative feelings or allow yourself to be manipulated into a relationship you resent, you are likely to explode. These explosions are what some people think of as confrontations. Confrontation is not only an infrequent high intensity response, but also a well-modulated, ever-present low intensity response useful to the counselor.

Feelings and Issues for the Treatment Worker

Workers can block themselves from effective use of confrontation because of their beliefs about how they ought to use it or how they ought to feel about confrontation. (See Table 15–1.)

Table 15–1. Confrontation Behavior Checklist

Rate the qualities of confrontation below for each confrontation used.
1 = appropriate use; 2 = inappropriate use; 0 = not present

Record the frequency of the behavior below:		Empathy	Genuineness	Conciseness	Immediacy	Timing	Changeability	Relationship intensity	Emotional readiness
	Self-confrontation								
	Guided self-confrontation								
	Shared perception								
	Clarification of consequences								
	Clarification of relationship								
	Shared feelings								
	Direct suggestions								

"He Deserved It; He Has To Face Facts. It's For His Own Good."

Some workers may use confrontation as a disguise for venting anger and hostility. This hostility may be displaced from some other person or situation. Or it may be a discharge of little irritations stored but not commented on.

Dumping this hostility is guaranteed to arouse defensiveness which may show itself in immediate anger from the child or in a more subtle, long-term passive-aggressive behavior. Such dumping of hostility is good for getting anger off your chest, but it is not good for developing and maintaining a therapeutic relationship. Workers can work through their hostility in other relationships.

"How Can I Tell Her That She's Wrong: Won't She Be Devastated?"

This belief can overprotect and deprive the child from experience with divergent feedback. The hidden assumption is that the child is unable to cope with feedback. When you have affirmed the child's emotional readiness to receive confrontation, then confrontation demonstrates your respect towards the child as worthy of your involvement. Also, following the overprotective mode of behaving, you may find yourself storing anger and venting it indirectly and incongruently. Rules against expressing feelings can, in the long run, lead to worker burnout.

"Confrontation Is A Qualitatively Different Response That Should Only Be Used In The Most Serious Circumstances"

This belief stems from the "doomsday" assumption that confrontations are a last resort to be used only if all else fails. If confrontations are saved for the most deteriorated situations, of course they will need to be intense to make an impact. In this case their intensity are more likely to arouse defensiveness. A better solution is to confront at low intensity continuously. Confrontation is not a qualitatively different response to everyday behavior. It exists at low levels all the time since we all have slightly differing perceptions about the world we live in.

"But I'm Not Mad At Him, How Can I Do An Effective Job Of Confronting?"

You need not be angry to confront. The implicit assumption here is that confrontation is akin to punishment and may be used only in the heat of anger. Because someone's perception differs from yours, you need not take that difference as a personal affront or insult. Likewise, if you are angry at a child's behavior, you need not build to a rage before you share your feelings. Sharing low-level irritations allows you a more flexible response. Placing limits on the child's behavior or defining the limits of your own behavior within the counseling setting can be done in a matter-of-fact way.

"There's Only One Reality, And I Know What It Is! Therefore Anyone Who Disagrees With Me Is Not Only Different, But Also Wrong And Maybe Even A Little Crazy As Well."

If you believe this, you will not learn from the children with whom you work. Also remember that "reality is in the eye of the beholder." If someone chooses not to change his perception on the basis of your confrontation, that does not mean that they are "bad" or "crazy." Better than labeling, point out the consequences to them in terms of feelings and behavior. Then, allow the child the choice of his own pain and frustration. Confrontation at this point can center around the child's owning his choice rather than changing his behavior.

"I Need To Confront People To Break Through Their Defenses Because People Have To Experience Pain In Order To Change"

This belief assumes that all change stems from conflict and suffering; "You've got to cry a lot in order to change." There is plenty of research and clinical evidence that shows the "cry a lot" assumption to be untrue. Thus, creating discomfort for a child through confrontation solely because you believe that is the way it "ought" to happen, does not match with research and experience about behavior change.

Extended Example—With a Parent

Type of Confrontation	
Guided self–confrontation	PARENT: Sometimes I just can't stand him—he's such a little devil. Ha, ha.
	TREATMENT WORKER: You're laughing about his antics in the same breath that you say you can't stand him.
	PARENT: Wow! I am, aren't I?
Self–confrontation	TREATMENT WORKER: Looks like you have some reactions to that.
	PARENT: Yeah! I don't really find his acting-up funny at all.
Shared perceptions	TREATMENT WORKER: My impression is that his behavior is cute or funny at low intensity, or that it was cute when he was younger. But it's not funny now when it gets out of hand.

PARENT: You bet! Sometimes he's cute but when he gets too worked up I can't stand him.

Clarification of consequences

TREATMENT WORKER: When you laugh at and get angry at him for the same type of behavior, it's very likely that he gets confused. He may even think you want him to do more of the very thing you want him to stop.

PARENT: Now wait a minute! Are you trying to tell me that I'm purposely making my child misbehave?

Clarification of relationship

TREATMENT WORKER: We're working together to try to deal with your child. Sometimes we will consider ideas and topics that will cause feelings of discomfort or anger. Sounds like this one raises your hackles. Are you willing to consider all relevant topics?

PARENT: I don't want to talk about me, it's my child that's the problem. You help me fix him up, but leave me out of it.

Shared feelings

TREATMENT WORKER: I'm irritated at the way you closed off the issue we were dealing with, and at the same time I feel sad that you won't recognize that your child's behavior *is* related to your behavior. You're too important to "leave out of it."

PARENT: Well, OK. What can I do?

Direct suggestions

TREATMENT WORKER: The first thing is to continue the discussion we started. I want you to allow discussion of all relevant information, even if it's uncomfortable. Will you agree to that?

Part III

THE BASICS

In our attempts to "cure" kids rapidly, some basic considerations are often overlooked. The basic skills outlined in Part III form the foundation upon which other change efforts are erected. The general goal of the skills in Part 3 is to create a therapeutic atmosphere of acceptance, safety, security, and predictability. Although these qualities are extremely important, they can be overshadowed by more dramatic and obvious treatment skills. In the past, treatment workers may have received instructions to "love your children more" or "be more caring." We will detail some specific behaviors you can *do* to follow these injunctions and thus create a therapeutic context from which behavioral change may proceed. We do not assume that all treatment workers inherently love their clients, nor that all children behave lovably. We do believe that you can create a physical and social environment that elicits from you the emotional responses of acceptance and caring. Thus, you may need to work for change for yourself before you can work for change for the child. Recognize that this sequence of events represents a high level of treatment worker functioning. You must learn to take responsibility for yourself as a treatment person as a precursor to your doing effective treatment.

Chapter 16

Basic Care

After mastering the information in this chapter you should be able to—

1. define basic nurturance, UPR, and supervision and explain how they demonstrate basic care;
2. list at least ten examples each of basic nurturance and UPR;
3. discriminate between *doing* and *being* as they are related to basic care;
4. identify the rationale for distant and close supervision;
5. explain the factors necessary for good scanning behaviors;
6. relate basic care skills to non-behavioral levels of worker functioning as illustrated by "Feelings and Issues for the Treatment Worker."

Urie Bronfenbrenner—

> The child should spend a substantial amount of time with somebody who's crazy about him. . . . I mean there has to be at least one person who has an emotional involvement with that child, someone who thinks that kid is more important than other people's kids, someone who's in love with him and whom he loves in return.
>
> (Byrne, 1977)

In the above quote, Bronfenbrenner describes the ideal relationship between child and treatment worker. His observations and research over many years in a variety of cultures has led him to conclude that aspects of what we call basic care are crucial to children. The important thing to remember here is not that you always need to feel warmth and love towards the child, but that the necessary physical caretaking behaviors are demonstrated to the child. Sometimes you may feel alienated from a child because of some odious or repulsive behaviors. Unfortunately, this may be the time he needs basic caring the most, and it may be a crucial factor in changing his rejection-seeking motivation. It is not required at these times that you become syrupy and ingenuine. It is simply required that recognition be given to the child's basic needs. This means, for example, supervision, food, a clean cloth for a dirty face, and a pleasant greeting in the morning. Every child has the right to basic nurturance, unconditional positive regard (UPR), and supervision. These contain specific identifiable behaviors, and thus may be defined as skills.

Basic Nurturance and UPR

Basic nurturance provides for the child's physical needs. Basic nurturance includes such elementary activities as feeding a hungry child, washing up, combing hair, and brushing teeth when basic hygiene has been neglected; first aid in the case of injury, and physical comfort when a child is afraid or hurt. Children with an especially low self-concept may need a lot of this input. They feel undeserving and demonstrate this by neglecting their needs. By providing basic nurturance, the treatment worker is teaching them to care for themselves. Also, this kind of physical ordering can help to "center" a child, thus assisting in setting him off in a positive direction. For example:

> Leonard inevitably arrived in the morning with a runny nose which he often wiped on people that he hugged. Rather than avoiding or neglecting Leonard, treatment workers supplied him with tissues and encouraged him to wipe his nose so that they could hug him wholeheartedly.

Unconditional positive regard (UPR) means positive verbal and physical attention and may involve giving food or objects, especially when a child discounts personal messages. Some common examples of UPR are touching, smiling, hugging, positive comments on a child's appearance, and attending to her conversation. Each child should be given this every morning, in the form of some sort of positive greeting, as well as intermittently throughout the day. This kind of attention is important for self-esteem; it says "You're an okay, valuable person regardless of your behavioral performance." UPR actively demonstrates to children the difference between *doing* and *being.* You may disapprove of what a child *does,* and at the same time, show that you can accept who he *is.* This requires that the treatment worker look upon the child as being okay and that she encourage him by focusing on the positive aspects of even the most seemingly negative behaviors (e.g., effort and improvement). For example:

> Louise has systematically destroyed her math seat-work assignment by poking designs in it with her pencil; now she is looking out the window. Treatment worker (bending down to give Louise eye contact, with hand gently on her back): "Having trouble with your math, I see. Do you realize how hard you concentrated on making your designs? I was really impressed at how well you stayed with it. I bet you can do the same with the math. I can still make out the problems. What do you need to help you get going on them?"

Basic nurturance and UPR are given to children as first priorities and without any behavioral expectations; that is, they are not contingent upon any specific behavior. These two skills are used throughout the day as the need arises, and are especially important in the morning as the child first enters. At this time, special care must be taken to survey each child closely for verbal and nonverbal cues as to his physical and emotional needs. This survey may be seen as the psychological equivalent of taking the child's temperature, a routine check that is invaluable in predicting the child's behavior on a specific day as well as providing information about what the treatment worker can do to intervene with each child on an appropriate level. In many instances, missing the relevant cues at this early stage can mean an unpleasant, chaotic day during which one constantly feels one step behind the game. For example, if a child enters showing low-level anger cues and the treatment workers miss them, the wrestling tournament scheduled later in the day may deteriorate into a physically harmful event. On the other hand, if a treatment worker catches the initial cues and allows the child to vent his anger early, the child may be able to use the later wrestling match constructively. (See Figure 16-1.)

UPR and basic nurturance are essential in building trust and self-caring. They guard against children becoming alienated enough that they resort to negativity for their only contact with others. They ensure an accepting environment necessary for treatment and help prevent those miserable days that devastate both children and staff.

Often kids will operate from a "zero-sum" assumption. This assumption says that there is only a limited amount of positive attention. Therefore, the child feels that if another child gets attention, she is *losing* attention. Liberal, consistent use of basic nurturance and UPR demonstrates that there is an infinite amount of positive attention for all. Thus, children can relax and become less negative and demanding.

Figure 16-1. Temperature Check

SUPERVISION

Supervision is *essential* in child treatment. The treatment worker should always know where each child in her care is. Supervision provides for the safety of the children as well as one of the most basic caring messages: "I care enough to be aware of your physical whereabouts and safety." Children often seek limits as a demonstration of caring from adults. Many children will try to test this basic caring by inobtrusively "slipping away" in a subtle game of hide and seek. The treatment worker must be alert to catch these instances, for they are primary in building trust and feelings of self–worth in the child. An ongoing head count is useful.

Distant versus Close Supervision

Although knowing the location of each child is central to supervision, it also includes much more. Each child is different in terms of responsibility and physical ability, and each can be allowed varying degrees of freedom and choice of activity. This means that the treatment worker must be making constant decisions about distant versus close supervision. A child who has been engaging in self-destructive behaviors, such as falling off the teeter-totter, must be watched closely in order to guard against these occurrences. Activities should be limited in this case. This type of "policing" provides the child with the needed security and caring of close supervision. For example:

> Treatment Worker: "Benji, I want you to stay out of that tree. I know you'd like to climb with the other kids right now, but you've been hurting yourself lately and I don't want you to be any place you might fall from. When you've shown that you're not hurting yourself, you can climb again."

On the other hand, close supervision for a child who has demonstrated self-responsibility and physical ability may only serve to inhibit his growth in terms of self-maintenance and learning through exploration and experience. He needs a greater degree of freedom within, of course, the visual field of the supervisor. For example:

> Treatment Worker: "Benji, this past week you've really taken care of yourself well—there've been no falls, no cuts, or bruises. I think you're ready to have access to climbing."

These limits need to be continually assessed for each child in terms of his present ability and activity. For example, a certain child may be allowed wider limits around tree climbing than around water activity.

Certain children are notorious for slipping out of the supervisor's view. These are generally the more quiet, inactive children who somehow fade into the scenery. Special care must be taken to make sure that these children are tracked.

Scanning the Environment

Supervision occurs in every setting and covers both the physical and emotional aspects of the child. It is easy to become absorbed in an interaction with a child or worker, thus "tunneling" attention and missing the fact that another child has left the room, is engaging in especially positive behaviors, or is sending the nonverbal message that he's about to hit someone. In order to pick up on these facts early, one must: a) "periscope" and scan the environment at frequent and regular intervals and b) position herself to see the entire setting whenever possible. Preventing problems is always preferable to picking up the pieces later, and only the quick eye of a good supervisor can ensure prevention. (See Figure 16-2.)

Figure 16-2. Periscoping

Feelings and Issues for the Treatment Worker

Personal beliefs and feelings can be hooks that lead treatment workers to resist using basic nurturance and UPR and to misuse supervision.

"If I Keep On Giving And Giving, I'm Going To Be Sucked Dry And Have Nothing Left."

This fear comes from the zero–sum assumption that people have only a limited amount of attention, affection and approval to give. The fact is that appropriate use of basic nurturance and UPR helps kids (and adults) to be better able to return positive conditions. If you are feeling "sucked dry," examine your ability to accept reciprocal positives.

"How Can I Give To A Kid Who Is So Yukky?"

Yukky kids may behave in repulsive ways to set themselves up for rejection. Your task as a treatment worker is not to allow the child to manipulate you into rejecting him. Yukky kids are good at what they do! You may be hard pressed to find things to feel positive about or ways to overcome the repulsive aspects of the child. However, we believe that there is no person without redeeming qualities. You must find those qualities. Use your creativity.

"I Just Don't Feel Like It And I Don't Want To Be A Phoney."

First of all, we are not asking you to be insincere. We are asking you find something, no matter how small, to be sincerely positive about. As with all skills, you will find that locating and commenting on such aspects of the child will become easier and easier with practice. Secondly, unfinished business with a child may block you from allowing yourself to be positive. As a treatment worker, you may carry anger, guilt, fear and other emotions beyond the source from which they came. Basic nurturance and UPR require a here-and-now presence. Taking care of past business or future worries allows you to function better in the present.

"I Know They're Going To Mess Up, And When They Do I'll Catch Them Red-Handed."

This sentence carries a punitive orientation to supervision rather than a protective-caring orientation. Treatment workers with this orientation become so tense and anxious fantasizing that a calamity is about to happen that they minimize their effectiveness.

"My God! They May Get Hurt. I Must Prevent Their Pain At All Costs."

Here, treatment workers would provide restrictive limits "for the child's own good." Such overprotection does not allow a child to benefit from his own mistakes and his own pain.

"They're Just Trying To Put One Over On Me. We'll See Who's Smarter."

With this orientation, the treatment worker takes the child's testing limits of supervision as a statement about the treatment worker rather than as a statement about the child's needs. Setting up a "me against them" relationship only leads to frustration and anger, especially when the child outsmarts the treatment worker.

"I Resent Having To Break My Concentration With Children Who Follow Expectations In Order To Track Those That Don't."

Timing of periscoping to coincide with breaks in conversation or transitions allows treatment workers to alternate between tunneling and scanning without taking attention away from other children. Also, when supervising in a team setting, the team might have one person responsible for supervision while others concentrate on the activity at hand. This issue resolves itself into a technical issue. It is quite possible to provide excellent supervision without taking away time and attention from other children.

"The Kids Are Doing So Well, I Can Just Sit Back And Talk To My Fellow Worker."

With supervision there is no such thing as "just" sitting back. Conversations with a fellow worker may take place; at the same time, an awareness of the children must also take place. After a while you become good at doing more than one thing at a time. Supervision may recede into the back of your mind. Yet, good workers, when asked to report where all of their kids are, will be able to do so accurately even if they seem to be occupied by other events. That awareness becomes a habit of perception. (See Table 16–1.)

Quality factors—Describe the worker's performance in relation to the following:

1. congruence of UPR
2. defines the degree of supervision necessary for each child with regard to the activity

Table 16–1. Basic Care Behavior Checklist

Rate these behaviors according to the following scale: 0 = never; 1 = seldom; 2 = moderately; 3 = frequently; 4 = almost always.

Positive performance	*Problematic performance*
____ Greets each child	____ Avoids obvious cues that child needs UPR and basic nurturance
____ Attends to and can describe cues indicating the child's emotional temperature	____ Allows early cues to go unattended
____ Basic nurturance needs attended to with each child	____ Attention only for behavioral output of child
____ UPR given to each child	____ Unable to state whereabouts of each child under his supervision
____ Knows whereabouts of each child under his supervision	____ Overprotects child
____ Scans frequently	____ Neglects child
	____ Uses tunnel vision

Chapter 17

INFORMATION-SHARING

After mastering the information in this chapter you should be able to—

1. explain the rationale for using information-sharing with children;
2. identify and describe four different types of information;
3. identify and describe four different aspects of the manner in which information is appropriately given;
4. relate information-sharing behaviors to non-behavioral levels of worker functioning as illustrated by "Feelings and Issues for the Treatment Worker."

In a very real sense, knowledge is power; not necessarily power to change events, but at least power to predict events and to prepare oneself for them. With information about the important events and people in their lives, children can learn to make connections and to form a somewhat predictable understanding of how their world works. Without that information the child's world is erratic, confusing, frightening, and even hostile.

All people have the right to be informed on issues relevant to them. An environment which promotes the open flow of information, both between and among staff, children, and parents, also promotes trust-building, an essential part of the treatment process. The meaning that a piece of information contains is conveyed by its content and its manner of delivery. This chapter will be addressed to the treatment worker/child interaction, although it can be applied to other interactions as well.

Figure 17-1. Information Sharing

Content

The kinds of information that a child needs runs the whole gamut from general to behavioral, emotional, and personal. Most children in treatment have lacked honest and complete information. Therefore, they are unclear or misinformed on the way in which the world works. Many times, in the absence of specific and honest information, they assume the worst—about events, people and themselves. In order to correct this situation, lots of information on all levels needs to be given. (See Figure 17-1.)

General Information

THE WAY THE WORLD WORKS. Information about the physical world, mechanical processes, etc. fills the child's store of knowledge and also tunes him into the predictability of natural events. "Oh yeah, when the sun reflects off of the rain, it makes a rainbow."

PREDICTABLE EVENTS. General information about the day's events and procedures should be given in advance, i.e., what will be happening, where it will happen, how it will proceed, who will be present, what the purpose is, etc. Also, account for changes in schedule, unfamiliar people, and their reasons for visiting. "First we'll have arts and crafts led by Clarence: then all those who have enough points will be going on the field trip, while others will stay here and contract for individual activities."

TRANSITIONS. Transitions may be routine or moment–to–moment changes in scheduling or setting. Many children in treatment have great difficulty in adjusting to any kind of change. Therefore, advance and repeated notice of these changes is important. For example, "In three minutes we'll clean up for lunch" (short-term transition) or "Next fall you'll be going back to regular school" (long-term transition, see the chapter on "Transitions").

EXPECTATIONS AND CONSEQUENCES. A child can obey the rules and make choices about his behavior if he has information about expectations and consequences for his actions in advance (see the chapter on "Setting Expectations and Contracting"). "Now, the expectation for the bus ride is that all kids will buckle their seat belts and keep them buckled so that no one will get hurt if we stop suddenly or have an accident. Those of you who follow expectations on the bus will get an extra snack when we get back."

Who Is Responsible

Often a child will interpret an event or feeling displayed by an adult as "his fault" when in fact it has nothing to do with the child. Clarifying the cause-and-effect relationship will stop the child's guilt and also demonstrate a more realistic connection between events. "Johnny, you didn't make me sad. I'm crying because my cat got run over last night."

Legitimization of Limits

Information about what behaviors lead to positive or negative consequences helps the child gain control of his behavior. Also important is knowing that the limits and consequences imposed on his behavior are not just a whim of the adults in his life but do have some logic. This will help him accept, though not necessarily like, those limits. "I'm insisting that you stay off of the monkey-bars because you have been putting yourself in dangerous positions, and I will not let you hurt yourself."

Emotional Information

Children need information about the feelings of the people around them. Since emotional information is conveyed through nonverbal as well as verbal channels, children are continually noticing feelings that they may not fully understand. Further verbal information helps to piece together the nonverbal cues and make sense out of them. This leads to a greater awareness of their own and other's feelings and the emotional consequences of human interactions. The treatment worker's being open and honest about his feelings helps to build trust between the worker and the child and gives the child the message that all feelings are okay. Reflecting your perceptions of the child's feeling state is the other part of emotional information (refer to "Reflection of Feelings"). For example:

> Norma, a treatment worker, has just been informed that one of her good friends is moving to another city. She comes to work feeling grieved and angry. In the morning meeting she tells the children, "Last night my good friend Sandy called and told me that she is moving to another city, and I'm feeling really bummed out about it today. I feel bad that we won't be sharing much time together any more, and I'm angry that she's leaving me behind. So, if I look like I'm moping around today, that's what it's all about."

Behavioral Information

Giving behavioral information means describing to the child his or your behavior, not making assumptions or ascribing intent. It is important to make these descriptions clear and concise, and it may be helpful to describe the behaviors step by step as they are occurring, thus talking the child through the process. In the beginning of treatment especially, it is difficult for many children to hear rambling orations on their behavior. These can be seen as threatening and scary. In a conference, Karen tells one of the kids, "I have noticed that whenever your mom walks in the room after her counseling session, you look down at the floor with a frown on your face and walk away from her. What's going on?"

Personal Information

This category involves the treatment worker's giving out information about his personal life as well as giving the child information about personal events occurring in her life. By disclosing personal information, the treatment worker becomes a "real person" and facilitates the building of a trusting, therapeutic relationship. He serves as a model and thus gives the child permission to be open. When the child discovers that she and an admired adult have had some common experiences, she may begin to feel that she is not so "strange" or "bad" as she had previously imagined. She may also find some helpful hints around problem-solving for disturbing personal issues. When giving a child this kind of information, the worker must do so with regard to the treatment goals for the child and the child's readiness to hear such information. It should not be done solely for the treatment worker's gratification (see the chapter on "Self-Disclosure).

Treatment Context Information

Our treatment philosophy says that a child has the right to information and treatment concerning his reality. Knowledge of the child's history and his present circumstances is essential to keep the therapist reality-oriented in her treatment. Be aware of the child's environment and what it takes to survive in that environment. Teaching a street kid never to use physical aggression and to trust everyone may deprive him of some essential survival mechanisms. The job here is to teach the child how to differentiate between one environment and the next. Certain behavior may not be allowed in the agency that may be allowed elsewhere and vice versa. Give the child ongoing information about these realities.

The child may deny his reality: what has happened, what is happening, and what will happen. This is true, for example, with foster children's fantasies of living with their parents. They may erroneously remember how happy they were with their parents and be convinced that their parents want them back when in fact the parents have no desire to take them back and their life together was tumultuous. The child should then be reminded of the reality of the situation. The treatment worker should sensitively choose an appropriate time and should take care to give the child only as much information as he can handle in his present emotional state. The treatment worker should then follow up with appropriate support messages (see "Confrontation").

Manner of Delivery

In order to be therapeutic, information must be given in a particular manner. For children in treatment, personal issues concerning their behavior and feelings are very loaded and can result in a negative emotional aftermath. In the following outline, the appropriate style of delivering information is discussed.

Specificity and Directness

Vague generalities and a roundabout manner convey the expectation to the child that the information may be too tough for her to handle (see "Use of Language"). They give the feeling of impending doom. Also, a hesitating style may lead the child to believe that there is some withholding of information and she may not trust what is being said.

Nonjudgemental Attitude

In general, personal, emotional, and behavioral information should be given in a matter-of-fact style. This aids in allaying the fear that a personal judgement is involved, especially about information that the child considers to be negative. Remaining nonjudgemental does not mean repressing feelings. If the treatment worker is feeling strongly about information that is being discussed, these feelings are being conveyed nonverbally. Trying to remain matter-of-fact will only lead to cue discrepancies and, thus, ingenuineness. At these times, the treatment worker should label his feelings and differentiate the emotional expression from value statements, e.g., "I'm saying I'm angry; I'm not saying you're bad." If the treatment worker is too emotional to remain nonjudgemental, he should give himself time away from the child specifying to her his reasons and when he will be back to discuss the issue. For example:

> After a fight on the playground, Jeanne storms into the art area, grabs Leon's painting and rips it apart. Treatment worker: "I really don't like that. I really get angry when you destroy another's work! It looks to me like what's happening is that you still have some unfinished business with Danny from recess, and instead of working out your anger with him, you're throwing it on Leon, who's a lot less big and scary. I want you to deal directly with both Danny and Leon and I'm willing to give you support if you want it."

Sensitivity to Overload

Refrain from giving the child more information than can be assimilated at one time. If there is a lot of information relevant to a particular issue, break it up and give it out over time.

Timing

Generally, immediacy is the key here. Information concerning a specific incident has greater impact and makes more sense when given as the incident is occurring. This is particularly true of behavioral and emotional information. However, there are times when the child is not ready to hear the information, and will therefore not use the information well. In this case, a delay is in order. Verbal and nonverbal cues (e.g., fidgeting and wandering eyes) will signal the child's receptivity. In some cases, especially when the child has continually been avoiding important information, it should be given "ready or not."

Thus it can be seen that information-sharing covers a broad area and is basic to treatment. It functions in facilitating behavioral changes, emotional acceptance and self-understanding, and trust-building, as well as making sense out of daily experiences.

Feeling and Issues for the Treatment Worker

Workers can both under-use and over-use the skill of information-giving.

"Oh, It Doesn't Matter Whether or Not He Knows, After All He's Only a Child."

In this case the worker discounts the importance of the child as a thinking, choosing, coping person. Children, just like anyone else, must respond to change. When they have information about changes in advance, they can prepare themselves appropriately. Even if they prepare themselves "inappropriately" by resisting or by becoming overwhelmed by the impending change, these issues can be dealt with before a transition so that the actual transition is less traumatic for both the child and the treatment worker.

"If I Tell Her In Advance She'll Only Raise a Fuss."

Fussing may be the child's way of expressing her feelings about the change. You can then deal with the fussing or the feelings underlying the fuss, or you can reassess whether or not the transition you have planned for the child is one that will ultimately work for her benefit. If treatment workers completely avoid arousing negative feelings in the children they work with, it is very likely that the children are not confronting some of the emotional issues they must cope with. The treatment worker statement above is really a justification for not dealing with the possible negative side-effects of the child's frustrations or fears of progress in treatment. The ultimate decision becomes a choice between the worker's comfort and the child's progress.

"Well, I'm Not Sure What's Going to Happen Myself, So How Can I Share Information With the Child?"

Some aspects of treatment or of the child's living situation are unpredictable. That is hard for the treatment worker to deal with, and certainly that is difficult for the child to deal with. However, rather than saying nothing about the situation, the treatment worker can model positive ways of coping with uncertainty. Such modeling may include listing the things that you know for sure, differentiating these from what you only imagine or hope. Likewise a treatment worker can share his feelings, i.e. that he is scared, worried, angry, frustrated, etc. Modeling will give the child permission to deal with his own feelings and provide possible alternatives for him in coping with his situation.

"I Can't Be Bothered Taking Time to Fill the Kid In On Everything. How Would I Ever Get Anything Else Done?"

First, it is not necessary to tell the child every detail of the coming day nor to fill her in on your every move. Over time children learn the daily routine and they know what to expect of you and the treatment setting. However, by following the information-sharing skill, you will find yourself telling the children you work with much more than you ever did before. Secondly, the treatment worker statement above also implies a choice between getting on with the daily schedule versus interrupting the schedule to deal with the child. We believe that the child comes before the schedule. Most of the time, with information-sharing incorporated into your daily routine and given constantly on a low-intensity level, you can plan information-sharing so that your daily schedule allows for necessary time given to the child.

"Well, If He Doesn't Already Know How He/I Feel/Behave, Then What Good Will It Do to Tell Him?"

This assumes that a child either knows or does not know some bit of information. If he knows, then there is no use in telling him because he already has the information; if he does not know, there is no use telling him because he is probably not smart enough to comprehend it since he did not figure it out by himself. Obviously the above pattern of thinking is a double-bind. There is no way the child can justify his receiving information. This kind of "Catch-22" reasoning leads treatment workers to behave in ways that only aggravate the child's mistrust and anger. Therefore, the child is more likely to act out and rebel. A treatment worker who withholds information will find himself using more controlling interventions because the child is consistently angry at him for putting him in the double-bind. This vicious cycle perpetuates itself indefinitely because the child feels justified in rebelling, and the treatment worker feels justified in continuing to control and to withhold information.

"It's My Responsibility to Make the Child Understand."

In one sense this is true. As a treatment worker you must give information in ways that the child can comprehend and use. However, some treatment workers translate the above statement into "It's my responsibility to make the child com-fortable with the information." In this case the treatment worker takes responsibility for something he has no control over: the child's feelings. We have seen treatment workers expend a great deal of energy trying to "make it all better." In these cases information-sharing can be over-used. If the child finds that she can vent her anger or delay some unpleasant consequence by not accepting your justifications for a particular action, further information-sharing only feeds the indirect feeling expression or allows avoidance of the consequence. In these cases the most important thing is that the child hear and can repeat your information, not that he agree with or like what you have said. (See Table 17-1.)

Table 17–1. Information-Sharing Behavior Checklist

Rate these behaviors according to the following scale: 0 = never; 1 = seldom; 2 = moderately; 3 = frequently; 4 = almost always.

Positive performance	*Problematic performance*
____ Gives all relevant general information	____ Withholds daily, routine information
____ Gives all relevant emotional information regarding the child	____ Withholds certain emotional and behavioral information
____ Gives all relevant emotional information regarding others	____ Avoids self-disclosure
____ Gives all relevant behavioral information–individual and interactional behaviors	____ Self-disclosure inappropriately
____ Self-disclosure in terms of general, behavioral, and emotional information	
Manner of delivery is:	Manner of delivery is:
____ Specific	____ Vague
____ Direct	____ Indirect
____ Nonjudgmental	____ Judgmental
____ Emotionally expressive	____ Inexpressive
____ Does not overload child with information	____ Repetitive and rambling
	____ Too much information for the child
Information timed appropriately in terms of:	____ Information the child is not ready for
____ Immediacy	____ Overprotective
____ Receptivity and need of child	

Part IV

BEHAVIOR MANAGEMENT

In this section of the book we address the very real and often crucial issue of behavior management. Sometimes treatment cannot go on until some of the noise and distractions in the therapeutic setting can be reduced, and some of the basic skills of coping and learning can be increased. In this section we will not go into great detail explaining the theoretical underpinnings and research associated with the various principles we introduce. Rather we will focus primarily on the nuts and bolts of applying the principles with troubled children. This choice on our part is not meant to diminish the value of understanding theory. Rather the choice represents our attempt to say what most other books on behavior management leave out. Experience is an excellent teacher; and experience has taught us that behavior management is a vital set of skills in any treatment worker's repertoire regardless of theoretical orientation. So, we hope to avoid waving a red flag in front of those of you who may have strong negative reactions to behavior modification by emphasizing techniques from several different theories in a practical way that will have positive results for you. Finally, although we separate the behavior-management techniques for ease of discussion and learning, they seldom occur in isolation in real life. We will attempt to illustrate some crucial and recurrent patterns of behavior which entangle the behavior-management principles.

Before getting into the specific skills you can use to increase behavior, we want to share some of our assumptions about behavior management which will help to put our presentations in perspective.

To begin with we assume that ultimate control of a person's behavior ought to come from internal sources and/or ought to be maintained by external factors in the "normal" environments of school, home, and job. We act on this assumption in a variety of different ways. First, we plan out interventions to move the child towards independence. That is, we exert our influence to advance the developmental stages that all individuals go through to become more autonomous within their capabilities. Secondly, we take advantage of the internal motivations that *do* exist within the child as a starting point. We do not undermine these positive motivations by imposing artificial external incentives which may lead the child to focus outward and discount his own existing motivation (Green & Lepper, 1974). For example, it would not be useful for a treatment worker to assume that a child needs an elaborate point system to learn reading skills when simply using the child's inherent motivation to learn and giving information concerning his progress would suffice. Thirdly, we arrange the least restrictive but effective method of behavior change. By doing this we allow more of the child's motivation to be used, and we have less controls to remove when the behavior reaches acceptable levels. We view behavior-management interventions as devices that temporarily bridge the gap between what the child can and will do now and what he needs to do to function effectively. Just as you would not deprive a child with a broken leg a crutch with which to gain mobility, neither would you allow the child to depend on that crutch after he could walk. Fourthly, because each individual and each environmental context is different, we expect that each application of intervention principles must take into account these differences.

Next, we suggest to you an "interactionist" view of behavior management. That is, we assume that the functional effect between behavior and environment goes both ways. We can influence our environment as much as we are influenced by it. Therefore, the dichotomy of choice versus control becomes a false distinction. We can adjust our environment so that it can help us, and we can teach children to do the same. If I want to lose weight, I can arrange my environment so that it makes weight loss more likely. Thus, I choose to have the environment control behavior. The key factor is knowing how your environment affects you so that you can get it to work for you.

Our third assumption is that environment has its effect whether we like it or not. Control issues cannot be escaped. Control is happening all around us everyday—yes, even now. So the question is not "Should I or should I not control?" but rather "How should I control?" One of the most tragic yet easily remedied errors we see people making falls into the category of accidental learning. Treatment workers can systematically and unknowingly intervene to increase the very behaviors that they believe they are working to decrease. Some people fear that systematic use of behavior management techniques will deprive people of freedom. Others may experience elation over the prospect of controlling others. In either case, control does not cease to exist. Our concern is how to use it technically correctly and in the service of positive values.

Finally, we assume behavior management does not account for all of child treatment. Certainly for some children and some treatment settings, behavior management will have a primary and continuing importance; yet there is more. The "more" that we refer to is related to the "more" that we have addressed in the beginning chapters of this book as it relates to you. And beyond that, the integration of behavior and beliefs, values, personality, and relationship dimensions represents a different level of functioning. Therefore, we call attention to the limits of behavior-management techniques.

Yet, even with the limits we have mentioned, it is unavoidably true that identifiable parts of the child's environment can be arranged in order to have predictable effects on that child's behavior.

Chapter 18

SETTING EXPECTATIONS AND CONTRACTING

After mastering the information in this chapter, you should be able to:—

1. formulate expectations for any given treatment context according to the guidelines of limit-setting;
2. discuss self-responsibility and self-management skills with regard to setting expectations;
3. discuss the rationale for providing choices and sharing the formulation of expectations;
4. identify and give examples of the ways in which delivery affects limit-setting;
5. discuss the desirable balance between consistency and flexibility;
6. identify and give examples of the use of limits as cues;
7. explain the concept of loopholing and ways of constructing loophole-free expectations;
8. relate setting expectations to non-behavioral levels of worker functioning as illustrated by "Feelings and Issues for the Treatment Worker."

Setting Expectations

Sometimes children do not meet expectations because they do not know what adults want. The easiest way to get children to cooperate is to tell them clearly and directly what you want them to do. Setting expectations and contracting are two ways to let the child know exactly what you want and what the consequences of his cooperation or non-cooperation will be. Desirable and undesirable behaviors and their consequences should be logical and understandable to the child, and should be based on the reasonable and fair requirements of the environmental setting as well as on the child's ability to meet the expectations.

Guidelines

When setting limits consider the following guidelines:

1. What behaviors does the child need to learn in order to function appropriately in his present and projected future environments?
2. What are the child's capabilities and limits, that is, what behaviors can he reasonably perform without undue stress?
3. What limits are important to the activity?
4. What are the safety needs of the setting?
5. What limits are necessary to protect the rights of the people in the environment?
6. Can the limit be enforced? Is there a consequence for the limit and can it be monitored?

If the limit does not appear to be reasonable in terms of the guidelines, it is most likely superfluous and should be discarded. Superfluous limits serve only to inhibit a child's learning processes and self-management skills. In addition, excessive limits and expectations arouse a feeling of being controlled and oppressed. Such feelings lead to rebellion. After answering the guideline questions, it will be possible to formulate positive behavioral goals. After formulating these goals, list undesirable behaviors that are incompatible with these goals and plan the social and physical environment to reduce the probability of the latter responses while encouraging the positive behaviors. This requires formulating the limits and verbalizing them to the children as well as providing a physical environment that facilitates these goals (see chapter on "Use of the Environment"). For example, it would be unreasonable to expect children to refrain from elbowing one another at the lunch table if they do not have adequate space between them.

Sharing the Power

Whenever possible, the child should have input on the limits and consequences and agree upon them. This teaches a child to provide for his needs and increases the likelihood that the limits will be followed without disruption. It also demonstrates that expectations are not arbitrary whims of the adult. Discussing and developing the rationale for the expectation provides legitimate logical reason for it; that is, it makes sense to the child.

WORKER: We have a new toy—a tricycle.
KIDS: Oh, boy! Let's ride it right now.
WORKER: OK, but first what should the expectations be about using the tricycle so that everyone gets a turn without fighting, and people who don't want to ride it can play with other things without being run over, or forced to move.
KIDS: Well, how about if we only ride it outside. Maybe we could use the timer to share the time on the trike. How about anyone who bumps someone else is off the trike for the day . . .

Providing Choices

Providing choices needs to be done only when the child has a compliance problem around a particular issue. In the absence of such a problem, it is superfluous and many times damaging to imply this degree of need for external controls. Given a history of the child's internalization of this choice process, the worker must respect the child's self-responsibility. In this case, a worker may need only to call attention to an upcoming event that implies an expectation. For example, a simple "It's time to clean up," or even less intrusive, "Play group is over," may suffice to convey the expectations of putting away toys.

When a child has not developed such internal processes or when non-compliance is most likely, choice-giving is a mediating step toward positive decision-making. The choice may be a series of acceptable alternatives, or a paired positive and negative alternative. Choice within limits provides the child with two or more actions that all fall within the acceptable range. For example: "You can pick up your toys first or clean up your crafts project first. Which will it be?" Even though this does not seem like much of a choice, children often experience more freedom than if the same requests were made individually.

With paired positive/negative choices the child hears that he can adhere to the rules and experience a positive consequence, or choose not to and experience a specified negative consequence. This builds self-responsibility. "Pick up the tinker toys in one minute!" poses a threat, denies choices, and may increase anger or fear, thereby inhibiting the desired behavior. "Pick up the tinker toys in one minute and you may go out for free time, or choose not to and stay in" offers a choice available and makes consequences clear.

Manner of Delivery

The manner in which expectations are stated will either help or hinder the child's ability and willingness to cooperate.

GIVE AND GET ATTENTION Attend to the child with your eyes and body as well as your words. Ask the child to do the same for you. Casting your expectations to the ceiling or to the child's back makes them less likely to be followed.

BREVITY Say it in twenty-five words or less. Too many words may lose the child or overwhelm her. If she is tuning out, she obviously can not hear and respond.

STATED WITHIN THE CHILD'S ABILITY TO COMPREHEND Again, if the words or concepts are beyond the child's ability to understand, she will not be able to cooperate.

MATTER-OF-FACT NONVERBAL CUES A condescending tone or hostile posture can raise resistance regardless of how well an expectation is otherwise expressed. A foot-tapping, hands-on-hips, impatient body position during the child's responding well to expectations, or during a delay before his responding may undo otherwise good expectation setting.

CLARITY Obviously the criteria outlined in the "Use of Language" chapter apply here: language that is non-equivocal, exact, descriptive, nonjudgmental. Also important with demands or requests for action from another is the imperative level of communication. When giving expectations the command or request should be direct and obvious, not implied. (See Table 18-1.)

The most common indirect command or request is the question implying choices that the adult does not mean to give as options. For example, how familiar is the following interaction?

WORKER: "Don't you want to help the other kids clean up for lunch?"
CHILD: "No!"

We do not mean to imply that you should never give commands or requests in the form of questions. Just remember to be precise about the choices you really want to offer.

Table 18–1.

The example below illustrates types of direct and indirect expectations.

	Indirect	*Direct*
Abstract rule	"We don't do that here."	"I don't want you to do that."
Question rather than statement	"Wouldn't you like to . . ." "How about doing . . ." "Would it be OK with you if you did the dishes?"	"Please do the dishes."
Discounting of feelings	"You really don't want to do that."	"Stop doing that." or "I want you to stop that."
Vague time expectation	"Some time when you get around to it would you please . . ."	"Before lunch I want you to . . ."

TIMING The key here is to give expectations in advance. By giving advance notice you stand in good position to follow through with the positive or negative consequences you have planned. If expectations are given during the heat of the activity, you will have to deal with distracted and frustrated children who feel you have changed the rules on them. Most settings have general expectations that must be explained to new members. Children will test these general expectations from time to time, and so, they will probably need to be repeated often enough for all the children to stay refreshed. If your group is engaging in a familiar activity which they have not done for a long time, general expectations would be best reviewed, for example, if the time between field trips has been long. Any new situation also calls for setting expectations.

Limits as Cues

As you give expectations, you must assume that expectations are made to be followed. Worker mediated consequences paired with the child's cooperation and non-cooperation teach the child to weigh the costs and benefits of choosing his course of action. Ideally, when an expectation is given clearly and directly, it will serve as a cue to appropriate behavior. You may from time to time have to remind the children or ask him to restate the expectations. Such reminding and restatement, if used *sparsely* and only with *new expectations*, will serve to prompt memory. At times, just a word or two or a nonverbal signal will suffice. For example, to remind the kids that they are to be quiet, a simple "Quiet time" or a finger over the lips will convey the message. Repeating expectations too often teaches the child that you expect him not to internalize expectations and, therefore, that he should depend on you to remind him.

Consistency

When working with a team it is especially necessary that rules be planned in advance and agreed upon in order to ensure consistency. Although changing expectations in midstream should be avoided if possible, it is sometimes necessary in a creative and flexible program that is designed around the needs of kids. In these instances, quickly get team consensus and inform the children of the change.

In order to help children follow your expectations, you will have to demonstrate over time that you mean what you say. Again, given clear and direct expectations, the factor that will convince children that you mean what you say is your follow-through with an appropriate positive or negative consequence. New workers sometimes have the mistaken notion that they can manage their children's behavior by using only words. Most workers quickly learn that the only way a worker can gain control over children through her use of words is to back those words consistently with actions. Expectations in a treatment setting are given with the intent that they be followed, and the recognition that they will very often be broken. Thus, expectations must be designed to accommodate a child's testing limits. The long-range outcome of limit-testing should be growth for the child. Therefore, each incident of breaking expectations may be seen as a treatment opportunity, not merely as a problem in management.

Loopholing

In addition to violating expectations to see if you mean what you say, some children become very good at finding the loopholes in your verbalized expectations. For example, a child may comply with an expectation that there be no running in the classroom by crawling, skipping, hopping, or turning cartwheels. After all, only running was restricted. In order to outmaneuver the "loophole lawyer" or the "worker deaf" child you can routinely make your expectations loophole free and ask the child to repeat the expectation back to you.

Components of a Loophole-Free Expectation:

1. Objectively-described behavior stated in positive terms: e.g., "Stay in your seat," versus "Don't get up to sharpen your pencil."

2. Statement of criteria of the behavior
   a) How much behavior: e.g., "Three math problems"
   b) Statement of how long the behavior is to last: e.g., ". . . until lunch."
   c) Statement of acceptable performance: e.g., ". . . all the toys in this room put back where they belong."
   d) Starting time limit: e.g., "Start after you finish reading that chapter."
   e) Completion time limit: e.g., "You have fifteen minutes to get done."
   f) Statement of method of performance: e.g., "Use the broom."
3. Objectively-described high-probability non-acceptable behavior: e.g., "I specifically want you to stay out of the cleaning closet."
4. Specify positive consequence paired with acceptable performance of expectation.
5. Specify negative consequence paired with non-acceptable performance of expectation.

For many children a loosely stated expectation will convey your intent, and that is enough to promote cooperation. Other children will make you work harder by requiring you to add some or all of the above loophole-stoppers to your intent.

A clear statement of expectations and consequences made in advance of the activity aids in creating the structure and predictability necessary to treatment. Within this structure, the probability of achieving positive behavioral goals is greatly enhanced.

Self-Fulfilling Prophecies and Expectations

Sometimes the anticipations that a worker has about how a child will behave (that is, her beliefs, fantasies and peredictions about a child's behavior in specific contexts) influences that child's behavioral performance. These beliefs are conveyed to a child subtly and usually through nonverbal channels, often outside the person's awareness. For example, if a worker feels that a child will behave positively, his body may be relaxed and open, his voice tone warm and positive, and his face soft and smiling. This kind of demeanor is felt as supportive by the child and creates conditions that maximize the probability of success. Conversely, negative beliefs have a negative, nonsupportive effect.

A well-known study by Rosenthal (1968) cited in *Pygmalion in the Classroom* clearly demonstrates the effects of preconceived expectations. In the study, teachers were, without their knowledge, given inaccurate I.Q.

scores on their students. At the study's conclusion, it was found that the students performed at their *believed* rather than *actual* intelligence levels. The author infers that the teacher's beliefs about performance levels were subtly conveyed to the children, thus influencing their self-concepts which in turn affected academic performance.

The lesson here is not that a worker should not expect a particular outcome or that she should fear the power of her beliefs. The lesson is simply that our assumption influences what will be, and that self-awareness and self-monitoring are important in carrying out and evaluating therapeutic programs.

CONTRACTING

A contract is a more formalized statement, either verbal or written, of expectations and consequences. Contracts aid in teaching children self-determination, responsibility, how to make decisions and choices, and aid in increasing their awareness of their abilities. Contracts can be devised for a child by the treatment worker or can be formulated mutually. They can be short-term (e.g., during an activity) or long-term (e.g., over a week or month). The behavior covered in the contract must be specific and easy to track. If the contract is verbal, it is important to *make eye contact* and have the child repeat the terms of the contract. If it is written, it should be reviewed with the child, verbally repeated or paraphrased by the child, and signed. Sometime treatment workers forget to track nonverbal as well as verbal cues when they ask the child for commitment to follow through with a contract. A child can agree to the contract verbally while contradicting himself nonverbally. Some typically nonverbal statements of non-agreement include breaking eye contact, disowning language such as "I guess," or "I'll try," fidgeting, whiny or angry tone of voice, and a nervous laugh. A treatment worker who accepts a nonverbal contradicted contract as valid invites frustration and anger at the child. (See Figure 18-1.) A positive example of how to handle such a situation follows.

WORKER: OK, I've reviewed the contract with you and you've been able to say it back to me. Now I want a commitment from you that you will abide by the contract.

CHILD: Yeah, I guess I will.

WORKER: "I guess" isn't going to make it. I want you to sit quietly, look me in the eye, and say, "I will abide by this contract."

CHILD: I'll try, that's all I can do.

WORKER: Not good enough. I want you to do what I just asked you to do.

CHILD: Sure, sure. I will abide by this contract, ha, ha!

WORKER: I can see you're having a hard time making a commitment right now. Your sarcastic tone and laugh tell me you're not ready. I'll get back to you later, or you can find me when you're ready to make a commitment. For now we don't have a contract.

This example is very confrontive, yet this confrontation reflects the necessity of getting complete commitment before accepting the contract as valid.

Example of a written contract:

I (child's name) agree to (objective statement of positive behavior and performance criteria). Upon completion I will receive (positive consequence).

Signed: (child)
(treatment worker)

Penalty clause: If I do, (objective statement of negative behavior) then I will earn (negative consequence).

I Robbie Jones agree to remove myself from all fight situations on the playground during recess each day from Tuesday to Thursday of this week by either walking away, playing with other kids, or talking to my treatment worker. Upon completion I will receive after each successful recess, 5 minutes of free play time with my treatment worker to talk or play.

Signed: Child: Robbie Jones
Treatment worker
Barney Bagle

Penalty clause; If I do get myself into a fight, then I will miss 15 minutes of recess time either that day or the following day.

For many children you may not need to include the penalty clause. The withholding of the positive for nonfulfillment may be enough. For other children, the penalty (response cost) clause is advisable (see "Decreasing Behavior" for guidelines).

Upon completion of the contract, it should be evaluated and continued, discontinued, or revamped. If a contract is not working, determine why and attempt to correct it rather than discard it. Some common reasons for contracts not working include: the contractual period is too short or too long: the behavioral expectations are too high for the child's skill level; the positive consequence is not appropriate; other responses or consequences interfere with behavior.

Figure 18-1. Invalidation of Verbal Contract

Feelings and Issues for the Treatment Worker

Both the proficiency at setting expectations and contracting, and the personality of the treatment worker affect the worker's ability to use these skills effectively.

"You will Follow These Expectations, or Else."

Setting and following through with expectations can lead to power struggles between treatment worker and child. If the treatment worker sees making the child comply as the major issue, then he is likely getting caught by his need to control. It may seem paradoxical that expectations and contracts are used to enhance a child's self-control; yet that is the goal. Coercion or external threat do not facilitate a child's learning self-control.

"But We Can't Change Our Plans Now Just Because Irving is Crying."

Irving's crying may indicate many different things, some of which may call for a change in expectations and some of which may not. However, to perceive adherence to a preconceived plan as more important than responding to the needs of a child puts the cart before the horse. Plans are made to treat children, not children forced to fit plans. If there is a conflict, the child always comes first. This does not mean that you abandon plans lightly at the first sign of a tear. Your team structure may allow you both to carry on and to minister to the individual child by having one worker focus on the child while the others stay with the group.

"If He Doesn't Learn to Mind, How Will He Ever Get Better?"

This statement implies that compliance and treatment are one and the same. This equation is not valid. Compliance is not a reliable indicator of mental health. Some chronic inmates of mental hospitals follow directions quite dociley. Certainly, both the child's life and your life may be made easier by his cooperative response to expectations, but that is not the ultimate goal.

"But I Asked Him Nicely At Least Twelve Times, Why Doesn't He Do It?"

There are at least two errors in this statement. First, twelve times is too many reminders. One or two reminders may serve as prompts for following expectations. More than that are grounds to label the child's behavior as non-cooperative. Secondly, the worker sounds as if she is expecting her voice and words to control the child's behavior. As mentioned before, words must be backed with actions.

"What Good Does It Do To Lay Out Expectations? I Have To Be On Her Back Anyway Because She Always Mucks Up!"

Consistent follow-through can be a drag. There may be times you would much rather be doing something else. Backing your words with actions takes most energy when the children are testing to see if you really mean what you say and whether or not they can trust you. This testing process is an important part of treatment for most children. The long-term payoff for them is worth the effort. If you find no reduction in the amount of monitoring you have to do after setting expectations, then examine the expectation-setting and follow-through process. Something is not right. If expectations are correctly used, the amount of testing and therefore the amount of follow-through you have to do will decrease over time.

"Well, Shouldn't Anyone That Age Just Know How to Act?"

The passage of time is no guarantee that a child will learn appropriate behavior. Children do not "just know" the rules of behavior relevant to specific situations; they learn those rules. Children who are more sensitive to unspoken messages and compliant to indirect commands may behave as if they "just know" what to do; they are unlikely to cause the adults in their life many problems. It would be easier for all of us if children knew how we wanted them to behave and then did so. But we do not live in that fantasy land, and children do not have instincts for expected behavior. Neither can children read our minds. So, the burden of providing education about expectations falls on the treatment worker.

"The Kids Will Think I'm a Bad Guy If I Really Enforce The Expectations."

Some treatment workers want so intensely to be liked by their children that they undermine their own effectiveness by failing to follow through effectively with expectations. Failing to follow through has two effects. First, the children learn not to trust your words. Therefore, you are constantly being pushed to ignore violations of your previously set limits. Secondly, the children come to disrespect you. Trust in children is built by being trustworthy, and part of trustworthiness comes from enforcing limits. Even if the children do not like the limits in the short run, your enforcement will build your credibility in the long run.

"If You Don't Come Here Right This Instant, I'll Knock Your Block Off."

Another related reason why some treatment workers fail to follow through on limits is that they have unenforceable expectations. That is, the behavior expected is beyond the child's abilities or the consequences are undeliverable. "Doomsday" threats or outlandish positive consequences cannot be delivered. Expectations and contracts must be performable by the child with whom they are made. Consequences must be realistic.

"He Said He'd Follow Through, But Now He's Not. How Can I Trust Him?"

If the child does not follow through on a commitment to a contract, then you must look to deeper levels of the child's personality for blocks to follow through. It is probable that the worker mistakenly thought that he had a valid commitment from the child when, in fact, he did not. Some ways of contradicting a verbal commitment are obvious and some not so obvious. Most contradictions, however, are observable during the contracting process if we pay attention to them. To ignore such nonverbal cues will lead the worker to mistrust the child and to frustrate himself. The treatment worker must also be able to confront the child about his contradictory behavior and must be able to stick by his guns about his perception of nonverbal commitment. The key for the worker's well-being and for the child's growth is that the worker *not* accept an invalid contract.

"I Can See That He's Reluctant to Give Me a Full Commitment, But I'll Accept It Anyway Because The Contract is Bound to Help Him."

This treatment worker wants the child to succeed so much that she undermines his learning to bear the consequences of his own behavior. Such a strategy, although done with the best of intentions, teaches the child how to manipulate others rather than how to take constructive control of his behavior. It also implies that the child is in fact unable to deal with his life without someone taking care of him. (See Table 18-2.)

Quality factors—Describe worker performance in relation to the following:
Setting Expectations—

1. loophole-free for "loophole lawyers"
2. safety factors considered
3. team informed of new limits—has team consensus
4. expectations supported by the physical environment

Contracting—
1. evaluates contract after brief passage of time
2. makes changes if necessary

Table 18–2. Setting Expectations and Contracting Behavior Checklist

For each occurrence of setting expectations or contracting, check which of the behaviors below occurred:

Positive performance	*Problematic performance*
Setting expectations:	Setting expectations:
____ Laid out in advance	____ Given after the fact
____ Stated positively when possible	____ Stated in judgmental, condemning, or threatening manner
____ Involves a choice	____ "Doomsday" threats
____ Stated concisely	____ Questions used where commands are intended
____ Stated clearly	____ Overly complicated statement
____ Logical and understandable	____ No follow-through or inconsistent follow-through
____ Important to child's present and future functioning	____ Too many reminders
____ Within child's capabilities	____ Superfluous limits
____ Can be enforced	____ No room for child input
____ Important to the activity	____ Harsh or tentative delivery
____ Child has input when appropriate	
____ Matter-of-fact or pleasant delivery	
____ Only as many limits as can be absorbed	
____ Consequences follow consistently	
____ Used as cues or prompts when appropriate	
Contracting verbally:	Contracting verbally:
____ Has child repeat contract correctly	____ Accepts contract with verbal or nonverbal disclaimers
____ Gets eye contact	____ No follow-through
____ Tracks behavior	
____ Follows with consequence	
Contracting in writing:	Contracting in writing:
____ Has child repeat contract correctly	____ Accepts contract without assessing child's understanding the terms
____ Signs with child	____ No follow-through
____ Tracks behaviors	
____ Follows through with consequences	

Chapter 19

INCREASING BEHAVIOR

After mastering the information in this chapter, you should be able to—

1. define and give examples of positive and negative reinforcement;
2. explain the concept of empirical definition and why it is important to understanding the principles of reinforcement;
3. explain the complications arising from viewing the consequent stimulus as the source of the positive or negative quality of reinforcement;
4. list five types of reinforcers and give examples;
5. list and explain eleven conditions of delivery of positive reinforcement;
6. explain the rationale for moving from external to internal labels for behavior being reinforced;
7. contrast and compare negative reinforcement and punishment;
8. define and explain the treatment significance of escape, avoidance, and coercion;
9. relate increasing behavior methods to non-behavioral levels of worker functioning as illustrated by "Feelings and Issues for the Treatment Worker."

Increasing Behavior Through Positive Reinforcement

If you want to increase behavior, use positive reinforcement. The process of positive reinforcement occurs when a stimulus delivered as a consequence of a behavior increases the likelihood of the behavior occurring again.

BEHAVIOR + STIMULUS = INCREASED LIKELIHOOD OF BEHAVIOR

The process of positive reinforcement is defined by the *effect* that the consequent stimulus has on the behavior. Thus, this empirical definition depends upon the result of the procedure. For example, if you give Johnny a cookie after he cleans up his toys, you will have to wait to see whether or not he cleans up his toys again before establishing that the cookie was in fact positively reinforcing. Recognizing the necessity of empirical definition will allow you to avoid the most often made error in using positive reinforcement: expecting a specific stimulus, such as a cookie, *always* to have positively reinforcing properties. Or even more commonly, to expect that seemingly aversive consequences, such as being yelled at or spanked, *never* to be positively reinforcing. The proof of the reinforcer lies in the effect of consequent presentation, not in the stimulus itself.

Finding Reinforcers

Beyond the basic definition many practical issues arise when using positive reinforcement. First, you will need to select some stimulus that is in fact positively reinforcing. You could arrive at this selection by trying a wide variety of stimuli to see what works, by asking the child what she likes and would work for, by observing what the child selects naturally, and by observing what the child does most frequently. In the long run you will have to try your selection to see if it produces the desired effect, but certainly you can narrow the choices by asking and observing.

In your search for positive reinforcers you can consider several categories. *Edible* objects come most often to mind as reinforcers: cookies, candy, fruit, juice, corn chips, etc. *Tangible objects* of the non-edible variety can be used: toys, models, books, games, etc. *Activities* can also be used as positive reinforcers: playing, watching TV, reading, sitting in a favorite chair, smelling perfume, etc. *Social reinforcers* are the most easily dispensed, are free, and come from a virtually inexhaustible supply: praise, smiles, hugs, tickles, winks, etc. Finally, *tokens* can be distributed as credit to be traded in on any of the above reinforcers: marks on a chart, stars, smiling faces, money, etc. The possibilities for positive reinforcers are limited only by your and the children's imagination.

Conditions of Delivery

You will have to arrange to deliver the potential positive reinforcers you have selected under certain conditions in order to have maximum effect.

The expectations must be given in advance, and must be stated *clearly* and *positively.* Reinforcement should not be used in a guessing game. The child needs to know exactly what is expected of him and exactly what he will get for following through with those expectations. Also, expectations must be put forth in a positive manner stating what a child *will* get for doing what you *want,* not what he *won't* get for doing what you *don't* want.

The reinforcer must be given *after* the behavior. This at first seems obvious, but how many times have you heard, "Okay, one more game, then join the meeting." This is the reverse of reinforcement. It should be, "After the meeting you may play one more game."

The reinforcer must follow the behavior immediately. Only then can one be sure that one is reinforcing the desired behavior. If there is a delay, the child may be performing an undesirable behavior at the time the reinforcer comes. For example, if a child is told that he can play with a favorite toy for cooperating with a peer, but delivery of the toy is delayed, he may be fighting with the child when the toy is finally given to him. This would reinforce fighting behavior rather than cooperation. Of course, verbal information, especially with older children, can aid in bridging a time gap in the case when reinforcement must be delayed. In this instance, verbal recognition becomes a reinforcer for the immediate behavior, and verbal information given with the major reinforcer links it to the desired behavior.

Reinforcement must be *consistent.* If a child is reinforced for one behavior at one time and not the next, or if incompatible behaviors are reinforced at different times, the child will become confused, and the desired behavior will not be fully learned.

The act of reinforcement must *match the reinforcing person's verbal and nonverbal behavior.* If praise is being used, then the voice tone and facial expression must be positive in order to match the words. Frowning and speaking in a harsh tone when praising will give the child a confusing double message and will weaken the reinforcer: we call this a split-reinforcer. It is your task as a treatment worker to find something to be genuinely positive about, even if it is only that the child is "breathing well!" (See Figure 19-1.)

The reinforcer must be of an *appropriate strength.* If it is too weak (e.g., a candy bar for a month of perfect group participation), the child may find that it is not worth making the effort. If it is too strong, (e.g., a banana split for one participation), the child may become satiated and may not be motivated to improve.

When a child is *first learning* a behavior, it must be reinforced *each time.* The expectations must be within his present capabilities and he must experience immediate success in order to make further growth. As the behavior becomes well established and easier for the child to perform, it must be reinforced *less often.* This kind of variable reinforcement strengthens the behavior (see chapter on "Transfer and Maintenance").

Figure 19-1. Split Reinforcer

Use a *variety* of reinforcers. The same old reinforcer gets boring after a while and loses its strength.

Pair verbal reinforcement, such as praise, with other kinds of reinforcers. This will eventually give verbal reinforcement strength to stand on its own. The behavior can then be maintained largely by positive comments. Descriptive praise also gives the child information about her behavior and its impact on the social environment.

Be *specific* when using verbal reinforcement. Tell the child *exactly* what you liked, e.g., "I like the way you went right to your desk without complaining when asked," rather than making a general comment, e.g., "Nice job."

Know which behavior you are reinforcing. Sometimes treatment workers reinforce positive behaviors that only can occur as a result of some previous negative behavior. For example, praising a child each time she pulls her thumb out of her mouth will probably increase both thumb-pulling-out-of-mouth behavior and the thumb-putting-into-mouth behavior that must precede it. Rather, find a behavior to reinforce that does not exist because of some other undesirable behavior.

Be aware of the possible *interfering effects* that the reinforcer might have on the behavior it is to reinforce. For example using licks of ice cream to reinforce pages of reading may lead to sticky fingers, sticky pages, and generally sticky situation. Likewise using high-sugar-content items to reinforce quiet behavior may lead to a "sugar high" which is incompatible with quiet behavior.

Positive Reinforcer Backlash

Upon presenting the selected reinforcer under the appropriate conditions, you may find the effect you want missing, or, in opposition to your intent. If this occurs, consider the following:

1. You have selected the wrong reinforcer for the specific moment. Kids can become satiated easily. Try a different one.
2. You may be arousing resistance to control in the child. If this is the case, you can become *less specific* about what it is you are reinforcing. For example, rather than praising a recently completed painting (knowing that in the past such praise was followed by the child's ripping the painting to shreds) you might suddenly remember a great game that you and the child might play, not mentioning at all the connection in your mind between the painting and the consequence of playing the game.

Discounting Reinforcers

Another response to reinforcers that can dilute their power is the discount. Discounts are demonstrations of non-acceptance of the reinforcement, and can occur in four ways:

1. By ignoring the reinforcement
2. By denial: "That's beautiful"
"No it's not."
3. By devaluing: "What a pretty dress."
"Oh, this old rag."
4. By shifting the credit: "I like that drawing."
"Oh, my treatment worker helped me."

These kinds of discounts may signal to the treatment worker that the child's self-concept needs to be improved. Also the reinforcer may be at a level that is too intense, or may be focusing on especially vulnerable areas for the child.

Flexible Verbal Reinforcement

You can aim the focus of your reinforcement at many different levels of the child's behavior. This focus varies along a dimension of external to internal behavior. For example, if a child has just completed a page of math problems, you can say, a) "Great math paper." (focus on the paper); b) "I like how quickly you finished your math." (focus on the speed of completion); c) "I'm impressed at how carefully you worked on your paper." (focus on the care he took); d) "I could see that you were thinking really hard while you were working—neat!" (focus on the process of thinking); e) "Isn't it fun to be done?" (focus on the joy of being done). Readjusting your focus to internal levels may also help you to avoid arousing resistance to control in children because you are merely bringing to their attention the positive events they are experiencing within themselves rather than to your attempts to get them to perform. Refer to the chapter on "Observation" if you have difficulty conceptualizing how this might be done. Those of you familiar with child-rearing approaches based on Adler's work (Dreikurs, 1958) will recognize this paragraph as addressing some of the issues raised with the concept of encouragement.

Another way to look at the flexible use of verbal reinforcement reflects different types of acknowledging and valuing statements. If a child builds a tower of blocks the treatment worker may respond on several different levels:

ACKNOWLEDGE THE PRODUCT: "I see you've built a tower."

ACKNOWLEDGE THE PROCESS: "That must have taken quite a bit of concentration."

VALUE THE BEHAVIOR AS IT RELATES TO FUNCTION: "That looks like the kind of tower that could be a boundary marker in a game of soccer."

VALUE THE BEHAVIOR IN TERMS OF HOW IT RELATES TO STANDARDS: "That's one of the straightest towers I've ever seen."

VALUE THE BEHAVIOR AS IT RELATES TO THE BEHOLDER: "I like it. I'm impressed with your tower."

VALUE THE BEHAVIOR AS IT RELATES TO THE EXPERIENCE OF THE CHILD: "I can see that you're pleased with your tower."

Selection of the level of reinforcement will depend upon the child's ability to accept that level and upon the child's treatment issues. That is, the worker may use one level when focusing on skill acquisition and another when focusing on self-awareness.

The non-evaluative attention given in the two types of acknowledging mentioned above, and relating the behavior to the experience of the child, helps to avoid social reinforcer backlash. By implying external control and by comparison of the child's behavior with standards other than his own, backlash may increase.

Consider phrasing your expectations and verbal reinforcers to make the most of attributing responsibility and choice to the child. Choices for behavior do in fact reside in the child no matter how tightly you have arranged the environment to produce a specific effect. Since you will be trying to move the child to greater and greater assumption of responsibility for his behavior, the ways in which you reinforce and set expectations should reflect the child's progress towards this goal. For example, you can reinforce the child for catching a negative behavior at an *early-cue* level before he exhibits a higher-level behavior. In addition, as a side-effect, the child will come to internalize his behavioral controls more and more as he comes to learn that he does have increasing control.

Arranging the Environment

A fundamentally and yet often overlooked procedure is to arrange the environment so that the behavior you want will be more likely to happen. You will have to work harder to get children to sit quietly in the middle of a noisy playground than in the middle of a small, quiet room. Each environmental situation has a set of behavioral "demand characteristics." Beware of these and use them to your advantage (refer to the chapter on "Use of the Environment").

INCREASING BEHAVIOR THROUGH NEGATIVE REINFORCEMENT

The process of negative reinforcement occurs when a stimulus removed as a consequence of a behavior increases the likelihood of that behavior occurring again. As with positive reinforcement, the empirical definition holds. Thus, the effect defines the process, not the quality of the stimulus. For example, the pain caused by George's hitting Sara can be removed by Sara's running away. The running-away behavior was followed by the removal of the pain-inducing stimulus; therefore running away is more likely to occur in that situation in the future. The usual model of negative reinforcement is based on pain or tension reduction: it is like hitting your head with a hammer; it feels so good when you stop. (See Figure 19-2.)

Figure 19-2. Increasing Behavior

Negative Reinforcement and Punishment

Theoretically the distinction between negative reinforcement and punishment is clear. Negative reinforcement *increases* behavior through consequent removal of an aversive stimulus. Punishment *decreases* behavior through consequent presentation of an aversive stimulus. However, in practice two things lead to confusion of the principles.

First, in usual practice the stimuli that are either presented or removed have adverse qualities. Therefore, people attribute the "negativeness" of negative reinforcement to the unpleasant quality of the stimuli rather than the process of subtracting that stimulus. Secondly, the adverse stimuli that children work to remove, thereby achieving negative reinforcement, have often been originally presented as a consequence for some other previous behavior. For example, if you were to hold the hands (presentation of aversive stimulus) of a child who was beating on your arm to get your attention, you could say, "I will let go of your hands (removal of adverse stimulus) as soon as you stop." In this example, the *presentation* of the stimulus was a punishment for beating on you; the *removal* was negative reinforcement for stopping. Thus, punishment and the opportunity to remove adverse conditions often go hand in hand.

Because negative reinforcement contains aversive stimuli, it falls subject to all of the potential negative side effects of punishment which we will discuss in the next chapter. Therefore, you must be alert to track its effects carefully.

Escape and Avoidance

People work to escape aversive stimuli. Anything they do which relieves the pain and tension becomes negatively reinforced. For example, a child's looking down or away while being scolded increases with its effectiveness at decreasing the intensity of the scolding. When a predictable cue announces the onset of an aversive condition, the child learns to avoid that aversiveness altogether. Thus, the avoidance is negatively reinforced. For example, children may lie in response to an angry, accusatory question or cheat in order to avoid the scolding that they predict will happen when they tell the truth. When you are observing a child, you may find no adverse stimuli occurring which could account for negative reinforcement of a behavior. Sometimes the absence of such stimuli means that the avoidance behavior has been learned so well that the child does not allow the aversive situation that once motivated the behavior to occur. This situation can be distressing to treatment workers when they try to help a child overcome a self-defeating avoidance behavior. For example, it may be difficult to arrange for a child to have a pleasant experience with a dog, thus showing him that not all dogs bite, once he has learned to avoid dogs because of past experiences.

Pain–Learning and Coercion

Much of our behavior is motivated by avoidance of pain and tension. Infants use this principle effectively by crying until their caretakers find and relieve the distressing condition: hunger, cold, wet, loneliness, gas. Troubled children also often excel in using their aversive behavior coercively to demand care and attention. It is amazing how well children learn what our "buttons" are, and how to push them. Pain-learning, as opposed to positively reinforced learning, occurs quickly and resists extinction.

Patterns of Behavior

Below is an illustration of a pattern of behavior that meshes the effects of positive and negative reinforcement (See Table 19-1.) This all too common pattern is explained and one remedy offered.

In the second version, the statement of the child's personal responsibility in maintaining his own unhappiness dilutes the potential for coercion.

Table 19–1. The Coercion Cycle

Child: (whiney voice) But why can't I go out and play?	Child's whining and nagging are aversive to treatment worker.
TW: I've told you twelve times now that you have to put your toys away before you go outside.	TW's keeping child in from playtime is aversive to child.
Child: (whine) But playtime is almost over. I'll put them away as soon as I come back in, honest.	Child's repeated aversives used as coercion on TW.
TW: Oh, all right. I don't want you to miss all of playtime. But you clean up as soon as you come back in.	TW's releasing child to play (a) negatively reinforces child for whining and nagging by removing tension of not playing and, (b) positively reinforces whining and nagging by following that behavior with play.
TW rubs her ears and gets a cup of coffee.	TW's not sticking to limits with child is (a) negatively reinforced by removing the whining and nagging and (b) positively reinforced by coffee drinking and free time. Notice that both the child and TW reinforce each other to maintain this cycle.
Remedy for the Coercion Cycle:	
Child: (whiney voice) But why can't I go out and play?	Child's whining and nagging are aversive to TW.
TW: You can exercise your choice to go outside by putting your toys away.	TW's keeping child in from playtime is aversive to child. TW describes the contingency as a choice for which the child is responsible.
Child: (whine) But playtime is almost over. I'll put them away as soon as I come back in. Honest.	Child's repeated aversion used as coercion on TW.
TW: First you put away the toys, then go outside. It's your choice how long it takes. Your actions, not your words, will show me when you're ready to go out.	TW restates the contingencies, restates the child's responsibility for choice, and indicates that deeds not words will have an effect.
TW ignores further nagging and whining and allows child to go out only after toys are put away.	TW attends only to behavior stated in the contingency, not allowing further aversive child behavior to have impact.

The treatment worker's follow-through allows the child only one way to relieve the tension of not playing. Therefore, putting-away-toys behavior will be reinforced.

Feelings and Issues for the Treatment Worker

"Isn't Positive Reinforcement Really Bribery?"

No, it is not. Bribery implies that someone is paid or rewarded as a result of illegal or unethical acts. That certainly is not the case here. The behaviors reinforced are positive ones leading to "healthier" functioning. However, positive reinforcement can be perverted to simulate bribery in that rewards can be made coercively positive. Consider the following example:

TREATMENT WORKER: Cheri, hang up your coat if you want a token.
CHERI: Aw, I don't care if I get one or not.
TREATMENT WORKER: Well, how about a chance to pick our next field trip, if you hang up your coat.
CHERI: I'd rather stay home.
TREATMENT WORKER: How about an all-expense-paid trip for two to Hawaii, if you'll hang up your coat.

In this somewhat exaggerated case, the treatment worker did not allow Cheri to forego her token. Rather, he chose to violate the initial expectations. The manner in which he violated the expectations has taught Cheri how to hold out for a bigger goodie, not how to take responsibility for hanging up her coat.

"These Behavior-Management Principles Are Just Too Simplistic."

Although the principles are relatively simply to understand when taken one by one, their application in the maelstrom of ongoing activity represents a complicated and ever-changing challenge. So many variables must be accounted for to make the simple principles work that simplicity soon becomes an asset rather than a liability. A major error that new workers make in applying the behavior-management principles is to attempt to force the complexity of the child and his situation into the simplicity of the principle. Most often the results of this effort demonstrate that such "forcing" does not yield the desired result. Rather than rushing to implement a behavior-management strategy, we suggest allowing your full awareness of the child and his situation to help you understand the complexities involved. The challenge is to tailor the application of the principles to the child rather than ignoring or disallowing information in your efforts to squeeze the child into the principle. Beware of your urge to solve the child's problems in the first five minutes.

"These Behavior-Management Principles Are Just Too Mechanistic; After All, Children Are Not Robots."

The idea of behavior-management principles being mechanistic assumes that all children receive the same treatment. If such were true, the principles would be violated. Since the proof of the effect of the principles lies in their effect on behavior, and since individuals react to stimuli differently, not all individuals will respond to the same stimuli in the same way. Sometimes people using praise as reinforcement, for example, use stock phrases which do not reflect their current feelings or interests. Thus, they respond mechanistically. Such responding on the treatment worker's part is not good practice. To sum up, appropriate use of the behavior-management principles responds to the individuality of both the child and the treatment worker.

"Don't the Behavior-Management Principles Take Away the Child's Freedom?"

Behavior-management principles can be used in the service of those in authority to increase docility, compliance, and obedience. After spending the day in the midst of a group of chaotic, non-compliant, acting-out children, you may want a little docility. But taken to an extreme, reinforcing compliance and docility runs counter to the values of autonomy and internal control. The task for treatment workers using behavior-management principles lies in finding the appropriate resolution for the continuing treatment issue of control versus autonomy. You may have to exert external controls initially in order to free the child from self-defeating patterns which prevent him from developing his own control. The artful encouragement of autonomous behavior on the one hand and fading of external control on the other hand requires intense concentration on the child with whom you are working.

"Why Should I Reinforce Kids for What They Ought to Do Anyway?"

Here is the contrast between internal and external control stated in yet another way. If children lack the internal motivation to perform a task, no amount of our bemoaning their not having the motivation will give it to them. Rather than continuing to worry because the way it "is" is not the way it "ought to be," we can think about how we might provide external motivation as a step toward the child's developing internal motivation. Thus we get away from idealized notions that easily promote blame and attack, and move towards more pragmatic steps to remedy the situation.

"Well, I Can Fix That Kid. All I Have to Do Is Apply My Handy-Dandy Behavior Mod Tool Kit."

This is the pitfall of the behavior mod zealot. The danger here is that the worker will make the child fit the program rather than design the program for the kid. Or, even more dangerous, will use behavior-management techniques when they are not warranted. This may happen, for example, when a worker attempts to decrease whining by ignoring the child's unmet nurturance needs. (See Table 19-2.)

Table 19–2. Increasing Behavior Checklist

Record the frequency of the following

Positive performance	*Problematic performance*
Positive reinforcement:	Positive reinforcement:
____ Reinforcer delivered after the behavior	____ Reinforcer not contingent on the behavior
____ Reinforcer delivered immediately	____ Reinforcement delayed
____ Verbal or other means used to bridge delays between behavior and reinforcement	____ Reinforcer withheld (forgotten, ignored, etc.)
____ Contingencies of reinforcement verbalized specifically	____ Reinforcer too large or too small
____ Reinforcer verbally and nonverbally congruent	____ Nonspecific reinforcement
	____ Split-reinforcer used
	____ Reinforcement of positive behavior that can only occur as the result of a preceding negative behavior
Negative reinforcement:	Negative reinforcement:
____ Behavior that will remove the aversive conditions is clearly stated	____ Behaviors which terminate aversive conditions are not stated, or stated clearly
____ Aversive condition terminated immediately after the desired behavior	____ Yielding to coercive demands
____ Escape and avoidance behaviors other than the desired behavior are eliminated	

Quality factors—Describe the worker's performance in relation to the following:

1. target behavior consistently reinforced
2. environment arranged to support behavioral goals
3. reinforcer backlash considered and delivery adjusted
4. adverse conditions such as time out, logical consequences, etc., used as opportunities for negative reinforcement
5. selected reinforcer is actually reinforcing to the child

Chapter 20

DECREASING BEHAVIOR
Punishment and Contingent Negative Consequences

After mastering the information in this chapter, you should be able to—

1. discuss four issues that treatment workers must keep in mind when using decreasing-behavior methods;
2. define punishment and give examples;
3. delineate six possible negative side-effects of using behavior-decreasing methods;
4. discuss the "criticism trap";
5. define response cost and natural and logical consequences and give examples;
6. cite thirteen rules for the delivery of behavior-decreasing methods;
7. list four guidelines for choosing a behavior-decreasing method;
8. define Time Out and discuss the variables affecting its effective use;
9. discuss the difference between Time Out and Cool Off;
10. relate decreasing behavior methods to non-behavioral levels of functioning as illustrated by "Feelings and Issues for the Treatment Worker."

One of the first things that treatment workers look for are methods to decrease undesirable behaviors of the children in their charge. Such a reaction is natural because all of us want to avoid situations that are painful or troublesome to us. Prior to explaining some of the techniques that may be used to decrease behavior, we will address a few issues that treatment workers must keep in mind to moderate this initial impulse.

First, just because an inappropriate or negative behavior decreases is no guarantee than an appropriate or positive behavior will emerge in its place. Behavior-decreasing methods are to be used in tandem with behavior-increasing methods aimed at a more positive behavior. The decreased negative behavior may allow more opportunity for the positive behavior to occur, but only methods to increase behavior (as listed in the previous chapter) will ensure that more positive behaviors will develop.

Secondly, the treatment worker must determine what are the central, as opposed to the peripheral, behavior issues. For the well-being of the child it is best to address key behaviors so that by decreasing one key behavior, other more peripheral behaviors drop out. For example, a child may nag other children, take away their toys, interrupt their games, and generally be a pain in the neck to his peers. You could deal with each of the separate peripheral peer-nagging behaviors, or you could work on the more central behavior of appropriatly asking for inclusion with peers and the larger issue of self-image. If the child learns how to get peer attention in a positive manner and feels good about himself, he will be much less likely to engage in the peer-nagging which might alienate those whose company he wants to keep. The issue of central versus peripheral behaviors also affects the well-being of the treatment worker. If you are spending all of your time working to decrease the entire set of peer-bugging behaviors, you will have little time for anything else because the child will create new behaviors as you work to decrease the others. You may become frustrated and feel like little more than a policeman apprehensively waiting for the next "crime" to be committed. (See Figure 20-1.)

Thirdly, the onus of developing positive behavioral goals falls on the treatment worker. Ultimately, treatment with children is aimed at developing processes that have been blocked or distorted. Thus, any method used to decrease behavior must reflect a step towards growth for the child, not just a convenience for the treatment worker. Working towards growth requires a basic understanding of the developmental process and an ability to convert the obvious behavior-decreasing situations into positive behavior-learning situations. Workers must "reframe" the decreasing of inappropriate behaviors into a step towards growth. Such reframing will affect the methods you use. For example, decreasing daydreaming and looking out the window during academic time may be reframed as increasing academic "on-task" behavior. Learning "on-task" behavior fits more directly into the developmental needs of the child. In the short run, such reframing may demand more effort, but in the long run the effort will be repaid many times over.

Fourthly, be aware of the potential hazards of over-using behavior-decreasing methods. The children will come to see you as someone whose

Figure 20-1. Decreasing Behavior: Punishment and Contingent Negative Consequences

very presence is inhibiting or restricting. If this is the case, your overall effectiveness as a change agent will have been decreased. Likewise, you can easily get into the mental set of a behavior-stopper. If that is the case, you will miss opportunities to enrich your treatment with more helpful methods. Also, children may perceive you to be aiming your behavior-decreasing efforts at a wider range of behaviors than you intend. For example, if you are trying to decrease fighting, and fighting is Johnny's only means of anger expression, he may perceive you as meaning he should not be angry. Especially concerning feelings, it is important to distinguish and help the child to distinguish between feeling reactions and feeling expression.

PUNISHMENT

When we talk about punishment, we will limit our discussion specifically to the process of consequent presentation of stimuli that decrease the likelihood of that behavior.

BEHAVIOR + STIMULI = DECREASE IN LIKELIHOOD OF BEHAVIOR

Typical examples of this process in everyday life are spanking, shaking, scolding, humiliation, yelling at the child. Again, the empirical definition holds, so that what seems to us aversive may not be so to the child. The proof lies in the effect on behavior. Sometimes compliments will decrease behavior.

Punishment is an effective way to decrease behavior. It seduces people into using it because the behavior punished usually ceases quickly, providing the person doing the punishing with negative reinforcement. The short-term relief provided is usually overridden by the destructive long-term consequences.

Negative Side-Effects of Punishment

CHILDREN LEARN TO ESCAPE AND AVOID PUNISHMENT. As explained in the previous chapter, people work to terminate aversive stimuli. Therefore, children will learn to increase any behavior that delays or avoids punishment, such as arguing, blaming others, lying, running away. Children also come to associate the people who punish them with the negative qualities of the punishment, and so learn to avoid those people.

CHILDREN LEARN TO MODEL AGGRESSION. One of the results of spankings or other corporal methods of punishment is that children learn that big people can hit little people and get away with it. Thus, you can expect to see them become more physically and verbally punishing.

USE OF PUNISHMENT ALONE AS A METHOD OF BEHAVIOR MANAGEMENT IMPLIES THAT THE PUNISHMENT WILL HAVE TO BE CONTINUED OVER TIME TO MAINTAIN THE UNDERSIRABLE BEHAVIOR AT A LOW RATE. Therefore, the person doing the punishing will have to continue suppressing behavior.

PUNISHMENT MAY AROUSE INTENSE FEELINGS IN THE CHILD THAT PERPETUATE RATHER THAN ELIMINATE UNDESIRABLE BEHAVIOR. The child may experience excessive guilt, fear, frustration, and anger, which may lead to other or more intense maladaptive behaviors. The child may withdraw or use counteraggression, thus perpetuating a cycle of punishment—maladaptive behavior—punishment. In addition, a behavior may have been so successfully suppressed that the child may not see that the punishing consequence no longer exists in his current environment. That is, the avoidance behavior may be unrealistic or maladaptive in a present circumstance. This is true in the case of withdrawn behavior and other fear-based behaviors.

PUNISHMENT MAY BECOME GENERALIZED SO AS TO INHIBIT BEHAVIORS THAT WERE NOT THE TARGET OF THE PUNISHMENT PROCEDURE. Punishing interruptions may decrease the number of interruptions as well as the number of appropriate verbal contributions. Punishment of hitting as an expression of anger may be mistaken as a punishment of the feeling of anger, or even the punishment of feelings in general.

PUNISHMENT MAY AROUSE NEGATIVE EVALUATIONS BY SELF AND PEERS. Children base their self-evaluation on the ways in which others react to them. Punishment for a specific behavior may be mistaken by the child as punishment for his whole being. Thus, he may come to feel and speak poorly of himself. Likewise, peers may follow the lead of the punishing adults and join in to scapegoat the child. Or, on the other hand, they may develop a rooting section for the underdog.

Although these side-effects apply most directly to punishment, they may also interfere in the use of other behavior-decreasing methods, especially if the methods are used in a "the kid deserves to suffer" manner.

Below is a behavior pattern called the "Criticism Trap" which illustrates the negative side-effects of scolding. (See Figure 20-2 and Table 20-1.)

The long-term effect of this pattern may strengthen the very behavior that the teacher wishes to decrease. The child, finding no approval for appropriate behavior, will get attention in predictable ways by engaging in rule-breaking behavior. The teacher, finding the short-term effect of her yelling negatively reinforcing, will continue to yell. Thus, both members of this vicious cycle receive reinforcement for continuing, in spite of the teacher's intent to decrease behavior. The obvious way out of this cycle lies in reinforcing appropriate behavior and ignoring (if possible) inappropriate behavior.

Now, after explaining some problems with behavior-decreasing methods, an explanation of more desirable ways to use the method is in order. Behavior-decreasing methods can effect behavior change when used conscientiously with positive techniques. They are many times the best techniques to use when the undesirable behavior is: 1) physically or psychologically harmful to the child or others (e.g., hitting, name-calling, or running into the street); 2) too prevalent, self-defeating, or intense to ignore because of the amount of time ignoring would take and the extent to which the child would disrupt others; 3) in itself a stronger reinforcer than any others that can be brought to bear on the behavior, making alternate behaviors ineffective; 4) being widely imitated by others; 5) so disruptive as to interfere with the rights of others (e.g., incessant loud vocalization during a study time); 6) impossible to ignore because the reinforcers are not under the treatment worker's control. In short, punishment is effective in quickly stopping behaviors whose continuance is too detrimental to be allowed.

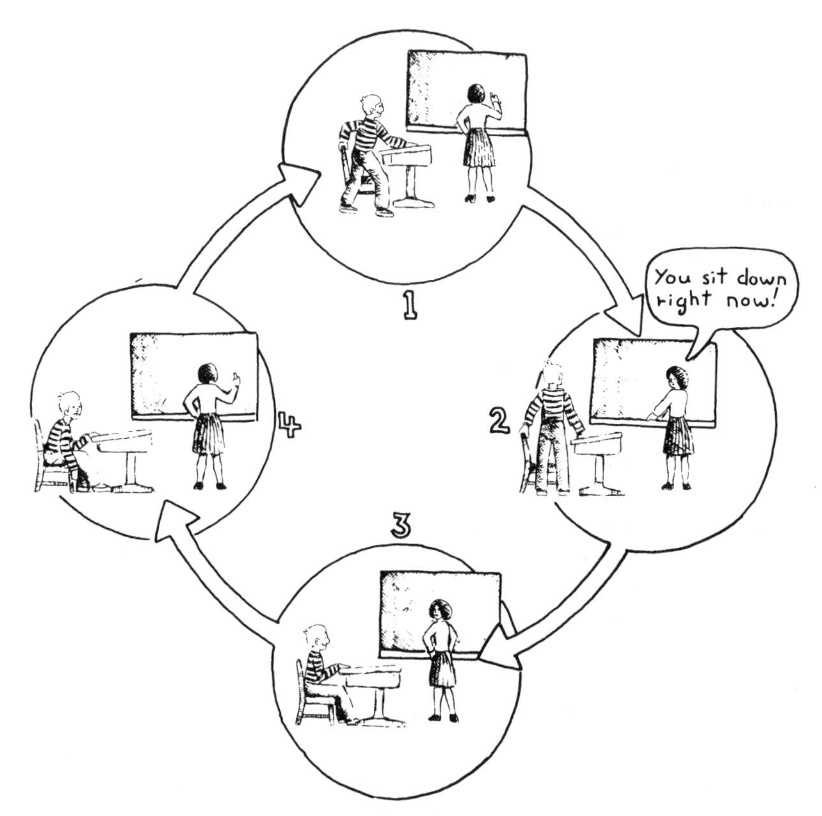

Figure 20-2. Criticism Trap

Table 20–1. Criticism Trap

1. Child gets out of his seat	The child's behavior violates the teacher's expectations, and is seen as an aversive event by the teacher.
2. Teacher yells, "You sit down right now. How many times do I have to tell you?"	Teacher provides a punishing consequence for violation of expectations. She moves to decrease out of seat behavior.
3. Child sits down and begins work.	Short term effect of the teacher's yelling decreases the behavior. The teacher is negatively reinforced for yelling.
4. Teacher ignores the child's working.	No positive consequence is given for appropriate behavior. The child's appropriate working behavior is extinguished.
1. Child gets out of his seat (and so on)	

The following behavior-decreasing methods, when used properly, aid in avoiding some of the aforementioned problems.

RESPONSE COST, NATURAL, AND LOGICAL CONSEQUENCES

Response Cost

Response cost occurs when the removal of a stimulus consequent to a behavior decreases the likelihood of that behavior occurring again; that is, when a particular response results in a particular cost.

BEHAVIOR – STIMULUS = DECREASE IN LIKELIHOOD OF BEHAVIOR

Here, you would withdraw reinforcers that a child has or which would otherwise be provided for him. In other words the child's response costs him something. These can take the form of withdrawing reinforcing events or activities, or token fines. For example, following an inappropriate behavior, a child may lose a free-time privilege, access to toys or games, or may lose points on her token card. In the case of token fines, a system of behaviors and corresponding fines should be set up in advance and, whenever possible, involve the children's input.

Natural Consequences

The physical world obeys natural laws. People who attempt to violate those laws find themselves inescapably faced with the consequences of their actions. If you attempt to fly off a cliff you crash; if you put your hand in a fire you get burned; if you walk in the snow without shoes your feet get cold. These natural consequences affect behavior. As far as your efforts at decreasing behavior for treatment purposes is concerned, we suggest the natural consequence as a model. That is, when consequences occur without your dispensing them, the child has to relate to the natural order rather than to you. This gets you out of the way as a middleman. One of the errors made by treatment workers which lessens their effectiveness is to intervene by trying to interrupt or save the child from potential natural consequences. For example, if a child refuses to bring his coloring book inside after he has finished playing with it outside, the treatment worker might bring it in for him, thus avoiding the possibility that the book might get wet, chewed on by the dog, or used or stolen by another child. The worker's action teaches the child to depend on others to monitor and care for his things. On the other hand, leaving the book outside, as the child had left it, keeps whatever consequences that do occur focused on the child and behavior.

Logical Consequences

Logical consequences most often follow the response-cost idea; that is, the child has some item removed as a result of his behavior. The treatment worker as the remover of the item makes a logical connection between the removal of the item and the child's behavior. For example: "If you keep throwing the ball inside, you're showing me that you are not willing to follow the rules about ball-playing; therefore, you will have to put the ball away." Another example might be: "Since Joan and Betty are pushing each other in the lunch line, they are showing me that they are not yet ready for lunch; so, they will have to go to the back of the line until they can stand in line quietly." Note the verbalized logical connection between the behavior and the consequence.

Another type of logical consequence is related to the behavior principle of *overcorrection.* If a child spills her milk, the most logical consequence for her is to clean it up. If she wets the bed, logically she would be expected to put the wet bedclothes in the washer and makes her bed with dry ones. Even children with limited physical abilities can attempt to correct their behavior. The concept of *restitutional overcorrection* extends this idea to include a logically related additional task as a consequence. For example, the milk-spilling child would not only clean up the part of the floor on which she spilled the milk, but also the parts that did not get spilled on. Finally, *positive-practice overcorrection* involves repeating and rehearsing the appropriate behavior that is an alternate to or incompatible with the offending behavior. For example, if a child runs along the side of the swimming pool, positive practice overcorrection would involve walking the same distance several times. This is the old "Do it over till you get it right" technique.

Time Out

If effective response-cost or logical consequences cannot be found, a time-out procedure can be an effective behavior decreasing tool. Time out (TO) means time out from reinforcement and involves removing a child from access to the sources of reinforcement and isolating her for a prescribed time period. This response-cost technique *removes the child from the reinforcer* rather than removing the reinforcer from the child.

What Behaviors and When

Time out is an effective tool for rapidly decreasing physically or psychologically harmful acts, such as hitting or name-calling, as well as noncompliance and extreme or persistent disruptive behaviors that are too intense to ignore.

Time-out behaviors are divided into those that require a warning, and those that do not. Generally, those that are physically or psychologically harmful are not given a warning. Thus, if a child hits another, she is immediately sent to time out. Ongoing disruptive behaviors, such as persistent loud singing in the middle of a group discussion, may require a warning so as to allow the child a choice concerning her behavior. In the beginning, a verbal warning presented with a choice is useful. For example, you may say, "Tim, your singing is disrupting the group. You can choose to stop and stay here or continue and go to TO." Remember, this is a *warning,* not a threat. It should be given in a matter-of-fact style using few words and little facial expression. After the child gets the hang of it, hand signals or a simple "Warning one" can be used to minimize attention to negative behaviors. One warning and *one warning only* should be given. Follow-through must be immediate. Warnings paired with TO become conditioned cues and will gain strength on their own. Warnings paired with warnings become meaningless. If the child makes a positive choice, remember to reinforce her after the warning, e.g., "I like it that you've chosen to stay with us." (See Figure 20-3.)

Where

In TO, the child is removed from the situation where he receives reinforcers and is placed in a dull, nonreinforcing environment—that is, manipulatable, or colorful visual objects, and social stimulation (including visual contact) are minimal. At the same time, the supervising adults must

Time Out Flow Chart

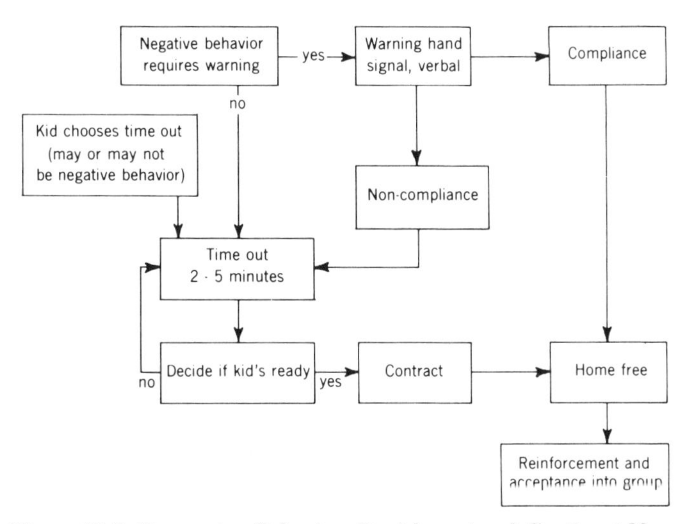

Figure 20-3. Decreasing Behavior: Punishment and Contigent Negative Consequences

be able to see the child. A small room off of the central activity area or a carrel in the corner make good TO Areas.

The above is a guideline and, like all guidelines, needs some adjusting in the face of unusual circumstances. With a destructive child or with a child who is deeply involved with the issue of separation or loss, a Time Out from the ongoing activity is effective. In this case, the child is asked to cease physical and verbal participation in the activity but stays in the group close to an adult supervisor. Likewise, a child who gains gratification from solitary self-stimulation is not a good candidate for Time Out since he carries a host of reinforcing activities into a solitary situation. In the end he may find the Time Out situation reinforcing and may work to be there more often.

How Long

TO is effective with children from two to twelve years when only for short periods of time—from one to five minutes depending on the age of the child. Research has shown that one to five minutes of TO is as effective as twenty to thirty minutes. A kitchen timer is a useful device to keep track of the time since the end of the interval is clearly signaled for both the treatment worker and the child.

What if the child pops in and out of TO before her time is up, refuses to go, or is disruptive in TO? Here it is appropriate to begin the timing of TO when he is sitting quietly. If he leaves TO before the bell rings, the TO period begins again. If the child refuses to go, use the "taxi fare" method; that is, give the child a choice between going by herself for five minutes, or being taken for seven minutes, two minutes being added to TO for "taxi fare."

The child may return to the group when he has: 1) stopped his disruptive behaviors; 2) sat for the prescribed period; and 3) given a verbal statement as to what circumstance got him to Time Out and a contract concerning the behavioral changes he plans to make to work through, avoid, or change that circumstance. When making the statement and contract, the child must give eye contact and demonstrate nonverbal compliance. The child is then given a low-intensity reinforcer such as "Thank you," or "You're showing me that you're willing to take care of yourself," and returned to the group.

Remember, Time Out is *not* solitary confinement. Avoid leaving a child there too long.

No Arguments or Conversations

When a child is in TO, he/she is ignored. Children frequently try to argue their way out or to involve a treatment worker in an interaction by saying such seemingly legal things as "When's my time up?" The bell or your verbal signal will tell them when Time Out is over. Of course, this assumes that the treatment worker is tracking the time closely. If not, the child may have a legitimate gripe. This is an important point in that troubled children are extremely sensitive to abandonment and being forgotten. Guard very closely against this pitfall.

Providing a Positive Environment

The environment that the child returns to from TO must be positive in order for TO to work. Time Out means "time out from positive reinforcement"; therefore, something must be reinforcing about the environment from which the child is removed. If the environment is negative, the child may choose to avoid it by setting himself up to go to TO. When the child returns, he should be warmly accepted into the ongoing activities without negative messages, and should be *reinforced for positive alternative behaviors whenever they occur.* He has paid his dues.

Dry Run

Before using TO, the child must know the answers to such questions as "Where?" and "How long?" With many children, it may be helpful to walk them through the procedures.

Time Out versus Cool Off

A word here needs to be said about the difference between "cool off" and "Time Out." It is many times useful to encourage or allow a child to "cool off" by removing himself from the group when he is in an emotional state that may lead to disruptive behaviors. This is a preventive measure. Nonverbal behaviors must be caught *early* in order for this to be effective. A gentle permission message can then be given, such as "You're face is frowning and red. Why don't you cool off for a few minutes?" Make sure that the child knows that this is *not* Time Out. In order to facilitate this distinction, it is useful to find a cool-off place other than the Time Out area that is quiet, calming, and comfortable. Again, toys should not be available because they distract from the child's focusing on and dealing with the issue, although this may vary from child to child. If the child makes the decision on his own to cool off and remove himself from the group allow his choice of placement within certain limits. Reinforce the child heavily for making this choice. It is a giant step towards self-control. At times, certain children may use cooling off to avoid the group. In this case, some limits need to be made on cooling off with this child. (See Table 20-2.)

Table 20–2. An Example of the Multiple Principles of Behavior Management Involved in Time Out

TW:	I've been noticing that you've been sticking your tongue out at Tommy at morning meeting. We've been ignoring you and encouraging others to ignore you, and that hasn't worked.	TW labels the behavior that she wants to decrease. TW has tried other means of decreasing it before using Time Out.
	Instead of sticking your tongue out, I'd like you to tell Tommy in words directly what he did to bug you and how you feel about it.	She also identifies acceptable alternate behavior that will avoid Time Out.
	Until you can learn another way of expressing yourself, we will use Time Out. Each time you stick your tongue out at Tommy at morning meeting, I'll give you one warning by raising one finger. You can choose to stop or use words, and stay in the meeting. Or you can choose to do it again and go on Time Out for three minutes.	TW sets expectations for the Time Out procedure, including a warning signal, and an indication of the duration of Time Out. These expectations are phrased as choices, placing responsibility for the child's actions with the child.
Child:	(2 minutes later) Neah Tommy! (Sticks tongue out at Tommy)	
TW:	(Raises one finger)	Warning signal given
Child:	(1 minute later) Neah! (Sticks tongue out at Tommy)	
TW:	Ok, that's Time Out. (Points to Time Out chair)	Immediate, mater-of-fact follow through of consequence.
Child:	(Stays in Time Out for 3 minutes)	Child is removed from reinforcing consequences.
TW:	Your 3 minutes are up, come here. Tell me what you did to get into Time Out.	TW uses negative reinforcement of escape from Time Out contingent on 3 quiet minutes of Time Out. TW asks child to demonstrate his awareness of the contingencies that lead to his Time Out.
Child:	I stuck my tongue out at Tommy.	
TW:	Tell me what you can do to stay out of Time Out.	TW asks child to demonstrate his awareness of alternate behaviors.
Child:	I can ignore his bugs, or I can tell him about it in words.	
TW:	Far out! Those choices will work for you. Remember, we'll have the same expectations throughout morning meeting.	TW praises accurate verbalization of alternative and labels their positive function. TW reminds child of continued expectations.
Child:	(Nods head) Okay.	
TW:	Okay, now you can join the group.	TW uses positive reinforcement of rejoining group contingent upon acknowledging expectations.

Conditions of Delivery of Behavior-Decreasing Consequences

In order for behavior-decreasing consequences to be most effective, they must be used precisely. Keep the following rules in mind when using them:

The behavior-decreasing consequence must be *contingent* on the specific behavior.

The contingencies must be made *clear* to the child *in advance* of delivery of the consequence.

A *warning,* stated as a *choice,* should be given when possible. For example, if a child is banging a ruler on his desk, give a warning by saying "You can use your ruler appropriately and keep it, or continue banging and lose it for the day" (using logical consequences). As a general rule, use warnings only once. Warnings help you avoid having to deliver continual consequences and help the child focus on his decision process.

The behavior-decreasing consequence must follow the behavior immediately. A consequence affects the behavior it immediately follows. If it occurs well after the behavior has stopped, a positive behavior may be decreased.

The child must have the opportunity to *regain the lost reinforcer.* When taking a reinforcer away, tell the child that it will be taken away for a *specific amount of time* and that she can have it back at a *specific time* or contingent on a *specific behavior.*

Make the consequence *short term* when possible. This gets the negativity over with so that you can get down to the positives. It also avoids lingering negative side-effects.

Deliver the behavior-decreasing consequence in a *matter-of-fact, nonjudgmental,* but firm manner. Blaming tones only serve to increase negative feelings and thus, negative behaviors.

Verbalizations during consequences should be *concise* and *minimal.* Give the child the necessary information without unnecessary orations. Avoid commercials and lectures. Also, fireworks may add interest that maintains rather than decreases behavior.

The child must be in a state of behavior-decreasing consequence-deprivation. Frequent consequences lead to satiation and become ineffective.

Consequences for specific behaviors must be *consistent.*

Appropriate, *incompatible behaviors must be positively reinforced.*

If the child does not have the appropriate alternate behaviors in her repertoire, she must be taught.

Once the consequence is over, the child's dues are paid; there are to be *no lingering, nonspecific, or indirect negatives.*

When choosing a behavior-decreasing consequence, consider the following points:

a) The consequence must be a behavior-decreasing consequence to the child, no matter how others may view it.
b) The consequence must be as free from negative emotional side-effects as possible.
c) The consequence should be logical when possible.
d) The intensity of the consequence must match the behavior.

Feelings and Issues for the Treatment Worker

"I'm Not Angry, So How Can I Give a Behavior-Decreasing Consequence?"

Although anger and punishment are often linked, there is no necessary connection at all between the feeling state and a person's ability to carry out a consequence. You do not need to feel angry to use any of the techniques listed in this chapter. As a matter of fact, calm, non-blaming follow-through increases the likelihood that the child will feel the impact of the consequence without the additional positive or negative stimuli resulting from your expressing your feeling state. This does not mean that you can never be angry. Anger is as valid an emotion as any other. We are only saying that there need not be a connection between that emotion and your actions. You can say "Go to Time Out" in a variety of tones of voice, all of which will convey the message.

"Well, The Kid Has a Good Point There; Maybe I'll Let Him Off Just This Once."

Debating the "fairness" of the consequence is a time-honored method of stalling and avoiding that consequence. If you have followed all the guidelines for the delivery of behavior-decreasing consequences then you are on good grounds to administer the consequence first and negotiate later. Of course, you are not infallible. And, from time to time the child will have a valid complaint. At these times you may wish to explore what the child presents. However, most often "it ain't fair" debates can be seen as avoidance tactics which should not be reinforced by your attenton.

"Oh, I Couldn't Let Him Fail, He'd Be Crushed."

The best learning comes through success. Therefore, arranging the environment to provide successes and positive experiences becomes a primary task for treatment workers. However, there are behaviors the child engages in which lead to defeat and failure for the child. No matter how you arrange the environment the child will find a way to fail. Or, your arrangement may move him backward in the developmental process to a less autonomous way of coping. If these conditions occur, your taking responsibilty to "save" a child actually damages his chances of moving beyond the self-defeating patterns. At these times remember the advice stated previously in this chapter: let the consequences have their effect. Work with the child around the pain or discomfort he experiences from the natural consequences rather than preventing these consequences.

"If It Was Good Enough for Me, It's Good Enough for Them."

We all grow up with some notions of the way the world "ought to be" based on our experience of how it was for us. There is a natural tendency to do unto others what was done to us. If we were lucky and had good care, then maybe that's okay. Usually, however, our parents or caretakers did not have the benefit of books such as this to explain information and skills. In additon, the children in your charge certainly are different from you and may have special needs that you did not. Although the reasons just mentioned promoting flexibility of response make good sense, people who believe the statement at the beginning of this paragraph may dismiss those reasons out of hand. Challenging old assumptions and changing one's own behavior can be difficult and scary, because if you acknowledge that there is another, possibly better way, then you also open the possiblity that your experience was not as "good" for you as you thought. Play with the image and get in touch with the feelings of how it would have been for you had your caretakers been able to do with you what we are asking you to do with the children in your care. We guess that such fantasy exploration will lead you to at least a tolerance for trying the techniques explained in this book.

"If I Take Things Away from a Child She'll Feel Deprived; If I Put The Child Into Time Out She'll Feel Rejected.

Kids may react to these consequences with many different emotions. Your task is not to refrain from delivering the consequences, but to make your efforts fit into the needs and understandings of the child. Behavior-management techniques must be integrated into the larger framework of treatment for the child. Sometimes you may choose to forego specific behavior-change efforts to work with other modes of treatment. Most often behavior-management principles can be incorporated into the total treatment. The child's issues of deprivation or rejection occurring in conjunction with behavior decreasing consequences usually signal a larger pattern of feelings aroused by the specificity of the behavior-management techniques. Use the child's responses as signals to attend to broader issues. (See Table 20-3.)

Table 20–3. Punishment and Contingent Negative Consequences Behavior Checklist

Record the frequency of the following behaviors:

Positive performance	*Problematic performance*
Response cost, natural and logical consequence	Response cost, natural and logical consequence
_____ Non-catastrophic natural consequences allowed without interference	_____ Natural consequences interrupted
_____ Relation between the consequence and the behavior made logical	_____ No logical connection between the consequence and the behavior
_____ Warning stated as a choice	_____ "Doomsday" threats
_____ Reinforcer regaining behavior specified	_____ Warning in non-choice terms
_____ Behavior decreasing consequence delivered contingently	_____ No warning signal
_____ Behavior decreasing consequence delivered immediately	_____ Too many warnings without follow-through
_____ Short duration	_____ Behaviors avoiding or delaying consequence allowed (e.g., debating)
	_____ Overly intense negative consequence
Time Out–All of above behaviors also apply to Time Out	Time Out–All of above behaviors also apply to Time Out
_____ Time Out location chosen is unreinforcing to the child	_____ Debate or other attention given to delays or Time Out rule violations
_____ Time added for delays or violations of Time Out rules	_____ Ending time forgotten, ignored
_____ Ending time tracked closely	_____ No exit contract made
_____ Contract made for child to exit Time Out	

Quality factors—describe the worker's performance in relation to the following:

1. matter–of–fact, nonjudgmental, and firm manner of delivery, i.e., non–aggressive model
2. no lingering, non–specific, or indirect negatives
3. environment from which the child is removed is positive
4. behavior decreasing consequence appropriate to the child (e.g., no Time Out for self–stimulating child)
5. expectations given in advance: first Time Out role-played

Chapter 21

DECREASING BEHAVIOR
Extinction and Reinforcing Alternatives

After mastering the information in this chapter, you should be able to—

1. list at least three reasons to favor extinction and reinforcing alternatives over punishment/response-cost methods of decreasing behavior;
2. explain the principle of extinction/ignoring and give an example;
3. identify the conditions under which to select and use extinction/ignoring;
4. identify three traps in using extinction/ignoring and suggest ways of avoiding them;
5. explain the rationale for favoring reinforcing alternatives over all other behavior-decreasing methods;
6. define reinforcing incompatible behavior and give an example;
7. identify four issues in selecting an incompatible behavior to reinforce;
8. define and explain how to use omission training and reinforcing a low rate of behavior;
9. Relate extinction/ignoring and reinforcing alternatives to nonbehavioral levels of worker functioning as illustrated in "Feelings and Issues for the Treatment Worker.

We suggest the first attempts to decrease behavior come from the principles elaborated in this chapter. Unless the behaviors you wish to decrease are potentially dangerous to the child or his peers, we feel that the techniques outlined here provide a more positive approach for a number of reasons. First of all, you remove yourself from the position of punisher/depriver. Thus, many of the side-effects of the punishment and response-cost methods are eliminated. Secondly, you do not need to maintain long-term efforts at keeping a behavior at low levels as you do with punishment/response-cost techniques. Punishment and response cost function in a reverse fashion to reinforcement. That is, if you stop reinforcing, the behavior will decrease. With punishment/response cost, if you stop delivering consequences the behavior will increase towards its level previous to your efforts. Thus, with punishment/response cost alone you will need continuing effort. Thirdly, the reinforcement of alternatives provides the child with a much clearer sense of what he *can do* rather than only what he *cannot do.*

EXTINCTION/IGNORING

In the extinction process reinforcement is withheld for a specific undesirable behavior.

BEHAVIOR + IRRELEVANT STIMULI OR NO STIMULI = DECREASE IN LIKELIHOOD OF BEHAVIOR

In most instances the stimuli being withheld is treatment worker attention. Therefore, we will discuss the process of extinction under the label of "planned ignoring." Be aware that reinforcing stimuli come from other sources as well. Treatment worker attention may not be the only source.

In comparison to punishment/response cost, ignoring takes a longer time to decrease behavior. However, once the behavior has decreased, ignoring requires less effort to maintain the behavior change. Therefore, extinction/ignoring has the advantage of more permanent and more complete behavior decrease, and fewer negative side-effects.

When to Use

Ignoring is to be used under certain conditions and with certain behaviors. Behaviors that are physically or psychologically harmful to the child or others (e.g., hitting and name calling) should not be ignored, while behaviors that are commonly agreed upon to be irritating or age- or situationally-inappropriate are prime candidates for this technique (e.g., interrupting, "clowning," talking out of turn, whining, having low-level tantrums, and manipulative crying). These behaviors are generally maintained by attention, positive and negative, and will thus weaken when they are ignored. Sometimes the conditions supporting the behavior are not quite so clear or easy. Other reinforcers may be maintaining the behavior or the behavior may be reinforcing itself. In these cases, the treatment worker must ascertain what the reinforcers are and be able to control them consistently in order for this technique to be effective.

How to Use

Behaviors that can be extinguished most easily are usually those maintained by continuous positive reinforcement. Behaviors maintained by variable schedules or by successful avoidance of aversive stimuli (negative reinforcement) are very resistant to extinction by ignoring. In these cases, another method may be preferred. If not, the behavior will have to be tolerated for a long period of time. Other behaviors that a treatment worker may decide not to ignore are those that are frequently imitated by other children.

To be effective, ignoring must be consistent and precise. One of the laws of reinforcement holds that a behavior reinforced intermittently is very resistant to extinction. Therefore, if you were to ignore a behavior most of the time but attend to it some of the time, you would actually be making the behavior last longer. Ignoring must be total! Because of this, it is important to get the other children's assistance in helping to carry out ignoring programs by reinforcing them for ignoring the disruptive behaviors of others; for example, saying to a child who is ignoring another child's interruptions, "I really appreciate your support in ignoring Rita." This kind of total ignoring may be difficult at times due to the persistance of certain behaviors and the paradoxical fact that behaviors actually *increase* in rate and intensity when reinforcement is initially withdrawn. Sometimes a child will even try a new and more disruptive behavior to get the desired reinforcer. The number of times a behavior will occur after ignoring begins depends upon: 1) the number of times the behavior has been reinforced, 2) the strength of the reinforcer, 3) whether it was on a continuous or variable schedule, 4) how deprived the child is of a reinforcer, and 5) the availability of alternate means by which the child can obtain the same or similar reinforcers. In any case, you can count on an initial increase so be patient, replay your favorite fantasy, hum a few bars of music, or preferably, reinforce a more appropriate behavior in another child. Remember, total ignoring means withholding both verbal and *eye* attention. Even short, intermittent eye contact has been found to be a strong reinforcer of undesirable behavior.

As soon as the undesirable behavior stops, give the child some positives. This is crucial at the beginning of an ignoring program. Ignoring teaches a child what *not* to do; it does not teach him what *to do* instead. In order for ignoring to be effective, it must be used in a program that reinforces positive behaviors that are incompatible with the behaviors being ignored. The reinforcement must be *immediate,* especially in the beginning. If you have ignored Shirley for whining, attend to her as soon as she stops with a comment on her positive behavior, e.g., "I like to listen to you when you talk to me in a pleasant voice," or "Thank you for being quiet."

Traps in Using Ignoring

The previous paragraph hints at several potential traps in the use of extinction. First, inappropriately used ignoring can shape a more disruptive behavior than was originally present. If the treatment worker cannot ignore the increase in behavior, she may inadvertently reinforce a more intense level of responding from the child. With a number of repetions of failed ignoring, the treatment worker may in fact have "created a monster" whose level of disruption is much more intense than when the first ignoring was instituted. (See Figure 21-1.)

Ignoring can produce not only a temporary increase in the behavior which is being ignored, but also more aggressive behavior. Visualize your behavior the last time you put money in a vending machine and got nothing. Swearing at, pounding, and kicking the machine illustrate types of aggression aroused when reinforcement is withheld. The disruptive behavior of a child may have been highly functional for him to coerce attention from his social environment. Not to respond to his most practiced behavior invites him to do more of the same, and to display frustration through other

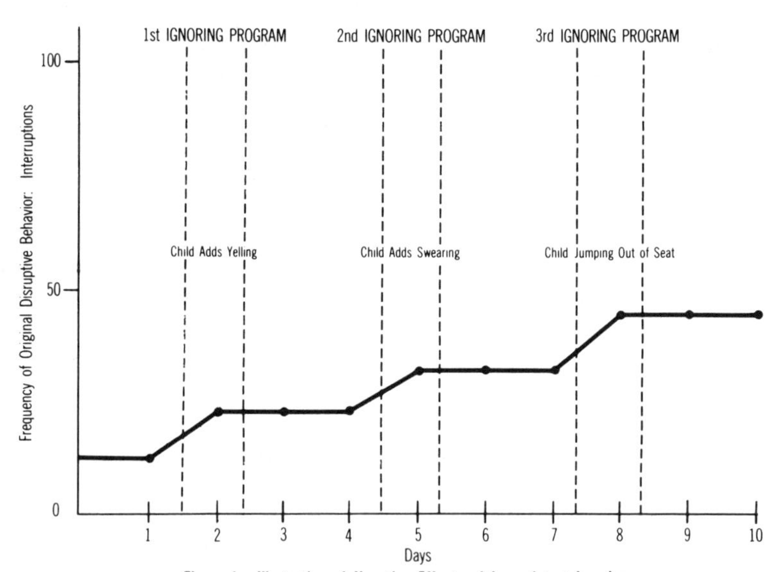

Figure 1. Illustration of Negative Effects of Inconsistant Ignoring.

Figure 21-1. Decreasing Behavior: Extinction and Reinforcing Alternatives

disruptive behaviors. Fortunately these disruptions are only temporary and will pass. The question is, can you tolerate them for that short time without reinstating reinforcement for them?

After a behavior has been ignored successfully so that the frequency of the behavior is zero, there may be one or two recurrences of the behavior (spontaneous recovery). If the treatment worker is not prepared for that possibility, she may attend to the old behavior, thus increasing it. Spontaneous recovery can be expected. Plan for it and you will be able to continue the ignoring, thus keeping the response extinguished. This vigilance for spontaneous recovery does not mean you have to labor to keep the behavior extinguished as you would if you were using punishment/response cost. The behavior will not recur very often. Extinction/ignoring causes a virtually permanent reduction in the behavior.

Acknowledged Ignoring

It is sometimes useful, particularly in the beginning of an ignoring program, to let the child know, verbally or with a hand signal, that you will be ignoring. This is called "acknowledged ignoring." You may want to verbalize why you are ignoring and how the child can obtain the desired attention. In this case, verbalize only when the behavior first begins, be concise, and do not repeat the verbalization, e.g., "I will ignore your loud voice. I will listen when it is quieter." If acknowledgment to the child is not desired, acknowledgment to others may be used, e.g., "I am ignoring David's screaming and will give him attention when he stops." When the child knows the expectations and consequences well, hand signals are preferred because the attention is minimal (e.g., a hand up with palm towards the child in a "stop" position may indicate that no attention will be given until he asks more appropriately). This acknowledgment should be given once and once only. The worker and whichever peers she has enlisted to ignore should then go about their usual business. Otherwise the ignoring procedure can disrupt the more positive behavior of others. Thus, the disruptive child can continue to control the group in ways as devastating as the original behavior which was to be ignored. (See Figure 21-2.)

In making the decision to use an ignoring program on an inappropriate behavior, use the following guidelines:

Is the behavior inappropriate and/or disruptive?

Is the behavior not harmful to the child or others?

Have all of the reinforcers maintaining the behavior been determined?

Do you have control of the consequences?

Is there an alternate behavior that the child can perform to obtain the same or a like reinforcer?

Figure 21-2. Handsignals as Acknowledged Ignoring

If the answers are yes, the behavior is likely to respond well to extinction. The following flow chart provides more decision-making information (Benoit & Mayer, 1974). (See Figure 21-3.)

Reinforcing Alternatives

There are several advantages to the behavior-decreasing method of reinforcing alternative behaviors. First, and most obvious, no aversive consequences need be given. This creates a more positive atmosphere for learning. It also allows for generalization of positive consequences to other child behaviors such as positive self-statements (self-esteem). Overall, the reinforcing conditions create a situation in which the child feels more comfortable and willing to work. Secondly, the child receives clear direction for what he can do to gain reinforcement; thus it is more potentially constructive. Finally, reinforcing alternatives is the least intrusive of the behavior-decreasing methods. It does not introduce punishment or frustrating consequences. Therefore, the negative side-effects of the other methods can be avoided completely.

EXTINCTION FLOW CHART

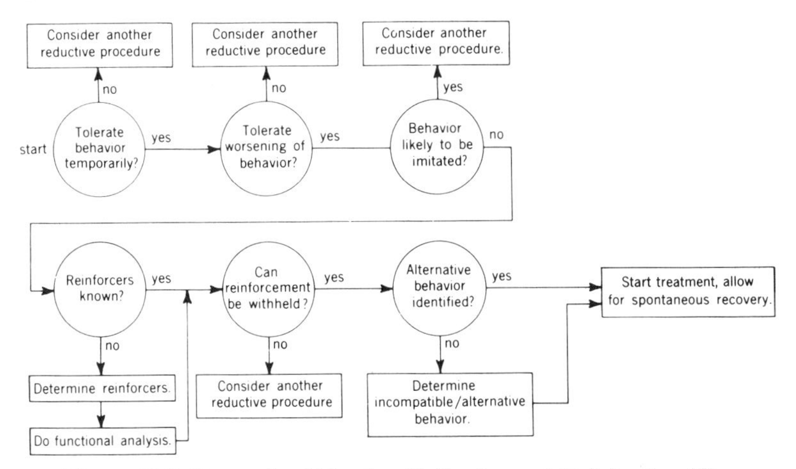

Figure 21-3. Decreasing Behavior: Extinction and Reinforcing Alternatives

Reinforcing Incompatible Behavior

The most elegant of the types of reinforcing alternatives is reinforcing incompatible behavior. Theoretically, there exist some behaviors which, when performed, preclude the performance of behaviors you wish to decrease. Obviously, incompatible behavior must be functionally useful for the child, and it must be able to be eventually maintained by naturally existing consequences in the environment. You could get a child to stop grabbing others' papers during math time by reinforcing the child for standing on his head. However, that would interfere with his ability to complete his own math and give him a headache. A more natural behavior that could be reinforced in the context is completing math problems. If the child were holding his pencil in one hand and his math paper in the other, he would have difficulty grabbing things from others. Some of these techniques could be referred to as "distracting" or "redirecting."

When considering an incompatible behavior, you may be able to come up with a variety of potentially incompatible behaviors. The key to your decision about which to choose may lie in the centrality of the alternate behavior. That is, some behaviors demand a greater effort or encompass a greater number of possible behaviors. When possible, choose a central rather than a peripheral behavior, because the "spread effect" of a central behavior will have a more far-ranging positive impact. For example, you may wish to decrease a child's non-participation in group activities. Several incompatible behaviors which might fit could be: reinforcing nonverbal participation such as sitting with the group, reinforcing verbal participation, reinforcing leading the group in some activity. Obviously leading the group would have the most far-ranging effects because not only would the child have to participate, but also he would have to monitor and respond to the participation of others.

Another consideration when selecting an incompatible behavior is whether or not the behavior already exists within the child's abilities. An already existing response is preferable. Shaping or modeling a new response takes time and effort which may interfere with the effectiveness of the new behavior in decreasing the behavior you wish to decrease.

Sometimes you may choose an alternate behavior that is not incompatible with the behavior you wish to decrease. If that is the case, then be very careful to reinforce the alternative behavior alone or in conjunction with other acceptable behaviors, and not to reinforce the alternative in the presence of the old behavior or some other potentially disruptive response. For example, you may want to reinforce a child for handing out papers, but would not want to reinforce this behavior when it is accompanied by talking to others, if talking to others is undesirable for that child. Pinpointed verbal reinforcement can help localize the effect of the reinforcement somewhat, but some of the reinforcing may in fact increase the negative behavior as well.

All of the guidelines for the conditions of delivery or reinforcement listed in the chapter on "Increasing Behavior" apply here.

Omission Training

Sometimes a child may engage in many specific behaviors that will lead to more constructive consequences for him. A problematic behavior may not affect a specific situation or intent, but may be pervasive enough to affect a variety of situations, for example, when a child makes continual disruptive nonsense noises. Therefore, a single alternative may not be appropriate. In this case, you may choose to use omission training and require only that the child not engage in the undesirable target behavior. Technically this is known as "differential reinforcement" of other responses. The typical strategy is to monitor the child at specific time intervals, and if the child is not engaging in the behavior you wish to decrease, you reinforce him. This method works well for a busy treatment worker who cannot continuously monitor a child. A kitchen timer set on a variable time schedule will cue both the worker and the child to attend to the child's behavior.

A second variation on this same theme requires that the child omit problematic behavior not only at the end of the time interval, but also all during the interval. This expectation radically increases the expectation of behavior change, and so you may wish to make the interval very small in the beginning in order to assure an adequate rate of reinforcement. For example, Susan picks her nose as she listens in group. Not only is this behavior ridiculed by the other children, it also gives her several nose bleeds a week. The treatment worker enlists Susan's cooperation in a program to reinforce non-nose-picking. The treatment worker may use a timer, or just choose random time periods during group time to look at Susan and record non-nose-picking. More intensively, the treatment worker may use interval recording (see the chapter on "Observation") with 15-second intervals to reinforce Susan for each 15-second interval in which she refrained from nose-picking altogether. Later the intervals would be lengthened until all of group time was included in one interval.

Reinforcement of a Low Rate of Responding

Sometimes the problem is not the behavior itself but the rate at which the child performs the behavior. Contributing to group discussion can be a positive response unless it occurs so often that nobody else can say anything. In such cases you may want to use differential reinforcement of a low rate of responding. In this procedure you would give the expectation to the child that if he reduced his problematic behavior to a specified level, then he would receive reinforcement. Initially, the reduction in behavior should be quite small in order to assure the child's success. As the child gains more and more reinforcement for behavior reduction, you can slowly move to acceptable levels or responding. This procedure reverses the shaping method to be explained in the next chapter. Behavior monitoring can take the form of noting the behavior in question until it exceeds the specified limit. In the beginning it may be useful to remind the child that he is approaching his limit. Later this reminder would be dropped.

Early Cues

Sometimes disruptive behavior can seem very volatile and explosive. Tantrums, or hitting and verbal abuse may burst forth with little or no warning. In these cases the child most likely cannot easily stop this behavior to perform more positive alternatives. If you focus only on providing negative consequences for that explosive behavior, you will find the changes more slow in coming than if you also look for early cues to that behavior. Explosive behavior does not usually spring full-blown; rather it is the end of an orderly chain of behaviors that increase in intensity until the explosion. For example, Greta seemingly explodes—kicking and screaming—at other kids from time to time. The links preceding the explosion may occur as follows: Greta leaves home late and forgets or does not make her lunch. She is silent and frowning during play time. She turns away from kids and pulls away from adults when they try to talk with or touch her. She begins to breathe in short shallow breaths; her face and neck become blotchy. A child approaches her to play and she kicks and screams at him. In order to help the child gain more control over her explosive behavior, you will have to locate the links in the chain, and help the child build alternatives to the explosive behavior. To locate and respond to early cues, consider the following:

Systematically observe the behaviors and the environment of the child which preceded the behavioral explosion. You are looking for patterns and sequences that advance the intensity of the child's behavior (use general sequence analysis as explained in the "Observation" chapter).

When you have identified the chain, draw the child's attention to an early link to it. As a first step, simply draw the child's attention to the sequence that has already developed, and inform him of your observation of the likely sequence to follow. This link in the chain must be at a low enough level of intensity that the child can stop his behavior relatively easily.

If the behavior escalates to the next step in the chain, you can problem-solve with the child about what else he could do instead of moving toward a blow out (see the later chapter on "Problem Solving and Conflict Resolution").

Next, you may suggest several alternatives in the form of a choice, and apply positive consequences for choosing non-escalating behaviors.

Finally, you can prompt alternative behaviors in the presence of behavior-escalating cues.

Obviously, you may not have the luxury of doing all of the above things in each and every incident, and some children will be ready for less intrusive methods while others will require more directive ones. In the long run your goal is to build into the behavioral chain new links that will help the child to gain what he wants without exploding.

Feelings and Issues for the Treatment Worker

Several beliefs about the way change happens, and feelings associated with the change process can short-circuit appropriate follow-through of the techniques listed in this chapter.

"I Can't Stand It Any More. I Don't Care, I've Just Got To Scream At This Kid."

Screaming is a very healthy release of pent-up feelings. However, if you are engaged in an extinction procedure, we suggest you find ways to deal with your feelings that do not risk attending to the response that you are trying to decrease. This may mean passing the child in question to a co-worker, taking a day off, talking out your feelings with a peer or counselor, sleeping late the next morning, or any of a million other things you can do to take care of yourself. Once you embark on an extinction program, you must respond consistently. You may have misjudged your ability to tolerate your aversion to the child's behavior. If so, you can change your behavior-reduction strategy. Just be clear on your approach so that you and your co-workers can be consistent. One other passing comment: People sometimes think that by expressing their dislike of a child's behavior, the child will automatically change that behavior. We suggest that you do not expect anyone to change his behavior only on the basis of your expressing some feeling about it. Behavior changes occurs by systematically following the behavior-management principles elaborated in this part of this book.

"I'm Just Going To Tune Out Completely. That Way I'll Be Able To Ignore All The Problematic Behavior."

Although tuning out completely sounds inviting, it does not work well as a mode of ignoring because everything is ignored, even positive behaviors. You will have to devise some way of paying attention without attending to the problematic behavior in order to be available to reinforce the positive behaviors that occur. Practice using your peripheral vision; learn to listen to kids without looking at them; orient your body towards kids who display positive behaviors. In addition, you may need to find a way to distract yourself: write notes, hum to yourself, respond to ap propriately behaving children, practice muscle relaxation. When used in the ongoing context of treatment, ignoring can fit very easily. When a dis ruptive behavior occurs that you wish to ignore, we suggest that you use the behavior as a cue to find something in some other child to positively reinforce.

"Even Though I'm Reinforcing An Alternative Behavior, The Problematic Behavior Is Getting Worse."

There may be a variety of reasons for this. The most common in our experience stems from reinforcing an alternate behavior that exists because of the problematic behavior. A common example is praising a child for stopping whining. The only way the child can get praise for stopping whining is to whine first. Paying a large amount of attention to a child immediately after he has thrown a tantrum runs the risk of the child believing that only after tantrums does positive attention come. Know what you are reinforcing.

Table 21–1. Behavior Pattern: Using Ignoring and Reinforcing Alternatives in a Group

TW:	Who knows what today is?	TW poses a question to the group.
Fred:	(Yelling) I know, I know, it's	Fred yells appropriately.
TW:	(Addressing the whole group) I'll listen to people with raised hands and quiet voices.	TW ignores Fred's yelling by speaking to the whole group. She defines expectations.
Fred:	(Yelling) But I know it's George Washington's Birthday.	Fred yells again.
TW:	Johnny, you have your hand up and are ignoring disruptions, what is today?	TW ignores Fred's yelling by focusing on a child with appropriate behavior and gives Fred cues as to desirable and undesirable behaviors.
Fred:	(Yelling and moving over to wave his hand in front of TW's face) Why didn't you call on me?	Fred continues to yell and add a different disruptive behavior.
TW:	(Turning her back to Fred and facing Johnny more directly) Good, Johnny. It is George Washington's birthday. And who knows why we celebrate his birthday?	TW continues to ignore. This time she has to use her whole body to ignore.
Fred:	(Yelling but sitting back in the group) Goddammit, you never call on me.	Fred still yelling but exchanges one disruptive behavior for another (swearing).
TW:	Georgette, your raised hand, quiet voice, and attentive face show me that you're ready to answer.	TW continued to ignore Fred but she labels what she is reinforcing, using the other children as models.
Fred:	(Scowls and raises hand about halfway up)	Fred meets expectations for being called on in the group.
TW:	That's right Georgette, he's called the Father of Our Country. Anything else? Fred, your hand is up and your voice quiet. What do you have to add?	TW reinforces appropriate response from another child. Then, ignoring the scowl she acknowledges Fred's appropriate behavior, and invites him to speak.

Table 21–2. Ignoring and Reinforcing Alternatives Behavior Checklist

For each incident warranting ignoring, check (√) each of the following behaviors that occur:

Positive performance	*Problematic performance*
____ Uses simple ignoring	____ Attends to behavior targeted for ignoring
____ No verbalizations	____ Gives eye contact with simple ignoring
____ No eye contact	____ Uses rambling verbalizations with acknowledged ignoring
____ No other non-verbal attention	____ Uses eye contact with hand signals
____ Uses verbal acknowledged ignoring	____ Ignores appropriate behaviors in others
____ Concise verbalizations	____ Ignores child's compliance
____ Specific verbalizations	
____ Uses hand signal acknowledged ignoring	
____ No eye contact	
____ Reinforces appropriate behaviors of others	
____ Reinforces child's compliance	

"People Have To Suffer In Order To Get Rid Of Pain-Producing Behaviors."

In some people's minds there is a rough equation which indicates that a person must suffer as much pain unlearning a behavior as she did learning it. Thus, they expect that behavior-change techniques ought to help people to suffer or cry a lot (Armstrong and Savicki, 1971). This belief may lead treatment workers to choose more painful or frustrating methods of decreasing behavior over those that create a positive atmosphere. Numerous studies in psychology show conclusively that people learn best under positive conditions. In addition, they can learn to interfere with or override problematic behaviors with positive means. Therefore, they do not need to cry a lot. As a matter of fact, the process and the outcome of behavior change becomes more direct and less potentially troublesome when positive methods are used. Some children may need behavior-decreasing methods other than the techniques suggested in this chapter applied to them before they can allow the positive approach to work. If that is the case, look to the child to show you when he is ready for a different approach. (See Tables 21-1, 21-2, 21-3)

Table 21–3.

For each incident warranting reinforcing alternatives, check (√) each of the following behaviors that occur:

Positive performance	*Problematic performance*
_____ Reinforces alternate behavior before child can engage in disruptive behavior	_____ Misses opportunity to reinforce alternative behavior
_____ Reinforces central rather than peripheral behavior when possible	_____ Chooses peripheral rather than central behavior
_____ Chooses incompatible behavior when possible.	_____ Reinforces a behavior in the presence of a disruptive behavior
_____ Reinforces an alternative behavior which does not occur in the presence of a disruptive behavior	_____ Uses omission when could reinforce an incompatible or alternate behavior
_____ Uses omission training when other strategies not available	_____ Lets the behavior go beyond early cues
_____ Reinforces a low rate behavior when this is appropriate	
When using early cues:	
_____ Catches the chain at an early link	
_____ Problem solves with child when appropriate	
_____ Gives child a choice	
_____ Prompts alternate behavior when appropriate	

Quality factors—Describe the worker's performance in relation to the following:

Behaviors chosen for ignoring are—

1. not physically or psychologically harmful
2. inappropriate and/or disruptive
3. behaviors whose maintaining reinforcers have been identified
4. behaviors whose maintaining reinforcers are under staff control

Quality factors—describe the worker's performance in relation to the following:

Chooses an alternate behavior that—

1. fits with the child's intent
2. the child is able to perform easily
3. diminishes self-defeat

Chapter 22

GETTING BEHAVIOR STARTED

After mastering the information in this chapter you should be able to—

1. give examples of shaping;
2. discuss how shaping provides a general design for behavior change;
3. identify and explain the shaping procedure;
4. explain and give examples of chaining;
5. discriminate between the process of shaping and chaining;
6. explain the function of prompts;
7. explain and give examples of verbal instructions, modeling, and physical guidance;
8. relate the techniques of getting behavior started to non-behavioral levels of worker functioning as illustrated by "Feelings and Issues for the Treatment Worker."

Once a behavior exists the principles of how to increase or decrease it can be applied. However, if we waited around for some behaviors to occur, we could wait forever. Therefore, it is useful to know how to start a behavior that does not now exist. Much of child treatment depends on teaching children new and more complicated behaviors. Of course, developmental processes place some limits on the abilities of a child to perform. However, given the appropriate applications of the principles in this chapter, even seemingly constitutionally limited behaviors may be extended in ways treatment workers may not have thought possible. For example, echolalic or previously nonverbal autistic children have been taught to converse meaningfully (Lovaas, et al., 1966).

In this chapter we will discuss three general ways of getting behavior started: shaping, chaining, prompting.

Shaping

Shaping takes a behavior that in some respects resembles the goal behavior and reinforces successive approximations of the goal until the goal behavior has been reached. For example, you may wish to shape a child's ability to verbalize his feelings. Ultimately you may want him to use "I" statements and feeling words, but you have to start where he is. Thus, you may find yourself reinforcing the child's screaming at you at the top of his lungs that you are "stupid" as a first approximation. Eventually you would withhold reinforcement until the child was able to go to the next step (e.g., screaming "you make me angry"). Then, you would raise your expectations of the child at successive steps along the way until the child's behavior matched your goal. With animals you might have to wait around until the next approximation occurred, but with humans you can use *prompting* to increase the speed of the process.

We suggest shaping as a general design for planning for behavior change because it embodies steps that can be applied to many types of interventions.

Shaping Procedure

DEFINE THE GOAL BEHAVIORS. In order to move successively closer to the final behavior, you will need to describe that final behavior clearly enough to recognize movement towards it. This goal behavior must be realistic. For example, expecting first graders to read at a fourth-grade level may push their developmental capacity; it may expend their energy on a task that could be delayed, thus taking their resources away from tasks that require current attention.

START THE SHAPING PROCESS WITHIN THE CAPACITIES OF THE CHILD. Obviously, you must consider the physical and mental limitations of the child. You cannot ask a child with a broken arm to swing from playground equipment. Even more important to consider is the current performance of the child. You must begin from what the child can do relatively *easily* in order to develop a history of success to encourage the child to attempt more difficult approximations later. Shaping can be a very encouraging experience for a child, because if reinforcement is delivered at a high rate, the child will feel that new challenges can be mastered.

FIT THE STEPS OF APPROXIMATION TO THE CHILD. Two questions must be answered in judging the appropriateness of the increments of approximation: how large is each step, and how quickly should you move the child to the next step. Too large a demand, and too quick a move to the next approximation may disrupt the approximations already learned, so you would fall back to reinforcing a previous step. On the other hand, too small steps and too slow a movement from one step to another will bore the child and may over-intensify a behavior of intermediate approximation. This approximation or step will then take longer to extinguish in favor of the next. For example, Fox and Azrin in *Toilet Training in Less Than a Day* suggest avoiding staying too long at the step reinforcing the child for urinating in the potty, because then the next step of reinforcing the child for dry pants becomes more difficult. The child develops a dependence on an adult to reinforce the urination rather than figuring out that dry-pants reinforcement requires self-monitoring, getting to the potty on time, and urinating. One key to determining the appropriate pacing of the steps is the percentage of successes the child experiences at each step. As a generalization, prone to all of the faults of generalizations, we suggest that 80–90 percent success at each step is enough to maintain both encouragement and challenge.

ARRANGE THE MAINTENANCE OF THE NEW BEHAVIOR. Once the goal behavior has been performed, you do not just assume that it will forever afterward be maintained. At that point refer to the behavior-increasing methods explained earlier. The behavior should be stable enough to be maintained by the environment in which it is to be performed. See the next chapter for more specifics about maintenance.

CHAINING

By the principle of chaining, you can take simple behaviors that the child can already do, and reinforce combinations of those behaviors to form more complex ones. The assumption here is that the simple component behaviors already exist within the child's repertoire. Of course, shaping additional component behaviors can introduce new links in the chain. However, the time taken to shape new component behaviors may interfere with the chaining process, and might best be accomplished separately prior to the chaining procedure. Complex chains of behavior include: getting dressed, preparing for math, eating a meal, driving a car, hitting a baseball.

The principle of chaining relies on the multiple functions of stimuli. That is, the same event may serve both as a reinforcer for the event which it follows and a cue for the behavior it precedes. (See Figure 22-1.)

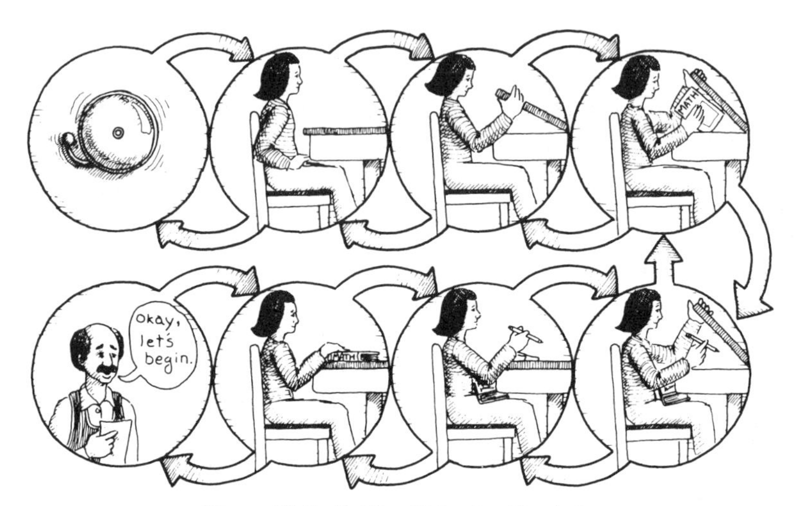

Figure 22-1. Getting Behavior Started

As you can see, the complex behavior of getting ready for in-class seatwork contains many sub-parts. In the chain each sub-part serves a multiple function. The teacher saying "Good, let's begin," is the only identifiable reinforcer, yet Jane's performance of behaviors occuring earlier in the chain have moved Jane closer to that reinforcer, and so have gained reinforcing qualities in relation to the teacher's statement.

Of ultimate importance in developing the chain is the sequence of behavior. If the behavior is taught out of sequence, the chain will break down. If the sequence is changed from time to time, the chain will break down. Therefore, when designing a chaining program you must first break the task into its logical steps. The steps need to be just large or small enough to fit the child's capabilities. This will help to determine which behaviors belong in the chain and in which order they should be taught. It would not make much sense to have a child brush his teeth before putting the toothpaste on the brush, but a child may do just that if one time you have him wet his brush before putting on the toothpaste, and one time you have him wet his brush after.

In theory, backwards chaining works most effectively because each link in the chain is built up from the effect of the previous reinforcers. For example, praise and a cookie at the end of the chain of shoelace-tying will make the ending behavior, i.e. tightening the bow, gain reinforcing quality for the preceding step, i.e. pushing the second loop through the hole under the first loop, etc. In this case of backward chaining, the treatment worker would complete all but the final link of shoe-tying; the final link being the one that the child is currently being reinforced for performing. The next step, occurring after the final link has been established, would be to complete the shoe tying up to the second to the last link, etc. Thus, the finished product is reinforced each time. Of course, forward chaining works, too. It just takes longer to get to the reinforcer that will naturally maintain the chain after the training is done.

PROMPTING

Prompts are additional stimuli that cue behavior in the presence of naturally occurring antecedents and reinforcers. For example, when a child is having trouble putting together a complicated puzzle, you might say "Try putting the outside pieces together first," as a prompt in the presence of the puzzle (antecendent) which will be followed by completing the puzzle (reinforcer).

Puzzle pieces (natural cues or antecedents)	(Prompt) "Try putting the outside pieces together first."	completion of puzzle (natural reinforcer)

Prompts are temporary cues that must be faded out in favor of naturally occurring cues. To use a prompt for an excessive period of time introduces artificial steps in the learning process that may interfere with the final learning of the child. For example, in response to a question, a child may look to an adult for a cue as to whether or not he ought to answer the question. The adult's encouragement, which may have been necessary in the beginning, may be carried on so long that the child seeks it regardless of any real need to do so. In this way, the adult may be inadvertently nurturing unnecessary dependence.

When selecting a behavior to prompt, pay attention to where the behavior falls apart in order to know which behavioral component to prompt. The final behavioral outcome may not occur for various reasons. You must find the correct reason and prompt the correct behavioral component in order to guide the child to success. For example, prompting a child to run faster in soccer (because he is always a few steps behind the play) may do no good at all if the problem is not one of speed but rather one of visually tracking the ball's movement. In this example, "Keep your eye on the ball," may work more successfully.

Prompts take three general forms: verbal instructions, modeling, and physical guidance. The order in which they are presented represents a movement towards more intrusive methods. As a general rule, attempt to use verbal instructions before modeling, and modeling before physical guidance. And, if you start with a more intrusive method, fade to a less intrusive one, then fade out prompts altogether.

Verbal Instructions

Verbal instructions may come in a variety of forms: Instructions on what to attend to in the antecedent stimulus, e.g., "Keep your eye on the ball," "Notice the way Johnny has asked 'please'?" "See how this letter curves around on the bottom." Instructions on what behaviors to perform, e.g., "Keep your wrist straight," "Lower your voice when you ask for what you want," "Say 'beee.' " Instructions on what to attend to in the consequent conditions, e.g., "See how when you follow through, the ball hits the back of the court," "How do you feel now that Johnny has given you what you asked for?" "Listen to how I say it and see if you said it the same way." Verbal instructions may be questions, requests, demands, hints, suggestions, etc.

The crucial factor in determining whether or not to use verbal instructions is whether the child does in fact do what you ask. You can hint, suggest, or demand all day, but if the child does not follow instructions, you will have to back up and teach the child that skill first. Following instructions is a skill, which, like any other, can be shaped and reinforced.

Modeling

Modeling means showing the child through demonstration what behavior to perform and how to engage in it. Used as a prompt, modeling primes the child by offering a sample of what is expected. Modeling can also teach altogether new behavior through vicarious learning. Several situations indicate that modeling may be appropriate. First, motor responses may best be modeled rather than described verbally. Secondly, complex responses may become overwhelming when described, but comprehensible when demonstrated. Thirdly, children with a limited receptive vocabulary or people who learn visually may better comprehend a model than a description. For example, trying to instruct a child in the individual steps involved in rolling a bowling ball may become so tedious to the child and the treatment worker that both give up. On the other hand, saying things such as "See how I'm holding my hands," "Now watch what I do with my feet," "Notice how I swing the ball," etc. will tune the child into the types of actions necessary to knock the pins down at the other end of the bowling alley.

The research on modeling has yielded the following principles to make modeling more effective:

Select a model who is similar to the child but who has greater status or prestige. Drawing the child's attention to a somewhat older child's behavior may serve both purposes.

Cue the child on what to look for in the model's behavior so that the child attends to the critical factors and can potentially "talk himself through" the modeled behavior.

Keep the modeled behavior within the capacities of the child. You can combine shaping and chaining with modeling so that complex behavior to be modeled can be broken into smaller portions.

Provide reinforcement for the model's behavior. The child observes not only the behavior in question, but also the positive consequences of the behavior. Thus, the child can anticipate similar reinforcement for his own performance of that behavior.

Choose a model that the child views as competent.

Choose behavior to model that the child has failed at or had difficulty with in the past. Such behavior is more likely to be seen as needing external aid.

Choose a model with whom the child has had previous cooperative experience.

For example, the treatment worker may want to teach Jeff some new dance steps so that he can receive reinforcement for social behavior. Jeff has had troubles at dances before. The treatment worker negotiates with Jeff to arrange to ask Alan, an older, popular basketball player with whom Jeff has worked in a band, to teach Jeff. The treatment worker asks Alan to begin with simple steps to slow music. As Alan demonstrates, the treatment worker labels Alan's movements "1, 2, 3 step back; 1, 2, 3 step forward," and praises Alan's speculating on how the girls must like that dance step.

Sometimes children do not know how to model, just as they may not know how to follow verbal instructions. If this is the case, you can teach imitative behavior as a precursor to using modeling as a prompt.

Physical Guidance

When the previous methods of prompting have failed, you may need to fall back on the use of physical guidance. As the most intrusive of the prompts it can cause the most negative side-effects. Wean the child off of this method as quickly as you can. This fading starts by using the minimum amount of pressure to guide the action that will be reinforced. Two general principles apply to physical guidance. First, arrange the environment so that the child can attend to the appropriate kinesthetic cues as he moves through the performance you are guiding. For example, a treatment worker teaching a child how to throw clay on a potter's wheel will need to be sure the child is physically comfortable, can reach the clay, and focuses his attention on the physical sensations in various parts of his hands. Secondly, the most important pitfall in using physical guidance is creating or magnifying resistance by the child. The best strategy is to create conditions in which the child will be cooperative. If the child resists and you struggle with him, several negative effects occur: the child becomes angry, frustrated, etc.; the physiological and kinesthetic cues developed in the struggle interfere with the cues you want learned; the child learns negative associations with the behavior you wish to teach. The object is to teach the child how to act so that he can reap rewards. Do not mistakenly persuade yourself that the goal is to " make the child do it." With a resisting child you may choose to wait until the child is relaxed, reinforce approximations of cooperation, maintain passive contact with the child until the child reduces struggling, or make an appointment to try the skill at a different time.

With many children, using more than one prompting technique simultaneously increases their success at learning new skills and new ways of learning. Some are especially weak or strong in the different modes. With these children, it may work well to pair prompts in order for them to learn to use new modes. For example, a child who is deficient in the auditory mode but strong in the kinesthetic mode may benefit from literally walking and talking her through a new behavior. By doing so, her chances of learning by verbal instruction would greatly improve.

Feelings and Issues for the Treatment Worker

Treatment workers can make assumptions about the way behavior ought to change and about what is legitimate for them to do in encouraging new behavior. These assumptions and rules may get in the way of a worker applying the getting-behavior-started techniques.

"A Kid That Age Ought to Be Able to Tie His Shoes, Get Himself Dressed, Etc."

Even though there are age norms for certain behaviors, each child is unique. Troubled children defy normative definition even more. Making rules about what "ought" to be can only lead to problems. If a person could shift the energy used to complain about what the child is *not* doing to carrying through a getting-behavior-started program, that person would probably have enough energy left over to go dancing until the wee hours for several nights. Even when a treatment worker chooses to use shaping, for example, the arbitrary rules about what the child "ought" to be able to do may lead the worker to expect too much from the child too fast. The saying "Little steps for little feet" captures the expectation that behavior programs must be tailored to the individual, not to some abstract notion of correctness. To expect too much from a child, even if the child encourages such overestimation, may teach the child that trying to change his behavior leads to failure. Rather than learning how to gauge his own abilities realistically, he learns to idealize his goals only to define himself as a failure for not reaching such goals. Kids learn to feel helpless in the change process because the first step of their past efforts at changing have been overly large. Modifying the change procedure slightly and allowing more time to reach goals can create feelings of mastery instead.

"Am I Going to Have to Tell/Show This Kid What to Do All His Life?"

If you find yourself feeling caught as the middleman between the child and the naturally occurring antecedents and consequences, that is a good sign that you may have stayed too long prompting or shaping a specific behavior. Fading yourself out may take some effort, but it can be done. The easiest way to avoid getting caught in that position in the first place is to move quickly to the next step. This strategy demands that you have a good grasp of what the treatment goals are and how those goals translate into specific action. It is sometimes amazing how quickly children move through parts of their treatment plans. Therefore, it is a good idea to peer into the future enough to develop an image of what you expect that child to look like, then develop concrete thoughts about your reactions to him as he progresses. Obviously, you will need to leave room for ongoing changes you have not anticipated, and for new input about modes of treatment.

"The Kid's Not Dumb! Why Can't He Learn How to Tie His Shoes?"

The answer to that question may include many factors, including the child's resistance and his response to expectations for complex behavior. First, the child may choose to refuse, directly or indirectly, to comply with an expectation. Playing dumb, finding distractions, becoming angry or anxious all may serve to restrict the child's performance. If the simple behavior that you are trying to teach the child represents a larger issue for the child, you may have to respond to that issue along with the behavior at hand. Expecting specific behavioral performance may call forth specific resistances and issues that have laid dormant for years. Rather than seeing such larger issues as irritating distractions, appreciate them as important materials for treatment that may not have otherwise surfaced and be prepared to include them as aspects of the child's treatment plan. Secondly, even the most simple behavior may appear very complex to a child. Be prepared to break performances into small chunks. Then be prepared to break the chunks into smaller chunks. In order to get a behavior started, there no chunk is too small to use.

"This Is Just Too Easy. How is She Supposed to Learn Anything When Everything is Made So Easy For Her?"

The assumption here is that for learning to be worthwhile, it must be difficult, frustrating, and painful. It is true that children must learn to cope with frustration in order to cope with the "real world." And, frustration tolerance can be shaped just like any other skill. However, if the goal is learning specific behaviors, then frustrations, and pain are not useful. A child's successes need not be diminished because she had fun during the learning process. The final behavior is the same. In fact, given a positive experience, the child's feelings about her final performance will make her more receptive to future learning. (See Table 22-1.)

Table 22–1. Getting Behavior Started Behavior Checklist

Record the frequency of the following behaviors:

Positive performance	*Problematic performance*
Shaping:	Shaping:
____ Final performance specified	____ Initial expectations of child's performance too high
____ Shaping begun within capacity of the child	____ Shaping steps too large
____ Shaping steps small enough to ensure success and large enough to create challenge	____ Shaping steps too small
Chaining:	Chaining:
____ Chain links sequenced properly	____ Inconsistent or improperly sequenced chain links
____ Links in chain fit child's capacities	____ Links in chain too complex for child
____ Behavioral links already in child's repertory	____ Links in chain too simple for child
Prompting:	Prompting:
____ Verbal prompts used to point out antecedents	____ Verbal prompts to irrelevant stimuli or consequences
____ Verbal prompt used to point out consequences	____ Verbal prompt kept too long
____ Verbal prompt faded as quickly as possible	____ Modeled behavior too complex for the child
____ Attention drawn to crucial part of modeled prompt	____ Model chosen not facilitative for the child
____ Model chosen has both similarity and greater status than the child	____ Too much pressure used
____ Modeled behavior given words or other symbolic referents usable by the child	____ Physical guidance used for too long
____ Physical guidance used with minimum pressure	

Quality factors—Describe the worker's performance in relation to the following:

1. behavioral approximations and new final performance behaviors reinforced continuously
2. prompted behavior selected for its centrality in repairing breakdown in behavior
3. prompts faded as quickly as possible
4. model chosen fits all the characteristics of a good model as listed in the chapter

Chapter 23

TRANSFER AND MAINTENANCE OF BEHAVIOR CHANGE

After mastering the information in this chapter you should be able to—

1. define the concepts of transfer and maintenance;
2. explain how to minimize the need to work toward transfer and maintenance;
3. explain how transfer and maintenance problems arise;
4. identify and explain possible solutions to transfer and maintenance problems;
5. define generalization and identify three ways to increase it;
6. define intermittent reinforcement and give three advantages for using it;
7. identify and give examples of four different types of intermittent reinforcement;
8. relate transfer and maintenance to non-behavioral levels of worker functioning as illustrated in "Feelings and Issues for the Treatment Worker."

Since most children you treat will not stay forever in your treatment setting, the issues of transfer and maintenance of behavior will emerge. Transfer addresses the problem of helping the child perform behaviors learned in the treatment setting to other non-treatment settings. Maintenance addresses the problem of keeping the behavior going in the face of non-ideal conditions. Consider these issues before you try to change behavior so that you can select methods that will best prepare the child for the world in which you expect him to live. Repeating here our rule of seeking the least intrusive-effective method of behavior change, we want to emphasize the view of treatment as a bridge to a more developmentally advanced behavior, not as an end in itself. Therefore, the methods used must take into account the context into which the child will eventually function, whether it be a continued treatment or a non-treatment setting. The final context as used in this chapter does not necessarily mean "normal" public school or family. Rather it means whatever setting in which the child can function at his capacity. Obviously this setting will be different for children of different capacities.

Transfer and maintenance of behavior change cannot be assumed. As a matter of fact, assuming non-transfer and relapse may be safer. A plan must be made to assure transfer and maintenance rather than leaving these phenomena to chance. There are several conditions in which you can minimize the difficulties of transferring and maintaining behaviors. First, if you devise and carry out a behavior-change program within the context in which it is to be finally performed, then there is no transfer problem. Secondly, if you use existing reinforcers at the levels at which they are already distributed in the final context, then you have no maintenance problems. Thirdly, if you can increase the quantity and quality of reinforcers available in the final context to a level that coincides with those of the treatment setting, then you have no maintenance problems. In other words, if you can rearrange the existing final context to distribute its reinforcers according to the conditions of delivery as explained in the chapter on "Increasing Behavior," and if that rearrangement is enough to change the behavior, then you eliminate transfer and maintenance problems by making an out-patient model possible. We suggest this model to you as an ideal, least intrusive-effective method.

Reasons for Transfer and Maintenance Problems

Not all children, not all behaviors, and not all final contexts fit the ideal described in the previous paragraph. Transfer and maintenance of behavior change become problematic under certain conditions. First, you may not know the final context for which the child must be prepared. With no parental, foster care, or other group care setting in mind, you can only make an educated guess as to where the child will be living. Secondly, the most desirable final context, family or school, may be unable to accept/tolerate the child's current approximation of positive behavior. The child may provoke negative reactions from his parents and siblings; he may severely disrupt the operation of a regular classroom. Therefore, the child's behavior must be changed significantly before the child returns to these contexts. Thirdly, the most desirable final context may contain cues for continued disruptive behavior. In a family, parents may show anger/rejection/passivity that provokes negative reactions in the child. His siblings may manipulate and scapegoat him. In school and in the community peers may provoke him. Therefore, maintenance of the child's progress would be extremely difficult if not impossible in those settings. Finally, a child may need extensive work on transference and maintenance of behavior change if her behavior is extremely stimulus bound. You can assume that all children will react very specifically to cues in specific situations. By virtue of their lack of experience in the world, children's behavior is responsive to environmental influences. They will react more to the specific stimuli in a specific situation rather than to the similarities across situations. That is, they do not generalize well. Moreover, some children react with extremely concrete tunnel vision which makes more pronounced the narrow range of the stimuli to which they will react with a given behavior. For example, if a child learns to dance to a specific record, he may not dance to another record even though the music may be similar. With them you may have to almost re-teach the behavior in each new setting.

Possible Solutions to Transfer and Maintenance Problems

At least five possible solutions may be considered to combat the problems raised in the previous section. Although we will consider each separately, note that in practice you might best do all of them at once.

First, develop the final context to which the child moves into a more supportive one. Such activities as parent training, family counseling, inservice training to teachers, consultation with community agencies, and advocacy for the child all may encourage a more positive response from the physical and social context into which the child moves.

Secondly, build on the child's strengths while continuing to work on his weaknesses. Most children will demonstrate an unevenness of behavior across academic, social, and emotional areas. Rather than waiting for all of these areas of behavior to even out, you can move the child towards the final context in one area while keeping another area in a treatment context. Special, individualized educational settings in the public schools capture the idea of providing special help in some areas while moving the child into "normal" contexts in others. As with the principle of shaping, if you allow the child to remain too long in one step, he will become bored and overlearn the behavior appropriate to that step, making it more difficult to move on. Moving with the child's readiness in a variety of areas of his functioning can avoid these problems.

Thirdly, teach the child to reinforce himself in the presence of nonreinforcement from the final context. Children can learn self-management skills which allow them to maintain and modify their own behavior in non-treatment contexts. Some of these skills include self-reinforcement, verbal mediation of skill behavior (talking themselves through difficult tasks), and others.

Fourthly, train the child to perform behaviors that will elicit positive reactions from the final context. These positive-reaction-evoking behaviors may or may not be related to the core issues of the child's treatment, but they will increase the likelihood that the people in that environment will react more positively towards him, and may even create a more tolerant attitude towards other low-level disruptive behavior. Reinforcing a child for participation in potentially rewarding activities may lead the child to experience the natural reinforcing contingencies available from peers. Training the child in fundamental skills necessary to engage in more complex rewarding activities may be a precursor for his engaging in those activities. For example, teaching a child how to throw and catch a ball may be necessary before encouraging him to join a baseball game.

Fifthly, several behavior-management principles can be used to aid generalization of behavior change and to innoculate the child, thus increasing the child's resistance, to behavior-disrupting factors. The concept of *generalization* indicates that to facilitate transfer of behavior change from situation A to situation B you must gradually approximate situation B within the context of situation A using as many different cues as possible. For example, in preparing a child to move from a small, quiet, individualized, informal academic setting to a large, noisy, group-oriented formal classroom, the treatment worker must begin to give the child experience with noise, formality, and group expectations within the more protected context. The concept of *intermittent reinforcement* indicates that to facilitate maintenance of behavior change you must gradually shift to types and amounts of reinforcers that currently function in the final context. We will now detail these behavior-management principles. (See Figure 23-1.)

Generalization

When generalization occurs, a behavior learned in one stimulus situation is performed in other stimulus situations. This effect can be increased by taking a number of specific steps.

EMPHASIZE SIMILARITIES BETWEEN THE TREATMENT CONTEXT AND THE FINAL CONTEXT. Verbalize the similarities; point to or show what things are similar and explain how they function similarly. Reframe apparent differences as functional similarities. For example, a child going home for a weekend visit may be told in the presence of his parents, who have been briefed earlier, what expectations, consequences, and daily routines will be the same both at home and at the treatment agency. Although the Time Out

Figure 23-1. Transfer and Maintenance of Behavior Change

location will be different in the two places, parents and the treatment worker can discuss the similarity in function of the two places.

IDENTIFY AND USE KEY CUES IN THE FINAL CONTEXT. The treatment worker may demonstrate to the parents the warning procedure for Time Out, showing a nonverbal hand signal that the child recognizes, and then have the parents demonstrate the hand signal or have them adapt a method of giving warnings that they feel is more natural for them. Likewise the treatment worker and the parents may negotiate a method to set expectations using a specific vocabulary which then would be similar across settings.

PRACTICE THE CHANGED BEHAVIOR IN A NUMBER OF SETTINGS, OR UNDER A NUMBER OF SETTING CONDITIONS. For initial home visits the treatment worker may suggest that the parents avoid trips or visitors. But later, these may be introduced gradually to vary the environments in which the changed behavior might be practiced.

Intermittent Reinforcement

As its name implies, intermittent reinforcement means that behavior does not receive reinforcement every time, but only intermittently.

ADVANTAGES. First, the child's behavior better resists breakdown in the face of non-reinforcement if an intermittent schedule has been used. The child becomes familiar with functioning for short periods of time while some behaviors go unreinforced. He develops the expectation that continued responding, up to a point, will yield eventual reinforcement. Secondly, intermittent reinforcement approximates levels of reinforcement available in the final context. Continuous reinforcement in the final context is highly unlikely; therefore, *slow transition* to a less than continuous schedule becomes advantageous. Thirdly, a shift away from external reinforcers allows the child to focus more on the intrinsic reinforcing qualities of the behavior and the context. Thus, the child moves his attention to more naturally occurring consequences.

Moving to intermittent reinforcement schedules follows the design of shaping. That is, the shift to leaner schedules comes about gradually. If you move the child too quickly to low levels of reinforcement, his behavior will be disrupted. The four schedules of intermittent reinforcement are explained below.

RATIO

1. Fixed Ratio. In this schedule a reinforcement is given after a specific number of behaviors. For example, for each three days of *keeping her room clean,* Cheryl receives 25¢. This ratio may be a reduction from 5¢ for each separate chore of hanging clothes, making the bed, putting away toys, and vacuuming the rug, performed each day. It may yet be diminished to 25¢ for each week of keeping her room clean.

2. Variable Ratio. In this schedule a reinforcer is given after an average number of behaviors. In the example above, Cheryl might receive her 25¢ after two days, after four days, or after three days, the average being three days. This schedule closely resembles the most typical natural reinforcement schedule. That is, in naturally occurring situations, reinforcement comes after every few behaviors in an unpredictable manner, and yet are contingent on performance.

In each of the above schedules, reinforcers are delivered after some number of behaviors performed. In the next two schedules the reinforcer is delivered for a behavior performed only after a passage of time.

3. Fixed Interval. In this schedule a reinforcement is given for performance after the passage of a specific interval of time. Thus, a treatment worker might praise George's contributions to group every five minutes. This might be down from praising him every one minute, which in turn might be down from praising every contribution. A further reduction might be praising George's contributions only after group is over.

4. Variable Interval. In this schedule a reinforcement is given for performance after the passage of an average amount of time. Thus, in the example above, the treatment worker could have praised after four minutes, or six minutes, or five minutes; the average being five minutes.

In selecting which schedule of reinforcement to use, you can consider several factors. First, work to approximate the type of schedule available in the final context. If an allowance is used, move the child towards a fixed interval schedule because that is how an allowance is given. If the response to desired behavior is random, such as praise in the classroom, then move towards a variable ratio schedule since it reflects this unpredictability.

Secondly, consider the type of final performance desired. Interval schedules promote a low rate of behavior that may accelerate at the ends of intervals. For example, note the rash of studying that occurs just before mid–term and final exams. Ratio schedules yield higher rate behavior since the reinforcer is clearly related to the amount of performance.

Finally, consider the ease with which a treatment worker or other person in the final context can maintain the schedule. Interval schedules are easier to track by the use of devices such as kitchen timers. Variable schedules may be easier to carry through because of their approximate rather than precise nature.

Feelings and Issues for the Treatment Worker

Treatment worker feelings and the mechanics of generalization and intermittent reinforcement *may* combine to block the worker from effective efforts at gaining transference and maintenance of behavior change.

"What If His School Blows Up? How Will He Handle That?"

There is no way for you to predict the future. You cannot possibly work with the child to overcome every potential problem in the final context. Likewise, at the end point in treatment you will not see the perfectly adjusted, perfectly behaving child. You must face the fact that changes for good or ill will continue with "your" child after he leaves you. Give it your best shot. Work to anticipate most of the reasonably predictable problems. Tinker with the transition process to encourage long-lasting positive change. Then, keep your hands out. Both the child and the people in the final context must learn through experience.

"He Does It So Well In The Agency, Why Doesn't He Do It At Home?" Or Vice Versa.

Different contexts elicit different reactions from children. The treatment setting is not "normal" and the home or school setting is not "treatment". Ultimately it would be nice if the child's positive behavior occurred in all settings. When working for this state of affairs, look to the context in which the positive behavior occurs to teach you how to develop that behavior in other contexts. Yes, even the most seemingly bizarre home or school environment may have something to teach you. Recognize also that with some behaviors it may be best to discriminate clearly between settings rather than to generalize. For example, full-blown temper tantrums that are allowed in the treatment setting may not be encouraged at home or in school.

"He's Just Not Trying. I Know He Can Do It; I've Seen Him."

A child may stop positive changes and even revert to previous problematic behavior while transfering out of the treatment setting. Such reactions can be a normal part of the transition process which we will discuss at length in a later chapter. In addition, treatment workers can expect that transitions will take much effort for both the child and the worker. Using the information in this chapter you can de-bug the recurrence of problem behavior. Expect problems to occur; expect to intervene with both the child and the people in the final context. Such problems do not ordinarily reflect a failure in treatment, but rather a natural stage in the extention of treatment results.

"But She's Not Ready Yet!"

Treatment workers may unrealistically recite the previous sentence for a variety of reasons. Workers may become very attached to a specific child and wish to keep her near. Workers may become over-attentive to the rule of taking small steps and miss the child's readiness to take a leap. Workers may wish to protect the child from failure or may be too perfectionistic in their expectations of how the child must behave in the new setting. One of the continually unresolved paradoxes of treatment can be found in the decision concerning a child's readiness to move on. On one hand, if you do not allow the child to take considered risks, you over-protect the child, teach her to mistrust her own judgment, and invite her to depend on others to do her thinking. On the other hand, if you allow a child to take too great a risk, she may experience overwhelming failure which creates pain and fear that blocks her from making further attempts when she is truly ready. There is no easy answer. Encouraging the child to take responsibility for small-step decisions and success or failure may pave the way for the child to make more realistic large-step decisions later.

"I Have To Bite My Tongue In Order To Cut Down On The Social Reinforcers I Give."

As effective treatment workers you are taught to use a high rate of positive social reinforcers. When you move to intermittent reinforcement, you must reverse your hard-won learning. You may in fact have to develop strategies to make more flexible the routine you have developed for delivering reinforcers. With the ultimate criterion of positive outcome for the child, this discomfort to you will pay off for the child in a greater ability to maintain his behavior in non-treatment settings.

"Oh No! I Forgot To Reinforce Him."

Intermittent schedules create a more complicated pattern of reinforcement. In that complexity rests the potential for forgetting or confusion. If you forget to reinforce a behavior according to a specific schedule and the behavior maintains, you may wish to use your "error" to readjust the schedule in a leaner direction. Often the child will tell you that you have stayed too long with a specific schedule by her ignoring or not cashing in her accumulation of reinforcers. She may move to request non-contingent reinforcers at times other than when she performs behaviors you wish to maintain. In that case, she is working on "credit" rather than on "piecework". This move on the child's part clearly signals her readiness to maintain that behavior without heavy external control. (See Table 23-1.)

Table 23–1. Transfer and Maintenance of Behavior Change Behavior Checklist

Record the frequency of the following behavior:

Positive performance	*Problematic performance*
Generalization:	Generalization:
____ Similarities between treatment and final context situation emphasized	____ Similarities between treatment and final context situation ignored or de-emphasized
____ Key cues in final context arranged to support treatment setting learning	____ Key cues in final context ignored or unnecessarily altered
____ Graded practice of performance to be maintained given under different conditions in the treatment and final context setting	____ No allowance for graded practice under different conditions
Intermittent reinforcement:	Intermittent reinforcement:
____ Intermittent reinforcement introduced in gradual steps	____ Intermittent reinforcement introduced too rapidly
____ Selection of intermittent schedule matches final context schedule	____ Perseveration of too much reinforcement
____ Intermittent schedule maintained consistently	
____ Schedule of reinforcement adjusted to the child's pace	

Quality factors—Describe the worker's performance in relation to the following:

1. behavior-change intervention carried out within the final context using rearrangement of existing reinforcers
2. transfer and maintenance issues addressed at the beginning of a behavior-change intervention when possible
3. final-context people consulted while treatment-setting interventions are developed
4. final-context people consulted while transfer and maintenance issues are planned for

Part V

TREATMENT FRAMEWORKS

The individual skills elaborated in the preceding three parts of this book must be combined in relevant ways to address crucial issues in treatment; otherwise the skills become isolated techniques with no broader application. In examining broader frameworks for treatment, we will step up a level in complexity and perspective. Because of this more abstract view of treatment, it is difficult to point to one discrete set of behaviors that exclusively advance the goals of treatment strategy. Rather, multiple skills are necessary. Therefore, we will drop the behavior checklists from this section in favor of guidelines and suggestions in the text.

The treatment frameworks included in this part address recurrent themes in child treatment: problem solving, conflict resolution, transitions, and tantruming. These themes have somewhat predictable patterns, and therefore, children can be guided and encouraged through a general sequence of steps to a positive outcome. Using the treatment frameworks is a little like taking a trip. The child is at the wheel; you, the navigator, have the map. You can help the child to decide which route to take to get to his goal: shortest route or scenic route. As the child embarks you can adjust the route according to the needs of the child, picking short-cuts when available. There may be some detours, dead ends, and back alleys, but with your broader view of the map, you can reassure the child of the overall progress he is making toward his goal.

Chapter 24

PROBLEM SOLVING AND CONFLICT RESOLUTION

After mastering the information in this chapter you should be able to—

1. identify the preliminary steps to problem solving;
2. explain and give examples of the steps in the problem solving strategy;
3. explain the notion of conflict as opportunity;
4. explain and give an example of how to use the gripe formula;
5. identify fair fighting guidelines to be used in the negotiation process;
6. identify patterns of behavior that violate constructive conflict resolution guidelines;
7. identify the advantages and disadvantages of the negotiation mediator role;
8. explain the transition of the mediator role from more to less intrusive;
9. identify options that can be used if conflict resolution is not concluded;
10. relate problem solving and conflict resolution to non-behavioral levels of worker functioning as illustrated in "Feelings and Issues for the Treatment Worker."

Problem solving and conflict resolution can be seen as personal and interpersonal events. As a treatment worker, you may be called upon to solve your problem with a child or you may wish to facilitate the process of a child's working through his own problem solving. You may wish to resolve a conflict with a specific child, or you may mediate between two or more children who want to work through their conflict. In each setting the problem solving and conflict resolution processes apply. Some factors need to be added as you step out of the direct participant role into the facilitator/mediator role. Keep in mind as you read this chapter that the skills also apply to co-worker relationships.

The diagram below illustrates some decisions that need to be made and some steps that need to be taken in solving a conflict that you might have with a child and in facilitating the child's developing solutions for a problem. Before addressing the steps in the problem solving process, two preliminary steps need to be addressed. (See Figure 24-1.)

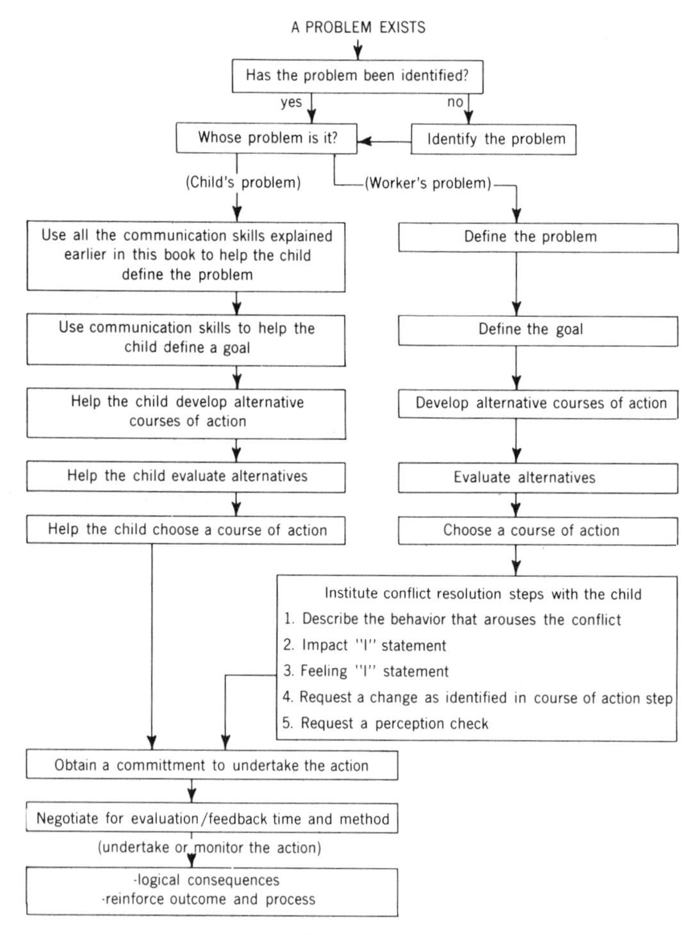

Figure 24-1. Problem Solving and Conflict Resolution

Is the Problem Identified?

If a problem exists for an outside observer but no problem exists for the treatment worker or the child, then you need to assess whether the observer has the problem (see the following step), or whether you are ignoring something that in fact must be addressed. We all have a tendency to avoid problems. Oftentimes we mistakenly think that by refusing to acknowledge them, we can make them go away. Also, some people hope against hope that if they wait long enough things will get better. Your task as a treatment worker is to evaluate which problems must be acknowledged and addressed.

Whose Problem Is It?

This step is crucial because treatment workers can spend much time and energy solving problems for children who do not wish those problems to be solved because they do not perceive them as problems. We elaborate the concept of problem ownership as follows:

CHILD'S PROBLEM. The child has a problem if he is thwarted in satisfying a need. It is not the treatment worker's problem because the child's feelings and behavior in no way interferes with him. Therefore, the child owns the problem.

NO PROBLEM. The child is satisfying his own needs. He is not thwarted, and his feelings and behavior do not interfere with the treatment worker. Therefore, there is no problem in the relationship.

WORKER'S PROBLEM. The child is satisfying his own needs. He is not thwarted but his behavior interferes with the treatment worker. Now the treatment worker owns the problem (Gordon, 1970).

Your discomfort alone does not define a problem for the child or vice versa. Embedded in this concept of problem ownership is the idea that we are all responsible for our own feelings, ideas, and behaviors. We must take care of ourselves rather than waiting for others to do so.

PROBLEM SOLVING

The problem solving process has two specific goals: the outcome goal is to cope with the child's immediate problem; the process goal is to help the child deal with his present situation in a way that increases his long-term problem solving abilities. Overall, the objective of problem solving is best reached when the treatment worker can help the child to cope with his own problems.

When problem solving meets the above goals, it occurs within a person-to-person relationship. This relationship implies an acknowledgment of the child's strengths and capabilities while focusing on his present problem. A child may be overwhelmed by many different kinds of distressing situations. Exploring the full range of problems and facilitating the child's own understanding of how the problem persists is necessary groundwork for the problem solving strategy.

Often problem solving has been thought of as "advice giving." When you give advice from outside of a relationship that promotes exploration and understanding, the child is usually discounted because the advice comes from your point of view rather than from an empathic understanding of the child. Such advice, if followed, may even cause additional problems. A "friendly piece of advice" may turn out to be anything but friendly when not preceded by an effort to promote exploration and understanding.

The steps outlined below for the problem solving strategy explain the factors involved in more detail than you will be able to address in a typical problem solving incident. Ideally, you will sit down with the child for some uninterrupted conversation leading progressively to a solution to the child's problem. In reality, you may engage in an abbreviated version of this process on-the-run or in the middle of a million distractions. Over a period of time you will need to address all of the issues elaborated here. If you find that you neglect some of these issues, we suggest that you make time for an individual conference with the child to touch all bases. Likewise, if it frequently occurs that the solutions the child develops do not work out, it is likely that some steps in the problem solving strategy have been slighted and need to be strengthened. The steps of the problem solving strategy follow:

Defining the Problem

Of the several problems that a child is likely to present, it is usually wisest to select the *one* that can make a difference in the person's life, but is simple enough to yield a high probability of success. Such early successes encourage the child to use the process again. Typical everyday misfortunes will raise many issues, e.g., "I lost my jacket," "Irv stole my football," "They won't let me play," etc.

When defining the problem, the goal is to break it down into specific, concrete terms. For example, rather than saying "people don't like me," one would say "Pat has it in for me," or even better (i.e., more specific and concrete) "Pat yells at me when I try to play with him." In addition, each concrete term has a positive or negative feeling attached to it. These feelings must also be pinned down as closely as possible. For example, "When he yells at me I feel lousy" could be more specific, such as "When he yells at me I sometimes get mad and feel like crying."

Define the Goal

The purpose of defining a goal is to provide a specific future reference towards which the treatment worker and child work and against which they measure the success of their final solution. Again, it is important to be as specific and concrete as possible. Goals should be related to the problem definition in the previous step. It is important to be as realistic as possible in setting goals. Often at this step the child must come to a clear understanding of what is changeable and what is not. For example, "I wish Pat would like me more," is a goal not directly under the child's control. "I'll try to play with him better," *is* under his control. In simple terms, the definition of a goal is the "flip side" of the definition of the problem. It is a statement of what he would like to do differently. Sometimes the goal as finally defined needs to be broken down into sub-goals to make successful goal attainment more likely.

Develop Alternative Courses of Action

The question in this step is "How can the child attain his goal?" Brainstorming all possible means of goal attainment is the first task. Initially, no course of action is too far-out or too outlandish. Practicality in this step may stifle creative possible solutions. After an initial list of alternatives is created, each must be examined to determine their relevance to the goal and their practicality. Care must be taken to include *all* workable and relevant courses of action, even those that do not seem immediately desirable. For example, to attain the goal of "playing soccer in ways that Pat approves of," the solution of "practicing soccer two hours every night," might at first seem an undesirable alternative, but it should be included because it is relevant and workable. You may wish to add alternatives to the list, being cautious not to subtly persuade the child by your nonverbal expressions of bias.

Evaluate Probable Consequences of Action Alternatives

In order to measure consequences of action, the child needs to develop his own yardstick. Since it is he who will be most affected by whatever course of action is chosen, it is he who must evaluate the personal consequences of the alternatives. The questions to answer are first, "What values will be met by each course of action?" and secondly, "Which alternatives will best satisfy my most important values?" To answer these questions the child must identify what aspects of his life are most important. What does he value? When he has made value statements, the values need to be sorted into a hierarchy, that is, ordered from most important to least important. For example, a child may value his family, his free time, success at school, and approval from his peers, in that order. Using this personal "yardstick" he can determine which alternative action choices maximize his most important values, and which minimize them. The treatment worker's role at this time is to be sure that all critical values are represented on the "yardstick," and that the values are weighted according to their true importance. Then, elicit from the child probable consequences for each alternative. You may need to serve as a reality check for the child. In this role, be cautious about including or excluding alternatives on the basis of *your* value system. Allow the child to weigh the alternatives against probable outcomes, not against your potential approval or disapproval.

Choose a Course of Action

The next logical step is to select the course of action that best meets the values of the child. Even at this point the child may be determined to follow actions that do not best meet the goals he has chosen. The child still has the right to choose, even if unwisely. It is the treatment worker's task to support the choice by offering help in planning how to carry out the chosen action. At this point knowledge of therapeutic interventions is necessary to facilitate the child's move towards solving his problem. Implementing a course of action depends on many factors: the severity of the problem, the child's ability to follow through, etc. In any case, a specific and concrete plan considering and anticipating as many factors as possible will be more likely to succeed than a simple injunction to "go do what you have to do." Simplifying the steps necessary for effective action will help the child attain his goal. Activities such as role-playing, trying out words, scheduling time, helping him write a letter, all will help the child be more impactful.

Obtain a Commitment

The child may have worked through the problem solving strategy up until this point, and then decide that the actions available to him to solve his problem are more problematical than the original problem. Or, he may be under the false assumption that if he does not do what he can to cope with his own problems, then someone else will do it for him. In any event, he may decide not to undertake the task he has selected. Many workers believe that understanding what to do automatically guarantees appropriate action. That is not so. You must get a commitment from the child to undertake the action he has selected within a specific time. Likewise, you may want to provide support for the child. He may be afraid to confront another child by himself. You can negotiate to sit down with both of them as a non-participating member. In the long run you want to get yourself out of the middle so that the child takes full responsibility for developing and carrying out his solutions.

Evaluation/Feedback Time and Method

You and the child need to evaluate the effectiveness of the child's action. Feedback may come naturally from the attainment of the child's goal, in which case brief congratulations are in order. The evaluation may be immediate such as debriefing after your observation of the child's action to solve his problems. At this time, you may wish to coach him on better technique. In any event, a scheduled time to get together and review what has happened allows the child an opportunity to reflect on his gain or recalibrate his efforts at change.

Aftermath

Most often aftermath means providing some feedback about the problem solving process as well as the outcome. It is a chance to recycle the problem that remains unsolved back through the problem solving strategy. The treatment worker will reinforce gains made and help the child redefine the problem as it still exists. With positive outcome, it is a time to notice how the child's behavior has changed. (See Table 24-1.)

Conflict Resolution

Although most of us consider it undesirable, we believe conflict itself to be inevitable. Only the manner of resolving conflict is desirable or undesirable. Conflict between people indicates some unresolved issue that must be dealt with, now or later. Thus, we look at conflict as an opportunity to notice something that must be dealt with and an opportunity to advance our development through constructive action aimed at the issue underlying the conflict. Since conflict cannot be totally avoided, we suggest that you adopt our *opportunistic* notion of conflict in order to take advantage of conflict incidents that will arise.

Conflict resolution, as presented here, has two parts: the method for presenting your gripe as a participator and the factors that facilitate good negotiation.

Presenting Your Gripe

Your task in presenting a gripe is to be as clear as possible about what your reactions are to the present state of affairs and to request a specific

Table 24–1. Example of Problem Solving

Child:	Nobody likes me.	Child states problem in general terms.
TW:	What do you mean?	TW asks for clarification.
Child:	The other kids won't let me play football with them.	Child is more specific.
TW:	You're feeling sad because the other kids won't let you play football with them.	TW reflects feelings and attaches the feelings to an event.
Child:	Yeah. But I don't blame them for not letting me play. I can't throw a football or catch one either.	Child continues to clarify the problem.
TW:	How would you like this situation to be different?	TW elicits a goal statement.
Child:	Well, I'd like the kids to let me play with them.	Child verbalizes a goal.
TW:	So you want them to let you play with them more. How do you suppose you could get them to do that?	TW paraphrases the goal and then elicits alternatives for solution.
Child:	Well I could read up on how to play football. I could ask to be included when they choose sides. I could get somebody to teach me how to play. Uh . . . . . I don't know what else.	Child generates several solutions.
TW:	That's a great list. I've been thinking, I've got some ideas to throw into the pot. Is that OK with you?	TW reinforces child for generating alternatives and asks permission to offer some of her own.
Child:	Sure.	Child allows TW to contribute.
TW:	Now I'm not saying that these are any better or worse than the ones you already said. Here's two I can think of: being with the kids as a non-playing member like a referee or manager, or being with them when they are not playing football. Can you think of any others?	TW takes pains to put her alternatives in as equal with the child's. Then she attempts to elicit more alternatives from the child.
Child:	No, not right now.	
TW:	Let's work with the ones we have, but any others we think of later we can include too. How do you feel about each of the alternatives? Will they get you what you want?	TW defines the list of alternatives as continually open, and moves on to evaluate them.

Table 24–1. Continued

Child:	Well, I don't like the ones you suggested because I want to be a part of the group when they're having fun playing. Being a referee wouldn't be the same. And I know that I can't learn football out of a book. And I already know that because I can't play very well, they don't like to pick me.	Child verbalizes his reasons for not accepting various alternatives from the list.
TW:	Sounds like playing with the group is what you really want and the ideas you just mentioned don't quite fit your idea of what it means to play with the group.	TW nondefensively allows the child to rule out her alternatives. She reflects the value embodied in the child's reasoning.
Child:	Yeah. Now I have a friend Ronnie who lives next door who could teach me how to throw and catch a football. I'm pretty sure he'd be willing to do it too.	Child acknowledges TW's reflection and goes on to consider the remaining alternatives in more detail.
TW:	So having a friend teach you seems to be the alternative that best meets your goal. What specifically will you have to do to get the other kids to let you play with them?	TW confirms the child's selection of an alternative and then elicits specifics on how that alternative will be carried out to attain his goal.
Child:	Well, first I have to ask Ronnie if he'd do it. Then I'll learn to catch and throw a football. Then when I'm good enough I'll ask to be picked again with the guys who play together.	Child articulates the steps he will have to take to attain his original goal.
TW:	Sounds like a very logical plan. When do you plan to ask Ronnie?	TW reinforces the plan and requests a commitment to ask Ronnie.
Child:	Well, I see him after school every day.	
TW:	Could you ask him either today or tomorrow?	TW asks for a specific commitment.
Child:	Yeah.	Child agrees.
TW:	Sounds great. Let's check back in a couple days to see how it's going, ok?	TW reinforces the child's solution and requests a follow-up meeting.
Child.	Ok.	

change that will remedy the situation for you. Remember that stating your reactions and your wants does not guarantee the child's responding as you wish. Your statement is merely a starting point for negotiation or for some other more unilateral action on your part. Below are the components of a formula to state a gripe effectively. (See Table 24-2.)

Negotiation

The formula for presenting a gripe embodies many positive behaviors that help to develop constructive negotiation. When you present your own gripe or when you act as a third-party mediator for conflict resolution, you will want to work for constructive negotiation and avoid the pitfalls that delay resolution or even escalate the conflict.

Patterson and Forgatch (1975) warn that the typical mode of conflict resolution relies on what he calls the "lawyer syndrome." In this pattern of conflict, three steps emerge: 1) prove fault, 2) induce guilt, and 3) sit back righteously and wait for the other person to change. Both sides of a conflict bring with them a vulnerability that they protect with defensiveness. When this defensiveness is breached, revenge and retaliation often follow. The negotiation process outlined here aims to eliminate the "lawyer syndrome" and all of its side-effects.

Fair Fight Guidelines

Below are fair fight guidelines that indicate how to avoid some of the more common errors made in negotiation:

Table 24–2. The Gripe Formula

Components	*Example*
Describe the behavior or situation that is a source of conflict.	"You know, you left the Tinker Toys out this morning all over the playroom floor,"
Describe the impact of the behavior or situation on you.	". . . and I tripped on some of them."
Describe your feelings about the impact of the behavior or situation.	"I am really irritated about that!"
Request a reasonable change that will relieve the conflict.	"So please put away the Tinker Toys when you're done."
Request a perception check to confirm that you were understood as you intended, and correct any misperceptions.	"Do you understand what I'm saying? Say back to me what I've just said to you."
Obtain a commitment to follow through with your request.	"Are you willing to do that?"

Be specific when you introduce a gripe. Describe a behavior and its impact on you. Also describe your feeling about the behavior.

Do not just complain, no matter how specifically, ask for a reasonable change that will relieve the gripe.

Ask for and give feedback on the major points to make sure you are heard, and to assure your partner that you understand what he wants. Be sure to paraphrase content and reflect feeling.

Confine yourself to one issue at a time. Otherwise you may skip back and forth, evading the hard ones.

Do not be glib or intolerant. Be open to your own feelings, and equally open to your partner's. Try to be honest and accurate in describing your own feelings and reflecting your partner's.

Always consider compromise. Remember, your partner's view of reality is just as real as yours, even though you may differ. There are not many totally objective realities.

Do not allow counter-requests to enter the picture until the original requests are clearly understood, and there have been clear-cut responses to them. Help your partner to clarify by asking him for behavior descriptions, feeling descriptions, and paraphrases.

Never put labels on a partner. Call him neither cowardly nor stupid. Do not make sweeping, labeling judgements about his feelings, especially about whether or not they are real or important.

Do not correct a partner's statement of his feelings or tell a partner what he *should* know or feel.

Do not mind-read. Ask! Never assume that you know what your partner is thinking until you have checked out the assumption in plain language; nor assume nor predict how he will react and what he will accept or reject.

Sarcasm is dirty fighting. It is retaliatory, thus resulting in further hostility and leading away from, rather than toward, resolution.

Forget the past and stay with the *here-and-now.* What either of you did last year or last month or that morning is not as important as what you are doing and feeling now. Furthermore, the changes you ask for cannot possibly be retroactive. Hurts, grievances, and irritations should be brought up at the very earliest moment, or the partner has the right to suspect that they may have been saved carefully as weapons.

Do not overload your partner with grievances. To do so makes him feel hopeless and suggests that you have either been hoarding complaints or have not thought through what really troubles you.

Meditate! Take time to consult your real thoughts and feelings before speaking. Your surface reactions may indicate something deeper and more important. Do not be afraid to close your eyes and think. Time is useful, take all you need.

Remember that there is never a single winner in an honest effective fight. Both achieve more closeness, or both lose it (Bach & Deutsch, 1970).

Counterproductive Fighting Styles

The guidelines for fair fighting may be violated in many different ways. Adler and Towne (1975) have identified patterns that treatment workers may wish to monitor in themselves and certainly must track as mediators for constructive negotiation. Adler and Towne's vocabulary refers to adults, so some translation for application with children will be necessary.

THE AVOIDER. The avoider refuses to fight. When a conflict arises, he will leave, fall asleep, pretend to be busy at work, or keep from facing the problem in some other way. This behavior makes it very difficult for the partner to express his feelings of anger, hurt, etc. because the avoider will not fight back. Arguing with an avoider is like trying to box with a person who refuses to put up his gloves.

THE PSEUDO-ACCOMMODATOR. Not only does the pseudo-accommodator refuse to face up to conflict; he pretends that there is nothing at all wrong. This really drives the partner who feels there is definitely a problem crazy and causes him to feel guilt and resentment toward the pseudo-accommodator.

THE GUILT MAKER. Instead of saying straight out that she does not want or approve of something, the guilt maker tries to change her partner's behavior by making him feel responsible for causing pain. The guilt maker's favorite line is "It's okay, don't worry about me . . .," accompanied by a huge sigh.

THE SUBJECT CHANGER. Really a type of avoider, the subject changer escapes facing up to aggression by shifting the conversation whenever it approaches an area of conflict. Because of his tactics, the subject changer and his partner never have the chance to explore their problem and do something about it.

THE CRITICIZER. Rather than come out and express his feelings about the object of his dissatisfaction, the criticizer attacks other parts of his partner's life. Thus he never has to share what is really on his mind and can avoid dealing with painful parts of his relationships.

THE MIND READER. Instead of allowing her partner to express feelings honestly, the mind reader goes into character analysis, explaining what the other person really means or what is wrong with the other person. By behaving this way the mind reader refuses to handle her own feelings and leaves no room for her partner to express himself.

THE TRAPPER. The trapper plays an especially dirty trick by setting up a desired behavior for his partner, and then when it is met, attacking the very thing he requested. An example of this technique is for the trapper to say, "Let's be totally honest with each other," and then when the partner shares his feelings he finds himself attacked for having feelings that the trapper doesn't want to accept.

THE CRISIS TICKLER. This person almost brings what is bothering him to the surface but he never quite comes out and expresses himself. Instead of admitting his concern about finances he innocently asks, "Gee, how much did that cost?" Thus he hints broadly but never really deals with the crisis.

THE GUNNYSACKER. This person does not respond immediately when he's angry. Instead, he puts his resentment into his gunnysack, which after a while begins to bulge with large and small gripes. Then, when the sack is about to burst, the gunnysacker pours out all his pent-up aggressions on the overwhelmed and unsuspecting victim. (See Figure 24-2.)

THE TRIVIAL TYRANNIZER. Instead of honestly sharing his resentments, the trivial tyrannizer does something he knows will get his partner's goat—leaving dirty dishes in the sink, clipping his fingernails in bed, belching out loud, turning up the television too loud, and so on.

THE JOKER. Because he is afraid to face conflicts squarely, the joker kids around when his partner wants to be serious, thus blocking the expression of important feelings.

THE BELTLINER. Everyone has a psychological "beltline," below which subjects are too sensitive to be approached without damaging the relationship. Beltlines may have to do with physical characteristic, intelligence, past behavior, or deeply ingrained personality traits a person is trying to over-

Figure 24-2. Counterproductive Fighting

come. In an attempt to "get even" or hurt his partner, the beltliner will use his intimate knowledge to hit below the belt, where he knows it will hurt.

THE BLAMER. The blamer is more interested in finding fault than in solving conflict. Needless to say, he usually does not blame himself. Blaming almost never solves a conflict and is an almost sure-fire way to make the receiver defensive.

THE CONTRACT TYRANNIZER. This person will not allow his relationship to change from the way it once was. Whatever agreements the partners had as to roles and responsibilities at one time remain unchanged. "It's your job to feed the baby, wash the dishes, discipline the kids, etc."

THE KITCHEN SINK FIGHTER. In an argument this person brings up things that are totally off the subject (everything but the kitchen sink): the way his partner behaved last New Year's Eve, the unbalanced checkbook, bad breath—anything

THE WITHHOLDER. Instead of expressing her anger honestly and directly, the withholder punishes her partner by keeping back something—courtesy, affection, cooperation, good humor. As you can imagine, this is likely to build up even greater resentments in the relationships.

THE BENEDICT ARNOLD. This character gets back at his partner by sabotage, by failing to defend him from attackers, and even by encouraging ridicule or disregard from outside the relationship. (Adler & Towne, 1975)

The Mediator Role

First on the list of *advantages* of putting yourself in the mediator position includes having the objectivity of a person not directly involved with the dispute being considered. Be aware of what your vested interests are, and keep out of the content of the negotiation as much as you can. Your primary role is to facilitate an effective conflict resolution process. Often people with something to gain or lose cannot maintain their objectivity. As an objective party interested in facilitating the negotiation process, you can call attention to and interrupt destructive processes such as those listed in the previous section. Likewise, you can direct, suggest, and model more constructive processes as embodied by the gripe formula. Finally, you can call a halt to a deadlocked, destructive negotiation process that, if left to continue, could create new conflict and injury.

The major *disadvantage* to the mediator role stems from the tendency of humans to form coalitions and triangles of interaction. With only two people in conflict, the parties have to deal with each other. Add a third person to the situation and each person in the conflict will try to get the third party on his side against the other. As a mediator you must avoid this because such action on the child's part does not resolve the conflict, it only justifies positions and assigns blame either overtly or covertly. Your credibility as a mediator plummets as children learn that you can be manipulated to "take sides."

Bandler, Grinder, and Satir (1976) illustrate three steps that a family therapist goes through when working with a troubled family. These same steps can apply to procedures that you can use to help children work through their conflict to constructive resolution.

1. The treatment worker contacts each of the parties, i.e., listens to and understands the source of their concern.
2. The treatment worker acts as a translator between the parties, i.e., rephrases the concerns of the one into language understandable to the other.
3. The treatment worker assists the parties in making direct contact. At this step interrupting destructive patterns and facilitating constructive patterns is the primary concern. (See Figure 24-3.)

What happens if the conflict remains unresolved? Sometimes, one or more of the conflicting parties will not be ready to settle the conflict. They may indicate this to you by refusing to follow the conflict resolution process

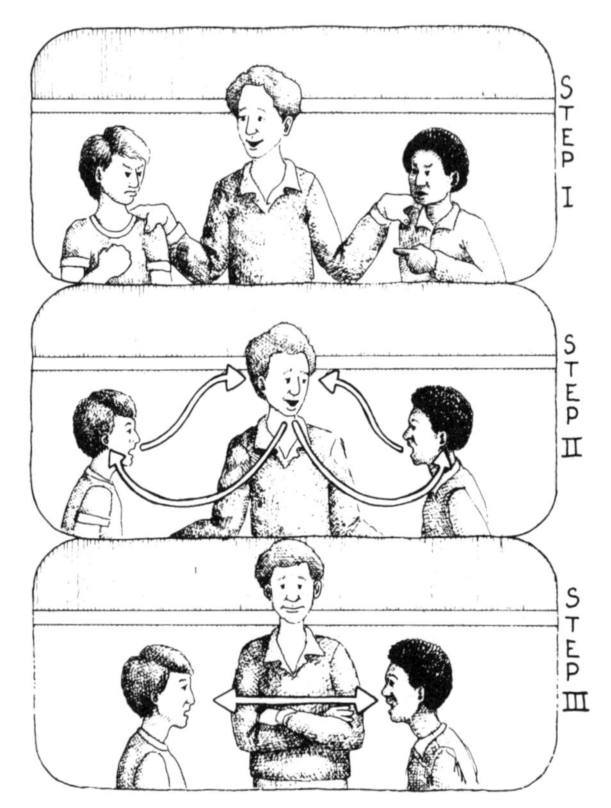

Figure 24-3. Mediator Role

even when you coach them, by refusing to accept or tolerate compromise, by using the negotiation process to develop coalitions and triangles, and by refusing to follow through with the agreements. You and the parties involved in the dispute have several choices of action:

POSTPONE THE NEGOTIATION UNTIL BOTH PARTIES CAN FOLLOW THE CONSTRUCTIVE PROCESS. Sometimes, emotions run too high for constructive response. A cool-down period may be advisable.

AGREE TO DISAGREE. If it turns out that the conflict does not bear immediate negative consequences to either of the parties, they may choose to avoid that part of their relating and agree to disagree. Many a marriage has been saved by refraining from trying to convince a spouse that his mother-in-law is really a "nice person."

DEVELOP UNILATERAL ACTION. When one party refuses to compromise, the other person has the choice of acting without the help or approval of the other. If a child refuses to stop stepping on your toes as he approaches to talk with you, you can take unilateral action by providing the logical consequence of turning away or having him engage in positive practice by walking up to you without toe-stepping.

PHYSICALIZE THE CONFLICT FOR DISCHARGE OF ANGER. Bach and Bernhard (1971) suggest using batacas (foam-rubber-covered sticks) to hit each other with. Other forms of physical contact such as pushing, wrestling, boxing, etc. may be used under controlled conditions. The key here is to provide a safe setting for release of aggression. One of the most important aspects of safety is some semblance of equity between the combatants. Therefore, holding one hand behind your back may equalize the abilities between you and a child.

SUBMIT TO BINDING ARBITRATION. Sometimes people become so committed to an uncompromising position that they feel they cannot budge for fear of "losing face." In such cases agreeing to abide by the decision made by a third party may be a graceful way out. This method takes responsibility off of the conflictees and puts it on someone else. For this reason we suggest that you avoid this solution if possible.

When the consequences of a conflict between two children involve others and the children are not willing to resolve it in an acceptable manner, you may wish to interrupt the conflict by assigning a temporary solution. For example, if two children engage in hand-to-hand combat on the bus, you may decide to break up the battle and place them in separate seats. (see Table 24-3.)

FEELINGS AND ISSUES FOR THE TREATMENT WORKER

"You've Got a Problem, So Face Up to It and Do Something About It."

In a very real sense, the child may have the problem. But the statement above implies a nonsupportive approach to the treatment worker role. When the above statement is expressed in an angry tone the child may rebelliously deny the problem. When the above statement is expressed in an indifferent tone, the child may feel not only the problem he started with, but also the problem of nonsupport from the treatment worker. Rather than debating with the child about whether or not he has a problem or detaching yourself from the child by denying your part in the problem solving process, help the child discover for himself the consequences of leaving the problem unsolved. Then require that the child take the responsibility to work through the steps of the problem solving strategy with you.

Table 24–3. Mediation Examples

Poor Example: "The Courtroom"

Speaker	Dialogue	Commentary
TW:	I can see that you two are having a hassle. What's the problem?	TW invites the kids to use her as a mediator.
Ron:	(Looking at TW) He stole my lunch and he won't give it back. I'm gonna break his arm if he doesn't give it back.	Ron presents his grips in an incomplete way with a threat attached.
Dick:	(Looking at TW) Well, he threw my baseball glove on the roof; now I can't play first base like I promised the guys.	Dick accuses in return without acknowledging Ron's gripe. Both talk to TW, not to each other.
TW:	Whoa, wait a minute. Now who started this?	TW interrupts process, then invites both kids to blame and justify to defend their perceptions rather than move into a constructive resolution.
Ron and Dick:	(simultaneously while pointing accusing fingers) He did!	Both kids respond accordingly.
TW:	Now, let's find out what really happened. I want the truth now! Ron, you threw Dick's glove on the roof?	TW implied that there is a right/wrong, win/lose answer to this conflict.
Ron:	I didn't mean to. I only did it because he pushed me off the swing.	Ron justified his position by blaming Dick.
Dick:	I pushed him off the swing because he took my place when I went to pick up my bat.	Dick justifies his position by blaming Ron.
TW:	Now Ron, you shouldn't have taken Dick's place on the swing. You'll have to stay in from play time this afternoon.	TW using right/wrong, "should" language, sides with Dick, and provides negative consequences for only one of the conflicted dyad, and she takes the responsibility for solving the conflict away from the children.
Ron:	(With tears in his eyes) That's not fair. He started it. (Walking away) I'll get you for this.	Ron invokes the injured "it ain't fair" justification for future revenge.
Dick:	(Smiling at TW) He'll get over it.	Dick gloats in the righteous vindication awarded him by the TW's siding with him.

Table 24–3. Continued

Good Example

Speaker	Dialogue	Commentary
TW:	I can see that you two are having a hassle. What's the problem?	TW invites the children to use her as a mediator.
Ron:	(Looking at TW) He stole my lunch and he won't give it back. I'm gonna break his arm if he doesn't give it back.	Ron presents his grips in an incomplete way with a threat attached.
Dick:	(Looking at TW) Well, he threw my baseball glove on the roof; now I can't play first base like I promised the guys.	Dick attempts a retaliatory accusation.
TW:	(Turning to Dick) Wait a minute, Dick. I want to hear what you have to say, but first I want to be sure I understand Ron. You'll have your turn too. Ok?	TW interrupts a getting-off-the-track maneuver. She moves to make clean contact with Ron by negotiating turn-taking with Dick.
Dick:	(Grumpily) Well, I guess.	Dick agrees to take turns.
TW:	(With hand on Dick) Thanks. (Turning to Ron) Ron, you sound really angry at Dick.	TW reassures Dick with hand. Uses a direct expression of the feeling implied by Ron.
Ron:	Damn right. Wouldn't you be if he stole your lunch?	Ron attempts to get TW on his side.
TW:	I'm interested in how you feel right now. Tell me how it happened.	TW avoids a coalition with a noncomittal reply, and request for more information.
Ron:	I came back from the field trip and my lunch was gone. Dick took it, I know he did.	Ron describes an ambiguous connection between the missing lunch and Dick.
TW:	So you're angry because your lunch is gone. And you think Dick took it, so you want him to give it back.	TW summarizes Ron's gripe in nonjudgmental terms.
Ron:	(Sulking) Yeah.	Ron agrees to the paraphrase.
TW:	(Turning to Dick) Now I'm ready to give you my full attention, Dick.	TW invites Dick's gripe.
Dick:	I'm angry too. That jerk threw my baseball glove on the roof. Now I can't play first base like I promised the guys.	Dick presents a fairly complete gripe with some name calling.
Ron:	(Looking at TW) See! See! He's trying to get back at me. Make him give me back my lunch.	Ron attempts to get TW on his side through "make him" language.

Table 24-3. Continued

Good Example (continued)		
TW:	(Glancing at Ron) Just hang on. It's Dick's turn. (Again looking at Dick) So you're angry because when your glove is on the roof, you can't play.	TW interrupts the attempt to sidetrack. TW rephrases Dick's gripe in nonjudgmental terms.
Dick:	Yeah.	Dick agrees to the paraphrase.
TW:	What did you want Ron to do?	TW invites Dick to complete his gripe with a request for action.
Dick:	I just want my glove back. Make him give me my glove.	Dick completes the gripe and moves to get TW on his side.
TW:	(Looking at both boys) You both have a problem. I'm not going to "make" either of you do things. I want you to work this out for yourselves. I want you to tell each other what no lunch or no baseball glove feels like. I want you to tell each other how you feel about it, and what you want the other to do about it. I'll be here to help with the words. Who'll go first?	TW removes herself from the possibility of coalitions. Then she places the responsibility on the kids, while directing the process. Finally she commits herself to support the process and moves to get it going.

"I Know You Feel Bad, I'll Make It All Better."

Although this statement reverses the angry or detached statements in the previous section, it too is nonsupportive in the sense that it assumes that the child cannot solve his own problems. Treatment workers who act on this assumption take away the child's opportunity to learn. Remember the goal is not only to decrease the suffering attached to the current problem, but also to teach a process that can be used to cope with the source of pain both now and in the future.

"You're Making Me So Mad; You've Got To Change."

Remember who owns the problem. Rather than persuade the child that he should change to make you feel better, take responsibility for your own feelings. One way to do this is by using the conflict resolution gripe formula.

"No, No! That Won't Work, Try This."

Treatment workers who find themselves saying this are interjecting themselves between the child and the consequences of his action. You must guide the child, of course, but do this by giving the child a good sense of the potential consequences of his actions, not by arbitrarily overruling his choices. The evaluation/feedback step of the problem solving strategy gives you and the child an opportunity to tinker with the solution if it does not work out well the first time. There is no rule that says you must solve a problem once and for all the first time. Give yourself and the child a break.

I'm Getting Impatient. Let's Get Off Your Feelings and Go On to Getting This Problem Solved."

Sometimes kids do not want problems solved. They may come to you with a problem only because they want you to listen to their feelings in a supportive way. Your pushing them to get on with problem solving may appear very nonsupportive to them. When in doubt, ask, "Do you want me only to listen to how you feel, or do you want to work for a solution?" If the child only wants you to listen, bite your tongue.

"Everything Must be Fair and Equitable."

This belief is the biggest stumbling block to conflict resolution. It establishes a standard that remains unattainable because each conflicting child views the conflict from his own perspective. Therefore, each has his own interpretation of "fairness." Compromise, not fairness, is the rule. Each must give more than they feel is fair. With unequals (aggressive child/passive child, child/adult) fairness becomes an issue only to the extent that one person not take advantage of the other. The above belief can emerge in full flower in response to the child's plaintive cry, "It ain't fair." Rather than trying to justify yourself by arguing about your fairness, agree with him that it is not fair and reflect his feelings about that fact.

"He Ought to Know What I Need and Give It to Me Without My Having to Ask."

This statement reflects a passive fantasy that you may come to see in yourself and kids you work with. People who truly believe this predictably become frustrated, disappointed, hurt, and revengeful. No one knows what another wants without some communication. The conflict resolution grip formula models a complete form of such communication.

"Oh No! They're Getting Into It Again. I've Got to Break it Up."

Stopping conflicts before they are resolved only perpetuates the conflict because the children have no direct outlet for their feelings and because the source of the conflict remains active. Rather than protecting the children, a treatment worker who consistently disallows conflict can in the long run make them feel worse by short-circuiting their potential resolution. Not all negotiations are calm and sedate. Yelling, jumping up and down, and finger waving are allowed so long as the process does not generate more hurt.

Chapter 25

TRANSITIONS

After mastering the information in this chapter you should be able to—

1. define the concept of transition in relation to large and small changes;
2. identify and explain the stages of the grieving process;
3. identify two common transitions that children in treatment settings face and explain steps which may ease those transitions;
4. identify eight guidelines to make daily transitions move smoothly;
5. relate the information about transitions to non-behavioral levels of worker functioning as illustrated by "Feeling and Issues for the Treatment Worker."

Transitions involve change and change involves stress. This occurs for the small, as well as the large transitions. At this time in our culture we are being bombarded with change, a fact that has been well documented in Alvin Toffler's *Future Shock* (1970). These accumulating changes bring with them physical and psychological stress. The research on Life Change Units (LCUs) shows that persons undergoing a great deal of change increase the likelihood of illness (Holmes & Rahe, 1967). This is true with positive as well as negative changes. The deleterious effects of transitions can be minimized by proper handling. In this chapter we will discuss some of the transitions children go through in a treatment agency and will present guidelines for dealing with them.

Transition and the Grieving Process

Inherent in any transition is loss, and grieving is our response to loss. This loss can run the continuum from the death of a loved one to the loss of a person who has moved away, to the loss of an object that has been misplaced, sold, or otherwise removed. Transitions from room to room and activity to activity also involve change and adjustment, and people have commonly been found to grieve for aspects of their personality that have been "lost" through change to more adaptive means of living. Thus, the concepts of grieving may be applied to everyday situations as well as major life changes.

There are many explanations for why people grieve. Some say that people experience abandonment, rejection, anger at being left; resentment at increased efforts of coping; or longing for a chance to complete unfinished business. In any event, people do go through a somewhat sequential reaction pattern in coping with the loss. If they do not go through the grieving process, or if the process gets side-tracked along the way, people may distort the feelings they experience and often retain the intensity of those feelings unabated over years and years. Thus, a "good grief" is very important in order for people to get on with living.

Stages of the Grieving Process

Elisabeth Kübler-Ross (1969) outlines the stages a dying patient passes through as he works to reconcile himself to his death. A modified form of the same process occurs in other transitions. These stages are not necessarily sequential; the order may vary. Some stages are dealt with rapidly and some slowly. Since each person has his own rate and style of progress, the important thing to monitor is whether or not the stages have been dealt with. (See Figure 25-1.)

Stage I: Denial and Isolation. Denial is often the initial response to uncomfortable and painful situations and may present itself as a total refusal to hear and deal with the information, a rapid changing of the topic, a minimizing of the subject's severity, or an emotional numbness to the issue. Denial is especially present in highly painful circumstances that occur very abruptly. It is a protective device that serves as a buffer, thus allowing the person time to integrate the information and call upon less extreme defenses. This stage should be respected as a healthy part of the process. With the support of your caring, awareness, and acceptance the child will most likely proceed to the next stage. Your denial or minimizing of the situation may lend to the prolonging of this stage. If the child remains stuck in denial, it is time to confront the child with the issue and help him work through it.

Figure 25-1. Grieving Process

STAGE II: ANGER. When denial can no longer be maintained, anger and resentment set in. This stage may be difficult to deal with due to the fact that the anger is projected onto the environment in all directions seemingly at random. There is always someone to blame for something: the snacks are lousy and there is never enough play time. Listen to the anger, give the child vents for her anger, direct her awareness back to the source of the anger, and attempt to remain unoffended by the attacks. You are not the target; you are just handy.

STAGE III: BARGAINING. This is the "if I'm real good, I can avoid the loss" stage. It generally occurs very briefly and is more apparent in more traumatic loss situations. As reality confronts the child with its immutability in the face of these pleas, the bargaining stage fades.

STAGE IV: DEPRESSION. As the child can no longer deny the issue, shake his fist at it, or believe in the power of his pleas, he begins to feel a tremendous sadness and emptiness. Often our initial response to such sadness is the "now, there," cheer-him-up approach. The fact is that loss hurts and expression of that hurt is healthy and necessary in order to accept it and work it through. Just being there and acknowledging the pain is far more facilitative to the process.

STAGE V: ACCEPTANCE. If the child has received support in working through the preceding stages, he will finally be able to accept the loss. This stage is not necessarily one of contentment. It may be void of feelings. Acceptance simply means that the child is no longer overwhelmed with denial, anger, and fear and has come to terms with the change that he is being confronted with. He sees the door and is ready to walk through it.

CHANGES IN THE CHILD'S LIFE

Many children in treatment have undergone more than their share of change and loss. Divorce, frequent moves, and foster home placements and replacements are common occurrences in the life of the disturbed child. Often these relationships are terminated abruptly without planned means for helping the child identify and deal with the losses. Thus, she may feel abandoned, angry, sad, and guilty, and will come to you with a storehouse of unfinished business. She will be extremely sensitive to loss, and seemingly mild occurrences, such as striking out in the softball game, losing out on snacks, or misplacing her favorite pencil, may tap into this unfinished business and stimulate a highly charged emotional reaction.

In a treatment agency, as in other aspects of life, change, loss, and transition are continual occurrences. There is a constant turnover of staff and children. There are vacations and sick leaves. Children who are especially sensitive to loss will react when an important staff person is absent during a certain activity or leaves the room to go to the bathroom. Because of this, it is important to give the children continual information about where you are going, what you will be doing, and when you will return. Information and follow-through will help the child in establishing predictability and developing trust (see the chapter on "Information Sharing").

The most common occurrences in the agency around which the child will deal with loss and grieving are the transitions of children into and out of the program. We will outline the procedures involved in these transitions. These outlines can serve as prototypes for other transitions, especially those involving staff turnover. The models we present apply to day treatment. Residential agencies will meet with their own, more extreme separation issues.

Entry into the Program

A child comes into treatment after having failed in the regular community. Often, he has been through several hoops—special programs in the classroom, counseling, special classrooms, tutoring—and has tripped on all of them. He is then referred to a special agency—your program—which is seen by his peers and others as a place for weirdos and freaks. His self-concept has plummeted to its depths: he feels lost, guilty, scared, helpless, angry, and deserving of punishment. Be on guard for "accidents." He may be oblivious to his safety or even seeking punishment.

Initial reaction to these feelings differ. Children use the whole gamut of defense mechanisms; denial, rationalization, identification, displacement, projection, and reaction-formation. It is common for some children to go through a "honeymoon" phase wherein they are on their best behavior. Other children display their fear, anger, or sorrow forthright.

As the child's treatment worker, you must be farsighted in arranging her entry. Knowledge of the child's background, visits to the school and home, and a pre-placement visit to your agency by the child and her parents should occur prior to entry. On the child's first visit, make sure that you are there to greet her and are available to her throughout the visit. We have found it helpful to ask for a volunteer from the children to show her around. It is our experience that children who have themselves gone through this painful process are very empathic and helpful. We have known children who have spontaneously shared their feelings and memories of their first visit with the new child.

The child will need you as a source of information and acceptance. Be sure to give him all the information he needs without overloading him. Feeling deserving of and perhaps expecting punishment, he may imagine all sorts of appalling practices in the absence of information. This is where your acceptance is essential. Assess his present state, recognize, and accept it. Long orations or in-depth therapeutic explorations, which may lead to the child's feeling intruded upon and scared, are contraindicated. A simple "First visits are scary," will do the job.

After entry, be prepared for the rush of issues and feelings that will emerge as the child relaxes. The skilled worker becomes adept at predicting these based on information of the child's background and on the worker's assessment skills. And, of course, watch for and facilitate the stages of the grief process.

Re-entry into the Community

Plans for the child's re-entry into the community should be made months in advance. In this way, the child can move towards the transition goal at his pace, and you will have the time to outline and implement the steps of generalization (see the chapter on "Transfer and Maintenance").

By anticipating the transition, the staff, child, and treatment group can engage in "pre-grieving." This is a process of continually addressing the change and loss so that it cannot be denied or avoided, working through unfinished business, and concluding the relationships. The "pre-grieving" process involves numerous scheduled and spontaneous group and individual meetings. During these meetings, you will be seen as a model of awareness and self-disclosure. Your most important job is monitoring and sharing your own and the group's feelings. The children will frequently express their grieving indirectly. For example, they may be inordinately angry at the departing child for missing a goal in the soccer game. This is your cue to bring the group together and ask, "Is the group angry right now at Jesse for leaving us?" Also, Jesse may be setting himself up for conflict so that he can leave angrily in an attempt to avoid the sorrow.

As the transition draws near, the child may display ambivalence. At one moment he is excited about having completed his treatment goals and about the prospect of going back to a "regular" school; at the next he becomes fearful of failure and fights leaving the security of the agency that has supported and accepted him. During these times, old behaviors may reappear as he attempts to show you that he is really not ready to go after all. Do not become too alarmed at this; it is just part of the process. Hang in there with him, letting him know that he *will* be leaving and that you will be there to see him through it.

Several months in advance of the termination date, the receiving agency (generally the public school) should be notified. Many teachers are apprehensive at the thought of including an emotionally disturbed child in her already overburdened workload. In-service training for the school staff concerning the child's treatment history, including effective methods of dealing with her, is useful at this point. We have found it especially helpful to include parents in these meetings. Frequent visits with the child and the parents to the receiving agency, as well as visits by their staff to your agency, are essential.

Once the grieving process has been worked through for the staff, child, and peer group, and once the receiving agency and child have been prepared for one another, the final "good-bye" ritual ensues. It is important that the child have something to take with her from the center. The children usually enjoy making gifts and cards, which helps them to make their good-bye tangible. It also may be important for the departing child to leave something at the center—an acknowledgment that she has been an important participant in the life of the agency. Also, during the last day or week, it is important for the child to have individual time with significant others.

Usually, good-bye parties become ritualized into a meaningful rite of passage: a particular song, a particular dessert, a particular time to say good-bye. Each staff member and child is to be encouraged to say good-bye one last time. We recommend that you have the child's parents pick her up early so that the children actually watch her leave the building. This not only makes the departure concrete, but also gives the staff and children time to see how the group feels without her. This aftermath process aids in putting closure on the separation.

After the final good-bye as a "center child," he comes back to visit as a "school or community child." This gives him a chance to receive recognition for his successes and provides a safety zone where he can vent frustrations without fear of rejection. This stabilizing period also helps the other children to see that people do not always go away forever and that the outside world does not gobble up children.

It is a good idea to deal with the loss of the departing child before bringing another one into the center. If the process has not been completed, an entering child may unwittingly be given some of the bitter leftovers, or may be expected to replace an especially admired child. The entry process is hard enough without having to follow that act. Different children leave different lingering effects. Some effects are short-lived; some are long. The group may feel relieved by one's absence and sad by another's. Whatever the feelings, they are legitimate. Telling the children they should or should not feel one way or another does not change the facts and may only induce guilt and anger.

During and after the transition process, one of your most important jobs is to monitor your own feelings. You may feel sad when leaving a child with whom you have a particularly strong connection; guilty with one whom you felt you slighted; resentful with another that you felt took from you without giving. As with the children, each of these reactions are okay. Recognize them and share those that you feel will be helpful to the children.

In spite of all the elaborate plans that you make for transitions, there are times when children will be pulled out of your program abruptly: a parent decides to move or becomes disillusioned or scared; the child runs away. In these instances, the stages of grief still apply and the processing of the loss will have to occur in one large chunk after, rather than before, the fact. You will not have the luxury of preparing the children that are left. Neither will the departing child be able to put closure on relationships. In addition, the children may fear being themselves suddenly torn from the agency. At such a time, use your own reactions as indicators of issues that the children will also be experiencing. Again, remain vigilant for subtle and not so subtle signals that your group is experiencing some side-effects of confused and distorted grief.

Daily Transitions

The same general principles apply to transitions that occur daily. Of course, the intensity of the feelings and reactions is much lower, and parts of the process may be missing. Therefore, some people mistakenly think that transitions on a daily level do not need special attention. Distrubed children become very unsettled in the face of any change, and special attention must be taken with transitions from activity to activity.

When one looks at the ways in which the environment sets the scene for positive and negative behaviors, the issue of bridging transitions from one setting to another is central. Planning for transitions is as important as planning for any other activity on the schedule. In fact, it should be seen as an aspect of the various activities. A poor transition may doom an activity to failure no matter how well planned that activity may be.

Providing for smooth transitions requires high-level coordination among staff members and information-sharing between staff and children. (See Figure 25-2.) To ensure the probability of a smooth transition, include the following:

Set up all activities in advance. This means having all materials available and placed for each child.

Have the pathway to this activity as short and free from distractions as possible.

Make sure that the children are in an appropriate state of excitation for the next activity. If a baseball game is next, it may be appropriate for the children to be at a high level of excitation, whereas they would need to be much quieter when going to lunch. If the group is not ready, have them sit down and excuse them only when quieted. In this instance, they may be excused individually when ready.

Provide the children with information and expectations about the next activity and the transition. This information includes: where the activity will be, what it will include, who will lead the activity, who will monitor the activity, the behavioral expectations of the activity, and the behavioral expectations of the transition.

Reinforce children listening to information and following through with expectations.

Have a staff member at the next activity ready to receive the children.

Have a staff member supervising the group or individuals through the transition. (With children demonstrating a high level of responsibility, this may not be necessary.)

Figure 25-2. Transitions

When possible, make the transition into fun and games. Such games as "follow the leader", "Red Light," or challenging the kids to be as quiet as possible are helpful here.

If all of these rules are being followed and transitions continue to be difficult, it may be that there are too many transitions. There is an optimal number of changes that individuals can go through without undue stress. This is especially true with emotionally disturbed children. A constant uprooting may be very disorienting for a child and may not provide the time a child needs to get involved with and put closure on an activity. This tolerance for change varies greatly from child to child. Each child should be tracked carefully to determine his tolerance levels. It is then possible to set up the environment in such a way as to provide greater or fewer transitions according to individual levels. As a general rule, a child first entering the program will have more difficulty. The number of transitions required by that child should be gradually increased until she makes the big transition, i.e., into public school, where she will be required to tolerate a large number of such transitions.

Another variable at work is the logical planning from one activity to another. The day should have an even rhythm and flow. If the children are programmed from high activity to low and back again, they may feel that they are riding a yo-yo, and appropriate behaviors may break down. On the other hand, they may become restless if required to be physically inactive for long periods of time, or tired and cranky if too active. Also, preventing the children from going back and forth between settings is desirable. For example, if a story reading is planned between recess and baseball and it is a nice day, it would be best to read the story outside in a comfortable spot rather than inside at the regular story reading spot. This would shorten the transitions and minimize adjustments.

Although the effects of grief and loss are more noticeable in the larger life transitions, on closer examination it becomes apparent that such effects are intrinsic to every transition that a child must make. This more comprehensive view of loss and transition provides a more general framework with which to interpret all forms of change.

Feelings and Issues for the Treatment Worker

"Why Pamper The Child? He'll Have To Deal With Change All His Life—He Better Get Used To It."

It is true that change is inevitable. We all attempt to deal with it. However, acknowledging the child's needs and preparing him for change do not fall into the category of pampering. The information about transitions needs to be tailored to each child. The ultimate goal is developing in the child the ability to cope with and prepare himself for transitions with minimum outside help. Troubled children do not have these skills. The modeling you can give and the skills you can teach will help children to forestall becoming overwhelmed by manageable changes. Finding growthful ways to bridge transitions means becoming skilled at preparing for and moving through changes without becoming blocked or permanently distracted.

"Now Children, Let's Ignore For the Moment the Fact That We've Just Had a Fire Drill. It's Time for Quiet Reading.

Ignoring transitions just completed or those yet to come may seem on the face of it to save time because you just do not talk about them. However, in the long run, such ignoring creates more time consuming problems by demanding behavior of children that contravenes their immediate past or future environments. In the case above, it is likely that the worker will spend more time trying to control the excited behavior created by the fire drill than by spending three to five minutes cooling the children down for the next task. Dealing with transitions works from the children's needs rather than against them.

"What's the Big Deal in Just Walking to Another Room?"

On an objective level there is no big deal. On a symbolic level the deal may seem very big indeed for a child. Loss is a pervasive issue for all of us. Some of us have suffered more frequent and intense losses than others. Troubled children usually have lived through intense loss at times when they were very poorly equipped to deal with it. Therefore, they have become more vulnerable to loss of any type, large or small. Until you can help them learn more adaptive ways of coping with loss so that they can build up their tolerance, your walking into another room may seem no different to a child than you walking off the face of the earth. Your task is to recognize and respond to the symbolic as well as objective realities in which you and the child live.

"I Know Clyde is Leaving, But Why Are We Having All These Meetings—After a While There's Nothing Left to Say."

Even though the number of words spoken in pre-transition meetings may be few, the meetings themselves can still serve their purpose. Simply recognizing the child's changes sets the stage for dealing with transition. Regularly scheduled meetings also help both the child and the worker avoid denying the child's eventual move. finally, you and the child may communicate powerfully about your relationship without words. Nonverbal cues and activities sometimes speak more eloquently than words ever could. We all say our good-byes in many different ways. It is important to allow time enough for everyone's full expression.

Chapter 26

PHYSICAL RESTRAINT AND THE TANTRUM

After mastering the information in this chapter, you should be able to—

1. identify when physical restraint is appropriate and how to decide what intensity of restraint to use;
2. identify how physical restraint is used most effectively;
3. identify steps to foster increase in internal control in the child;
4. identify methods of physical restraint for partial to complete restraint;
5. discriminate between two types of tantrums;
6. list the stages through which tantrums move and the interventions appropriate at each stage;
7. relate physical restraint and the tantrum to non-behavioral levels of worker functioning as illustrated by "Feelings and Issues for the Treatment Worker."

Mary comes in looking grumpy. The first thing she does is put her candy bar in the goldfish bowl. When she is asked to remove it, she throws the soggy candy on the floor and shoves the child nearest to her. In response to the treatment worker's labeling her feelings and giving choices and alternatives, Mary looks the other way and starts pushing the goldfish bowl toward the edge of the counter. On her way to Time Out, she trips another child; while in Time Out, she starts banging her head against the wall and yelling, "I hate you, I hate everybody, I hate me!"

The above incident shows a prime example of a situation in which physical restraint may be used.

Physical restraint consists of physically controlling part or all of a child's body when he cannot or will not do so himself. It is used when the child's or another's safety and/or rights are being jeopardized, and when the child is repeatedly behaving in ways that show a need for external control.

The goals of physical restraint include providing protection so that the child can work on emotional issues in a secure setting while learning ways to develop internal control.

In general, physical restraint should be used in ways that minimize intrusiveness and maximize effectiveness. Thus, the worker would select the least possible restraint that works. When emotions swell to highly intense levels, and when control issues are primary, physical restraint is the bottom line. Intense protection and control offered by the treatment worker counteract the destructiveness and out-of-control behavior of the child.

Partial Control

Children with defiance and/or impulse-control problems continually test limits and display non-compliant behaviors. In these cases, the issue of control is central. When other intervention techniques are not successful in decreasing the behaviors, it can be useful literally to "take them by the hand" in order to terminate the inappropriate behavior. This commonly occurs around Time Out when a child refuses to go by himself, and thus is physically taken. In another instance, a child may refuse to comply with a demand that he take his hands off of another child. As a consequence, the part of the body that is "out of control" is physically controlled by the treatment worker, in this case, the hands. It is a kind of logical consequence applied to the body and is accompanied by a short verbal statement of the reasons for it and how the child can regain control, such as, "You are not properly controlling your hands right now, so I will control them for you. When you have them in control, I will release them." The child may then attempt to pull away and struggle and may become more physically and/or verbally defiant. He then needs to have repeated the information that he will be given back control of his hands when he stops struggling, is quiet, and makes a verbal contract to control them properly. (See Figure 26-1.) Follow-through with return of control must occur upon compliance. This sequence follows a negative reinforcement pattern in which an aversive event, being restrained, is ended when the child completes specific behaviors.

Figure 26-1. Partial Control

When holding the child, make every effort to avert eye contact and ignore him verbally after giving sufficient information on the central issue. Attend to other children who are behaving appropriately. With a particularly defiant child, this process may take a great deal of time, and it may be advantageous for the treatment worker to take the child with her during the course of her activity so that the child is limiting the treatment worker's movement and choices (thus controlling her) minimally. It is especially important in this case to pour out the positives to the other children, thus demonstrating the desirability of self-management.

To be fully effective, this technique must provide an alternate behavior and must incorporate the concept of responsibility. It is a good way to establish physically and concretely the idea that freedom and privilege come with taking responsibility for personal actions. Eventually, other less physical and direct means of control, such as verbal requests and hand signals, must be substituted, which will finally lead to self-control. Given enough feedback, the child will recognize early cues to his escalation and be able to deflect himself into alternative behaviors earlier and earlier in the chain of responses that leads to out-of-control behavior. If physical control is becoming a standard procedure with a child rather than the first step in a shaping program, reevaluation is in order. It may be that this is the child's major source of physical attention, or that other techniques may be more effective.

THE TANTRUM

Although a well-planned, positive program reduces the incidence of tantrums, they are inevitable when working with emotionally disturbed children. Indeed, it is questionable whether prevention is always desirable. A tantrum may bring to the surface certain feelings and issues that were lying dormant, thus providing a situation in which to deal with them therapeutically. Or, a tantrum may be the outcome of this surfacing. In any case, the issue is not preventing tantrums, but developing alternative coping mechanisms in the child.

Many emotionally disturbed children have what is called "poor ego control"; that is, they have not developed the behaviors and internal processes necessary to deal effectively with certain issues and feelings. They feel a sense of powerlessness and throw a tantrum in an attempt to gain some final control or to rid themselves of pain. The purpose of treatment is to establish safe conditions during these times, and to present alternatives and more effective ways of dealing with these feelings and issues.

Feelings and Issues for the Child

Different children have tantrums over different feelings and issues, which become very apparent after one becomes familiar with particular children. One child may become fearful over change, while another may react to loss situations with grief and anger. Still another child may have a low frustration threshold over task mastery and may "blow" in anger. Tantrums commonly erupt over control or defiance issues, as described previously. These partial control situations sometimes become total control situations. Tantrum issues and feelings are many, and occur in varying combinations and intensities during various stages of the tantrum.

Tantrums are of two types: explosive and implosive. In the *explosive* tantrum, the most common type, the energy and feelings are directed outward. The child focuses her rage towards others, and "I hate you," statements are frequently heard. In the *implosive* type, the child directs the energy inward, and may roll up into a fetal position and display self-destructive behaviors such as banging her head or scratching herself. The child will sometimes verbalize this self-hatred by projecting it on the treatment worker, saying, "You hate me." The types sometimes overlap, and a child will intermittently lash outward, then inward. The implosive child, especially, needs permission to act out her rage. Any non-permission or judgmental messages will only increase the self-destruction.

Stages

Every tantrum proceeds through various stages, which differ slightly from child to child. Intervention can occur at various stages and will be determined by those stages. The most important decision happens at the very early stages when the treatment worker must decide whether or not to prevent, allow, or even push for the tantrum. This decision involves many variables, foremost being the child's needs. Will a tantrum at this point serve to perpetuate this inadequate means of coping and further contribute to an already poor self-image, or will prevention only suppress an issue that needs to be dealt with? In the first case, giving the child alternatives so that he can deal with the issues and develop positive self-esteem is essential. In the second, a tantrum may be necessary to surface and air the issues that can then be worked through. Another consideration is the environment's resources in terms of handling the tantrum. The treatment worker should be in an emotional and physical place to give the necessary support messages that the child needs at this time. Also, there should be adequate time and space. Five minutes before the bus leaves would be an inopportune moment to allow or push for a tantrum. Of course, tantrums may occur in any circumstance regardless of the intervention used, and the environment must be flexible enough to handle them.

The following is a sketch of the stages of a "typical" tantrum and some corresponding intervention techniques:

THE SET UP. As a precursor to the tantrum, the child is generally experiencing some sort of vulnerable internal state. This can be apparent in his nonverbal behaviors. He may have a sullen or angry appearance as he enters the room, or may be constantly "hyped" and laughing. Each child has his own signal which the sensitive and aware treatment worker will know. At this point, preventative intervention takes the form of filling the empty bucket or providing a vent for pent-up feelings. This may mean a hug and warm word, a labeling of the behavior and feeling with permission and acceptance messages, a proposed wrestling match, or a one-to-one conference.

> Example: Worker to child: "Hey! (Hand on shoulder) I'm guessing you're a little angry right now and that's okay. Let's talk about it while we throw these pillows over there in the corner."

THE PRECIPITATOR. If the first stage goes unattended or if the child does not respond to the intervention, an issue inevitably arises over which the child begins to "fall apart." The precipitating event may be a command to work out a hassle with another child, a mention of figures in her home life, or simply an ill-timed joke. At this stage, the child may seem to be searching for an external situation over which to "break." This stage is ripe for the substitution of alternatives. The treatment worker can present a read-out of the child's current process and some choices available to her. A brief "cooling off" period may be advisable before focusing on choices and decisions. If it is appropriate to the situation, redirecting the behavior or humor can be used.

> Example: "You're using your anger to set Gini up. The more you bump her while she's writing, the more irritated she's going to get at you. I think you'd be able to get your anger out, without getting yourself into trouble, by talking about it, or by hitting the punching bag."

If a command has been made at this stage, it is important to follow through, although a delay for dealing with the issue may be indicated.

THE WARM UP. Here the behaviors escalate and things start getting noisy and active. Verbal and physical assaults and expressions of distress are profuse. "That's not fair!" "You motherfucker!" "I'm gonna smash your face in!" "Nobody cares what happens to me," and related phrases are common. The child will usually need to be removed from the group at this point. Time Out may be in order. During this phase, the child may require partial control as she may refuse to remain in the prescribed area. In any case, the adult needs to stay in close proximity. This will provide the child with a person with whom to work out the issue when she is ready or to provide physical restraint. Use restraint only if the child needs it, that is, if he is becoming very aggressive or noncompliant. The main objective is still to allow the child to provide his own controls and to reinforce these.

> Example: Worker to child: "I like the way you're staying in the Time Out area. You'll have to stop banging the window because it might shatter. You can choose to control your feet or have me control them for you. (pause) It looks like you're not able to control your feet. So I'm taking control of them."

FULL TILT. In this stage, the child's physical and verbal lashing out have escalated to such a point that holding is required. The beginnings of this stage typically involve intense anger expression. The child will try to escape, bite, kick, spit, scratch, and do whatever he can to destroy and inflict pain, that pain being an outward manifestation of his own internal state. The child begins wildly thrashing in an attempt to exert the power he feels he is losing. He verbalizes this anger by such phrases as, "I hate you—I'm going to kill you," and "Just wait til I get loose—you'll be sorry." He loudly demands to be released. At this point the child is not receptive to much information and will generally negate whatever he hears. Give only the necessary information concerning what is happening. This information must include the following: 1) *Permission*—for example, "You're really angry and hurt right now, and that's okay. Go ahead and get it out." With a particularly contrary child, the "get it out" part may have to be deleted in that it may stimulate him to do the opposite. Permission would then be implicit in your allowing it to occur and your matter-of-fact attitude towards it. 2) *Support and Safety*—for example, "I am going to control you until you can control yourself. I will not allow you to hurt yourself or me. When you stop struggling and are in control, I will release you." The child needs to know that you will stick with him. He also must know what he has to do to terminate the holding when he feels ready to do so. These should be stated as information, not expectations. 3) *Potency*—These are the "I can hold you," and "We'll both be okay," messages. This allows the child to trust and reduces the fear that he will cause something horrible to happen.

Give all of this information as matter-of-factly as possible. If the child feels that he has caused anger or grief in others, it may cause a great deal of fear about the power he has unleashed and over which he has no control. In general, "I like you" and "You're a good person" messages may serve to instill guilt and should be avoided in this case. Arguments over his negations should also be avoided. If the child begins to verbalize unrealistic perceptions about why he is being held, focus back on the precipitating issues and feelings in a unargumentative fashion.

Example:

CHILD: "You hate me. You just don't want me to go on the field trip. My mom put you up to this, she hates me too."

WORKER: "I hear your anger and your hurt. It's all right to get it off your chest. I'm holding you because you will not control your feet and hands. When you can get your body in control, I will let go."

The "Let me go, you're hurting me" phrases translate more accurately into "Please don't stop, I hurt inside." Children have been seen pulling staff members' arms *around* them as they are saying these words. Sometimes though, a treatment worker may be holding a child more tightly than is needed to control, especially if the worker is angry. To prevent this, the staff member must keep a close check on her feelings. Passing the child off to another who is emotionally ready to do the job is preferable to inflicting further emotional or physical pain on the child. Here you may also be providing an inadequate model for self-control.

Example:

Worker to co-worker: "Hey, Joan, I need a break right now, I'm getting hooked into being angry. Can I pass Georgie on to you for ten minutes?"

Towards the end of the "Full Tilt" stage, the child many times begins to express a combination of grief and rage and may vacillate between the two from moment to moment. Care must be taken to track those feelings and to respond accordingly.

THE COMEDOWN. Now, the child begins to relax. Either the feelings have run their course, suppression has occurred, or physical exhaustion has set in. He is getting ready to take charge of his own body. Control of his body is given back piece by piece as he relaxes and shows control of each part. Total release takes place only when he has stated verbally in a congruent tone of voice that he can control himself. The treatment worker should verbalize what she is doing at each step. At this point, the child may be depressed, guilty, and possibly relieved and may express that he wants to withdraw and be alone for awhile. Respect this wish. He may need this time to pull himself together and may need a respite from the intensity of the relationship. Be sure to keep a constant watch on the child during this time. In some cases, the child may need a close and positive physical holding or some other positive interaction with the adult to tell him that he's okay. Be sure to expend only enough time and intensity as is needed to help him pull it together. An excess may reinforce the interaction and lead to the "Who's Afraid of Virginia Woolf" syndrome, in which the child may believe that intense positives come only after throwing tantrums.

Example:

WORKER: "Your feet are relaxed and under control. I will release them. Your whole body feels relaxed and your face shows me that you are ready to be responsible. I'd like you to tell me how you're feeling." (gently rubbing child's body)

CHILD: "Tired and a little sad."

WORKER: "Yeah, you've just been through a whole lot. What do you need for yourself right now?"

CHILD: "I need to be alone on the pillows."

WORKER: "That sounds like a good choice. As soon as you look at me and contract to be responsible for your body, I will release you and you can do that."

CHILD: (looking at worker) "I'm ready to be in control of my body."

WORKER: "Okay—sounds like you're ready. You may go to the pillows."

The comedown period may be a powerful intervention point for many children. For especially control-avoidant children, this may be one of the few points at which defenses are broken down, thus providing a situation ripe for hashing out the issue.

THE REENTRY. When the child's behavioral cues signal that he is ready to join the group, it is important to rehash the tantrum, the issues and feelings involved, and his resulting embarrassment and guilt. The treatment worker will then share her feelings, making it clear to the child that she cares for him. The child now is ready to hear about alternatives that he can use in the future at various phases of the process. Some children benefit from ritualizing the end of the tantrum, thus "laying the feelings to rest" by some concrete act such as tearing apart boxes and throwing them in the garbage. Just before joining the group is a good time to provide some basic care such as providing food and/or washing his face and combing his hair. Take special care to set up conditions that are conducive to peer acceptance. Then, get a verbal contract that he is ready, and move him into the group. The peer group and co-workers should maintain the status quo, and include the child matter-of-factly.

THE AFTERMATH. At some later point, the child may be ready to follow up on the tantrum issues in a conference. He may be more receptive to relevant information on alternatives after having some time to sort it all out. This is a time for the treatment worker to do some more in-depth read-outs and predicting. For example, if grief over loss is an issue, a review of the grief process will be helpful to the child. By this time, the treatment worker also should have "come down" from the intensity of the holding session. Left-over negative feelings may induce guilt and undo some of the permission and growth achieved during the session.

HOLDING TECHNIQUES

We recommend two holding techniques that are effective in different circumstances. The first is the *all-encompassing hold* which consists of sitting with the arms and legs around the child so that the child is fully encompassed by the worker's body. The child's legs are held down by the worker's legs and his arms are wrapped across his body so that the worker's right hand holds the child's left, etc. This allows for minimal movement. Ideally, the worker should lean against some support to prevent being thrown backwards. This type of hold should always be used when the child is expressing a lot of grief. From this position, one can easily move into a nurturant "hugging" hold. As the difference in body sizes between the child and worker decreases, this hold becomes more difficult. Therefore, a second hold has been devised. This is called the *prone hold* and is used when a worker cannot maintain the former. Here, the child is placed in a prone position, face down on the floor with his arms held behind his back. This hold is more secure but less comfortable for the child, and is more appropriate in intense defiance and anger situations. When the child calms down, becoming more manageable and showing more grief, a switch to the all-encompassing hold should be made. (See Figure 26-2.)

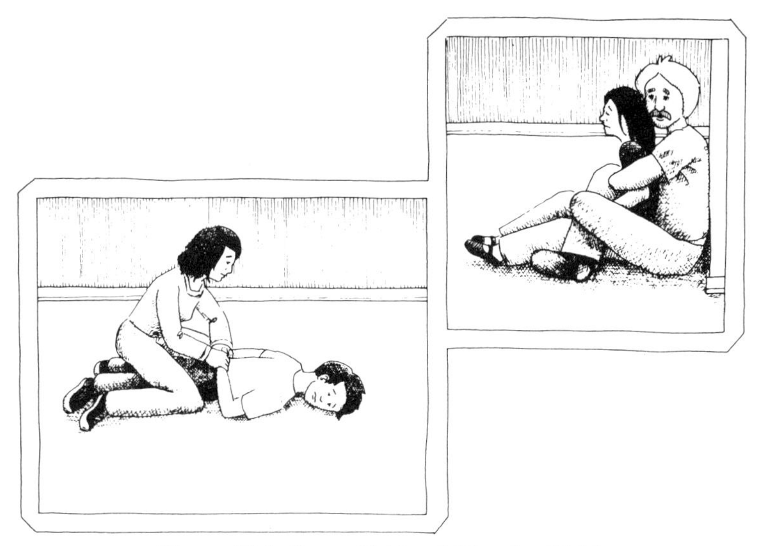

Figure 26-2. Prone Hold and Hugging Hold

Additional Comments

Care should be taken to track a child's tantrums over time. If they are not decreasing, or are actually *increasing,* the intervention technique must be closely examined. Some children require a high intensity level of stimulation and may be getting this only through the tantrum. The tantrum may be self-perpetuating rather than releasing. It may be that a daily wrestling match would provide the necessary intensity and a positive alternative. Or, a system of rewards and, if that is not effective, possible punishment may be considered.

Tantrums should not be punished after the fact by the treatment worker's snide remarks or indirect anger. Acceptance of the tantrum as okay must be conveyed at the same time that you suggest alternative behaviors and express your own anger or other negative feelings. Because physical restraint of a tantrum and even partial restraint require intense contact, intense feelings will arise. Accepting and dealing with those feelings in yourself will help you be more potent in use of this intervention.

Feelings and Issues for the Treatment Worker

"Is This Kid Going to Go Crazy on Me?"

An out-of-control child may look crazy or "act like a wild man." This can provoke fear in the initiate. To these workers we give words of comfort.

In our collective sixteen years of experience, we have yet to see a child "go crazy" (that is, permanently lose touch with reality) from a tantrum. In fact, out-of-control behavior is many times a necessary step to saner, less wild, more stable behavior. This is especially true when the issues at the base of the tantrum are allowed to surface and are dealt with therapeutically. Suppression of these issues through fear on the worker's part (which the child will most certainly pick up on through nonverbal channels) will only delay the progress of treatment.

"What Did I Do to Cause Such Pain and Agony?"

Many times workers feel guilty for a child's tantrum. They feel that they caused the tantrum by somehow neglecting to do their job correctly. This kind of worry over responsibility is very common in the field, especially with new workers. In fact, many children who are bent on a tantrum are going to have one no matter what the external circumstances are. They are like "an accident looking for a place to happen," and will gravitate towards any cause available to them at the moment. Of course, if the child is continually having tantrums, it may be time to sit down and examine the situation. It may be that the child pushes the worker's "buttons" or that the worker has issues in common with the child. In these cases, it is time for the worker to look at and work on these buttons and issues.

"Will I Lose Control When This Kid Tantrums?"

The intensity of feelings poured out by the child will lead to intense emotional reactions on the part of the worker. If you are afraid of, or somehow believe yourself not permitted to experience intense feelings, or fear your own loss of control, then you will find yourself closing off tantrum possibilities when, for the child's sake, they would best be allowed to progress. In such cases, we might consider closing off as a missed opportunity for both the child and the treatment worker.

"What Will I Do When I Can't Take It Any More? I'm Afraid I Might Physically or Psychologically Hurt the Kid."

Tantrums commonly entail physical and verbal assaults on the treatment worker. These assaults many times elicit strong reactions in the worker which can minimize her effectiveness. Some of these reactions could come out of fear, anger, grief, or helplessness depending upon the individual. When these reactions occur, awareness, acceptance, and close monitoring are important. If the reactions become too strong, it may be well for the worker to ask for staff assistance.

"Will Going Through This Tantrum Harm My Relationship With The Child?"

Just after the tantrum you and the child may have some negative feelings towards one another. This is the purpose of the aftermath period: to deal with these feelings. After dealing with these feelings, we have found that rather than harming the relationship, the fact that you have actually stuck with the child through, as he sees it, the display of the most negative part of himself, conveys a caring and acceptance of the total child which leads to increased trust and a more positive self-concept. It has been our experience that children in a treatment program often respond to a new worker by saying "Will she be able to control me?," revealing the importance they place on this kind of security and acceptance.

Part VI

TREATMENT CONTEXTS

In the beginning of this book, we examined the personality, beliefs, and observational skills of the worker, and discussed the dimensions of the worker/child relationship. These levels of functioning were integrated into the various skills represented in the sections on "Communication," "The Basics," and "Behavior Management." "Treatment Frameworks" provided a further integration by detailing the blend of skills used in dealing with larger treatment issues and strategies. In this section, we look at some of the contexts of these various interventions.

All behavior takes place in a context. The character of that context interacts with and affects behavior, which in turn affects the context. This interactional model is at the base of our treatment philosophy. Treatment is not a static process of applying one skill or the next. Rather, it involves combining the various behavioral and non-behavioral factors that exist at a given moment. The context which contains that moment can be viewed on various levels, and is powerful in influencing the impact of the treatment interventions. To illustrate this concept, we have chosen to examine the peer group, play, and the physical environment to represent a social, an activity, and a physical treatment context.

Chapter 27

THE GROUP

The major portion of treatment with disturbed children occurs within the basic unit of the group. It is the essential context into which fit the skills mentioned in previous chapters. To deliver effective treatment, the treatment worker must understand its dynamics and be able to facilitate the formation of an effective and positive peer group.

The greatest common element found among disturbed children is that they lack positive social skills, and thus function poorly in their social groups. Individual treatment is limited in its ability to deal with these issues. Interpersonal effectiveness and positive interdependence are learned through experiences in the group. This learning occurs because of the strong influence peers have on one another as well as the child's need for power and dignity that occurs through the recognition and respect of others.

A group is an interdependent collection of individuals—not merely a number of people with some degree of proximity. Knowles and Knowles (1959) define a group as having a definable membership, a mutual perception of belonging, a shared purpose, an interdependence in needs satisfaction, frequent interaction among members, and an ability to act in a unitary manner. Beyond this definition, an effective treatment group is a *primary* group. That is, it is a personal, intimate group with trust and caring, a group whose members feel emotionally involved and fulfill one another's basic social needs. Many disturbed children have never been a part of such a group, and it is the treatment worker's task to aid each child in becoming a member of a primary group.

An effective group has three essential core activities: (1) accomplishing its goals, (2) maintaining itself internally, and (3) developing and changing to improve effectiveness (Johnson & Johnson, 1975). Related to these core areas are several dimensions or properties that we will discuss in detail in this chapter. These include: cohesion, interaction, communication, structure, norms, goals, roles, leadership, stages of development, problem solving, and decision making.

Cohesion

Johnson and Johnson (1975) define cohesion as being the sum of all the factors influencing members to stay in a group. Cohesiveness depends upon common norms and goals, a sense of identification, and the frequency of interaction (or attraction) among the members (Bonner, 1959). The following list shows several indicators of high group cohesion. Group members—

demonstrate an openness which is based on mutual trust and support;
show high attendance and are on time for meetings and activities;
help one another;
plan and solve problems together;
resist disruption from without and within;
have fun together.

These are somewhat idealistic states. We do not mean to imply that they all must be present at all times. Even the most cohesive group will move in and out of one or more of these states in the natural flux of events and member turnover. In examining group cohesion, we will look at the group in terms of its interaction process, structure, norms, and goals.

Interaction

Interaction is the process through which the group is formed. In the early stages of group formation, one of the treatment worker's most important tasks is to facilitate this interaction through the development of an open communication network which gives the children access to one another. Hare (1962) discusses the following six characteristics which affect interaction.

PERSONALITY. Predicting and aiding interaction will depend upon knowing the personality composition of the group and how it determines which individuals interact most frequently.

SOCIAL CHARACTERISTICS. Factors such as age, sex, ethnicity, and friendship will also affect interaction. A blend of these characteristics gives the group diversity but may also lead to subgroups and cliques.

TASK. Activities that are fun, rewarding, lead to success, and give members access to one another will result in high interaction and cohesion.

COMMUNICATION NETWORK. Knowing your group's communication pattern (who speaks to whom over what), and encouraging group members to direct comments, questions, and feedback to the group rather than you, will increase interaction.

GROUP SIZE. Groups of from four to nine members are optimal for rich but not overwhelming interaction possibilities. Be aware of the "odd man out" phenomenon of the triad.

LEADERSHIP. Strong direction from a leader inhibits interaction. Be aware of how much leadership is needed at a given moment.

Structure

Structure refers to the members' relative social location. It is determined by the patterns of interaction which create the social stratification and hierarchy of power and status. The group's structure can promote or block cohesion, and it is your job to ascertain the existing structure and to promote one which will result in maximum cohesion.

THE SOCIOGRAM. Sociograms are tools that aid in the discovery of the group's structure. *Residential Child Care* (1977), a basic training course for child care workers, shows how such tools reveal friendship patterns and the social structure of the entire group through mapping patterns of interaction. These maps are based on the children's answers to questions about who their first, second, and third choice of partners would be for a certain activity. From this information, a *target sociogram* is constructed that connects children who *mutually* choose one another. The following is an illustration of such a sociogram and examples of the kind of information that can be obtained from it (See Figure 27-1.)

The circles which constitute the "target," are popularity quartiles, with the most frequently chosen children in the center. Examining Figure 27-1, a number of structural dimensions emerge. Those listed below are, perhaps, the most useful in terms of the peer treatment group:

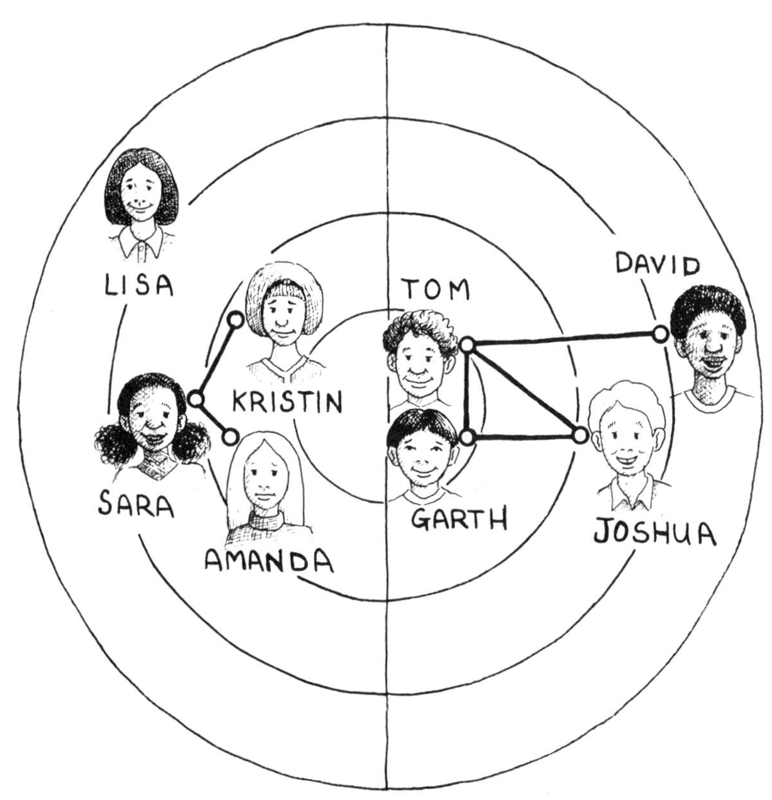

Figure 27-1. Target Sociogram

"The Stars" (e.g., Tom). These are the children in the center—the group with leadership, power, and status. Such central positions may be based on the person's ability to *reward* and *coerce;* her *legal or formal* position; her *likeability;* her *expertise,* or her *information* (French & Raven, 1959). Johnson and Johnson (1975) suggest that groups are more effect ive when power is widely spread among group members and when it is based on competence and information. We would like to add that along with these qualities, *caring for others* is important in leaders of a treatment group.

In groups of children, *likeability* or attraction is a strong determin ant of status and can be affected by sex, age, looks, special abilities (such as athleticism), and material possessions (Bany & Johnson, 1964). The last quality is an interesting one in that it is changeable and can pro vide rapid movement up and down the hierarchy. In our work with children, we have seen a group member's status and power move from the bottom of the pecking order to the top simply by bringing a tape recorder from home. This kind of manipulatable factor can be useful when a treatment worker sees the need for a child to move to another position in the group.

Other key questions in looking at this dimension are: "How do 'the stars' use their power and leadership constructively/destructively?" "How can I best work with their influence on the group?"

There are times when you, the worker, will need to put limits on the "star's" power. But there are two pitfalls that warrant close watching: 1) using them as puppets, and 2) vying with them for power (Mayer, 1958).

Friendship Chains. Chains are direct or indirect linkages of children. In the examples in Figure 27-1, one chain involves Tom, Garth, Joshua, and David. David, in the fourth quantile, is indirectly linked to Garth and Joshua through his friendship with Tom, who is in the first quartile. You can use this information to work with David's social relationships.

Isolates and Neglectees. These are located in the outer circle. In the example given, Lisa and David inhabit these positions. Your job here is to find the determinants of their status and work to improve their peer relationship. For example, structuring cooperative relationship or placing these children in positions of leadership (providing that they have the necessary skills to succeed) may be indicated here.

Rejects. Rejected children are those chosen by no one, and who, in addition, receive frequent "get lost" messages. These children may need intensive individual work to improve their self-concept and develop social skills that will enhance their value to the group.

Cliques (e.g., Tom, Joshua, and Garth). Cliques are exclusive subgroups whose members mutually choose one another. They can be disruptive to whole group cohesion and harmony, depending upon how they relate to one another and "outsiders." You must bridge their interaction with others and encourage alternative ways of dealing with others when their interactions are destructive.

Cleavages. The most common cleavage among eight- to twelve-year-olds is gender, as illustrated in Figure 27-1. These large subgroups choose members of the other subgroup very infrequently. When the cleavages become very rigid, regrouping may be necessary.

Sociometric tools can give useful information on the existing group structure. It is important to keep in mind that these scores and positions are relative to the questions asked and should not be seen as being written in stone. That is, a child may choose one person for a swimming buddy, and another to read with. Also, the structure tends to shift over time: what's "out" at one time is "in" the next. After some experience with small groups, you may develop the ability to assess the group structure without a complicated examination. You may also wish to use another kind of sociometric tool. For example, a simple "who's interacting with whom and over what" question can reveal important information.

Norms

Norms are behavioral rules which emerge in the course of group interaction, have general group acceptance, and involve social pressure to produce adherence. They provide frames of reference and controls that guide group behavior, and take forms such as customs, traditions, codes, values, standards, rules, and fads. They preside over areas as diverse as the prescribed attitudes members demonstrate towards specific activities and people, and what color socks to be worn in order to be "cool."

THE POWER OF NORMS. Since norms are at the base of all group action, they are essential for a high degree of cohesion and a growthful treatment environment. Most of us have experienced at some time the disruption and lack of progress that occurs in a group that cannot agree on standards and rules, or in a group whose norms are not conducive to group goals.

The norms of a child's peer group exert a powerful influence on his behavior. In studies reported by Bany and Johnson (1964) children's judgments were found to be more influenced by the opinions of other children than they were by the opinions of teachers. This peer influence becomes stronger as the child reaches adolescence. The proponents of Positive Peer Culture and Guided Group Interaction have used this influence as a powerful therapeutic tool. Vorrath and Brendtro (1974) found that in creating a therapeutic environment it was important to stress the expression of caring as a positive value among delinquent adolescents. However, it was not enough, and was often counterproductive, for the adult therapists to push the value. Rather, they had to get the group to accept this norm by modeling it and by linking the group's existing values of toughness, savvy, and autonomy with caring. They did this through relabeling caring and support as being smart and strong. In this way, the youths integrated the value into their culture and used it to create some dramatic therapeutic effects.

Murray and Ebner (1972) stress three basic values as essential in children's treatment groups: *respect* for members, *commitment* to members, and *concern* about members' worth. In addition, Johnson and Johnson (1975) assert that values encouraging psychological safety, individual creativeness, conflicts in ideas, and growth and change are important to therapy groups. In order to inculcate these norms, you must stress them early in the group's development. Once developed, therapeutically negative norms are very difficult to turn around. Promotion can be done by continually feeding back to members how their behaviors affect one another in terms of these basic values. For example, if the children want to take a field trip to a farm in the summer and Rachel has severe hay fever, inform the group how the trip would affect Rachel and ask them to take responsibility either to change the field trip, or find another activity that she could engage in.

The process of promoting positive norms can be tricky. You must be careful to stress their importance and enforce them without judgmental or punitive overtones which elicit guilt, anger, or resistance. This is especially difficult when the values are especially important to you. When they are, closely monitor your feelings and value system (see chapter on "Values and Beliefs").

Once norms are well established, they become codes which will perpetuate the culture over time. Old members will see to it that the culture is passed on to new members. Such a strong and cohesive group will greatly reduce the "enforcer" role of the treatment worker.

NORM DEVELOPMENT. Norms can develop deliberately or spontaneously. Deliberately developed norms are those that are overt, understood, and have been examined and accepted. Spontaneously developed norms arise out of a particular situation and can become a part of the culture simply by going unchallenged.

> For example:
> The "Tigers" have not developed rules to deal with physical pain. One day while playing soccer, Charlie is knocked down by the ball. He falls to the ground crying. The group is silent for a moment, unsure about what to do, when suddenly, Jason begins laughing. The rest of the group quickly follows suit.

In this example, the first responder sets the flavor for the group. If this reaction remains unchallenged, it rapidly becomes a norm and difficult to reverse. In such an instance, the alert treatment worker will immediately call a meeting and examine the reaction in light of the basic values.

Another point to remember in norm formation is that group members with higher status and power have a greater influence on group norms.

NORM ADHERENCE. Groups of children (as well as adults) push hard for conformity. A particular signal from a group member that requires a particular response will usually get it whether or not that response receives a negative consequence from the adult. Deviation from the group's expectation may result in loss of prestige or exclusion. Positive values, such as "The 'Bears' don't steal," will also carry a great deal of weight in the group.

Norms can be enforced either by positive sanctions for adherence or negative sanctions for nonadherence. Bovard (1948) found that groups demonstrating a high degree of tolerance for individuality and using positive rather than negative consequences produced more cohesiveness. You, as a treatment coordinator, can greatly influence the group in this aspect by modeling a positive approach, and by demonstrating how to accept and value individuality.

Murray and Ebner (1972) have developed a technique to deal with the ultimate negative sanction: ostracism. When such a threat is imminent, they suggest applying "protective punishment." For example, if a child is making lewd comments about another's mother, an act in violation of a strong group norm and risking group rejection, you can step in and provide a consequence for the behavior, thus stopping it and saving the child's group membership.

Group norms, once established, have a strong influence on individuals' behavior. It is important to know what they are and to promote values that aid positive treatment outcome. Once established, you must respect them and respond in a manner that shows the children that you see their norms as being important.

Goals

Goals are guides for group action. They direct, motivate, channel, and coordinate group energy. Successful goal achievement is powerful in creating cohesion and a positive group atmosphere. Treatment groups are unique in that their over-all goal is to change the members themselves. This can be done through a number of activities with goals of their own. For example, successfully cultivating a garden can aid in establishing a feeling of unity, cooperative social skills, and an increased sense of value and worth.

The task of the treatment worker is to assist the group in setting goals, in defining steps for goal achievement, and in evaluating goal achievement. As the group works towards goal achievement, you act as a supporter giving ongoing feedback and encouragement. You should not get into a "do for" pattern where you make all the decisions in the process and mechanically run the children through hoops. The group needs to *own* its activities. This is the only way the members will feel a sense of pride, competence, and self-responsibility.

GOAL ACHIEVEMENT. To reach its goal, the group must be motivated and committed to goal accomplishment. This can be difficult with a group of children who see themselves as losers with nothing to offer. To counter this attitude and promote participation in the group, you must oversee the process of goal setting by asking the following questions:

Is The Goal Relevant To The group? A group of pre-adolescent "street" kids may find the game of "Hoky Poky" pretty hoky.

Do Individual Goals and Group Goals Mesh? Giving a quiet child a part in a play increases his verbal interaction, which is an individual goal, and at the same time, works towards the group goal of creating a successful play.

Does The Group Have The Ability To Achive The Goal? Successful goal completion is a *must,* especially in the beginning of group formation. Having a group of six-year-olds with motor problems perform gymnastic routines in a talent show might prove to be disastrous.

Is The Goal Challenging? Just as a difficult goal can produce a sense of failure, a goal that is too easily accomplished will result in boredom.
Are The Goals And The Steps To Attainment Clear? Clear, concrete, and behaviorally definable statements must be made as to what the goal is, how it is to be obtained, and how the group is to know when it has been accomplished.
Is The Goal Rewarding? Some goals are rewarding in themselves, e.g., making and eating chocolate chip cookies. Others need to be enhanced by the treatment worker.
Is There A Built-in Structure For Feedback? In order for a group to be successful, it must receive information on its performance at each step in the process. It is best to provide times for the children to give feedback to one another as well as for getting feedback from the treatment worker.
Do All Members Have A Task? A member without a task becomes an outsider. Each child must feel that she is important, and feel that others are important to her. In this way, each child will learn how to function in a positive, mutually interdependent social structure. With caring and creativity, a group can always find something for even the most unskilled group member to do.
Do All Members Contribute To The Goal Attainment Process? When a child helps create a goal, he is more likely to work towards that goal. Take the time at some point to look at the difference in group spirit and productivity when the treatment worker defines the goals and procedures versus when the children do.
Is There Time Set Aside For Evaluation Of Goal Attainment? Evaluation reviews the process, thus putting closure on the activity and finding ways to improve group functioning.

COMPETITION VS. COOPERATION. Numerous studies have compared competitive and cooperative group practices, and have clearly indicated that competition breaks down group cohesion, attractiveness, productivity, and interaction, and inhibits communication. They also indicate competition leads to anxiety and hostility. Such results have obvious implications for disturbed children who are already hostile and anxious and who see themselves as losers and outsiders. The sensitive worker will take this into account when planning activities. A book from the New Games Foundation called *New Games* (Fluegelman, ed., 1976) is full of activities that do not involve winning and losing.

ROLES

Each group member takes on a role or function in the group. These roles can contribute to cohesiveness and a positive group atmosphere, or they can be disruptive. The effective treatment group teaches its members how to perform roles that give them positive value in social organizations.

Goal achievement and *group maintenance* are the two basic objectives of a group, and various positive group roles can be categorized under these objectives. *Task roles* are those roles required to get the work done. *Maintenance roles* are concerned with maintaining, supporting, and strengthening the group. A balance between these two functions is necessary for healthy group processing. These task and maintenance dimensions can be seen as leadership functions (Johnson & Johnson, 1975); that is, they are the elements that define leadership. Viewed in this manner, the children in the group can each perform acts that help them learn positive leadership skills. As a treatment worker, it is important that you promote each child's development of various roles. An imbalance in the distribution of leadership and role performance leaves some children lacking in terms of developing social skills.

Many sources have delineated specific task and maintenance roles (Johnson & Johnson, 1975; Bonner, 1959; Knowles & Knowles, 1959). For our purposes, we have synthesized these as follows: (See Table 27-1.)

Most disturbed children lack the skills needed to perform these roles. As a treatment worker, you can model these skills and attend to and support primitive approximations of them. Many children have parts of these roles in their repertory, and need guidance in expressing them appropriately. Oftentimes you simply need to rephrase or give a child the words necessary to express the roles positively. Workers sometimes make the mistake of reprimanding a child for his crudeness in performing a role rather than attempting to help the child find alternatives. The following example illustrates how this technique might work:

> The group is discussing where they want to go for a field trip. Meagan suggests the park.
> MATTHEW: That's dumb!
> (Meagan looks hurt and withdraws)
> TREATMENT WORKER: It sounds like you don't think the park is a workable idea. Meagan, it looks like having your idea called "dumb" hurt you.
> (Meagan nods)
> TREATMENT WORKER: Matthew, I would like you to tell Meagan what it is you like and don't like about her idea.
> MATTHEW: Oh, the park's an okay place to go. I like the park. But it's January and *freezing* outside. I'd rather go when it's warm.

Thus, Matthew is learning how to express his critical abilities in a more acceptable manner by evaluating the feasibility of the idea. His role in the group process can now be categorized as "reality testing."

Table 27–1. Group Roles

Task roles	*Maintenance roles*
Giving information and opinions	Encouraging and supporting
Seeking information and opinions	Harmonizing and compromising
Initiating	Relieving tension
Summarizing	Setting standards
Coordinating	Gatekeeping
Energizing	Expressing feelings
Reality testing and evaluating	
Elaborating	

Disruptive and Self–Directed Roles

Disturbed children have histories of unmet needs. Because of this, their behavior in groups tends to be largely self-involved. To a degree this is okay. Individual needs cannot and should not always be eliminated; they are there and should be dealt with. However, when members become excessively self-involved, they jeopardize the group effectiveness as well as their own position in the group. Knowles and Knowles (1959) identify six roles that treatment workers should be aware of and which can be dealt with by intervention and retraining; these are *blocking, aggression, recognition seeking, social pleading, withdrawing,* and *dominating.* Individuals can act out parts of these categories of responses, or they can synthesize them at different times and in different situations.

Fritz Redl (1966) describes some disruptive roles which disturbed children take on as styles or characters. Over time they may become stabilized personality characteristics. The following list presents some familiar ones: *the teacher's pet, the model child, the black sheep, the scapegoat, the janitorial assistant, the bully, the isolate, the group executioner, the attorney at law, the seducer, the appeaser,* and *the rabble-rouser.* When a child becomes stuck in one of these roles, you need to intervene individually or in the group to protect the child and the group from the destructiveness of the role.

The Treatment Worker as Leader

Johnson and Johnson (1975) define leadership as a process of influencing occurring among mutually dependent group members, and they make the point that all members provide leadership for one another through the task and maintenance roles. We take no issue with this point of view, but for the sake of clarity, in this section we wish to confine the term *leadership* to the role of the treatment worker in directing, guiding, and influencing the behaviors, thoughts, and feelings of the group. That is, we wish to discuss the worker as leader-therapist. Our ideal is for group members to lead one another. We recognize, however, that with disturbed children, the leader-therapist must provide more direction, at least initially, than with normal children and adults.

As a leader-therapist, you not only provide guidance and direction for the group, but also model and train effective leadership, and oversee and nurture the children's use of leadership skills. To do this, you must be aware of positive leader function and your own style. A quick check of your own role behaviors in groups may provide you with some insight.

Functions and Roles of Leader–Therapists

The general function of the leader is to facilitate the formation of a positive and effective group with regard to the previously mentioned variables. The following list combines definitions of leader functions from a number of sources:

The leader initiates the structure. Early in group development, the leader takes an active role in setting up positive patterns of interaction. He promotes a positive group atmosphere and cohesion.

The leader promotes growthful norms and is the guardian of the group norms.

The leader plans treatment activities that are consistent with the goals and objectives of the group.

The leader helps the group analyze, organize, and carry out its plans.

The leader serves as a resource to the group, providing it with information and feedback.

The leader facilitates communication and interaction among group members.

The leader keeps individual and group goals in harmony.

The leader models positive group functioning.

The leader trains the group in leadership skills. This will diffuse functions and aid the group in becoming self-directing and self-maintaining.

As the above definition demonstrates, the leader provides direction and protection while respecting and promoting the group's norms and goals. In this way, the leader is truly "the servant of the people."

Leader Roles

The leader moves in and out of various roles as the group grows and develops, backslides, and grows and develops again. The various roles imply various degrees of control and, as a leader, you must remain continually aware of the group's whereabouts in this undulating process. The state of the group defines the leader role. In order to achieve the goals of growth and self-responsibility, a delicate balance must be maintained between too little control, leading to fear and disruption, and too much control, leading to hostility and unhealthy dependence.

Murray and Ebner (1972) describe leadership roles that imply various levels of control and are used in various stages of group development. These include the *Controller, Director, Initiator, Facilitator, Motivator, Teacher, Consultant, Confidante,* and *Resource Person.* We will talk more about these roles later as we relate them to group development.

Leadership Styles

Leadership styles have a dramatic effect on the group's entire functioning. A number of studies have compared the effects of *authoritarian, democratic,* and *laissez-faire* leadership practices on groups of children and adults. These studies attest to the hostility, dependency, competitiveness, and scapegoating resulting from authoritarian styles. These results are also true for the kind autocrat, or "Patriarchal Sovereign," in Redl's terms (Redl, 1966). Such outcomes contrast sharply to the motivation, satisfaction, friendliness, and cooperation resulting from the democratic groups.

This general statement is tempered by situational variables. There will be times when, for example, urgent decisions such as those involving safety need to be made and authoritarian leadership is required. Likewise, in a highly self-motivated group with plentiful resources and skills, the *laissez-faire* state may be the most productive. Of course, the composition of the group in terms of age and developmental level will also dictate the degree of leader control. Working from a democratic base, the treatment worker must be sensitive to the group and flexible in style.

The leader's style sets the climate of the group. Observe and get the "feel" of the group. Is it supportive, critical, perfectionistic, fun, confusing, competitive, warm and friendly, threatening of emotional blackmail, etc.? The climate will give you a lot of data about yourself and your team.

Stages of Group Development

All groups proceed through various phases of development. From the many models of the development of treatment groups we have constructed our own model of relating the leader-therapist role to the developmental stage. In doing so, we have relied heavily on the work of Murray and Ebner (1972).

The developmental process has four stages. Each stage is described in terms of its issues and indicators: examples of goals and tasks that the group needs to learn before proceeding to the next phase are outlined. The role of the treatment worker is explained with regard to the goals. (See Figure 27-2.)

Stage I—Orientation, Participation, and Inclusion

In the first stage, the group is a collection of individuals who are just beginning to find out how to relate to one another. They are exploring and looking for information about how relationships are to occur, what meaning the group has to them, and what meaning they have to the group. Each child is asking questions such as, "Will I fit in?" "Will they like me?" and "What's allowable and not allowable?" Interaction among group members is limited and there is virtually no total group interaction. Most of the children have few social skills and make clumsy efforts to offer the skills that they have. Misunderstandings abound as the members start getting to know one another.

GOALS AND TASKS. learning agency rules; developing group norms around basic issues of concern, such as sharing treats and property rights; seeking personal relationships; having fun; learning that others have relevance.

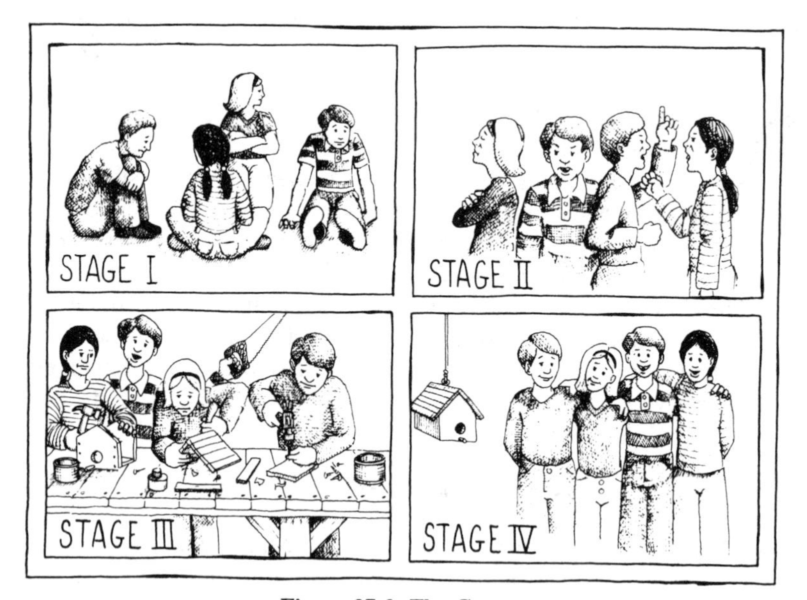

Figure 27-2. The Group

TREATMENT WORKER'S ROLE. Initiator, Director, Controller. As the leader, you will be the central figure of the group or the "hub" of the wheel, playing a "linking" role for the children. In this phase, you will actively promote interaction. The children will be directing most of their communication towards you, and it will be easy to slip into a pattern of multiple dyadic interactions. Watch for and avoid this. When you catch yourself doing this in situations that do not warrant such interaction, quickly attempt to *bridge* the communication through you and on to another child.

One of the most important functions you will serve in Stage I is to promote healthy group norms. Implicit in each interaction is a relationship value. Identify these values and encourage the group to examine them in light of their needs. Allowing destructive norms to creep into the culture unchallenged will inhibit growth and make your job harder in the long run. Below are some suggested interventions appropriate to this stage:

Gather and communicate information relevant to the group. Do not overload the group with data that they cannot yet use.

Promote, but do not push, interactions through activities of mutual interest. Pushing interactions or irrelevant activities may serve only to turn the children off to one another.

Use the children's common bonds to aid in identification with one another. Disturbed children have common problems around disrupted family and peer relationships, and common desires to be happy, have fun, and learn.

Create *fun* and *easy* activities and tasks that call only for the degree of interaction and social skills that the children can successfully achieve. Successful task accomplishment will provide the positive shared experiences necessary for identification.

Point out each child's skills and attributes. This will help the others to see each person's relevance to the group.

Attend to, encourage, and comment positively on each group member's verbal and nonverbal contributions to the group. Devaluing or putting aside such contributions will inhibit participation and the development of trust that is so important at this stage.

Develop a home base for the children to work from. This is typically a group meeting area.

Respect each child as a valuable group member.

Stage II—Involvement, Control, and Conflict

As the children begin to involve themselves with one another, conflicts and power struggles arise. There are many petty grievances, short-lived alliances, and sometimes full scale hates. The children are testing one another and you. As they work to identify the group's norms and structure, they want to know the answers to such questions as "Who's in charge here?" "Will I be powerless?" "Will I get my needs met?" "Are you really committed to the group rules?"

Sometimes the children will fight with one another and try to make you take sides. At other times, they will band together against you. As tiring as this can become, it is a positive sign that they are identifying and becoming cohesive.

Territory also becomes an issue, especially when there is more than one primary group in the agency. Clashes over territory may also occur within the group and indicate subgroups or cleavages.

The group is not always so tumultuous. There are lulls of real togetherness and community. Then, it is off to the races again.

GOALS AND TASKS. group identification; developing the group structure; asserting power and learning to control the environment; developing trust; learning to plan together; learning to solve problems; and resolve conflicts.

TREATMENT WORKER'S ROLE. Participant, Teacher, Motivator. This stage is often seen as negative, and treatment workers sometimes work hard to take control in order to stamp out disruptions and non-compliance. This is a mistake. Just as a two-year old needs to assert her power and independence to continue her development, so too does a group. Conflicts are positive indicators of group involvement. Where there is no conflict, there is no investment. The thrust here is to teach the children to work through and resolve conflicts rather than inhibit or ignore them.

The children will be watching you for cues and modeling. You will be called upon to teach decision-making, leadership, and planning skills. You will have to be especially sensitive to what degree of control is needed when. Below are some suggested interventions that are appropriate to this stage:

Provide frequent opportunities for shared experiences that demand a higher level of interaction.

Give constant feedback to the group on its pro-cess.

Train children in leadership roles. This may involve sitting next to the child and giving cues and support.

Teach the children to resolve conflicts by modeling and directing (see chapter on "Problem Solving and Conflict Resolution").

Make frequent requests for the children to make decisions and plans. Oversee and guide the process. Request each child's input.

Show enthusiasm for group ideas and plans. Participate in these activities to model and encourage involvement.

Direct children to build on rather than berate one another's ideas.

Stage III—Working Together, Belonging, Shared Purpose

As the conflicts begin subsiding, there will be more group play and emotional investment. Alliances will last longer and the children will begin to finish projects and show pride in their accomplishments. The longed-for pronoun "we" will begin to emerge. As the group takes greater responsibility, the members will begin to demand new skills and make frequent requests for information and equipment pertinent to their activities. Conflicts continue, but for shorter durations and the children begin to resolve them on their own. The group will begin to watch the treatment worker to see if he will take control or turn problems over to the group.

GOALS AND TASKS. resolving conflicts with minimal intervention; suggesting and planning activities with minimal intervention; learning to support others; learning to self-maintain in groups without treatment worker participation.

TREATMENT WORKER'S ROLE. Facilitator. Here, you will be moving in and stimulating activities and processes, and moving out again. Instead of initiating, you will be taking your cues from the group and building on and facilitating their ideas. Information and guidance will still be needed in new and difficult projects. Remain vigilant to notice cues that signal this need. Below are some suggested interventions that are appropriate to this stage:

Stimulate an activity and leave the rest to the group. For example, "Here are some passes to the planetarium. If you want to go, plan it."

Give the group greater opportunities to control their environment, e.g., let them rearrange the activity room. This will increase their sense of belonging.

Expand the boundaries, privileges, and responsibilities in accordance with their skill level.

Request that the children deal with individual problems as group problems. For example, "Sharon is really withdrawing right now. What do you want to do about that?"

Increase the need for sharing, e.g., put one bottle of glue on the table rather than three.

Stage IV—Primary Groupness, Affection, Single Organism Functioning

In this stage, the members begin seeking each other out and leaving the adults out of their activities. They carry out their responsibilities without direction, request greater boundaries, and go for long periods of time without disruptions. The children develop an elaborate scheme of symbols, particular to the group, with regard to rituals and taboos. A culture has emerged. Members begin giving feedback to one another, and the feedback is used. Protection of one another begins as children inform the treat ment worker of others' needs, and they grieve over the loss of group members.

GOALS AND TASKS. autonomy; self-direction; self-maintenance, organizing; planning and carrying out plans; expressing affection and concern for members; problem solving without adult intervention.

TREATMENT WORKER'S ROLE. Consultant, Resource. At this point, your interaction with the group has decreased markedly. Some workers at this stage feel useless and somewhat rejected. Most of us in the helping profession have strong self-imposed expectations that they should always be "doing" something ("Don't just stand there, *do* something!"). When the group has reached a state of autonomy, the best thing you can do is to sit back, watch, and enjoy the fruits of your and their labor. To overinvolve yourself at this point gives the group the message that perhaps they cannot do it after all.

Other workers risk the opposite reaction: dropping out of the picture to the point of being unaware of what the group is doing. This danger should be guarded against. The worker should *always* be aware of what is happening. The group can move in and out of this stage quickly and the treatment worker must respond at a moment's notice. Below are some suggested interventions that are appropriate to this stage:

When appropriate allow the group to create activities without your participation and involvement.

While hanging back, be aware of the group's activities.

Honor requests for autonomy by members.

Have equipment and resources available for the group. 1

These stages are not meant to be a chronological ordering which you can expect your group to go through step by step. It is more likely that your group will move in and out of them even within a day's time. Or, they may show several stage indicators simultaneously. Also, in most treatment agencies, members are phased out of the group at the completion of treatment and others are added. These changes in composition affect stage development. Your job is to assess and continually reassess the developmental level of the group and to respond accordingly. If the group does not show movement, it is time to examine your procedures with regard to the leader-therapist role.

Problem Solving and Decision Making

Conflicts

Conflicts are inevitable in any group. They are two-sided coins and can have constructive or destructive results. The conflicts themselves do not lead to destructiveness—the inability to deal with them does. Suppressing conflicts can result in frustration, avoidance, and withdrawal. Some of the positive effects of conflicts are listed below:

The group examines its procedures and goals.
Issues are kept up to date.
Interests are stimulated.
Problems are brought into the open, resolving tensions and leading to increased understanding.
Creativity and curiosity are encouraged.
The group readjusts its balance of power.

If conflicts are resolved by "win/lose," "right/wrong," and "me versus you" methods, positive group processing can break down. The following model, based on methods proposed by Johnson and Johnson (1975) and Bany and Johnson (1964), provides procedures that can be used to bring about positive effects.

Steps to Problem Solving

(See the chapter on "Problem Solving and Conflict Resolution for more detailed information on this process.)

Define the Problem. The important question to answer here is: "When is a problem a *group* problem? When one person defines it to be two people; half the group?" The general guideline is that individual problems become group problems when they disrupt the group's functioning. This may be a difficult line to draw at times.

PROPOSE SOLUTIONS AND STRATEGIES. A technique called *brainstorming* comes in handy at this step. Brainstorming is a technique that encourages divergent thinking and creativity. To be effective, *all criticism must be ruled out* and wild ideas are to be encouraged. The principle here is "quantity, not quality." The process proceeds as follows: *record all ideas* on a blackboard or sheet of paper so that the group sees their ideas recognized. *Encourage participation from all members;* involvement in the process will heighten commitment. Ask the children to *build on ideas.* Trimming or devaluing ideas is not allowed. Some children will use this opportunity to get pretty outlandish when discussing, for example, field trip ideas. Perhaps they are also testing to see if you really will accept virtually anything, as you say you will. Relax, they will settle down when they find that you will not buy into the "discouraging word" phenomena. And, perhaps a field trip to Antartica would be interesting after all.

EXAMINE AND APPRAISE THE SOLUTIONS. List each idea, or, if the list is too long, ask the children to decide which ideas they want to examine. A *force field analysis* technique, developed by Kurt Lewin (cited in Johnson & Johnson, 1975) is a convenient method for evaluating the feasibility of each proposed solution. The objective of such an analysis is to identify the pros and cons of each idea. After listing these, attempt to reduce or eliminate the cons and increase the pros.

DECIDE ON A SOLUTION AND MAKE PLANS TO CARRY IT OUT. Now it is time to make a decision (see next section on "Decision Making"), list the steps to be taken, *assign responsibilities to each member,* and develop a time sequence and dates for implementation.

EVALUATE SUCCESS. The last step involves reconvening the group after implementation for feedback on both the process and the outcome of the solution.

If the outcome or the process was not effective, look at the following list to aid in identifying blocks to problem-solving effectiveness (Johnson & Johnson, 1975):

Lack of clarity in stating the problem.

Not getting the needed information.

Poor communication within the group.

Premature testing of alternative strategies.

A critical, evaluative, competitive climate.

Pressures for conformity.

Lack of inquiry and problem solving skills.

Inadequate motivation.

Decision Making

Decisions are continually being made in groups. These decisions run from everyday housekeeping details (such as what to have for snacks) to larger decisions (such as where and when the summer outings should take place). The first decision is made by the treatment worker and involves whether or not the decision should be turned over to the group. Several questions concerning available time, skill level, the issue itself, and need for commitment need to be asked in order to make this initial decision. You should make the decision if it: 1) is about routine, boring issues that will only bog down the group; 2) requires too much time; 3) requires greater skill than the children possess; 4) may lead to consequences that are too severe to risk (e.g., whether or not to use life preservers in the row boats); 5) does not require a high commitment level by the group. Otherwise, the group should be involved. Numerous studies show that there is greater change in group behavior when members participate in decision making (Bany & Johnson, 1964).

When decisions are turned over to the group, a number of decision making methods are available to it. The effectiveness and efficiency of these methods can be assessed in terms of 1) costs and requirements, and 2) benefits. The methods that make the greatest demands on the group also reap the greatest benefits.

CONSENSUS. A consensus decision is one in which all members reach agreement on the decision.
Costs And Requirements— Lots of time, energy, skill, and group cohesion. These requirements exist at Stage IV of group development.
Benefits— Greater use of group resources; stimulation of creativity; skill enhancement; the highest degree of group commitment.

MAJORITY VOTE. This is the method most commonly used.
Costs and requirements— Skill in group discussion; may alienate the minority, leading to subgroups; less commitment than with consensus method.
Benefits— Useful when there is not a great deal of time and when a high degree of total commitment is not essential; avoids going around in circles when consensus cannot be reached.

DECISION BY COMMITTEE OR EXPERT. This method delegates the decision making to a person or committee knowledgeable on the issue.
Costs and requirements— Does not use all resources; lowers group com mitment; unresolved conflicts and resentments can occur; group does not interact; there may be arguments over who experts are.
Benefits— Efficient use of time; when only a few members have the information, the group is not inconvenienced; useful in simple, routine decisions

where broad commitment is not needed; useful when whole group cannot meet.

In addition to these methods, the group can simply agree to disagree and postpone the decision, or engage in a discussion of the issue and leave the decision up to the treatment worker.

All decision-making methods should rely on group discussions that positively emphasize contributions. The leader's role in these discussions is to oversee the process by *reflecting* ideas presented, *deflecting* questions and comments back to the group, making sure that ideas are *accepted without initial evaluation, pulling ideas together,* and *debriefing* the process and outcome. After discussing and making the decision, the group should be asked for commitment to the decision.

The lion's share of treatment takes place in the group. Knowledge of group process and structure is necessary for facilitating its formation as a therapeutic milieu. Hopefully, the information presented in this chapter will provide a framework with which to contain and organize such a complex and dynamic entity.

Chapter 28

PLAY

Play is an essential part of being a child. It is the major context of his or her activities. You must understand this context in order to know how to appreciate and nurture its richness. Presumably, you will increase your own ability to play and have fun in the process—an extra benefit of the job that can revitalize your energies and increase your effectiveness and well-being.

Often, in programs dealing with children, play is viewed not as a meaningful and fruitful activity, but as useful only in providing a reprieve from the work of learning and growing. Play time often ends with the message, spoken or unspoken, "Now, let's get down to business." This attitude could not be further from the truth. Play *is* business; it is the joyful and serious business through which the child comes to terms with reality, thus learning who he is, what he can do, and what the real world is like. With play as his means of self-expression and self-discovery, the child builds his own philosophy of life. He continually retests the reality of his beliefs and makes revisions accordingly. The world that he tests and retests is extremely complex, and play offers the child a tool for *managing* and *regulating* so that he will not become overwhelmed. Erikson emphasizes this point when he says, . . . "play is the infantile form of the human ability to deal with experience by creating model situations, and to master reality by experiment and planning" (Erikson, 1950). This mastery is the precursor to adult competence and self-fulfillment.

Dennis differentiates work from play. Work, he says, emphasizes the *product* while play emphasizes the *process.* "The objective [of play] is an *internal* and organic one and not necessarily one of *external* modification" (italics added) (Dennis, 1970). As the child's actions become directed by intentions and external products, play becomes work. This occurs naturally as the child gains assurance and mastery, and feels the competence necessary to accomplish successful outcomes. As the child matures, it is to be hoped that he will not lose the enjoyment of fully experiencing the moment.

This kind of experiencing and enjoyment in adult life is contingent on the ability to play as a child, and to carry that playful attitude into our work. In a thirty-year follow-up study, Erikson found that of the people he studied, those who were most playful and creative as children had the most fulfilling lives (Bruner, 1975). This is an important point to remember as you work with children. Many helpers are oriented towards outcome and are trained to reward children for results. Although we recognize that this is important, we also recognize that this style of responding to play can disrupt the child's focus on the process, thus disrupting her self-motivation and feelings about engaging in the moment with her whole being. Continual emphasis on outcomes tells the child that she has validity only for the results that she can create through *doing.* Validation of the child's *being* occurs through emphasis on the process as an intense, rich aspect of life through which she can experience not only her external products, but also her feelings, thoughts, and desires. This kind of validation is central to the treatment process.

Play and the Emotionally Disturbed Child

Emotional disturbance affects the child on all levels of development, including the ability to proceed through the developmental stages of play. Almy (1966) points out that play experiences stabilize the child's concept, and adapt his perceptions, actions, and information to others in his world. If the developmental process proceeds unhindered, this occurs by the time the child is school-aged. Not so for the disturbed child. Sutton-Smith and Sutton-Smith say that, "When life is too demanding, dangerous or anxiety producing, there is no room for play." (1974). Normally, children will master a process, concept, skill, or issue, and move on to the next. The disturbed child, failing to master a task, process or issue will persevere in an attempt to conquer it and gain freedom. Alden adds, "If a child has too few experiences and ideas or if the adults in his life limit his opportunities to deal with them too severely for whatever reasons, his developing idea of reality is likely to be distorted and will hamper his future happiness and well-being." (1961).

By playing, a child can find relief from his powerlessness and helplessness. He can find strength in creating his own reality, overcoming obstacles, and safely experimenting with solutions without the risk of failure that is so common in his life. Play reduces the pressure and anxiety that comes with having to achieve, thus facilitating the ease with which new, difficult skills are learned. In an interesting experiment, Bruner (1975) had four groups of children fish for an out-of-reach prize, with only two short sticks and a clamp. He found that children who had only the opportunity to play with the materials without instruction did as well as children who observed an adult solve the problem, and both of these groups did better than children who received instruction only. Bruner concludes that the anxiety involved in the pressure to produce results interfered with learning, while play reduced frustration. Emotionally disturbed children are especially sensitive to the effect of anxiety, and the integration of play into their lives is even more strongly indicated.

Almy (1966) discusses the role of play in Piaget's theory of intellectual development. Piaget postulates that a child must first take her experiences in the world into her egocentric concepts (assimilation) before she can adapt to them (accommodation) and learn to think conceptually. Assimilation occurs through play. Without completion of the developmental play process, the child will be intellectually hindered.

Functions of Play

Play is discovery and expression. The child discovers herself, her strengths, weaknesses, skills, attitudes, and feelings, and discovers the world. She can then express her impressions, desires, frustrations, fears, and joys. The end product is the power and mastery necessary to deal adequately with the world. These functions occur on the physical, mental, social, and emotional levels.

Physical

In vigorous play, the child uses her whole body, thus developing gross motor coordination and body awareness. In quiet, manipulative play she develops fine motor skills. Hand-eye coordination, essential for functioning in the world, is continually practiced in play. All of the senses (auditory, visual, tactile, olfactory, and gustatory) are developed and refined through the intense and vivid contacts that play provides with the world. Each of these senses is important in carrying messages to the brain. Thus, the child can be seen as a kinetic information absorber. It may look like the child is "goofing around" when she wildly, and seemingly without purpose, runs, jumps, climbs, balances, swings, etc. Look again with a keen eye and observe all of the muscles and senses that are being used. If the child is noticeably lacking in a particular skill, for example, balance, you may want to introduce a low beam in the play area that will invite her exploration and practice.

Mental

The skills gained through play lay the groundwork for cognitive learning. In terms of readiness for academic skills, the child develops the previously mentioned abilities of auditory and visual discriminations, fine motor and hand-eye coordination skills. Also, he begins to play with symbols and language. Through language, facts and ideas are expressed, and concepts are developed. The child begins to play with numbers as he notices that he will need to get six cookies if he wants himself and his two friends to have two apiece for a mock backpacking tour into the wilderness. And, as he sees and feels the "roundness" of balls, the "longness" of sticks, and the "curvedness" of boomerangs, he prepares himself to identify shapes that will aid in making sense out of numerals and letters. The absorbing nature of play also lengthens attention span and increases concentration, both of which affect memory.

Play often requires problem solving, reasoning, and organization skills. The previously mentioned experiment by Bruner (1975) illustrates this. It does not take experimentation to attest to the everyday occurrence of such circumstances: a treatment worker watches a child figure out how to get the inner tube through the small opening into the tree house. Once he is in the tree house, the gang begins to decide who will take what role in the pirate fantasy—who will go where and when, etc., thus developing organization skills. (See Figure 28-1.)

Nowhere is the connection between play and cognitive skills more apparent than in the area of creativity. Loosened from the boundaries of what is, the child expands into the realm of what could be. Artists and great thinkers take this aspect of play into adulthood.

Beliefs, attitudes, and self-knowledge come to the child through play. Answers to the questions "Are big people accepting or critical?" "Will I be taken care of?" "What can I do well?" and "What are my limitations?" are answered in the child's interactions with the world in play.

Social

Through interactions with others in fun, playful activities, children learn to value one another and develop important and close relationship. In groups children learn to share, take turns, empathize, ask, request, receive, and all the other innumerable social skills necessary for harmonious living. Imitative role playing, e.g., playing mom and dad, creates situations in which understanding of others can be gained.

Children go through four stages of social development: solitary, parallel, associative, and cooperative. Each stage must be completed before they can move on. Emotionally disturbed children may be stuck in one of these, or may vacillate back and forth between various stages.

Figure 28-1. Mental Stimulation of Play

SOLITARY PLAY. Very young children play by themselves, piling up blocks, playing with dolls, pulling wagons, dumping cans of marbles on the floor, and sticking crayons in their mouths.

PARALLEL PLAY. As they grow older, children enjoy being close to one another, perhaps using the same materials, but not too close. At times, they contact one another, and these brief contacts may be awkward and seem "socially inappropriate." Quite the contrary, these attempts are appropri ate for this stage. Disallowing them will only prolong the developmental process.

ASSOCIATIVE PLAY. Growing further, children begin to play in small groups with a common purpose. Although they are together, they may not always be in "synch." They often engage in "collective monologue"; that is, what one says may not follow what the other says and may in fact be totally irrelevant. At this stage, children are still more tuned into their individual needs than to those of their companions. For example, Leta and Corey are playing at the table with the doll dishes. Leta, playing mom, asks Corey, playing dad, about his day at the office. Corey replies, "I'm driving my motorcycle," while scooting the fork across the table. Leta then continues on about her day with the kids, seemingly without regard to Corey's response.

COOPERATIVE OR GROUP PLAY. Now, the children are playing in larger groups with some pattern of organization and cooperation. This is where tag and other games make their appearance.

Each child differs in his social development. Some show a strong desire for social contact very early. Others stand on the sidelines for a long time before entering. Some may never take a very active part in group play. Every child's style must be respected. One thing is clear—pushing will gain nothing. The child must feel comfortable before taking the leap. Hymes suggests to "begin at the beginning" (1963) with the socially distant child by playing with her before encouraging and facilitating her contact with other children.

Emotional

Play provides a safe means of dealing with complex emotional issues. The disturbed child can recreate experiences in which he was passive and helpless, gain mastery over them, and work towards resolution. He can do or be anything in play, and can thus experiment with various means of handling frustration and failure. He can also find undestructive ways to release unacceptable impulses, e.g., he can kill a daddy doll without damaging his father in the least.

Play therapy is a treatment modality that has made use of this level. It is an extremely powerful modality that we highly recommend for any children's treatment program. It is our opinion that training in play therapy requires information, guidance and supervision beyond which this book can offer. If you wish more information on the subject, refer to the works of Virginia Axline and Haim Ginott.

Most important of all, play is a time to have *fun* and enjoy life fully. Isn't that a major goal of treatment, after all?

The job of the treatment worker is to see that opportunities for play on all these levels is provided, and that materials are available which will facilitate physical, mental, social, and emotional exploration. Some activities have broad applications. For example, making pudding for finger painting requires taking turns, sharing the pudding, making sure that no one's diet restricts certain flavors (social); sequencing, measuring, using language to describe the process, observing the effects of heat and cold on the pudding, creating designs (mental); manipulating utensils and using fingers to make forms (physical); feelings of power in mastering a process, the expression of feelings in drawing and painting, and having fun (emotional). You may find it useful to observe children in different spontaneous and structured play activities and list the various levels that are involved.

Modes of Play

Sutton-Smith (1971) suggests that children learn through various modes: imitation, exploration, prediction, and construction. Each mode is a way of discovering truth. All of them may be involved in a given act of play, but generally one will be dominant.

Imitation

A child gains understanding of the people and processes around him by copying them. Some modeling is covert, as in latent learning, and some is overt, as in mimicry. Fantasy, through which the child becomes mother or police woman, is a form of imitation. Some fantasy involves taking bits and pieces of modeling from various sources and sticking them together in new and creative ways; thus, we have fairy tales and science fiction.

Exploration

Another means of understanding the world is through causal analysis: "How do things work?" "How did they come to be the way they are?," and "What can they do?" The child takes apart a clock to find out "what makes it tick," laughs at objects that shake up the order of the world (such as candles that will not blow out), and plays with water from a hose to discover that, yes indeed, what goes up, must come down.

Prediction

A child finds validation through testing and retesting his behavior and its impact. Exploration focuses on the existing interconnections of the objective world, while prediction focuses on the possibilities. This especially can be seen in physical play, as the child tests his strength, speed, and agility. In social play you can see children measuring their progress and achievements against one another. Also, games can test one's fear and power (Hide-and-Seek); anger, agility, and endurance (Dodge Ball); sensory functions (Simon Says); and impulse control (Statue Tag).

Construction

By putting things and concepts together, a child plays with and learns about his world. Children often make these constructions in fantasy play. Erikson (1950) suggests that this mode is analogous to adult planning and organizational activities. The example of the boys organizing a game of pirates in the club house illustrates this mode.

Observing these four modes of play may help to focus your attention and ascertain what and how the child is experiencing the learning.

Guidance

Children generally select objects and activities that are relevant to them at particular moments in time. Therefore, they need to be provided with opportunities for such selection. As a treatment worker, you will be a behind–the–scenes coordinator that makes appearances but quickly fades away as indicated. The coordinator role requires that you neither unnecessarily protect the children from experiences or overburden them with difficulties beyond their present capabilities. This juggling act takes knowledge of the play process and sensitivity to the children's needs. This section outlines areas to be aware of in guiding children's play.

Safe Limits

The environment must provide for physical and psychological safety. This means regulating the physical boundaries as well as expectations and rules. Children will feel more freedom in the absence of anxiety over their own or other's destructiveness. For example, limiting the children's practice of tying up and locking their "prisoners" in a small chest is important in avoiding excessive fear.

Acceptance

Accepting a child's feelings and world view gives the child a feeling of value for who she is. The message to the child is that it is okay for him to live out his concepts and experiences. Play time is not the time, for example, to criticize a child's drawing for being anatomically incorrect.

Observation

Although you will often be excluded from the actual play, you should always know what is going on and what each child's play needs are in terms of issues, levels, social stages, and modes. Without this kind of assessment, you will have no base from which to plan and manage.

Planning and Management

Your central "doer" role will be in setting up the environment and schedule. You will see to it that opportunities for all kinds of play are available. You will regulate and time those opportunities so that they are relevant at the moment, and so that the difficulty involved neither leads to boredom nor failure. Many agencies have activity centers, such as large-motor areas and dress up areas, that provide such variety. These centers need to be replenished and regulated from time to time so that they remain interesting and reach a balance on the overwhelming/"underwhelming" scale. In this role, your services in giving information and providing resources will often be requested.

Direct Involvement

There are times when direct involvement in unstructured play is warranted. In these circumstances, you will serve as a facilitator, bridge, or encourager. You should never take over and show them how something is "supposed to be done," but rather should let the child take the lead. Children who have few skills in playing with others need someone to interact with who will accept their clumsy efforts. These children may also need an adult to act as an intermediary and bridge their interactions with other children. In this process you should continually ask yourself how much of your involvement is indicated, and when it is inhibiting to their growth. And of course there are times when you and a child, or group of children, just want to have a good time together, and that is reason enough in itself.

Process versus Product

As was stated earlier, play is an involvement in the moment. Achievement and accomplishment should be de-emphasized—play should not become an anxiety-provoking performance. Rather, nonjudgmental acknowledgments (no goods, or bads) of process and enjoyment take the place of praise. These acknowledgments (e.g., "Those blocks are piled so high they almost touch the ceiling" or "Splashing in that water sure looks like fun.") serve to encourage rather than restrict play.

Awareness Training

Comments on the process, as illustrated above, can serve to increase a child's awareness. Paraphrases and reflections of feeling are useful in this process (see part 2 on "Communication"). Care must be taken to avoid interpretations unless you know the child and his issue very well.

Awareness training involves "read-outs" to the child about her play process. For example, when watching Sara angrily throw a "baby" doll against the wall, you can say, "You are really mad at the baby and are throwing her against the wall and hurting her." If you know that Sara's mother has just had a baby, and that Sara is experiencing grief, anger and fear, you might take a plunge into interpretation and say, "You are hurt and scared that the baby will take all of mom's attention. You want the baby to go away." Beyond providing awareness, these "read-outs" may give the child permission and encouragement to increase the intensity of the play, especially if the treatment worker is expressive and nonjudgmental in his comments.

Another awareness technique is called "overtalk," wherein two workers discuss the child's process in his presence at a time when the child seeks to avoid the issue. For example, when a child has retreated under a blanket after being rejected by the group, two workers can discuss and validate the child's hurt feelings. This technique must be used sensitively and timed according to the child's readiness to deal with the issue. Also, it must be done in such a way as to avoid the child's feeling belittled or intruded upon.

Although play time is ideal for awareness training, it can also be helpful in other situations. Novice treatment workers can overload children with this technique, having found it to be *the* therapeutic device. Used excessively, it can become irritating, if not countertherapeutic.

With information on the value, function, and guidance of play, you will be able to add to the richness of your program, and yourself. In the world of play, children have a lot to teach us about the process and enjoyment of life. In learning this lesson, you can improve your effectiveness as

Figure 28-2. Play

a worker and a whole person by increasing your feelings and expression of joy, and by providing a way to recharge your energies. The business of treatment can be playful business. After reading all of the justifications for play, we encourage you to remember just one thing: having fun is reason enough. (See Figure 28-2.)

Chapter 29

USE OF THE ENVIRONMENT

Environment is a broad term that applies to those objects, events, and processes around us that we can experience with our senses. Most of this book has focused on the social environment, that is, people and their effect on one another. In this chapter we acknowledge that "social relationships occur in a physical environment that in itself is a dynamic part of the process of change" (Ittleson, et al., 1974). Therefore, we will examine the physical context of the treatment process.

The social and physical environments act together and mutually affect one another. This process of dynamic interchange was recognized by Winston Churchill when he said, "We shape our buildings and afterward, our buildings shape us." That is, the physical setting has a *demand quality* that structures behavior patterns and implies which actions and events are and are not possible or appropriate. This demand quality can be immediate, such as a sand dune making roller skating impossible, or *symbolic,* such as a church suggesting, through custom, that the congregants are to be quiet.

The context of the physical environment has been conspicuously absent in discussions of human behavior, and, specifically, as it relates to child treatment. This is largely because of the complexity of the variables at work in the environment which make it difficult to understand and explain in any prescriptive way. Also, the environment often works on us outside of our awareness. Add to this the fact of mankind's immense adaptive ability and individual variability, and it becomes clear that environmental effects are difficult to categorize in a cookbook "how to" fashion. Our intention here is to increase your awareness of the physical environment and to invite you to examine your physical treatment context in light of your treatment goals.

Environmental Complexity

Research on the physical environment points to the difficulty in isolating specific variables and identifying their specific effects. The environment is dynamic and interactional. Each part has meaning only in relation to the other parts: color, texture, temperature, lighting, size, shape, noise, and design interact to produce a given quality or effect. In addition, activities and individuals in a particular context interact with the environment and affect that quality in various ways at various times. Here, we can clearly see the impossibility of a cause-effect model of determinism, and instead, must talk about multideterminism and "environmental probabilism" (Porteous, 1977). For example, we cannot say that blue walls will create a quieting effect in any setting. What if someone put loud disco music on the record player? We can say that all things being equal, we can *expect* the color blue to have a quieting effect relative to other variables. In this example, the music will *probably* be the salient feature. We also might guess that the disquieting effects of the sound might be more dramatic in a red room. So, it becomes apparent that the environment works as a gestalt with different aspects taking the foreground at different times with regard to the existing variables.

Different *levels* of environmental objects, as well as the objects themselves, come in and out of focus as needs shift. Ittleson et al. (1974) identify five levels on which any physical object, or conglomerate of objects, can be viewed: physical, affective, functional, cognitive, and social. For example, a large wooden playground structure can be seen as a large, rough, and sturdy *physical* object; can induce joy and security on the *affective* level; has *functional* value as a climbing structure; has a maze-like quality that can be thought about on a *cognitive* level; and serves as a place for *social* interaction.

The unique characteristics of the individual within the environment will also determine what features of the environment, and what levels of those features, she will attend to and what their affects will be. Her personality, temperament, physiology, biorhythms, beliefs, history, and cultural background will lead the individual to various responses. Hall (1966) talks at length about the differences in environmental preferences between the Japanese, Arab, and American cultures, and Porteous (1977) describes the widely discrepant homes chosen by personality types that he categorizes by the labels extrovert, introvert, social mixer, and misanthrope. As well as inter-individual differences, there are intra-individual differences; that is, a person's internal gestalt (mood, physical status, etc.) that fluctuates over time. Internal events that are "foreground" will affect what he sees as "foreground" in the environment. Barring something as dramatic as a tornado, different individuals may attend to different aspects of the environment at a given moment.

Environmental Awareness and Adaptability

Much of the environment's impact occurs outside of our awareness. "It is when our environment changes that we become most aware of it because it is at this point that we consciously begin to adapt" (Ittleson, et al., 1974). Many times we are aware of how a place "feels" (cramped, spacious, warm, cold), but are often unaware of how it affects us behaviorally until we look at the circumstance in retrospect. For example, in reviewing your reaction to a lecture, you may discover that you were bored and inattentive because the lecturer was too far away to hear and see well, and that the room was stuffy and warm, which induced drowsiness. This out-of-awareness quality of environmental impact can be insidious. Birren (1978) documents that the "errie" effects of blue-green lights have been used to force confessions from persons convicted of crimes.

Another possible insidious quality of our response to the environment stems from the fact that human beings are highly adaptive to their surroundings. This adaptive nature is a mixed blessing. One one level, it allows us to survive under the most adverse conditions; on the other, it creates a lack of awareness of conditions that have a negative effect on our being. For example, the country boy moving to Los Angeles will initally experience watery, stinging eyes in response to the smog and will cringe at the traffic noises. Over time, these responses will adapt out, but this does not mean that the poisons and noises will affect his physiology and hearing any less. So too with the executive who becomes emotionally oblivious to the stress of his job, but who develops ulcers and heart problems. In order to adapt, the organism uses a tremendous amount of energy and experiences stress. In applying this to treatment, you can guess at the level of stress created by expecting a group of children to be quiet and relax in a well-lit, large room with noise and object distractions.

Users of the Environment

Most of our physical environments have been created without regard to the user's behavioral needs. Buildings are designed and erected by architects and builders who, for the most part, are oblivious to emotional and social needs. They are built mostly for economy, convenience, utility, and aesthetics. A number of sources have cited the housing projects which have taken the place of the ghetto as an example of this. Although they may be clean and efficient with regard to utilities, appliances, and space, they neglect social needs and thus are generally less preferred than the slums. The high value on maintenance can be seen in school supply catalogues that often use the "easy to maintain" sales pitch. Sommer emphasizes this point in stating that schools are made for janitors rather than children and quotes Lady Allen, who pioneered the "adventure playground" in Great Britain and described the American playground as "an administrator's heaven and a child's hell . . . asphalt barracks, yards behind wire screen, mesh barriers" (Sommer, 1969).

The amazing fact is that the user is rarely consulted when environments are constructed. In a bold experiment, nursery school teachers in Milwaukee allowed their preschoolers to arrange their own environment. They proceeded, very cooperatively, to put all the objects against the walls so that they would have a large central area in which to play (Sommer, 1972). The surprising element is not that the arrangement worked so well, but that such an approach is so uncommon. Here, we make a pitch for involving the children, parents, and staff—the users—in the design and implementation of environmental renovations.

This kind of involvement of the users in creating the environment is difficult. Most of the buildings we inhabit were built for another time and use. There is little opportunity in the building process to give feedback, reevaluate, and restructure, as we continually do in other parts of treatment. This fact of our physical environment is even more problematic at a time when our culture, needs, and approaches are evolving so rapidly. Our physical structures just cannot keep up. Ask any doctor who has just invested in the latest equipment only to find that, within months, it has become obsolete.

Sommer (1972) suggests that we look at the possibility of including *environmental managers* in our agencies to ensure that our structures remain updated. Stan Honn, at the Child Center in Springfield, Oregon, an agency for emotionally disturbed children and their families, occupies such a position on their staff. In an innovative approach to remodeling their facility, the entire staff comes together and problem-solves around treatment needs and how they can best be facilitated environmentally. The environmental manager then takes the input and integrates it into the design. After trying it out, they reconvene, evaluate and redesign. In this way, the physical setting suits their needs and therapeutic approach (Honn, 1979).

The Environment as a Treatment Facilitator

In viewing the complexity of environmental affect and effect, you can see that the question of "what determines what" is extremely difficult if not impossible to answer. Rather, the question is, "Are the variables facilitating or hindering goal achievement?" Ittleson, et al., make the point that ". . . environments have physical limits. These can be described as resistive, supportive or facilitative. Behavior in the total environmental context will always be affected by the physical opportunities that exist for expressing a desired behavior" (Ittleson, et al., 1974).

Gump (1971) coined the term "synomorphic," which means similarity of shape, to describe the concept of environmental and behavioral fit. To illustrate this concept, we will look at some treatment areas in terms of environmental facilitation. This selection is not all-inclusive, prescriptive, or definitive, and only a limited number of examples are given. The categories are somewhat arbitrary and overlap here and there. Our intention is to stimulate you to see your physical surroundings in terms of your treatment goals. Your process will be unique and will take into consideration your treatment philosophy and client population. As Sommer says, "... man himself and what he wants to do [his value system] represents the yardstick by which design solutions must be measured" (Sommer, 1969).

Safety

As *basic care* is the fundamental aspect of treatment, safety is the fundamental dimension of the environment. Care should be taken to see that nails are picked up in the woodworking area, that breakables are not found in physical activity areas, and that sharp knives are not left out unsupervised in the kitchen. Plexiglas may be expensive, but it saves pain, injury, and the expense involved in replacing windows. Also, it prevents the "prison" effect of wire mesh and bars. Wrestling matches and tumbling should be confined to the mats; ropes are standard items for rock climbing excursions, as life jackets are for boating.

Accessibility and *supervision* are essentials for safety. Have you ever needed a first-aid kid only to find that it is under lock and key in the office on the upper level? In terms of supervision, check the environment for "blind spots." Children need privacy *and* safety. Make sure that areas of privacy are readily and quickly available to observation when necessary.

Autonomy, Self-Responsibility, and Competence

One of the major goals of treatment is to produce self-responsible individuals competent in living. One of the best ways to facilitate this goal is to provide an environment on the child's scale which he can manipulate without adult intervention. For example, if you expect the children to self-maintain, but put the games and art supplies on a high shelf that can only be reached by an adult, you are working against yourself and the child. In viewing your environment in terms of required adult mediation, you may be surprised. Ittleson, et al. (1974) describe such a reaction by an architect who, after completing a psychiatric facility for children, found that the doors were too heavy and large for his five-year-old to operate. This certainly would not lend itself to autonomy and competence. (See Figure 29-1.)

Look at your environment with regard to manipulation and mobility. Can the children move and manipulate the chairs, tables, pillows, scissors, pencils, and balls? Are the stairs too big for them? Can they affect and change their environment? Sommer (1974) quotes a study showing that the open, rather than closed, classroom encourages self-maintenance and self-direction by encouraging children to rearrange it, and by providing opportunities for free movement to various learning centers as their needs dictate. C. E. Lewis says,

> "If the recitation and reproduction of lessons is considered the chief aim of teaching, the traditional equipment of the classroom is perhaps sufficient. But if teaching is guiding children to do their own thinking, proposing, planning and executing and appraising . . . then the classroom becomes a workshop, a library, a museum, in short, a 'learning laboratory.'" (Sommer, 1969).

Figure 29-1. Use of the Environment

Stimulation

The environment has a dramatic effect on distractability and activity level. Studies show that both sensory overload and sensory stimulation create stress (Porteous, 1977; Toffler, 1970). The goal of environmental structuring is to create a level of stimulation appropriate to the activity. The skilled treatment worker knows that if he passes out the materials and equipment before explaining the activity, the children will be too distracted and excited to listen. Or, on the other hand, that trying to create group enthusiasm in a cold, dark, quiet, empty room is like trying to sell snowmobiles to the Sierra Club.

Hyperactive and brain-damaged children have been studied with regard to the environment. Porteous (1977) reports that brain-damaged children learn more and faster when facing blank walls without windows. It seems that such children are unable to screen out excessive stimuli. Although not as affected, normal children also learned more in low-complexity surroundings. In an impressive study by Ott (1978), the effects on hyperactivity of white fluorescent lights were compared with those of full–spectrum lights rigged with lead foil around the cathode ends to stop suspected soft X-rays. His dramatic results showed that the full spectrum lights without X-ray emissions lowered distractability markedly.

A number of sources have attested that conversational noise level and movement increase with increased light intensity. Most teachers know this and use the "lights out" technique to quiet the room.

The color research reported by Birren (1978) is interesting in terms of stimulation. For instance, red lights were found to produce a 12 percent quicker muscle reaction than normal lights, while green lights retard such reactions. In another study, blue lights had a quieting effect on mental patients and yellow lights stimulated depressives. Blood pressure was also found to be affected by color.

Mood

Birren's overview (1978) of color research also demonstrates its relationship to mood. Tranquility was related to yellow-green and green, excitation to orange and scarlet, and subdued moods to violet and purple. Gibson (1978) reports that painting a black bridge over the Thames green reduced suicide ateempts by one-third. Temperature, duration of sunlight, and weather change have also been related to suicide rates (Porteous, 1977).

Maslow and Mintz (1956) compared the effects of "ugly," "pretty," and "average" rooms on the subject's perception of the mood of others. The groups in the "pretty" room rated faces in photographs as having more energy and well-being. Thus, it can be conjectured that the aesthetic conditions actually influenced the *subject's* moods. However, the subject attributed these moods to the photographs.

To experience the power of the environment, track your own mood shifts as, in imagination, you move from a traffic jam in a hot city to a cool, green, lakeside mountain setting; or, on a less dramatic level, from a bright yellow and orange activity room to a blue, pillowed therapy room.

Self-Image

Our environment is an extension of ourself and reflects, in part, our self-image. Children who see that their environment is respected—well-maintained, clean—will be more likely to respect it themselves, will identify with it, and will see themselves as worthy of respect. Involving the children in the redesigning and maintenance of the environment will increase their identification, as will displaying their art works and crafts. A treatment agency is a place for children and parents, and this should be reflected in every part of the setting.

Interaction, Privacy, and Territorality

The children should have time together and time alone. Large open spaces that provide for group interaction should be balanced by soft, quiet, private spaces. Just knowing there are alternatives provides security and may reduce the need to choose. In a study of hospitals, Ittleson (1974) found that the provision of private spaces actually *increased* the patient's interactions.

Open floor plans have been found to produce more frequent and more diffuse interaction. Spaces that are subdivided into individual closed spaces reduce diffuse interaction while increasing social cohesion. Closed spaces have also been found to produce more isolates (Ittleson et al., 1974).

Strong leadership reduces interaction, and certain group arrangements have been shown to produce various degrees of leadership. Leavitt found that a circular arrangement had no effect on producing a particular leader while in a wheel arrangement, the leader was almost always identified as the one in the middle (Sommer, 1969). The wheel arrangement reduced interaction and group satisfaction. Many studies conclude that the circular arrangement increases interaction. This also has implications for the traditional, columnar classroom seating arrangement.

Territorality is a part of being human. It provides security, identity, and a sense of control. Witness the common phenomenon of staff members choosing the same chairs in the staff lounge from meeting to meeting, and watch the reaction of surprise or indignation when someone else sits in their chairs or spots on the floor. So too with children. Each group should have a "home base." This will increase their sense of identity and cohesion. Each individual should also have his own space—a tub, locker, or cubbyhole.

Cooperation, Competition, and Aggression

Crowding and group size has been linked with cooperation and aggression. In an experiment involving the effects of hot, crowded conditions, Griffitt and Veitch found that there was a high probability that strangers entering a room of high density and temperature would be met with hostility (Ittleson et al., 1974). Ittleson et al. (1974), also report studies showing that male juries deliver more severe verdicts when deliberating in small, crowded rooms. A number of sources have found that women are less affected by such conditions in terms of hostility and aggression. The same authors cite reports describing how, when small groups of patients at the Napa Valley State Hospital were moved into tents after the 1906 earthquake, cooperation and morale increased markedly. These behaviors quickly returned to "normal" after the patients were returned to large groups in the repaired facility. The positive affects of small group size in terms of cooperation was also shown in studies involving children. Findings consistently show that large groups and high densities lead to aggression and withdrawal, while the opposite conditions elicit cooperation (Ittleson, et al., 1974).

Sommer (1969) conducted a study on the effects of rectangular and circular tables on the cooperation, conversation, co-action, and competition between two people. Generally speaking, competition increases with distance and face-to-face positioning; cooperation is maximized in side-by-side arrangements. Circular seating patterns are conducive to cooper ative ventures in that each person has access to the other, and the built-in, territorial feature of the rectangular or columnar patterns is avoided.

There are a number of ways in which you can place environmental demands for cooperation on your group. The simplest is by limiting or centralizing resources. For example, rather than giving the children snacks in individual plates or cups, you can place one large container on the table. The same is true for project materials. Of course, in each of these cases, aggression may result if the particular group does not yet have the skills necessary for this level of cooperation.

In programs for disturbed children, adequate outlets should be available for aggression, and an aggression area should be standard equipment. Such an area would include wrestling mats, batacas, punching bags, dolls that can be torn apart, and rags and papers that can be ripped up. A "rage doll," consisting of clothing stuffed with rags, is a particularly satisfying item to kick and throw.

Learning

As the section on "Stimulation" suggests, the environment has a profound effect on learning. In addition, a number of sources have found that environmental novelty stimulates interest and exploration in children. Therefore, it is important to equip the learning area with a variety of materials. Care must be taken to limit the number of materials at a given time in order to guard against over-stimulation. The out-of-doors environment provides numerous opportunities for stimulation and involvement. In this way, the teacher need not *make* the children learn; the environment will naturally elicit questions and interest.

The environment may limit learning in some obvious, although sometimes overlooked, ways. Sommer (1969) recounts how he improved his "C" in geometry simply by having his seat moved from the side of the room to the center of the room where his weak eyes could see the blackboard.

The environment also affects learning in some dramatic and surprising ways. Studies at Munich's Gesellschaft für Rationelle Psychologie have clearly indicated the influence of color on I.Q. Children who were tested in rooms painted light blue, yellow, yellow–green or orange—colors the children described as "beautiful"—raised their I.Q. score an average of 12 points. Those that were tested in "ugly" colors—white, black and brown-dropped an average of 14 points. Carrying their studies further, the experimenters tested groups of children after they had played in "beautiful" rooms. After six months, the experimental groups outstripped the controls by 15 points. The margin increased to 25 points after eighteen months (Blue Is Beautiful, 1973).

Transitions

Transitions from room to room and activity to activity can be greatly facilitated by environmental manipulation. For example, pathways must be clear of obstacles and distractions; a place to hang coats and leave muddy shoes should be situated by the entryways, and activities must be set up in advance.

In terms of the child's transition into the community, the center should be located close to community resources. The reentry process is facilitated by the child's having the opportunity to become familiar with materials and objects that she will be confronted with in her new environment: desks, educational materials, lunch tables, play equipment, etc. To reduce isolation from the community, the agency's appearance should be "de-institutionalized." In this way, the child will not see herself a separate oddity.

These are just samples of treatment goals and means of environmental facilitation. We invite you to experiment with your environment in terms of design solutions to your unique problems and interests. Explore your environment with all of your senses: how does it feel, smell, look, and sound? What is its sense of movement? What is the mood, texture, variety, feeling of privacy or excitement, etc.? To illustrate the concept of environmental demands, take a look at the three setting designs in the illustration below. Without verbalizing any expectations, predict what kinds of behavior patterns would be elicited by the setting arrangement itself. (See Figure 29-2.)

Sommer (1972) describes objects as having three levels of messages: *emotional, action,* and *communication.* An object may say to you that it is warm, happy, or angry (emotional message); it may invite you to come close and touch it or demand that you stay away (action message); it may tell you that it is weak or strong (communication message). Explore your physical setting and decipher its messages to you. These messages will differ as your internal state and mood shifts. Look at what is foreground and background from one moment to the next. With environmental sensitivity, you will better understand how your surroundings affect your treatment population. Based on the data you collect, play with your setting to create various effects. Then observe the children and assess the accuracy of your predictions. In the end, "the proof of the pudding is in the eating."

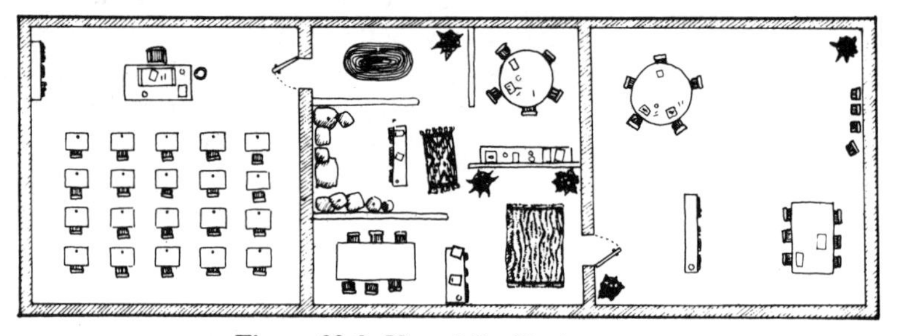

Figure 29-2. Use of the Environment

REFERENCES

Adler, R., & Towne, N. *Looking out/Looking in.* Corte Madera, Calif.: Rinehart Press, 1975

Alden, E. Guiding the young child's play. *Nursery School Portfolio,* Leaflet No. 66. Washington, D.C.: Association for Childhood Education International, 1961

Almy, M. Spontaneous Play: An Avenue for Intellectual Development. *The Bulletin of the Institute of Child Study.* Vol. 28, No. 2. Toronto: University of Toronto, 1966.

Altman, I., & Taylor, D. A. *Social Penetration: The development of interpersonal relationships.* New York: Holt Rinehart & Winston, 1973.

Armas, J. Adapted from Leary, T. *Interpersonal Diagnosis of Personality.* New York: Ronald Press, 1957.

Armstrong, H., Jr., & Savicki, V. *Precision Behavior Change Manual.* Unpublished manuscript, University of Washington, 1971.

Azrin, N. H., & Foxx, R. M. *Toilet Training in Less Than a Day.* New York: Simon and Schuster, 1974.

Bach, G. R., & Deutsch, R. M. *Pairing.* New York: Avon Books, 1970.

Bach, G. R. & Bernhard, Y. *Aggression Lab: The fair fight training manual.* Dubuque, Iowa: Kendall/Hunt, 1971.

Bandler, R., & Grinder, J. *The Structure of Magic, Vol. I.* Palo Alto, Calif.: Science & Behavior Books, 1975.

Bandler, R., Grinder, J., & Satir, V. *Changing with Families.* Palo Alto, Calif.: Science & Behavior Books, 1976.

Bany, M. A., & Johnson, L. V. *Classroom Group Behavior.* London: Collier-Macmillian Ltd., 1964.

Becker, W. C., Englemann, S., & Thomas, D. R. *Teaching: A course in applied psychology.* Chicago: Science Research Associates, 1971.

Benoit, R. B., & Mayer, G. R. Extinction: Guidelines for its selection and use. *The Personnel and Guidance Journal,* 1974, *52,* 290–295.

Birren, Faber. *Color Psychology and Color Therapy.* Secaucus, N.J.: The Citadel Press, 1978.

Blue Is Beautiful. *Time,* Sept. 1973. p. 66.

Bonner, H. *Group Dynamics: Principles and Applications.* New York: The Ronald Press Co., 1959.

Bovard, E. W., Jr. Social Norms and the Individual. *Journal of Abnormal and Social Psychology,* 1948, *43,* 62–69.

Bruner, J. S. Play is Serious Business. *Psychology Today,* 1971, *5,* 67–70.

Byrne, S. Nobody Home: The erosion of the American family. *Psychology Today,* 1977, *10,* 41–47.

Carkhuff, R. R. *Helping and Human Relations: A primer for lay and professional helpers.* New York: Holt Rinehart & Winston, 1969.

Combs, A. W., Alvila, D. L., & Purkey, W. W. *Helping Relationships: Basic concepts for the helping professions.* Boston: Allyn & Bacon, 1971.

Culbert, S. A. *The Interpersonal Process of Self-disclosure: It takes two to see one.* New York: Renaissance Editions, 1967.

Dennis, L. Play in Dewey's Theory of Education. *Young Children,* 1970, *25.*

Dreikurs, R. *The Challenge of Parenthood.* New York: Hawthorne Books, 1958.

Ellis, A., & Harper, R. A. *A Guide to Rational Living.* North Hollywood, Calif.: Wilshire Book Company, 1961.

Erikson, E. *Childhood and Society.* New York: W. W. Norton & Co., 1950.

Fluegelman, A. (ed.) *The New Games Book.* Garden City, N.Y. Dolphin/Doubleday, 1976.

French, J. R. P., & Raven, B. H. The Basis of Social Power. In *Studies in Social Power,* ed. D. Cartwright, pp. 150–167. Ann Arbor: University of Michigan, 1959.

Gazda, G. M. *Human Relations Development: A manual for educators.* Boston: Allyn & Bacon, 1973.

Gibson, John E. Leadership and the Spatial Factor in Small Groups. *Journal of Abnormal and Social Psychology,* 1957, *54,* No. 2, pp. 269–272.

Gordon, T. *Parent Effectiveness Training.* New York: Wyden, 1970.

Green, D., & Lepper, M. R. Intrinsic Motivation: how to turn play into work. *Psychology Today,* 1974, *8,* 49–54.

Grinder, J., & Bandler, R. *The Structure of Magic II.* Palo Alto, California: Science & Behavior Books, 1976.

Gump, P. Milieu, environment and behavior. *Design and behavior,* 1971, *2,* No. 8, 48–52.

Hall, E. T. *The hidden dimension.* Garden City, N.J.: Doubleday and Co., Inc., 1966.

Hare, P. A. *Handbook of Small Group Research.* N.Y.: Free Press of Glencoe, 1962.

Holmes, T. H., & Rahe, R. H. The social readjustment rating scale. *Journal of Psychosomatic Research.* 1967, *11,* 213.

Honn, S. Personal communication, 1979.

Hymes, J. *The Child Under Six.* Englewood Cliffs, N.J.: Prentice-Hall, 1963.

Ittleson, W. H., Proshansky, H., Rivlin, L. G., & Winkel, G. H.: *An Introduction to Environmental Psychology.* New York: Holt Rinehart & Winston, 1974.

Ivey, A. E. Cultural expertise: toward systematic outcome criteria in counseling and psychological education. *Personnel and Guidance Journal,* 1977, *55,* 296–302.

Ivey, A. E., & Authier, J. *Micro counseling: innovations in interviewing, counseling, psychotherapy, and psycho-education.* 2nd ed. Springfield, Ill.: Charles C Thomas, 1978.

James, M., & Jonegeward, D. *Born To Win.* Reading, Mass.: Addison-Wesley Publishing Co., 1971.

Johnson, D. W. and Johnson, F. P., *Joining Together.* Englewood Cliffs, N.J.: Prentice-Hall, Inc., 1975.

Jourard, S. M., & Resnick, J. L. Some effects of self-disclosure among college women. *Journal of Humanistic Psychology,* 1970, *10,* 1, 84–93.

Knowles, H., and Knowles, M. *Introduction to Group Dynamics.* New York: Associated Press, 1959.

Kübler-Ross, E. *On Death and Dying.* New York: The Macmillan Co., 1969.

Lazarus, A. A. *Multi-Modal Behavior Therapy.* Fort Lee, N.J.: Sigma Information, Inc., 1972.

Lewin, K. *Field Theory in Social Science.* New York: Harper and Brothers, 1951.

Lovaas, O. I., Berberich, J. P., Perloff, B. F., & Schaeffer, B. Acquisition of imitative speech in schizophrenic children. *Science,* 1966, *151,* 705–707.

Luft, J. *Of Human Interaction.* Palo Alto, Calif.: National Press, 1969.

Luthman, S. with Kirschenbaum, M. *The Dynamic Family.* Palo Alto, Calif.: Science & Behavior Books, 1975.

Maher, B. *Clinical Psychology and Personality: The selected papers of George Kelly.* New York: Wiley, 1969.

Maslow, A. H., & Mintz, N. L. Effects of esthetic surroundings: 1. Initial effects of three esthetic conditions upon perceiving 'Energy' and 'Well-Being' in faces. *Journal of Psychology,* 1956, *42,* 247–254.

Maultsby, M. C., Jr., *Help Yourself to Happiness through Rational Self-counseling.* Boston: Esplanade Books, 1975.

Mayer, M. F. *A Guide for Child-Care Workers.* New York: Child Welfare League of America, 1958.

Mehrabian, A., Communication without words. *Readings in Psychology Today.* Del Mar, Calif: CRM Books, 1969.

Murray, W., & Ebner, M. *So you Want to Work with Kids.* Unpublished manuscript, Portland, Oregon, 1972.

Ott, J. N. Influence of florescent lights on hyperactivity and learning disabilities. *Readings in Emotional and Behavioral Disabilities. Guilford, Conn.: Special Learning Corp., 1978, pp. 102–106.*

Patterson, G. R., & Forgatch, M. S. *Family Living Series: Part One.* Champaign, Ill.: Research Press, 1975.

Peterson, R. "The professional development of child care workers." Paper presented at 15th Annual Oregon Association of Child Care Workers Conference, Portland, Oregon, 1975.

Phillips, E. L., Phillips, E. A., Fixen, D. L., & Wolf, M. M. *The Teaching Family Handbook.* University of Kansas Printing Service, Lawrence, Kansas, 1975.

Porteous, D. J. *Environment and Behavior: Planning and everyday urban life.* Reading, Mass.: Addison-Wesley Publishing Co., 1977.

Powell, W. J., Jr. Differential effectiveness of interviewer interventions in an experimental interview. *Journal of Consulting and Clinical Psychology,* 1968, *32,* 210–215.

Raths, L. E., Harmin, M., & Simon, S. B. *Values and Teaching.* Columbus, Ohio: Merrill, 1966.

Redl, F. *When We Deal with Children.* New York: The Free Press, 1966.

Residential Child Care. *Basic Course for Residential Child Care Workers.* Chapel Hill, N.C.: Group Child Care Consultant Services, 1977.

Rosenthal, R., & Jacobson, L. *Pygmalion in the Classroom: Teacher's expectation's and pupil's intellectual development.* New York: Holt, Rinehart & Winston, 1968.

Satir, V. *Peoplemaking.* Palo Alto, Calif.: Science & Behavior Books, 1972.

Savicki, V. Outcomes of non-reciprocal self-disclosure strategies. *Journal of Personality and Social Psychology,* 1972, *23,* 271–276.

Secord, P. F., & Backman, C. W. *Social Psychology.* New York: McGraw-Hill, 1969.

Somer, R. *Personal Space.* Englewood Cliffs, N.J.: Prentice-Hall, Inc., 1969.

Somer, R. *Design Awareness.* San Francisco: Rinehart Press, 1972.

Somer, R. *Tight Spaces.* Englewood Cliffs, N.J.: Prentice-Hall, Inc., 1974.

Steiner, C. M. *Scripts People Live.* New York: Grove Press, 1974.

Sulzer-Azaroff, B., & Mayer, G. R. *Applying Behavior Analysis Procedures with Children and Youth.* New York: Holt Rinehart & Winston, 1977.

Sutton-Smith, B. Child's Play: Very Serious Business. *Psychology Today,* 1971, *5.*

Sutton-Smith, B. & Sutton-Smith, S. *How To Play with Your Children (and When Not to).* New York: Hawthorne Books, Inc., 1974.

Thomas, A., & Chess, S. *Temperament and Development.* New York: Bruner Mazel, 1977.

Thommen, G. *Biorhythm.* New York: Award Books, 1964.

Toffler, A. *Future Shock.* New York: Random House, 1970.

Vorrath, H., & Brendaro, L. K. *Positive Peer Culture.* Chicago: Aldine Publishing Co., 1974.

Wasickso, M. M. A research-based teacher selection instrument. Unpublished paper, Columbus College, 1978.

Watzlawick, P. *The language of Change: Elements of therapeutic communication.* New York: Basic Books, 1973.

Watzlawick, P., Beavin, J. H., & Jackson, D. D. *Pragmatics of human communication.* New York: W. W. Norton & Co., 1967.

Watzlawick, P., Weakland, J., & Fisch, R. *Change.* New York: W. W. Norton & Co., 1974.

Wolpe, J. *The practice of Behavior Therapy.* 2nd ed. New York: Pergamon Press, 1973.

INDEX